Ethical Consumption

A not-so-quiet revolution seems to be occurring in wealthy capitalist societies – supermarkets selling 'guilt free' Fair Trade products; lifestyle TV gurus exhorting us to eat less, buy local and go green; neighbourhood action groups bent on 'swapping not shopping'. And this is happening not at the margins of society but at its heart, in the shopping centres and homes of ordinary people. Today we are seeing a mainstreaming of ethical concerns around consumption that reflects an increasing anxiety with – and accompanying sense of responsibility for – the risks and excesses of contemporary lifestyles in the 'global North'.

This collection provides a range of critical tools for understanding the turn towards responsible or conscience consumption and, in the process, interrogates the notion that we can shop our way to a more ethical, sustainable future. Written by leading international scholars from a variety of disciplinary backgrounds – and drawing upon examples from across the globe – *Ethical Consumption* makes a major contribution to the still fledgling field of ethical consumption studies. With a foreword by Mike Featherstone, this collection is a must-read for anyone interested in the relationship between consumer culture and contemporary social life.

Tania Lewis is a Senior Research Fellow in Sociology in the School of Media and Communication at RMIT University, Melbourne. She is author of *Smart Living: Lifestyle Media and Popular Expertise* (Peter Lang, 2008) and editor of *TV Transformations: Revealing the Makeover Show* (Routledge, 2009).

Emily Potter is a Research Fellow in the School of Communication and Creative Arts, Deakin University, Melbourne. She is co-editor of *Fresh Water: New Perspectives on Water in Australia* (Melbourne University Press, 2007), and has published widely on questions of culture and the environment.

Ethical Consumption
A critical introduction

Edited by
Tania Lewis and Emily Potter

Routledge
Taylor & Francis Group

LONDON AND NEW YORK

First published 2011
by Routledge
2 Park Square, Milton Park, Abingdon, Oxon, OX14 4RN

Simultaneously published in the USA and Canada
by Routledge
270 Madison Avenue, New York, NY 10016

Routledge is an imprint of the Taylor & Francis Group, an Informa business

Typeset in Times New Roman
by Keystroke, Tettenhall, Wolverhampton, UK
Printed and bound in Great Britain
by CPI Antony Rowe, Chippeham, Wiltshire

British Library Cataloguing in Publication Data
A catalogue record for this book is available from the British Library

Library of Congress Cataloging in Publication Data
Ethical consumption : a critical introduction / edited by Tania Lewis and
Emily Potter.
p. cm.
Includes bibliographical references.
ISBN 978-0-415-55824-2 (hbk.) — ISBN 978-0-415-55825-9 (pbk.)
1. Consumption (Economics)—Moral and ethical aspects.
2. Consumption (Economics)—Social aspects. 3. Consumer behavior—
Moral and ethical aspects. 4. Social choice. I. Lewis, Tania. II. Potter, Emily.
HB835.E84 2010
174—dc22
2010008187

ISBN 13: 978–0–415–55824–2 (hbk)
ISBN 13: 978–0–415–55825–9 (pbk)
ISBN 13: 978–0–203–86778–5 (ebk)

Contents

Notes on contributors

Fiona Allon is an Australian Research Council (ARC) Future Fellow in the Department of Gender and Cultural Studies at The University of Sydney. She is the author of *Renovation Nation: Our Obsession with Home* (University of NSW Press, Sydney: 2008), and her current research focuses on cultures of home and households, sustainability and everyday life.

Frances Bonner is a Reader in Television and Popular Culture in the English, Media Studies and Art History School at the University of Queensland. She is the author of *Ordinary Television* (Sage, 2003) and co-author (with Graeme Turner and P. David Marshall) of *Fame Games: The Production of Celebrity in Australia* (Cambridge University Press, 2000), as well as many articles on non-fiction television, celebrity and magazines. She is currently writing a book on television presenters.

Benjamin Coles is a Research Associate on the European Research Council-funded 'Consumer Culture in an Age of Anxiety' research programme, based in the Interdisciplinary Centre of the Social Sciences (ICOSS) at the University of Sheffield, UK. In this role he is examining cultural, economic and place-based understandings of food systems, with particular interest in poultry and aquaculture in Thailand. More generally, he is interested in the role of place and place-making in the production and consumption of foods.

Geoffrey Craig is an Associate Professor in Communication at the University of Canberra. He is the author of *The Media, Politics and Public Life* (Allen & Unwin, 2004), the co-author of *Slow Living* (Berg and UNSW Press, 2006), and the co-editor of *Informing Voters? Politics, Media and the New Zealand Election 2008* (Pearson, 2009).

Philip Crang is Professor of Cultural Geography within the Social and Cultural Geography Research Group at Royal Holloway, University of London. His research interests centre on the geographies of commodity culture and the character of the geographical knowledges circulated within cultures of consumption.

Robert Melchior Figueroa is Associate Professor in the Department of Philosophy and Religion Studies at the University of North Texas. His principal areas of research are environmental justice studies, environmental identity and heritage, Latino/a environmental issues, critical race theory, political ecology, restorative justice and climate refugees, and science and technology studies. He is co-editor of *Science and Other Cultures: Issues in the Philosophy of Science and Technology* (Routledge, 2003), and editor of the *Environmental Philosophy Journal: Special Issue on Ecotourism and Environmental Justice* (2010).

Adrian Franklin is Professor of Sociology at The University of Tasmania, Australia. His books include *Tourism* (2003), *Nature and Social Theory* (2002) and *Animals and Modern Cultures* (2009). New books include *Collecting the Twentieth Century* (UNSW Press, 2010) and *City Life* (Sage, 2010). His work focuses on social and cultural change in modernity, and includes writings on city life, material culture and collecting, the sociology of nature and environments, our relationships with animals, posthumanism, and travel and tourism.

Michael Gard is an Associate Professor in Charles Sturt University's Faculty of Education. He teaches and writes about education, dance, sport and the science of human health. He is the author of two books: *The Obesity Epidemic: Science, Morality and Ideology* (with Jan Wright) (Routledge, 2005) and *Men Who Dance: Aesthetics, Athletics and the Art of Masculinity* (Peter Lang, 2006). His new book, *The End of the Obesity Epidemic*, will be published by Routledge in 2010.

Chris Gibson is Professorial Fellow and ARC Future Fellow at the Australian Centre for Cultural Environmental Research, University of Wollongong. His research interests are in the fields of human geography and cultural economy, with an empirical focus on cultural industries such as music and fashion. He is currently chief investigator on a number of federal government-funded projects exploring everyday cultural responses to governmental sustainability imperatives.

Cathy Greenfield is Associate Professor of Communication at RMIT University and General Editor of the interdisciplinary journal *Communication, Politics & Culture*. She researches the relations between media, politics and the government of populations. Her most recent published work includes a range of articles with Peter Williams on media rhetoric and neoliberalism, the role of media in financialization, the relations between communication and sustainability, and the role of mediated sport in the governing of everyday social relations.

Ann Hill is a doctoral researcher in the field of economic geography in The College of Asia and the Pacific, The Australian National University. Her doctoral research – a series of action research interventions in relation to community food projects in Australia and the Philippines – is concerned with conceptualizing what might constitute a 'community food economy'. Prior to taking up her PhD studies, Ann co-ordinated an ANU research project on local economic development through community partnering in Indonesia and the Philippines.

Kersty Hobson is lecturer in human geography and environmental politics in the Fenner School of Environment and Society, The Australian National University. Her research to date has focused on issues of sustainable consumption, behaviour change and participatory methodologies, with papers published in journals such as *Space and Polity*, *Geoforum* and *Environmental Politics*. Her current research – as part of an interdisciplinary ANU project – is examining social responses to climate change scenarios in the Australian Capital Region.

Kim Humphery is Associate Professor of History and Social Theory at RMIT University, Melbourne, Australia and he has been researching and writing on consumption for nearly two decades. His books include *Shelf Life: Supermarkets and the Changing Cultures of Consumption* (Cambridge University Press, 1998) and *Excess: Anti-Consumerism in the West* (Polity, 2010).

Tania Lewis is a Senior Research Fellow in the School of Media and Communication at RMIT University, Melbourne. She is the author of *Smart Living: Lifestyle Media and Popular Expertise* (Peter Lang, 2008) and editor of *TV Transformations: Revealing the Makeover Show* (Routledge, 2008). She is currently conducting research on sustainable lifestyles and green citizenship, and is a chief investigator on an Australian Research Council-funded project (2010–13) examining the role of lifestyle advice television in shaping social identity and consumer-citizenship in Asia.

Jo Littler is Senior Lecturer in Media and Cultural Studies at Middlesex University, UK. She is the author of *Radical Consumption: Shopping for Change in Contemporary Culture* (Open University Press, 2009) and co-editor, with Sam Binkley, of a special issue of *Cultural Studies*, 'Cultural Studies and Anti-Consumerism' (22:5, 2008). She is also co-editor, with Roshi Naidoo, of *The Politics of Heritage: The Legacies of 'Race'* (Routledge, 2005) and editor of *Mediactive 2: Celebrity* (Lawrence & Wishart, 2004).

Richard Maxwell is Professor and Chair of the Department of Media Studies at the City University of New York, Queens College. He has published widely on a range of topics: television in Spain's democratic transition, Hollywood's international dominance, and media politics and surveillance systems in the post-9-11 era. His current work focuses on the environmental impact of information and communication technologies and consumer electronics.

Toby Miller is Chair of Media and Cultural Studies at the University of California, Riverside. He is the author and editor of over thirty books, and he edits the journals *Television & New Media* and *Social Identities*. His latest book is *Television Studies: The Basics* (Routledge, 2009).

Wendy Parkins is a Senior Lecturer in the Department of English at the University of Otago, New Zealand. She is the author of *Mobility and Modernity in Women's Novels, 1850s–1930s* (Palgrave Macmillan, 2008) and the co-author, with Geoffrey Craig, of *Slow Living* (Berg, 2006).

Emily Potter is a Research Fellow in the School of Communication and Creative Arts, Deakin University. Her publications include an edited collection of interdisciplinary writing on water cultures and communities, *Fresh Water: New Perspectives on Water in Australia* (MUP, 2007), and numerous book chapters and journal articles. She is currently undertaking an Australian Research Council-funded collaborative study of bottled water as a biopolitical object in the context of global water politics.

Elspeth Probyn is a Research Professor at the University of South Australia where she directs The Centre for Postcolonial and Globalization Studies. Her work has focused on questions of identity and embodiment in terms of gender, sexuality and, now, eating. Her books include *Carnal Appetites: FoodSexIdentities* (Routledge, 2010), *Blush: Faces of Shame* (University of Minnesota Press, and University of New South Wales Press, 2005) and *Remote Control: New Media & Ethics* (Cambridge University Press, 2003). She is currently working on a new book entitled *Feeling Global Consumption: Land, Soil & Sea*.

Timothy J. Scrase is Professor of Sociology and the Associate Dean for Research, Faculty of Arts and Sciences, Australian Catholic University. A comparative sociologist, he researches and writes on social change and development, globalization, and social impact assessment focusing on the Asia Pacific region, especially India. He has previously published five books and over fifty papers. His current projects explore the impact of neoliberal globalisation on the Indian middle classes; the social impact of the transformation of Asia Pacific Ports; globalisation and artisan labour in Asia; and the commodification of water and its domestic use among the urban middle classes in India.

Elyse Stanes is Human Geography Technical Officer at the Australian Centre for Cultural Environmental Research (AUSCCER), University of Wollongong, Australia. Her research interests include sustainability, cultural industries (especially fashion) and household consumption. She is part of a large team of researchers at AUSCCER examining household consumption and cultures of sustainability.

Paul Starr completed a PhD in cultural studies at the University of Queensland, and a Master of Sustainable Management at the University of Sydney. His research and writing interests include social and cultural aspects of environmental issues, commodity biography and approaches to measuring sustainability. He is an independent scholar based in Canberra, where he is also involved in growing and making wine.

Gordon Waitt is Associate Professor in the School of Earth and Environmental Sciences at the University of Wollongong, New South Wales. He is a member of the Australian Centre for Cultural Environmental Research. His research interests include gender, place and cultures, tourism geographies and cultures of natures. In addition to numerous articles and book chapters he co-authored *Introducing Human Geography* (Longman-Pearson Education Australia, 2000) and *Gay Tourism: Culture and Context* (Haworth Press, 2006).

Peter Williams is a Senior Associate of RMIT University, Australia and has taught in the Honours and Masters programmes of the School of Media & Communication since 2002. He researches the relations between culture and power, especially in Australia since the 1930s. Current scholarly projects focus on the consequences of the uses of a range of communication technologies for the government of different populations.

Acknowledgements

We would like to thank the contributors whose intellectual labour and goodwill have made this collection possible. We are grateful to Gerhard Boomgaarden at Routledge for supporting the publication of this collection and Jennifer Dodd and Emily Senior for their friendly and professional editorial assistance. We would like to acknowledge funding support from the Australian Research Council's Cultural Research Network which enabled us to conduct a workshop at the University of Melbourne in December 2008 out of which this collection emerged. Thanks are also due to Alison Huber for her organizational support and critical feedback along the way and to Victor Albert for providing editorial assistance with the production of the book.

Foreword

Mike Featherstone

The title of a recent book by Zygmunt Bauman, *Does Ethics have a Chance in a World of Consumers?* (2008), raises an important question.[1] Here he suggests we have to face up to a stark choice. Either we continue to pursue our multitude of individual and personal portmanteaus, each designed 'like all consumer joys for utterly individual lonely enjoyment even when we relish company'. Or we endeavour once more to develop a public space of lasting engagement – 'a space of dialogue, discussion, confrontation and agreement' (Bauman 2008: 28). This new global public space is one based on a notion of 'planetary responsibility' in which the only lasting effective solutions to planetary problems are those that involve the development of 'a politics that can catch up with global markets'. In an age of increasing global flows of people there is also a growing *ressentiment* towards strangers – refugees, asylum seekers, impoverished exiles. To deal with such conditions Bauman suggests we need a new ethics, a way beyond the belief that happiness is linked to our volume of consumption. Such an ethics, Bauman believes, can be grounded in the philosophy of Levinas in which the self is conceived as 'being for the Other', as woven through with responsibilities to care for the Other beyond the anticipation of any reciprocity or redress. The ethic of caring for another is a necessary corrective to the manifold accumulated problems of modernity: egoism, loneliness, isolation and social disorganization, which are seen as destructive of the social bond. The expansion of consumer culture in what Bauman sees as our intensified 'hyper' or 'liquid' modernity only serves to heighten these processes.

Consumer-based lifestyles have proliferated on the back of the current wave of globalization since the 1980s. They can be related to the rise of neoliberalism and the view that the extension of the market is the sole guarantor of economic growth, wealth generation and political stability. They are linked to the assumption that only a life lived via the accumulation of consumer goods will allow greater personal fulfilment, human development and happiness. The inability of such a narrowly economistic model to deliver the good life or build positive human values has drawn a good deal of hostile critique from Zygmunt Bauman and others. The planetary consequences of the spread of more intensive consumption with the acceleration of global warming also brings home the limits to growth in a profound way. Yet the new information technologies which sustain global financial markets and transnational corporate production also make possible greater flows of information between consumer-citizens. The reverse side of a globalizing consumer culture is a growing concern to interrogate the ethical and planetary consequences of human action. The set of papers in this volume tackles these concerns by addressing a wide range of substantive issues and case studies in consumption drawn from various parts of the world. The topics considered range from ethically branded bottled water, to fair trade markets, to organic food, slow living, obesity, food markets and place making, the global electronics market, wine, fashion, eco-home renovation, neighbourhood gardening projects, eco-tourism, lifestyle television and second-hand goods.

The editors are to be congratulated for bringing together such a variety of perspectives on the issues surrounding ethical consumption. As they suggest, the politics of consumer culture, alongside a broader critique of consumer culture, is back on the global agenda, now combined with a burgeoning interest in some of the ethical questions raised above by Bauman. The ethics of consumption is now becoming a timely emergent field. Yet, it is clear that until recently issues such as over-consumption, the ethics of waste, radical consumption and climate change failed to penetrate very far into sociology, cultural studies and media studies (notable exceptions include Hawkins 2006; Binkley and Littler 2008; Humphery 2009; Littler 2009; Szerszynski and Urry 2010). Sociology in particular operated with an overly strong human-centric model of social life, in which questions such as the limits of growth and the question of the ethical consequences of human consumption for the planet and other life forms were generally bracketed out.[2]

Yet, as the editors of this collection note, aspects of the sociology of consumption are useful for thinking through the recent ethical turn. Bourdieu's work for instance usefully links ethics to questions of class, taste and aesthetics. In this context it is important to note the centrality of the social in one of the most influential sociological works on consumer culture, Pierre Bourdieu's *Distinction* (1984), which sought to counter economic and popular views of individual consumer sovereignty as playing the key role in the formation of taste. The book was based on French research in the 1960s which mapped cultural practices on to the field of class fractions and occupations, focusing on the socially structured reproduction of consumption. Its main assumption was that cultural goods and practices were used to generate social distinctions, with the types of goods and experiences consumed related to different groups' access to economic and cultural capital. An increase in the supply of new goods could threaten the structured differences in the field of existing social distinctions. Class fractions within the new middle class or new petite bourgeoisie (such as the new cultural intermediaries), although possessing limited economic capital, became arbiters for new lifestyles through their capacity to discuss and interpret the new goods and experiences through the media to wider audiences (see Featherstone 2007). Indeed, as Frances Bonner in her discussion of lifestyle television in this book reminds us, Bourdieu is disdainful of this group's desire to create 'the perfect consumer' thirsting for the latest things. At the same time, the new middle class habitus predisposes them to identify with nature and environmental issues and to adopt an ethical stance towards consumption. Yet how this group's concern for style and the general question of how aesthetics relates to ethics has not always been clear (see Eder 1990; see also Maffesoli 1991).

Of relevance here is Michel Foucault's quest to theorize an 'art of living' in the *History of Sexuality* volumes 2 and 3 (Foucault 1997, 1998; also his lectures 2009, 2010), in which he discussed the techniques of care of the self in Ancient Greece. Foucault's focus is not, of course, on consumption or consumer goods, being centred on the ethics and aesthetics of existence.[3] It would be useful to briefly examine his ideas, given the centrality of Foucauldian ethics to the concerns of this book and the utility of his work for understanding the place of goods in contemporary lifestyles, along with the environmental consequences of materialism. In part Foucault's interest in the topic was motivated by his concern to investigate and think through forms of subjectivity which go beyond notions of fixed identity. Through this exploration of alternative relations to oneself, the notion of 'way of life' became important, as it went against normative and institutionalized versions of the self. In a way of life, differences between the self and an other are not objectified and reduced to a common denominator – rather a way of life can involve people from different age, status and social backgrounds with the emphasis put upon the decentring of oneself towards an other; on the sharing of intense relationships and 'invention of oneself' (Foucault 1991a; 1998; Revel 2009; see also discussion in Featherstone 1995: chs 3 and 4; 2007: ch 11).[4]

Important for our purposes is his argument that a way of life can generate a culture and an ethics, for Foucault implies that a way of life is an ethics, a way of being together, of being with others which generates a shared space. This space is one of experimentation in forming a *polis*, that is, in making politics, which emphasizes the political character of ethics. As Revel (2009) argues, this means that Foucault's view of ethics is not a return to individualism, or a self-centred egoism; instead it is the opening of a space for problematizing a commonality that could be formed on the basis of differences and yet yields the potential for becoming a singularity. This is the opposite of the contemporary 'enterprise man', the neoliberal subject, driven by a calculative self-interest, with little concern for the general good. Foucault (2008), in his lecture course on *The Birth of Biopolitics*, traces the rise of the enterprise subject back to the development of liberalism in the eighteenth century, to show the way in which state power became grounded in laissez-faire economic theory, with its call for the freedom of the market providing the impetus for a new analysis of the forces governing populations and the formation of social life. Important here is Foucault's analysis of the conjunction of nature, life and the market which provided the basis for a new social ontology and epistemology in the economization of biopower. In the late twentieth century with the emergence of neoliberalism, a further shift in biopolitics is suggested, one which points to the environmentalization of power as Massumi (2009) argues (see discussion in Venn and Terranova 2009; Venn 2010).[5] Foucault, then, sought to mount a radical critique of contemporary neoliberal biopolitics and its emergent tendencies, as well as working towards potential alteratives via his analysis of 'way of life' and 'care of the self'.

Foucault's concern for the care of the self and body along with the development of a socially rewarding way of life with others has clear implications for an ethics of consumption. For Foucault (1997) such an ethics means moving beyond the world of material goods; as he remarks:

> What strikes me is the fact that in our society, art has become something which is related only to objects and not individuals, or to life. That art is something which is specialized or which is done by experts who are artists. But couldn't everyone's life become a work of art? Why should the lamp or the house be an art object, but not our life?

Foucault goes on to emphasize the importance of creative activity, that one should create one's life by giving style to it through long practice and regular work. Here Foucault minimizes the importance of objects or goods, in favour of working on the ordering of one's life (appearance, feelings and trajectory of lived life, or life course). His views combine insights from Antiquity with the artistic modernist imperative for an ascetic reinvention of the self (Baudelaire 1964), taking oneself as an object of careful and disciplined elaboration. Yet where does this leave our relationship to things?

Cultural commentators influenced by anthropology clearly see the centrality of things and their role in maintaining the social, interpersonal and personal ordering of life as an important dimension of the ethics of otherness. In her essay 'Housework as Magic' – in which the influence of Mary Douglas (1966) on 'dirt as matter out of place' is evident – Bernice Martin (1982, 1984), for example, elaborated on the importance of caring for mundane things, cleaning the lavatory, putting the house in order to restore a sense of personal order. Arjun Appadurai (1986) provided the classic analysis of the social life of things by examining the biographical trajectories of things and their transformations from active to passive, from mundane to sacred and back, over long periods of time. More recently, Daniel Miller (2008, 2010) has further developed the anthropology of things, to focus on the everyday lives of ordinary people by analysing their complex relationship to possessions, to show the difficulties in distinguishing between subjects and objects. Consumer culture, then, may be about not just the excitement of the new supply of enticing goods, but the more mundane use of goods to maintain the fabric of everyday social order, through familiarity with physical surroundings (place) and the layout of things that are 'to hand'. In short for many people there is already an ethic of consumption implicit in our relationship to the material world, which as Bauman's Levinasian critique implies, asks us to respect the other, to care for 'an other'. But while this injunction to care can be contrasted to contemporary intensified consumer culture, it should not be regarded as opposed to consumption per se; people care for others mediated by caring for things. Things are not necessarily superficial distractions; the materiality of 'stuff' has important implications for ethical conduct. Yet, can this ethical conduct be stretched beyond the social and the human – what would it mean to think of the things in our world, as not just objects for the human will to power, but to have an ethical encounter with things, to allow things to dwell in the world in their own right?

Lucas Introna (2009) explores this possibility; he begins with a critique of actor network theory's (ANT) view that all beings in the socio-material network – human and non-human alike – end up circulating as objects, as 'things-for-the-purposes-of the-network'. One of the limitations of the 'ethics of hybrids' put forward by ANT in the context of ethical consumption for instance is that the complexity of the socio-material networks with their intertwined agencies and competing incommensurable values often makes ethical purchase decisions difficult for the consumer – for example, airfreighted Fair Trade products may compete with locally sourced goods. This is something which Benjamin Coles and Philip Crang in their paper in this collection on 'Placing alternative consumption' elaborate on: ethical consumption depends upon place, knowledge of where goods come from and how they are made, their geographies of transformation and re-packaging; but it also involves attending to the 'fetish of de-fetishizing' commodities in which place, and the images of both the place of production and place of sale, are intrinsic to the consumption of things. Yet, Introna wants to take the analysis further: he regards the 'ethics of hybrids' position as anthropocentric, as it does not address the question of our relationship with things, *qua* things. He cites Heidegger (1977: 208 in Introna 2009: 30) in support:

> [I]t is important finally to realize that precisely through the characterization of something as 'a value' what is so valued is robbed of its worth. That is to say, by the assessment of something as a value what is valued is admitted only as an object for man's estimation. But what a thing is in its Being is not exhausted by its being an object, particularly when objectivity takes the form of value.

The problem is that we presume a framework of valuation that sees things as objects for our own use; they are always and already 'things for us', inscribed with our intentionality. They are valued as things for our disposal, to be sold in the market as in the case of works of art, or dumped at the garbage tip when they fail to be deemed useful. In forging a more-than-human model of ethical consumption we need to move beyond such limited understandings of and engagements with the object world; we need to build on the ethics of Levinas and the attempt to appreciate the radical singularity of our fellow human beings, to broaden it into an ethos of the 'letting-be of all beings'.

The problem of waste is an important site for addressing questions of the ethics of otherness and our relation to materiality. The rapid turnover of goods and the encouragement of a throw-away mindset within contemporary consumer culture means that we are only beginning to consider the implications of the accumulation of discarded things and their by-products. In this collection of papers there are a number of insightful discussions of the strategies adopted to deal with waste and discarded or second-hand goods. Adrian Franklin, for example, in his piece on 'The ethics of second-hand consumption', discusses the rise in the UK of gentrification, renovation and heritage, as part of a broader interest in reconstructing the past through artefacts and the collecting of older objects. As Walter Benjamin and others have indicated, collecting and aestheticization resonates strongly with memories and loss. The contemporary interest in collecting and archiving practices, in ordering and classifying music, photographs, etc. through new media devices such as personal computers, iPods and mobile phones, suggests that there remains a strong interest in curating not just 'the past' but our own pasts. In consumer-dominated societies, it is not surprising that consumer objects themselves can summon up strong affective, aestheticized and fetishized responses, as people seek out various modes for exploring the proximity, handling, contemplation and classification of goods and experiences (see Featherstone 2000; 2007: ch 5; 2009a; 2009b; 2010).

The rapid turnover of goods can act as an impediment to this potential. The turnover of fashions can limit the potential for self-fashioning, for customizing and reworking goods, for critically evaluating their potential contribution to our way of life prior to the act of purchase. Juliet Schor (2008: 595) argues that the rising volume of goods bought and discarded clearly creates ecological problems of waste, but that it also creates aesthetic and lifestyle problems too. A greater use of localized craft designs, to produce higher-quality, better-made, longer-lasting goods with greater sensory-aesthetic qualities, would encourage the kind of small-scale, artisanal and sustainable forms of consumption required to support more ethical and aesthetic ways of life.

As it stands, however, the present global economic system not only generates massive amounts of waste, it still holds up conspicuous consumption and mobile lifestyles as the ideal. While, as Maxwell and Miller discuss in this collection, some corporations have sought to appear more 'green', the overall trajectory within the current phase of neoliberal globalization remains, as John Urry (2010) remarks, tied to 'high carbon mobility systems'. These are implicated with capitalist overconsumption, archetypal images of which are found in new consumption spaces such as 'gated communities of excess' like Dubai, with their spectacular signature architecture and simulational leisure resorts for the new global rich which have been dubbed 'evil paradises' by critics (Davis and Monk 2007). The media tend to constantly feature and extol the virtues of the luxury lifestyles of celebrities and the new rich which, although utterly unattainable for the majority of people, continue to be presented as an aspirational ideal. At the same time, these overtly wasteful lifestyles and sites of excessive consumption have fuelled significant popular debates over global warming and ethical consumption. As many of the papers in this collection suggest, there are signs that increasingly people's concerns about the threat of catastrophic climate change mean they are willing to contemplate more restricted forms of consumption. Others seek to incorporate such self-limitations within more comprehensive regimes, adopting different ways of life and modes of sociability, which amount to new ethical modes of conduct. The appeal of satisfactions beyond consumption, the calls for a shift towards simplicity and more frugal lifestyles (the slow food movement being but one example), as Kim Humphery suggests in his contribution to this collection, are growing and we need to theorize more carefully the various modes of living they entail.

One major problem is that although there is clear evidence of the demand for ethical approaches to consumption which are environmentally sensitive and aware of the implications of climate change, the solutions to the problems of consumption and waste are generally couched in economic terms, the main language of value used by governments, business and other agencies. Because 'economics' is the most influential social science, it has largely monopolized the ways in which social issues are conceived, with its rational-choice assumptions that people are individualistic and calculative. This favours technological approaches to the problem (new energy saving inventions, low carbon goods and more efficient forms of transportation) along with the development of new markets to encourage and regulate (carbon-trading, weather derivatives, etc.). Yet, for the most part people's approaches to consumption are not governed by rational economic calculation, as the prior discussion of theoretical approaches to social life suggests; consumers are people who follow regular social routines and habits, but also who employ a range of values beyond economic calculation in their imaginative invention of ways of life. All discussions of climate change and the impending planetary catastrophe necessarily depend upon a broader vision of social life, on how society is and should be. This in turn also raises questions about the past, the sense of indebtedness to others, or exploitation, as we find with colonialism (Park and Roberts 2010). There are clearly problems in reconciling different social visions and theoretical frameworks employed to understand climate change, which have surfaced in the high-profile media disputes about data and modelling. Climate scientists are under pressure to conform to the predominant public positivist vision of science to frame discussions of the evidence and the technical solutions (Wynne 2010). At the same time there is a growing use of complexity theory and awareness of the difficulties of calculating unanticipated feedback effects in the face of the need for strategic 'scenario planning' (not least by the military); the sense of a unified linear global future in which long-term planning works gives way to an unstable future intelligible only through constructing scenarios, compounding the sense of 'multiple future worlds' (Cooper 2010). It is, then, by no means clear what, if any, modes of concerted action will emerge and the type of outcomes that will face humanity and other planetary life forms. One unintended consequence of the process could well be a greater appreciation of the interlinking of life forms and a greater humility with regard to human beings' place in the world.

Finally, in this context, a radical hypothesis to be considered is that of James Lovelock who sees the earth, or Gaia, as 'a biotic-planetary regulatory system', in which the biosphere is regarded as a superorganism, with homeostasis as an emergent property (Hird 2010). Yet this does not mean that nature and life harmoniously continue to work for us, to maintain the human species. Rather symbiosis suggests that humans are not the central players: instead ubiquitous bacteria are more essential. It is also significant that bacteria routinely cross species and geopolitical boundaries: they are the most important environmental actants. Bacteria do not just engage in mutual symbiosis with other species, but continually engage in symbiogenesis: that is, they generate novelty and variation. Perhaps Gaia theory's key insight is the indifference of non-human life to human life. As a species we utterly depend upon bacteria, but we cannot say the same for bacteria. As Donna Haraway (2008: 3, cited in Hird 2010) remarks:

> I love the fact that human genomes can be found in only about 10 percent of all the cells that occupy the mundane space I call my body; the other 90 percent of the cells are filled with the genomes of bacteria, fungi, protists, and such, some of which play in a symphony necessary to my being alive at all, and some of which are hitching a ride and doing the rest of me, of us, no harm. I am vastly outnumbered by my tiny companions; better put, I become an adult human being in company with these tiny messmates. To be one is always to become with many.

This suggests that domestic animals such as dogs and cats are by no means the only companion species; it should also be noted that Donna Haraway (2008) frequently returns in *When Species Meet* to discuss eating, for the human gut shows our dependence on bacteria, our key companion species. If humans were to disappear planetary life would continue, but if microbial life were to disappear the planet would instantly die. The implications here suggest a further ethical consideration, one that reaches well beyond how we usually conceive an ethics of consumption, or an ethical way of life. Such a Gaia-inspired 'ethics of globality', Hird (2010) argues, implies the confinement of humans to small geographical islands, where their threat to other life forms could be minimized.

The sense of greater connectedness with other forms of non-human life which live in and interpenetrate human bodies is not of course new, as we find in various strands of vitalism and particularly the pantheist writings of Goethe (Bleicher 2007; Simmel 2007). The rejection of humanism for a single ontology may well encourage greater humility on the part of human beings to other life forms and stimulate the 'ethical urge to tread more lightly upon the earth' (Bennett 2004: 364). Certainly it points towards the opening up of a greater appreciation of the intertwined social life of things and an interest in where things come from, how they live for us and find their place in our world and what happens to them when they leave it. There is clearly an aesthetic dimension to this appreciation, not just of the elegance of other life forms as we find in television wildlife documentaries, their vitality, colour and obstinacy, but also in their capacity to surprise us. There is already an inventiveness and creativity in life which can help us rethink the image of nature in modernity, as a number of theorists advocate (Latour 2004; Guattari 2008; Haraway 2008; Bennett 2010). The questions raised by an ethics of consumption are not just about how to live a life of more regulated consumption, they ask us to think about the nature of the things we consume and their fate, their potential, or right to be something more than waste.

Maybe it also asks us to consider more the balance between material and immaterial consumption, with a shift involving more contemplative knowledge: to connoisseurship, the play with classifications and the education of the senses, as opposed to ostentatious display, waste and excess (Featherstone 2009b). It also asks us to interrogate the implications of our human projections on to nature, to think not just of the destruction of things downgraded to soon-to-be-waste, or to overemphasize the destructive and defensive nature of other life forms. We began with Zygmunt Bauman's question, and it would be fitting to end with another reflection taken from his book.

At one point Bauman (2008: 5) discusses the striking case of wasps. In a Panama study, London Zoological Society researchers found that a majority (fifty-six per cent) of 'working wasps' change their nests in their lifetime. They moved to other nests not just as unwelcome temporary workers who were resented, discriminated against and marginalized. Rather, they were accepted as full members of the adoptive community, and freely allowed to feed and groom the native brood. As Bauman remarks, '[t]he inevitable conclusion was that the nests the Londoners researched were *as a rule* "mixed populations", inside which the native-born and the immigrant wasps lived and worked cheek by jowl and shoulder to shoulder – becoming indistinguishable from one another, at least for the human outsiders, except through the help of electronic tags'. The conclusion for Bauman is that all too readily our reflections on 'the state of nature' have been a projection of our own practices. Fluidity of membership and mixing, then, may well be more the norm in both the insect and human worlds than we customarily credit. The Panama research is a welcome counter-example to the accustomed view in both science and popular culture of living colonies or bodies as akin to nation-states, which endeavour to maintain their borders to repel invaders that threaten their fixed identities.[6]

The main lesson of Bauman's use of the example of wasp receptivity and care for outsiders is as an analogy, providing a critique of the projection of our own rigidly constructed insider/outsider categories on to other life forms. For Bauman it is our responsibility to build a counter-ethics to combat neoliberal market economics, overconsumption and planetary threat. Yet as we have argued, there is also a further lesson, about the things we consume and which form part of our world. An appreciation of other life forms and our interconnectivity with them can lead to greater solidarity with things, a sense of the importance of the lives of other things: non-human ways of life have much to teach us about ethics and aesthetics, as Goethe and others have long suggested.

Notes

1 This piece is dedicated to Zygmunt Bauman for his 85th birthday on 19 November 2010 and is also in memory of Janina Bauman who died on 29 December 2009.

2 Discussions of the limits to growth gathered pace in the 1970s, especially in the wake of the 1972 Club of Rome report on 'The Limits to Growth' and the 1973 Oil Crisis. Earlier books such as Galbraith's *Affluent Society* (1958) and Marcuse's *One-Dimensional Man* (1964) provided social and economic critiques of the implications of

affluence and capitalist consumption. Marcuse and other critical theorists, such as Adorno and Benjamin, had focused on the negative effects of the domination of nature in terms of the domination of man. The 1960s counter culture also was important in stimulating a critique of consumerism.

3   There is not the space to discuss the intriguing suggestion made by Elspeth Probyn in her piece in this collection 'Feeding the world: Towards a messy ethics of eating', that in some ways food and eating have taken up the imperative for self-regulation that sexuality played in the nineteenth and twentieth centuries.

4   Foucault (1998) mentions the example of gayness: 'To be gay is not about identifying oneself with the psychological trait and the visible masks of the homosexual, but to seek to define and develop a way of life' (cited in Revel 2009: 48). Paul Rabinow (2009) also discusses the relation of this concern for 'care of the self' and experiments with new forms of friendship and sociability to Foucault's time spent in Berkeley and elsewhere in the US.

5   Massumi (2009) argues that the dominant regime of neoliberalism is now an environmental one, since it is no longer a matter of normalization but a government of conduct. This 'becoming-environmental' of power works through the 'regulation of effects', suggesting we may be entering a period of post- or neo-biopolitical politics, with forms of power institutionalized in the course of the nineteenth century now problematized. What is different is that man-as-species can no longer be considered as a relatively autonomous or separable element of the 'environment'.

6   A similar argument is made by Aryn Martin (forthcoming) who investigates bi-directional cell-trafficking between foetal and maternal bodies – foetal cells can be found in women's bodies long after pregnancy is over (microchimerism). Microchimerism researchers tend to liken the cells to human migrants, which Aryn Martin argues contributes to the 'state-ness' of bodies. Donna Haraway (Gane 2006) and Emily Martin (1992) have previously discussed the conception of the body as a defended nation-state in constant conflict with threatening intruders, as a dominant metaphor in immunology discourse. The related metaphor of the body-at-war has been tremendously productive in the fields of organ transplantation and pharmaceuticals in the late twentieth century. Yet, as Aryn Martin (2010) remarks, in microchimeric bodies, cells that are coded not self ('foreign' cells) live and reproduce happily in 'body nations' that are not their own.

Bibliography

Appadurai, A. (1986) 'Introduction', in A. Appadurai (ed.) *The Social Life of Things: Commodities in Cultural Perspective*, Cambridge: Cambridge University Press, pp. 3–63.

Baudelaire, C. (1964) *The Painter of Modern Life and Other Essays*, Oxford: Phaidon Press.

Bauman, Z. (2008) *Does Ethics Have a Chance in a World of Consumers?*, Cambridge, MA: Harvard University Press.

Bennett, J. (2004) 'The force of things: steps towards an ecology of matter', *Political Theory*, 32(3): 347–72.

—— (2010) *Vibrant Matter: A Political Ecology of Things*, Durham, NC: Duke University Press.

Binkley, S. and Littler, J. (2008) 'Introduction: cultural studies and anti-consumerism', *Cultural Studies*, 22(5): 519–30.

Bleicher, J. (2007) 'From Kant to Goethe: Georg Simmel on the way to *Leben*', *Theory, Culture & Society*, 24(6): 139–58.

Bourdieu, P. (1984) *Distinction*, London: Routledge.

Cooper, M. (2010) 'Turbulent worlds: financial markets and environmental crisis', Special Issue on Changing Climates, *Theory, Culture & Society*, 27(2–3): 167–90.

Davis, M. and Monk, D.B. (eds) (2007) *Evil Paradises: Dreamworlds of Neoliberalism*, New York: New Press.

Douglas, M. (1966) *Purity and Danger: An Analysis of Concepts of Pollution and Taboo*, London: Routledge.

Eder, K. (1990) 'The rise of counter-cultural movements against modernity: nature as a new field of class struggle', *Theory, Culture & Society*, 7(4): 21–47.

Featherstone, M. (1995) *Undoing Culture: Globalization, Postmodernism and Identity*, London: Sage.

—— (2000) 'Archiving cultures', *British Journal of Sociology*, Special Issue on the Millennium, 51(1) January 2000.

—— (2007) *Consumer Culture and Postmodernism*, 2nd edition, London: Sage.

—— (2009a) 'Ubiquitous media: an introduction', *Theory, Culture & Society*, 26(2–3): 1–22.

—— (2009b) 'Luxury: consumer culture and sumptuary dynamics.' Special issue on Le Luxe, *Les Cahiers Européens de l'Imaginaire,* No. 2, CNRS Editions, March 2010: 166–72.

—— (2010) 'Body, image and affect in consumer culture', *Body & Society*, 67(1): 193–221.

Foucault, M. (1991a) 'What is enlightenment?', in P. Rabinow (ed.) *The Foucault Reader,* Harmondsworth: Penguin, pp. 32–50.

—— (1991b) 'On the genealogy of ethics: an overview of work in progress', in P. Rabinow (ed.) *The Foucault Reader*, Harmondsworth: Penguin, pp. 340–72.

—— (1994) 'Le Sujet et le pouvoir', texte no. 306 in *Dits et écrits*, vol. 4. Paris: Gallimard; also 'The Subject and Power', in *Michel Foucault: Beyond Structuralism and Hermeneutics*, edited by Hubert Dreyfus and Paul Rabinow, Chicago, IL: Chicago UP.

—— (1997) *History of Sexuality Volume 3: The Care of the Self*, Harmondsworth: Penguin.

—— (1998) *History of Sexuality Volume 2: The Use of Pleasure*, Harmondsworth: Penguin.

—— (2005) *The Hermeneutics of the Subject: Lectures at the Collège de France 1981–2*, Houndmills: Palgrave Macmillan.

—— (2008) *The Birth of Biopolitics: Lectures at the Collège de France 1978–79*, Houndmills: Palgrave Macmillan.

—— (2009) *Le Courage de la Verité*, Paris: Seuil.

—— (2010) *The Government of the Self and Others: Lectures at the College de France 1982–83*, Houndmills: Palgrave Macmillan.

Galbraith, J.K. (1961) *The Affluent Society*, Harmondsworth: Penguin.

Gane, N. (2006) 'When we have never been human, what is to be done?: Interview with Donna Haraway', *Theory, Culture & Society*, 23(7–8): 135–58.

Guattari, F. (2008) *The Three Ecologies*, London: Continuum.

Haraway, D. (2008) *When Species Meet*, Minneapolis, MN: University of Minnesota Press.

Hawkins, G. (2006) *The Ethics of Waste*, Lanham, MD: Rowman & Littlefield.

Heidegger, M. (1977) *Martin Heidegger: Basic Writings*, San Francisco, CA: Harper Collins.

Hird, M. (2010) 'Indifferent globality: Gaia, symbiosis and "other worldliness"', Special Issue on Changing Climates, *Theory, Culture & Society*, 27(2–3).

Humphery, K. (2009) *Excess: Anti-Consumerism in the West*, Cambridge: Polity Press.

Introna, L.D. (2009) 'Ethics and the speaking of things', *Theory, Culture & Society* 26(4): 25–46.

Latour, B. (2004) *Politics of Nature*, Cambridge, MA: Harvard University Press.

Littler, J. (2009) *Radical Consumption: Shopping for Change in Contemporary Culture*, Maidenhead: Open University Press.

Maffesoli, M. (1991) 'The ethic of aesthetics', *Theory, Culture & Society*, 8(1): 7–20.

Marcuse, H. (1964) *One-Dimensional Man*, London: Routledge.

Martin, A. (forthcoming) 'Foreign cells in the mother(land): blurring the borders of body and nation in fetomaternal cell trafficking', *Body & Society*, 16(3).

Martin, B. (1982) *A Sociology of Contemporary British Cultural Change*, Oxford: Blackwell.

—— (1984) '"Mother wouldn't like it!" Housework as magic', *Theory, Culture & Society*, 2(2): 19–35.

Martin, E. (1992) 'Body narratives, body boundaries', in L. Grossberg, C. Nelson and P. Treichler (eds) *Cultural Studies*, London: Routledge.

Massumi, B. (2009) 'National enterprise emergency: steps towards an ecology of powers', Special issue on Michel Foucault, *Theory, Culture & Society*, 26(6): 153–85.

Miller, D. (2008a) *The Comfort of Thing*, Cambridge: Polity Press.

—— (2009) *Stuff*, Cambridge and Malden: Polity Press.

Park, B. and Roberts, J.T. (2010) 'Climate change, social theory and justice', Special Issue on Changing Climates, *Theory, Culture & Society*, 27(2–3): 134–66.

Rabinow, P. (2009) 'Foucault's untimely struggle: towards a form of spirituality', Special Issue on Michel Foucault, *Theory, Culture & Society*, 26(6): 25–44.

Revel, J. (2009) 'Identity, nature, life: three biopolitical deconstructions', Special Issue on Michel Foucault, *Theory, Culture & Society*, 26(6): 45–54.

Schor, J. (2008) 'Tackling turbo consumption: an interview', *Cultural Studies*, 22(5): 588–98.

Simmel, G. (2007) 'Kant and Goethe: on the history of the Modern Weltanschauung', *Theory, Culture & Society*, 24(6): 159–91.

Szerszynski, B. and Urry, J. (2010) 'Changing climates: an introduction', Special Issue on Changing Climates, *Theory, Culture & Society*, 27(2–3): 1–8.

Urry, J. (2010) 'Consuming the planet to excess', Special Issue on Changing Climates, *Theory, Culture & Society*, 27(2–3): 191–212.

Venn, C. (2010) 'Foucault: Special Issue: Interview by Mike Featherstone', *Theory, Culture & Society*. Online. Available HTTP: www.sagepub.net/tcs/default.aspx?page =interviewee25 (accessed 10 January 2010).

Venn, C. and Terranova, T. (2009) 'Thinking after Michel Foucault', Special Issue on Michel Foucault, *Theory, Culture & Society*, 26(6): 1–11.

Wynne, B. (2010) 'Strange weather, again: climate science as political art', Special Issue on Changing Climates, *Theory, Culture & Society*, 27(2–3): 289–305.

Part 1

Introduction

1 Introducing ethical consumption

Tania Lewis and Emily Potter

In a small courtyard at the University of Melbourne, there is an unprepossessing, somewhat makeshift-looking café called KereKere. The coffee on offer is organic, Fair Trade, Rainforest Alliance-branded and sustainable: a list of options we've increasingly come to expect even in corporate café chains such as Starbucks. But at this café, customers are also asked to decide how the profits from that sale are distributed every time they buy a coffee. As customers are handed their order, they are also presented with playing cards that allow them to choose from a list of causes where the café's profits will go. Operating in the spirit of 'kerekere', a Fijian custom in which a relative or neighbour can request something that is needed and it must be willingly given with no expectation of repayment, the café sees itself as fostering 'a culture that promotes community wellbeing'.

Figure 1.1 A chalk stencil of the KereKere logo on a pathway at Melbourne University, by Andrew Aston.

At this café, the traditional economic exchange associated with the purchase of a cup of coffee has been subtly moved into other territories through the introduction of questions of gift giving, and of responsibility, care and even love (the café's logo is a coffee cup with a series of hearts rising from it) into the exchange ritual. Such attempts by social justice-oriented businesses to reconfigure the privatized moment of spending as a communal act, thus positioning consumer choice as a site of responsibility, are increasingly commonplace in today's marketplace. No longer purely associated with fringe politics or hippie lifestyles, terms such as 'ethical' and 'responsible' shopping and 'conscience consumption' are increasingly entering into the everyday language as well as the shopping experiences and practices of so-called 'ordinary' consumers.[1] Whether through injunctions to buy 'guilt-free' Fair Trade chocolate, to minimize the consumption of energy and water on behalf of the planet, or to recycle or swap goods as a means of reducing consumption overall, mainstream consumer choice is increasingly marked by questions of 'care, solidarity and collective concern' (Barnett *et al.* 2005a: 45).

This broadly ethical turn within consumer culture, however, is not necessarily marked by a coherent set of shared politics or values. As both Littler and Humphery note in this collection, what we are terming here as 'ethical consumption' is not a clearly defined set of practices, but is rather a convenient catch-all phrase for a range of tendencies within contemporary consumer culture today. Books written for a general audience like Naomi Klein's *No Logo* (2000), Eric Schlosser's *Fast Food Nation* (2001), Peter Singer's *The Ethics of What We Eat* (2006) and Raj Patel's *Stuffed and Starved* (2007) can be seen as part of a broader fundamental critique of capitalism and consumer culture. In contrast, self-help guides like Sophie Uliano's *Gorgeously Green: 8 Simple Steps to an Earth-Friendly Life* (2008) and Christie Matheson's *Green Chic: Saving the Earth in Style* (2008) aim to 'change the world' while operating within the logic of consumer culture.

Similarly, a glance at the myriad websites and consumer organizations that have emerged around the issue of political consumerism also reveals the difficulty of defining or containing the field as well as aligning it with any particular political valences. The Freegan website (http://freegan.info), for instance, offers a radical critique of consumption-as-usual, suggesting as it does 'alternative strategies for living based on limited participation in the conventional economy and minimal consumption of resources', while ethical food-oriented website *The Ethicurean* blends politics and pleasure in asking consumers to 'chew the right thing'. Meanwhile, more pragmatic informational websites like *Ethiscore* offer to 'provide information on the companies behind the brand names and to promote the ethical use of consumer power', while the *Fair Trade Federation* website points to the limits of a purely individualist consumer-driven approach and the need to articulate such practices to a broader 'global Fair Trade movement'. Less politically badged is the website *Big Green Purse*, which offers lifestyle and shopping tips, as well as a blog space, for consumers wanting to 'shop green'.

The diversity and breadth of popular manifestations of concerns about contemporary materialism and overconsumption points to the limitations of definitional approaches to ethical consumption, and the problems inherent in attempting to draw boundaries around a 'field' that touches upon everything from questions of North–South consumer–producer relations, to concerns with buying locally, to issues of sustainability. As we discuss below, the emergent scholarship around ethical consumption likewise reflects the inchoate nature of 'the field', with work in the area drawing upon and moving between political economy, geography, sociology, cultural studies, business studies and sustainability studies. Among other things, the tendency towards an intermixing of theories and methods here reflects a healthy recognition of the need for an object- or practice-centred approach to mapping the rise of ethical practices and concerns within consumer culture, rather than privileging the often limited logics of any particular disciplinary or theoretical rationale.

Such an approach also reflects a shift in how the ethical is conceived in recent scholarly work. Foucault's location of ethics in 'regimes of living' (Collier and Lakoff 2005) and self-governing has influenced a range of articulations that do not understand ethics in terms of external moral codes and values, but instead ground ethical practice in the terrain of the everyday: the network of relations in which we are each caught up. This is what Gay Hawkins refers to as 'the ubiquity of ethical work' (2006: 13), which requires a variety of methodologies to track and analyse its multiple and situated manifestations.

Having highlighted these definitional difficulties, one shared point of commonality that arguably marks the various practices and concerns framed within the ethical consumer turn is the growing politicization of life and lifestyle practices. Michel Feher notes that this expanding realm of non-governmental activism is forcing a redefinition of what counts as politics today, highlighting too the 'open-endedness of the political process' (2007: 26), which is no longer limited to the classical sphere of the *polis* defined against the *oikos* or household. Collier and Lakoff describe how this distinction, a traditional basis for moral philosophy, is no longer tenable in the contemporary world, where ' "living" has been rendered problematic' by a host of concerns around the regulation of life itself, from genetically modified humans and crops to climate change (2005: 22).

Given this political context, why are we using the term 'ethical consumption' rather than, say, 'political consumerism' to label this trend? In part this is purely to reflect the popular currency of this term beyond the realm of academia. But we also want to signal something of a shift in the nature and status of consumer politics today. While, as we discuss below, there are clearly strong links between ethical consumption and political consumerism, we suggest that it is useful to make connections to, but also distinctions between, what has traditionally been associated with political consumerism – forms of activism, 'boycotts', consumer organizations, etc. – and more recent forms of responsible or conscience consumption, which we would see as being particularly oriented to the contemporary moment and its problematization of living. In the following two sections then, we will briefly discuss the development of political consumerism before turning our attention to the distinctive social, cultural and political context from which ethical consumption has emerged as an increasingly mainstream practice today.

Historicizing political consumerism: from boycotts to brands

While the mainstreaming of ethical consumption is a reasonably recent phenomenon, it can clearly be linked to a range of longer-term struggles around consumer politics. As Humphery notes in this collection, the mass market has long been the subject of political and cultural critique by Marxist, liberal and conservative critics alike. Likewise consumer culture has been marked by active political struggles since its beginnings. Here, boycotts can be seen as some of the earliest forms of political consumerism. In the eighteenth century, for example, during the American War of Independence, consumers refused to buy English goods as a way of breaking free from English colonialism. Thus, private consumer experiences were converted into public rituals, as 'neutral' consumer items such as imported British tea and clothing become politically charged objects.

One of the more important examples of organized political campaigning around consumption was the US White Label Campaign of 1899, driven by the women's consumer leagues that had first developed in the UK in the late nineteenth century and subsequently spread to the US and Europe. Initiated by middle-class women concerned with the conditions of workers, these consumer leagues worked to compile white (as opposed to black) lists of products and department stores associated with good labor practices. Representing an early example of 'buycotting' and an antecedent to the kinds of practices employed by Fair Trade and No Sweat campaigns today, the White Label Campaign took over from these earlier 'white lists', with campaigners positively labelling the products of factories that passed the League's inspection. It was during this period, too, that corporations began to take notice of consumer dissent and an increasing suspicion of corporate practices. The visible social impacts of the industrial revolution were met with new forms of corporate philanthropy, such as the trusts dedicated to social reform established by Joseph Rowntree in 1904 (Frankental 2001: 20).

Negative modes of campaigning in the form of boycotts also continued through into the twentieth century, with 'Don't buy where you can't work' campaigns for black civil rights impacting on the hiring practices of firms like Woolworths in the US during the 1920s–1940s. As Naomi Klein points out (2000: 336), one of the more recent boycotts and the first case of global brand-based activism was the targeting of Nestlé (1974–84) by various consumer, church and action groups in response to their marketing of infant formula in Africa and Asia, which the company pursued despite medical research which pointed to its associations with higher infant mortality when compared with breast milk. What the Nestlé case also signalled was the shift towards a different kind of political activism around consumerism. Nestlé was targeted because it was a highly visible corporation. Not only was it the largest multinational to make infant formula, it also had a particularly strong brand presence and promoted itself along the lines of 'family values', making it especially vulnerable to attack on this issue.

One of the central arguments Klein makes in her book *No Logo* (2000) is that the mainstreaming of political consumerism today is integrally connected to the centrality of brand culture. As she explains, global anti-consumerist movements have been around since the 1970s, yet the shift towards an everyday mode of ethical consumerism has ironically been enabled by the rise of branding as a central corporate strategy and the growing presence of corporate brands in everyday life. While contemporary branding has enabled corporations to seamlessly integrate themselves into spheres of life that were once relatively free of market logics, as Klein argues, the flip side of brand strategies that position corporations as good, responsible citizens is that they are increasingly being held to account for their social responsibilities to customers and the community at large. The culturally and socially immanent nature of the brand today is thus at once both the strength and the Achilles heel of the contemporary corporation. While Klein links the anti-globalization movement and its highly visible forms of activism to the rise of brand culture, the more ordinary, everyday politics associated with ethical consumer practices today can be linked clearly to the simultaneously ubiquitous and quotidian nature of brand culture.

The mainstreaming of ethical consumption

Aside from Klein's argument regarding the centrality of the brand, the distinctive quality of what counts as political consumerism today – and in particular its integration into the consciousnesses and shopping habits of ordinary consumers – can also be linked to a range of other contemporary developments. One important context for the ethical turn in mainstream consumerism has clearly been the increased focus within popular media culture on the impacts and risks of capitalist modernity, particularly in relation to the environment (Lewis 2008). The global success and impact of Al Gore's *An Inconvenient Truth* (2006) alongside youth-oriented 'green' entertainment spectacles such as Live Earth has seen the growing coverage of green issues by popular media.

Marketers and advertisers have been quick to jump on the green bandwagon, increasingly embracing the language of corporate responsibility and incorporating green rhetoric and imagery into media-marketing strategies, a trend that has in turn seen rising concerns about corporate 'greenwashing'. Closely linked to and overlapping with environmental critiques of modernity, a range of critical commentaries on materialism and 'affluenza' in wealthy developed nations (De Graaf *et al.* 2005) have recently made their presence felt in the mainstream cultural landscape, from media interest in anti-consumerist activism around corporate practices (particularly the targeting of major transnational corporations (TNCs) like Nike and McDonald's) to popular cultural critiques of over-consumption, such as that offered up in the 2004 film *Super Size Me*.

The rise of ethical consumption thus connects to a broader popular critique focused on a range of concerns around environmentalism, anti-materialism and unsustainable lifestyles. Barnett *et al.* also contend that Fair Trade organizations and campaigners played a central role in the mainstreaming of ethical consumption, using strategies such as survey data to actively work 'to mobilise "the ethical consumer" as a newsworthy narrative figure' (2005a: 48). Alongside the No Sweat campaigning of the mid 1990s (see Ross 1997), the media-savvy strategies of organized consumer groups saw the growing mainstream coverage of ethical issues.

Perhaps what was most crucial here in terms of normalizing the figure of the ethical consumer was the mode of address adopted by the ethical consumption lobby. As Barnett *et al.* argue, while grounded in 'wider programs of mobilization, activism, lobbying and campaigning' (2005a: 50), various organizations sought to impact on and shape everyday consumer practices by addressing the consumer in the media as a privatized, informed individual. Connelly and Prothero likewise note that in the past two decades the 'green consumer' has become an increasingly popular concept (2008), with government initiatives over the past decade targeting consumers as informed, calculative agents through domestically based campaigns such as 'reduce, reuse and recycle', thereby privileging the home as a site of politico-cultural change (Hobson 2006; Potter and Oster 2008).

The prominent figure of a savvy, reflexive consumer-citizen within the media and in government policy has inevitably found the attention of marketers concerned with exploiting the cultural shift towards 'affirmative purchasing' (Carrigan *et al.* 2004: 413). As the following quote from the marketing journal *Brand Strategy* suggests, the ethical consumer has become an important demographic entity for marketers.

> The 'Yuppies' defined lifestyle marketing in the 1980s. Emotional marketing came to the fore in the 1990s, typified by consumer 'cool hunters'. But the noughties will be judged by the 'New Premium Consumer' (NPC). This customer group has values that combine bohemian creativity, a rock 'n' roll attitude, diversity, ethical consumption and socio-political consciousness. Its members are early adopters, prepared to pay more for the individuality inspired by leading-edge cultures.
>
> (Hujic 2005: 32)

The perceived importance of this emergent, affluent consumer demographic is reflected in the rise of publications like *New Consumer* magazine, which offers green lifestyle advice on everything from food to fashion complete with glossy images of celebrity greenies. Describing itself on its website as 'the UK's hottest ethical lifestyle magazine', *New Consumer* tells prospective advertisers that '[o]ur readers are switched on, committed and active, geared up to support and buy from our advertisers, which are businesses changing the world'. As these examples indicate, in the paradigm of ethical consumption as it is represented by marketers, 'self-gratification is no longer defined in opposition to civility' (King 2006: 38). The emergence of ethically branded products and the expansion of ethical markets is a direct result of this recognition that consumption is a prominent site of political concern and exercise among citizens.

Though grounded in a longer history of political activism around consumer issues, what has been crucial to the mainstreaming of ethical consumerism is its integration into lifestyle and consumer culture, and its articulation with the dominant modes of agency associated with late modernity – that is, to forms of agency tied to conceptions of risk (both personal and collective) (Beck 1992), to reflexive, choice-based modes of identity (Giddens 1991), and to the decentring of the state as the recognized site of civic responsibility. This shift has resulted in the emergence of new forms of citizenship and agency as, increasingly, 'the inefficiency, the limits and the inevitable failings of state provision' incite 'individuals, families, communities [and] employees [to] take back to themselves the powers and responsibilities that have been acquired by states' (Rose 1999: 2–3).

This loss of public trust or investment in the state, caught up with the state's own retreat from social service provision, is a crucial factor in the rise of ethical consumption. In contrast, non-governmental organizations (NGOs) and organizations associated with 'good works' have gained in status and influence. While critics such as Lauren Berlant see such developments in negative terms as '[d]ownsizing citizenship to a mode of voluntarism' (1997: 5), our interest in this collection is, at the same time, to understand consumer-citizenship as a field of action, experience and effect that is both constraining and productive in terms of enabling new forms of political governance and agency.

A further and key context for the uptake in ethical consumerism is the widespread biopoliticization of Western culture, which connects to a growing 'ethicalization of existence' under advanced liberalism (Rose 1989: 263–64). Here, questions of lifestyle are imbued with questions of life and death, both literal and metaphoric. Climate change, for instance, threatens the well-being of many millions of people around the world. Clive Hamilton describes the processes involved in altering current unsustainable consumption as 'experiencing a sort of death' for the subject: if 'consumption activity is the primary means by which we create an identity and sustain a fragile sense of self', he writes, then when 'we are asked to change the way we consume . . . we are being asked to change who we are' (2007: 1). While consumption studies has long understood consumer practice as a mode of self-fashioning, the biopolitical tenor of contemporary existence means that human life itself, its constitution and its sustainment, is the underlying concern of the contemporary *polis*. Furthermore, and as we later discuss, actor-network theorists – influenced by the work of Bruno Latour and Michel Callon – have foregrounded the role of non-human agents (such as animals and the environment) in posing ethical questions and constituting ethical subjects, a strategy which de-privileges the human in the constitution of life (Marres 2009) while challenging the shape of ontological politics.

Our use of the term 'ethical' rather than 'political' consumption in this collection, then, is tied both to its broader currency in contemporary culture today and also to its utility for marking this aforementioned shift in the nature of politics.

The notion of ethical consumption for us addresses a cultural turn in advanced liberal societies around the world whereby political questions have become increasingly linked to people's ordinary domestic lives, that is to an *ordinary ethics* (Barnett 2005b). The notion of the 'ethical' here, as we have indicated, is not necessarily tied to a stable external moral framework but rather speaks to what is at once a more pluralized and privatized moral universe. The ordinary and often individualized nature of the ethical – drawing from Foucauldian work on governmentality – indicates a changing relation between citizen and society in which 'the government of conduct' increasingly operates 'on a territory marked out by the vectors of identity, choice, consumption and lifestyle' (Rose 1996: 344).

A reflexive, risk-oriented perspective on ethical consumption similarly implicates 'life politics' in a growing sense of connection between personal life choices and community, national and global concerns. Here, the ethical entails a turning outward to 'others', whether distant producers of commodities or non-human others such as the environment, thus locating the act of private consumer choice within a space or network of relations. In utilizing the rhetoric of 'choice', however, our concern is not to overemphasize the calculative rational dimensions of consumer practices, or in turn to underplay the structural constraints on consumers as social actors. Rather the notion of the 'ordinarily ethical' as we are using it here also aims to speak to the routinized and habitual nature of consumption, and to the ways in which ethical conduct is increasingly becoming tied to everyday practices, relations of being and ontological production.

Mapping the scholarly field

As we have noted, it is hard to draw a clear definitional line around the phenomenon of ethical consumption within contemporary culture. Equally, in emergent scholarship on the topic, it presents as a complex shifting object that requires a range of critical tools and approaches. In this next section we want to map briefly some of the work being done in the field, and to explore some of the disciplinary and scholarly frameworks that are emerging as particularly useful and relevant for thinking through consumer ethics today.

A number of monographs and edited collections touching on issues related to consumption, ethics and sustainability have been published within and across a range of disciplines. Key monographs in this burgeoning field include the work of two contributors to this collection, Jo Littler's *Radical Consumption: Shopping for Change in Contemporary Culture* (2009) and Kim Humphery's *Excess: Anti-consumerism in the West* (2010) (which both draw upon cultural studies/cultural theoretical approaches), and that of Swedish political scientist, Michele Micheletti's *Political Virtue and Shopping: Individuals, Consumerism, and Collective Action* (2003). A number of edited collections have also begun to address questions of ethical and alternative forms of consumption including Kate Soper *et al.*'s *The Politics and Pleasures of Consuming Differently* (2009), which discusses the ethics and politics of consumer choice within the broader frame of alternative conceptions of the good life and in particular 'alternative hedonism';

David A. Crocker and Toby Linden's *Ethics of Consumption* (1998), which draws upon a range of disciplinary approaches from philosophy to economics; and Rob Harrison *et al.*'s collection *The Ethical Consumer* (2005), which brings together the perspectives of academic theorists with campaigners and business practitioners. In addition, Jo Littler and Sam Binkley's guest edited issue of *Cultural Studies* (2008) on anti-consumerism tasks cultural studies to explore the ethical consumption phenomenon.

Aside from these more prominent interventions, work on ethical consumption is starting to emerge from a range of disciplines. The many fields engaged in scholarship around the question of consumer ethics – economics, marketing, political economy, business, geography, sociology and cultural studies – are often also concerned with a range of other parallel and overlapping questions and concerns including 'green capitalism', corporate social responsibility and the social life of objects. A crucial parallel literature is growing on sustainable consumption, including key texts such as *The Earthscan Reader on Sustainable Consumption* (2006), Cohen and Murphy's edited collection *Exploring Sustainable Consumption* (2001) and Gill Seyfang's *The New Economics of Sustainable Consumption: Seeds of Change* (2009), which, with their focus on policy concerns, political economy and the collective impact of consumer practices, offer an important corrective to excessively individualized lifestyle-oriented approaches. It is hard to do justice to all the scholarly approaches and debates around ethical consumption and related issues here, but it is possible both to summarize some of the main areas in the humanities and social sciences out of which work has emerged, and to point to the fields and approaches that we see as offering potential for grasping the complexity of the ethical turn in consumer culture.

Consumption studies

One of the more obvious fields where one would expect work to be undertaken on ethical consumption is in consumption studies although, ironically, scholars in this area have been somewhat slow to pick up this issue. What this field offers, however, is a range of explanatory frameworks for conceptualizing consumption as it is practised more broadly, some of which have considerable utility for comprehending the current ethical moment. Without rehearsing the well-trodden path of debates around consumer agency, for instance, one important line of argument within consumer studies of relevance to ethical consumption has been the critique of rationalist models of consumer behaviour (the consumer as sovereign) on the one hand and psychologized Frankfurt school conceptions (the consumer as passive dupe) on the other. What has emerged out of such debates is a range of more nuanced and shifting notions of consumers and their relation to identity construction and to everyday consumption practices.

Featherstone's classic account in *Consumer Culture and Postmodernism* (1991) of the growing symbolic role of consumption and of a broader stylized lifestyle culture through which one experiences and performs identity, offers one such hermeneutic for making sense of ethical consumption. Likewise, as we have indicated, more recent work on the centrality of branding to contemporary culture has extended this work on the symbolic dimensions of consumption in fruitful ways (Klein 2000; Lury 2004; Arvidsson 2006). Arvidsson, for instance, contends that brands are playing an increasingly central role as a source of shared beliefs, meanings and social connectedness within contemporary capitalism. In today's thoroughly branded world, consumption can be seen to have taken on an enabling and productive quality, as a site or set of practices through which consumers construct 'the common social world that connects them to each other' (Arvidsson 2006: 19). Under this model, ethical consumers and their relation to ethical brands such as Fair Trade and Oxfam can be seen in many ways as archetypal consumers within a branded environment which relies on the immaterial and emotional input and labour of consumers.

Another seminal text on consumption that offers potential for locating 'alternative' consumer practices is Colin Campbell's *The Romantic Ethic and the Spirit of Modern Consumerism*, first published in 1987. Here, the recent ethical turn can be linked back to a longer romantic strain in consumer culture. Revisiting debates about the origins of consumer capitalism, Campbell complicates Weberian arguments concerning the split between romantic ideals and modern materialism. Rather than seeing modern consumer capitalism as a site of disenchantment and alienation, Campbell argues that romanticism was and continues to be a central force within consumer culture. The romantic emphasis on developing one's moral character through creative hedonism and aestheticism is carried through for Campbell into the contemporary consumer world with its emphasis on imaginative desires, beauty and endless novelty. Although Campbell's focus is on the romantic underpinnings of consumer culture as a whole, such a frame is particularly useful for conceptualizing ethical and other alternative modes of lifestyle and consumerism associated, as they often are, with romantic concerns around re-enchanting modernity, connecting with nature, and with creative identity-shaping forms of engagement with the commodity world. Other scholars have similarly sought to re-think consumption; Kate Soper (2008), in her more recent work, writes about 'alternative hedonism' and the 'sensual pleasures of consuming differently' while Jane Bennett's research foregrounds 'commodity enchantment' as a trigger for ethical practice (2001).

A range of anthropologists of consumption, from Douglas and Isherwood to Appadurai, have also worked to challenge conventional and narrowly economistic models of consumerism and material culture. Anthropologist and consumption theorist Daniel Miller's work in particular seeks to frame consumer practices as productive of social, rather than just calculative and marketized, relations. Like Soper and Bennett, Miller emphasizes the affective dimensions of consumption, and talks about shopping for others as a marker of 'love and care' (Miller 2001: 230), rather than viewing practices of ethical consumption as being completely subsumed within the economic logic of commodity capitalism.

While the symbolic and emotional aspects of consumption have been increasingly brought to the fore in consumption studies, another important and underdeveloped strain in the field is a focus on ordinary consumption. Drawing upon cultural studies and sociological work on everyday life, the turn to the 'ordinary' offers some useful models for thinking through the ways in which ethical consumer and lifestyle practices are often not about conscious choices or overtly symbolic modes of communication, but rather are tied to the rhythms and habits of everyday life (Gronow and Warde 2001; Hawkins 2006). As we discuss below some of these concerns about the affective, non-symbolic and everyday nature of consumption are being further developed and explored in other areas, such as cultural geography and Latourian studies of material culture.

In thinking through the everyday modalities or, more specifically, the *habitus* of ordinary consumption, a final important line of thought within consumption studies – touched upon by several contributors in this collection – concerns questions of class and distinction. A recurrent theme within both popular and scholarly discussions of ethical consumption is its bourgeois connotations, with journalist George Monbiot warning in a 2007 article that '[e]thical shopping is in danger of becoming another signifier of social status'. Veblen's theory of status emulation would seem to continue to hold some utility for conceptualizing the more conspicuous, performative dimensions of green and ethical consumer practices, such as the strategic placement of Fair Trade products in middle-class homes.

Bourdieu's arguments about distinction, however, offer rather more nuance to the classed dimensions of ethical consumption. As Littler notes in this collection, claims made for the democratic nature of consumer-based politics (the notion that all consumers have free choice) continue to be undermined by the recognition of the class barriers to consuming the 'right goods' (such as access to organic produce), barriers that are not just economic but related to the kind of class dispositions or cultural capital and forms of taste people bring to their consumption practices. Much of what gets defined as 'good' forms of consumption and lifestyle today, then, are not so coincidentally tied to middle-class virtues. Such debates about class and consumption point to some of the structural inequities and cultural values that frame the field of consumption complicating a one size fits all model of the consumer.

Geography

While consumption studies has been relatively slow to take up the challenge of alternative consumer practices, the discipline that has perhaps contributed most to the emerging scholarship on this topic has been geography, particularly cultural geography. The global cultural and political contexts to which alternative and political consumerist practices inevitably speak clearly point to the relevance of forms of analysis that emphasize questions of space and place. These analyses frame such questions in terms of a range of interconnected concerns around the politics of post- and neo-colonialism and global economics, as well as the 'non-representational' and 'more-than-human' politics associated with the work of the 'new cultural geographers' such as Nigel Thrift and Sarah Whatmore.

Geographers have brought a range of different critical lenses to questions of ethical consumption, but one of their primary contributions has been to map what has been called the 'commodity chain': that is, to expose the connections between production processes and consumption practices and the various activities, relations and politics in between. As Hughes and Reimer discuss in the introduction to their edited collection *Geographies of Commodity Chains* (2004), the rise of commodity chain analysis has gone hand in hand with increasing popular interest in the social lives of commodities. The recent emergence of a flurry of films such as *Black Gold* ('As westerners revel in designer lattes and cappuccinos, impoverished Ethiopian coffee growers suffer the bitter taste of injustice') and popular exposés such as the book *Bitter Chocolate: The Dark Side of the World's Most Seductive Sweet* speaks to a growing concern among political activists and consumers alike regarding the provenance and the politics of the goods they buy.

In the context of globalized commodity production, the growing length of commodity chains and the increasing disconnection between consumers and producers, geographic approaches are becoming crucial to understanding the complex relations underpinning consumption today. As Hughes and Reimer note, a range of approaches to mapping the commodity chain have emerged from the field. The more conventional global commodity chain approach seeks (like the popular exposés of commodity production mentioned above) to reveal the hidden geographies embedded or masked within the social relations of contemporary consumption, reflecting a Marxist-inspired concern with commodity fetishism and with foregrounding processes of commodity production in peripheral regions of world economy for retail and consumption in the 'centre'. The political economy of the global agri-food industry, particularly meat production, is often seen as exemplary of this disconnect between consumers and the exploitative realities of production. Loans from the World Bank to Central America, for instance, have seen traditional forms of farming and use of land increasingly tied to broader globalized and industrialized systems of meat production, which increasingly treat cattle as commoditized biological goods in feed lots and large ranches.

As Hughes and Reimer note, however, global commodity chain approaches are not without their limitations. Questions of the role of the consumer and the retail dimension of the commodity chain are often treated as trivial matters – purely starting points for moving on to discuss the more important exploitative relations of production. The focus of global food chain analysis, for example, is invariably trained on the industrialization of labour processes at the level of production rather than taking into account the broader role of retailers, restaurants, nutritionists, advertisers and other players in the global food industry. Such approaches tie into a fairly narrow understanding of consumer society as driven by Fordist logics of economic efficiency and standardization, with consumers configured as mindless and passive, uncomplainingly embracing a massified experience of food. A more complex commodity chain model, by contrast, endows consumers with significant influence to impact on sites of production, both close and distant, as in the case of pressures towards monocultivation of foods in Brazil and Thailand to supply the desires of fickle Western markets.

Another significant dimension of consumer influence relates to the growing visibility and impact of the political and ethical dimensions of consumption within and on commodity chain processes. Geographers have highlighted the ways in which consumers' geographical knowledges can play a central role in progressive social change through notions such as 'caring at a distance'. Such concerns with revealing the spatial politics behind commodities likewise often underpin the rationale and marketing strategies behind ethical brands and products such as Fair Trade, whose advertisements frequently feature images of first world consumers alongside farmers, weavers and textile makers from the global South. Similarly, strategies employed in relation to labelling products as locally produced also speak to the rising concern with food miles – that is, the amount of carbon dioxide emitted in the transportation of a product from source to consumer – and the generation of new auditing techniques and marketing devices that certify and label products as 'ethical' in this regard, such as Tesco's placement of 'air-mile' stickers on fresh produce in the UK. The defetishization of commodities here, then, is placed side by side with notions of consumer sovereignty and moral agency (Goodman 2004).

At the same time critical geographers like Ian Cook and Philip Crang have also pointed to the limits of such consumer-centred approaches (1996). Critiquing the idea that knowledge about commodities will somehow reveal their 'essence', they argue that ethical consumption is often involved in a process of double fetishization in which consumer knowledge about commodities is at once restricted at the same time as marketers and retailers emphasize particular geographic knowledges as a way of adding distinction to products. Here undue weight is given to the ability of first world consumers to understand and impact on the 'realities' of life for producers in the global South – an emphasis that also tends to reinscribe rather than undo the colonizing power relations between (agentic) northern consumers and (passive) southern producers.

Cultural geographers have also attempted to capture further the complexity of the relations between production and consumption and other dimensions of the commodity chain through non-linear models such as commodity circuits and, drawing upon Latourian or actor-network approaches, commodity networks. Such approaches are again sceptical of the objectivist notion that one can simply unveil the 'real' conditions of production. They are also particularly critical of human-centred models of consumer sovereignty; instead their focus is on the role of a range of human and non-human actors (actants) and practices in the construction of commodity relations. Much work in this field has accordingly sought to track the operations of non-human materials and objects (such as plastic bags) as social actors in themselves – possessing 'agency' not because of what humans do or do not do with them, but because of their specific material qualities and what these trigger or afford (Hawkins 2006; Foster 2008).

Lastly, and relatedly, the British geographers Clive Barnett and Nick Clarke, along with fellow researchers Paul Cloke and Alice Malpass (2005a and 2005b), have sought to critique narrow conceptualizations of ethical decision-making by consumers in their research on ethical consumption in the UK. While they focus primarily on the role of consumers in terms of the ethics and politics of responsibility in contemporary neoliberalism, their work emerges out of a growing recognition in cultural geography that the ethical dimensions of consumption are enacted and produced through everyday practices, as well as being figured as 'ethical' through their wider framing as practices of 'good citizenship'. This recognition has led to a shift in focus from the informed consumer as rational agent to a growing emphasis on the networks, organizations and the material contexts that shape people's consumption practices.

Political theory

This understanding of everyday consumption practices as a space of politics and citizenship brings us to another scholarly field of interest that is central to understanding ethical consumption today: debates concerning civic culture and political citizenship. As we have already noted, one important context for the mainstreaming of political and ethical forms of consumerism is the emergence of diverse forms of citizenship under neoliberalism. These include consumer-oriented modes of citizenship (Miller 2007) and also ecological or sustainable forms of citizenship, whereby a recognition of planetary limits informs an ethos of responsibility to, and rights for, non-human others (Dobson and Sáiz 2005). Scholars such as Aihwa Ong have pointed to a fundamental transformation in the ethics of citizenship in this context, characterized by governance regimes 'concerned less with the social management of the population . . . than with individual self-governing' (2006: 501). Accordingly, the ascent of micropolitics, or 'the relational arts of the self' (Connolly 1999: 146), as a scholarly interest over recent years, provides an important frame for understanding the phenomenon of ethical consumption that moves beyond a blanket critique of neoliberal impacts.

Similarly, Michele Micheletti (2003) argues that – in a 'post-political' world – we are seeing the rise of a range of new forms of micro-political and lifestyle-based modes of civic agency and citizenship based around people's personal lives and relations with others. Viewing the growing role of lifestyle politics or 'sub-politics' from a European social democracy perspective, for Micheletti the rise of political and ethical questions around consumption 'encourages, empowers, and allows citizens to take more responsibility for their personal and collective wellbeing' (2003: 9), a process she sees in terms of 'individualized collective action' (29).

Micheletti's perspective sits alongside a range of recent debates by scholars concerned with rethinking political citizenship and civic agency in order to account for the ways in which people's everyday lives today are increasingly embedded in questions of civic values and concerns around social responsibility. As we have indicated earlier, these reconfigurations of political form and practice complicate oppositions between public issues, citizenship and private interests

(Couldry 2006; Dahlgren 2006; Miller 2007). For numerous scholars, rather than reflecting the decline of civic culture, the rise of consumer-driven politics can be seen instead as heralding 'increases in various forms of lifestyle politics' (Bennett 1998: 745) forged at the level of everyday 'interpersonal bonds' and 'micro-mobilization' (Carty 2002: 132).

Conclusion

In his article, 'From ethical consumerism to political consumption', Nick Clarke wonders why ethical consumption is not referenced in the same terms as political consumption and suggests that it is because 'until recently, we have failed to recognize the political character of such consumption' (2008: 1877). As we have argued, the contemporary politics of consumption today has to be understood as emerging out of a broader politicization and ethicalization of everyday life, with 'the political' now referencing multiple arenas of action and concern, from the civic entanglements of the *polis* to micro-practices of the self and domestic lifestyles.

As we've noted, this recognition of lifestyle politics has understandably not been without its critics. The refiguring of consumption as a site of ethical and political engagement has been regarded suspiciously by some as a classic characteristic of advanced liberal governance, in which civic responsibility is reframed in terms of individual choice, 'self-realization' and the 'stakeholder society' (Pringle 1999: 267) at the expense of state care and conventional understandings of civic participation and citizenship. Critics also point to the limitations of a politics defined by and through the logics of the market. Monbiot, for instance, has little time for what he sees as the superficial platitudes of ethical consumption which, to his mind, encourage people to continue consuming while simply replacing less 'caring' products with others. 'It does not matter whether we burn fossil fuels with malice or with love he writes,' (2007: 4).

Monbiot's criticism, while having considerable validity, relies on reducing a complex field of practices and politics to a caricature. As we note, the reality is that the politics that constellate under this term range from those that operate merely within the logic of consumer culture to those that aim to radically reform it. Monbiot's critique also underestimates the reflexive awareness of consumers, many of whom are adept at discerning between ethical products, and who are becoming increasingly aware of 'greenwashing' tactics employed by marketers. The growing expectation that the ethical claims of products will be backed up by systems of audit and accreditation reflects this awareness. But as Humphery's arguments about anti-consumerism and Parkins and Craig's discussion of slow living in this collection suggest, where ethical consumption becomes potentially much more interesting and challenging as a cultural force is not so much through its impact on markets and products but rather through the questions it poses more broadly around styles of living, and the fashioning of new ethico-political realities. As such, it cannot be glossed over simply as a mere marketing ploy or fashion trend for bourgeois bohemians. Instead it asks to be approached through a broader political frame, which reveals not just its affordances, but also its limitations and inequities. These limitations are linked to foundational questions around the ongoing sustainability of existing social and economic organizational structures in the global North. Can we live 'the good life' within a narrowly materialist culture? As Joel Bakan puts it, can capitalism have a conscience? (2004: 31). What the practices and politics of ethical consumption at its most radical can bring us to then is a rethinking of the 'good life' and of ethical living in ways that fundamentally challenge the logics of consumer culture itself.

Critical perspectives on ethical consumption

Given our emphasis on the broad and variegated nature of ethical consumption, this collection is less concerned with defining the field than with offering a variety of perspectives into the diversity of politics, practices, sites and actors that constitute this cultural turn. Reflecting the complex and evolving nature of the area, the essays in this collection offer a range of methods and modes of analysis. As we have noted, as an object of study or enquiry ethical consumption has little respect for academic disciplinary boundaries and requires a multi-modal approach. Within the broad confines of the humanities and social sciences, this collection attempts to offer just such a multi-focal and interdisciplinary engagement with the topic at hand.

Part 2, 'Politics', offers a range of perspectives on the political concerns and contexts out of which the ethical turn in consumer culture has emerged. Jo Littler provides an overview of the various and contradictory ways in which ethical consumption is viewed, as at once a field of radical potential and political limitation. For her, the political efficacy of ethical consumption is not a given but can only be assessed through the specificities of particular, localized practices. Kim Humphery places the phenomenon of ethical consumption in the broader context of contemporary anti-consumerist movements in the West, from 'culture jamming' to 'slow living'. Humphery thus explores how ethical consumption relates to, bolsters and contradicts these other forms of contesting consumerism. Timothy J. Scrase's essay examines the politics of global Fair Trade through a discussion of the marketing of Fair Trade goods on the web. Discussing the 'competitive entrepreneurialism' normalized in Fair Trade markets, Scrase suggests that processes of commodification pose challenging questions to the ethical claims of Fair Trade products and their consumers. Michael Gard links the question of ethical consumption to contemporary concerns around the so-called 'obesity epidemic' in the global North, examining to what extent the rise of neoliberalism accounts for the emergence of this perceived 'epidemic'. Documenting the complex 'ideological contestations' within obesity debates, Gard concludes that the 'obesity epidemic' is not the product of any single ideological enterprise nor is it fully explainable via any single theoretical framework.

The chapters in Part 3, 'Commodities and Materiality', focus on a range of goods in relation to broader questions around commodity chains and networks, the 'placing' of ethical products, in terms of both local and global contexts, and the broader political economies that frame consumer 'choice'. Benjamin Coles and Philip Crang argue that the dynamics of place and place-making play a central role in ethical and alternative forms of consumption. Drawing upon fieldwork at London's Borough Market, they examine the ways in which the performative and representational space of the market works to produce an experience of 'alternative' cultures and geographies of food consumption for consumers in which commodities are both de- and re-fetishized. Broadening the focus to a discussion of the global food industry, Elspeth Probyn pushes the debate concerning the ethics of eating beyond the black and white terrain of moralized conduct. Critiquing the narrow 'reification of choice' which spotlights the responsibilities of the individual eater, Probyn instead locates questions of consumer ethics within the broader context of government policies, global agri-business, and the rise of 'un-natural foodstuffs' to foreground the limitations of choice-based models for understanding 'the complexities of eating'. Ethically branded bottled water is the subject of Emily Potter's chapter, in which she discusses a range of such brands as characteristic of the ethical turn in marketing this environmentally suspect product. On the one hand, 'ethical water' sits within paradigms of responsibilized consumption, where the consumer is invited to perform certain subjectivities through their engagement with 'ethical' bottled water. Yet it also indicates the ways in which the administration of life has been foregrounded in advanced liberal economies, as producers actively position themselves as biopolitical agents in their claims to 'do good work'. Paul Starr turns his focus to the wine industry. Comparing the politics and debates over sustainability and social responsibility in Australia and the UK, he teases out distinctions between ethical consumption and sustainable consumption, while foregrounding the limits of rational choice models of consumer sovereignty. Richard Maxwell and Toby Miller employ an internationally oriented political economy approach to consider questions of ethical consumption posed by the global electronics market. The complex geographies of electronic commodity production, and the ambiguous nature of electronic technology framed simultaneously as a solution to sustainability challenges, and as a significant contributor to pollution and waste, mean that determining the 'eco-ethical' nature of electronics is far from straightforward. The final two chapters in the section address the issue of ethical consumption and fashion. Adrian Franklin looks at the ethics of second-hand consumption given the contemporary popularity of vintage and retro goods, and changing associations with the purchase and use of second-hand products. Providing a complex historical account of this consumer market and practice, Franklin shows that the emergence of this market is a result of much more than just 'ethical' or sustainability concerns. Gibson and Stanes similarly present a complex picture of ethical fashion as an alternative market in what is increasingly identified as an environmentally unsound industry. They note, like Franklin, that while sustainable fashion practices are on the rise the motivations behind these practices are difficult to ascribe to purely ethical purposes.

Part 4, 'Practices, Sites and Representations', focuses on how ethical consumption is conducted, promoted and portrayed in people's lives, homes and neighbourhoods and through leisure activities such as tourism and watching television. In their chapter, Wendy Parkins and Geoff Craig look at the question of ethical lifestyles examining, in particular, the concept of slow living. They argue that practices of sustainable living – manifested in changing modes not only of consumption but also of food production, transportation and energy generation – require a slowness that carries with it a more acute consciousness or ethical sensibility in relation to place and the rhythms of everyday life, including weather patterns and seasonality. Fiona Allon turns her attention to the rising popularity of green home renovations as an example of individualized politics under advanced liberal governance. However, as she argues, this does not necessarily represent a turn away from civic engagement. Drawing on interviews with eco-home owners, Allon illuminates the intersections of individual and public interest that arise in the practices of green home-making. In their chapter, Kersty Hobson and Ann Hill position the rise of organized gardening projects around the world in the context of government interventions into community health and well-being. In a close empirical study of two such projects, one from Australia and one from the Philippines, they seek to complicate a straightforward reading of organized gardening initiatives as disciplining modes of governmentality, and instead elucidate the ways in which participating subjects resist and intervene in predetermined outcomes. Using Bourdieu's theory of cultural intermediaries, Frances Bonner takes a look at lifestyle television as a site in which various modes of ethical consumption are explored and promoted. Gardening and food-related programmes in both the UK and Australia form the particular focus of her chapter, which views cultural intermediaries as productive of consumption patterns that move towards reduced and alternative forms of consumption. Cathy Greenfield and Peter Williams offer a historical account of the practice of ethical investment, tracking its origins to the emergence of finance as a 'virtuous' profession in the seventeenth century, and more recently with the conjunction between discourses of sustainability and finance literacy. The chapter considers the cultural formation of the 'ethical investor' through media presentation of injunctions to make profits through doing good. Finally, in their essay, Robert Melchior Figueroa and Gordon Waitt analyse the phenomena of ecotourism as a mode of consumption that implicates a range of ethical concerns including environmental sustainability, postcolonial relations, heritage and development. Uluru in Australia provides a case study of what they call 'the moral terrains' of ecotourism in which the multiple interests that cluster around the practice of tourism in such a site are negotiated. Appropriately their essay ends the collection with a focus on the shifting and 'relational' nature of ethics – an approach which decentres the conscious human subject from ethical decision-making, framing ethical practices as processes produced through and in relation to broader social, cultural, political and economic networks.

Acknowledgements

Thanks to Jo Littler and Alison Huber for their extensive critical comments on this chapter.

Note

1   As Harrison notes, by 2001 'sixty-six per cent of UK consumers in their thirties and forties claimed to have boycotted brands because of their unethical behaviour, and eighty per cent of all consumers thought that companies should attach at least as much importance to "social responsibility" as profits when making business decisions' (2003: 129).

Bibliography

Arvidsson, A. (2006) *Brands: Meaning and Value in Media Culture*, London and New York: Routledge.

Bakan, J. (2004) *The Corporation: The Pathological Pursuit of Profit and Power*, London: Constable & Robinson.

Barnett, C., Clarke, N., Cloke, P. and Malpass, A. (2005a) 'The political ethics of consumerism', *Consumer Policy Review*, 15(2): 45–51.

——(2005b) 'Consuming ethics: articulating the subjects and spaces of ethical consumption', *Antipode*, 37: 23–45.

Beck, U. (1992) *Risk Society: Towards a New Modernity*, London: Sage.

Bennett, J. (2001) *The Enchantment of Modern Life: Attachments, Crossings and Ethics*, Princeton and Oxford: Princeton University Press.

Bennett, L. (1998) 'The uncivic culture: communication, identity, and the rise of lifestyle politics', *PS: Political Science and Politics*, 31: 740–61.

Berlant, L.G. (1997) *The Queen of America Goes to Washington City: Essays on Sex and Citizenship*, Durham, NC: Duke University Press.

Campbell, C. (2007) *The Romantic Ethic and the Spirit of Modern Consumerism*, Oxford, Blackwell.

Carrigan, M., Szmigin, I. and Wright, J. (2004) 'Shopping for a better world? An interpretive study of the potential for ethical consumption within the older market', *The Journal of Consumer Marketing*, 21(6): 401–17.

Carty, V. (2002) 'Technology and counter-hegemonic movements: the case of Nike Corporation', *Social Movement Studies*, 1(2): 129–46.

Clarke, N. (2008) 'From ethical consumption to political consumerism', *Geography Compass*, 2(6): 1870–84.

Cohen M. and Murphy, J. (eds) (2001) *Exploring Sustainable Consumption: Environmental Policy and the Social Sciences*, Amsterdam: Pergamon.

Collier, S.J. and Lakoff, A. (2005) 'On regimes of living', in A. Ong and S.J. Collier (eds) *Global Assemblages: Technology, Politics, and Ethics as Anthropological Problems*, Malden, MA: Blackwell.

Connolly, J. and Prothero, A. (2008) 'Green consumption: life-politics, risk and contradictions', *Journal of Consumer Culture*, 8(1): 117–45.

Connolly, W.E. (1999) *Why I am Not a Secularist*, Minneapolis and London: University of Minnesota Press.

Cook, I. and Crang, P. (1996) 'The world on a plate: culinary culture, displacement and geographical knowledges', *Journal of Material Culture*, 1(2): 131–53.

Couldry, N. (2006) 'Culture and citizenship: the missing link?', *European Journal of Cultural Studies*, 9(3): 321–39.

Crocker, D. A. and Linden, T. (eds.) (1998) *Ethics of Consumption: The Good Life, Ethics and Global Stewardship*. Lanham, MD: Rowman & Littlefield.

Dahlgren, P. (2006) 'Doing citizenship: the cultural origins of civic agency in the public sphere', *European Journal of Cultural Studies*, 9(3): 267–86.

De Graaf, J., Naylor, T.H. and Wann, D. (2005) *Affluenza: The All-Consuming Epidemic*, San Francisco, CA: Berrett-Koehler.

Dobson, A. and Sáiz, A.V. (eds) (2005) *Citizenship, Environment, Economy*, Abingdon, Oxon and New York: Routledge.

Featherstone, M. (1991) *Consumer Culture and Postmodernism*, London: Sage Publications.

Feher, M. (2007) 'The governed in politics', in M. Feher (ed.) with G. Krikorian and Y. McKee, *Nongovernmental Politics*, New York: Zone Books.

Foster, R.J. (2008) *Coca-Globalization: Following Soft Drinks from New York to New Guinea*, New York and Basingstoke: Palgrave Macmillan.

Frankental, P. (2001) 'Corporate social responsibility – a PR invention?', *Corporate Communications: An International Journal*, 6(1): 18–23.

Giddens, A. (1991) *Modernity and Self-Identity: Self and Society in the Late Modern Age*, Cambridge: Polity.

Goodman, M.K. (2004) 'Reading fair trade: political ecological imaginary and the moral economy of fair trade foods', *Political Geography*, 23(7): 891–915.

Gronow, J. and Warde, A. (2001) *Ordinary Consumption*, London and New York: Routledge.

Hamilton, C. (2007) 'Building on Kyoto', *New Left Review*, 45(May–June). Online. Available HTTP: www.newleftreview.org/?view = 2671 (accessed 15 February 2009).

Harrison, R. (2003) 'Corporate social responsibility and the consumer movement', *Consumer Policy Review*, 13(4): 127–31.

Harrison, R., Newholm, T. and Shaw, D. (eds) (2005) *The Ethical Consumer*, Sage: London.

Hawkins, G. (2006) *The Ethics of Waste: How We Relate to Rubbish*, Sydney: UNSW Press.

Hobson, K. (2006) 'Bins, bulbs, and shower-timers: on the techno-ethics of sustainable living', *Place and Environment*, 9(3): 317–36.

Hughes, A. and Reimer, S. (2004) 'Introduction', in A. Hughes and S. Reimer (eds) *Geographies of Commodity Chains*, New York: Routledge.

Hujic, L. (2005) 'Brand papers: luxury leaders', *Brand Strategy* 32.

Humphery, K. (2009) *Excess: Anti-consumerism in the West*, Polity Press.

Jackson, T. (2006) *The Earthscan Reader on Sustainable Consumption*, Earthscan.

King, S. (2006) *Pink Ribbons, Inc.: Breast Cancer and the Politics of Philanthropy*, Minneapolis and London: University of Minnesota Press.

Klein, N. (2000) *No Logo: Taking Aim at the Brand Bullies*, New York: Picador.

Lewis, T. (2008) 'Transforming citizens: green politics and ethical consumption on lifestyle television', *Continuum*, 22(2): 227–40.

Littler, J. (2009) *Radical consumption: Shopping for change in contemporary culture*, Open University Press.

Littler J. and Binkley, S. (eds) (2008) 'Anti-consumerism and cultural studies', *Cultural Studies*, 22 (5).

Lury, C. (2004) *Brands: The Logos of the Global Economy*, New York: Routledge.

Marres, N. (2009) 'Testing powers of engagement: green living experiments, the ontological turn and the undoability of involvement', *European Journal of Social Theory*, 12(1): 117–33.

Micheletti, M. (2003) *Political Virtue and Shopping: Individuals, Consumerism, and Collective Action*, New York and Basingstoke: Palgrave Macmillan.

Miller, D. (2001) 'The poverty of morality', *Journal of Consumer Culture*, 1(2): 225–43.

Miller, T. (2007) *Cultural Citizenship: Cosmopolitanism, Consumerism and Television in a Neoliberal Age*, Philadelphia, PA: Temple University Press.

Monbiot, G. (2007) 'Environmental feedback: a reply to Clive Hamilton', *New Left Review*, 45 (May–June). Online. Available HTTP: www.newleftreview.org/?view = 2672 (accessed 15 February 2009).

Ong, A. (2006). *Neoliberalism as Exception: Mutations in Citizenship and Sovereignty*, Durham, NC: Duke University Press.

Potter, E. and Oster, C. (2008) 'Communicating climate change: public responsiveness and matters of concern', *Media International Australia*, 127: 116–26.

Pringle, H. and Thompson, M. (1999) *Brand Spirit: How Cause Related Marketing Builds Brands*, Chichester, West Sussex: John Wiley & Sons.

Rose, N. (1989) *Governing the Soul: The Shaping of the Private Self*, London: Routledge.

—— (1996) *Inventing our Selves: Psychology, Power, and Personhood*, Cambridge: Cambridge University Press.

—— (1999) *Powers of Freedom: Reframing Political Thought*, Cambridge: Cambridge University Press.

Ross, A. (1997) *No Sweat: Fashion, Free Trade, and the Rights of Garment Workers*, New York: Verso.

Seyfang, G. (2009) *The New Economics of Sustainable Consumption: Seeds of Change*, Palgrave Macmillan.

Soper, K., Ryle, M. and Lyn, T. (eds) (2009) *The Pleasures and Politics of Consuming Differently: Better Than Shopping*, London: Palgrave Macmillan.

Soper, K. (2008) 'Alternative hedonism, cultural theory and the role of aesthetic revisioning', *Cultural Studies*, 22(5): 567–87.

Part 2
Politics

2 What's wrong with ethical consumption?

Jo Littler

My opening question is somewhat loaded. To ask what's wrong with ethical consumption is to foreground its problems, its failures, its inabilities to live up to the promise of its name. This chapter does aim to consider the criticisms – which are many, and varied – of ethical consumption. Such criticisms are widely circulated in day-to-day discourse. They include, for example, the following ideas: that ethical consumption is ultimately ineffective because it is merely used by a minority as a panacea for middle-class guilt; that it is an individualistic form of politics, a means through which neoliberal governments encourage consumers to become 'responsibilized' amidst the atrophying of wider social safety nets; that it is produced primarily through the whitewashing and profit-seeking actions of corporations, and as such can have little radical purchase; and that it is, in itself, a fractured field of often dissociated and contradictory practices, or simply too large a category to be meaningful.

Such issues are important and deserve to be addressed. However, in looking at 'what's wrong with ethical consumption', the aim of the chapter is somewhat broader, as I want to consider some of the key criticisms which have commonly (and not so commonly) been made of the practice as a way of *navigating* this often quite complicated area. This means that the chapter is also open to the potential or 'progressive' possibilities that ethical consumption may have at the same time as looking at its contradictions, pitfalls and dead ends. The chapter therefore summarizes different *attitudes* toward these positions, and draws on a number of theories from media and cultural studies and adjacent disciplines to contextualize and interpret them. Charting some of the nascent lines of debate which are emerging around this expanding area can help emphasize how we need to use a broader range of theory in order to consider the complexities of the zone of ethical consumption as a space which, the chapter argues, can be colonized and stratified by both reactionary and progressive forces.

Contradictory consumption

To begin with, I want to engage with the issue of whether or not ethical consumption is a field that is simply too large and fractured to be meaningful. It is certainly the case that an extremely wide range of practices has come to be grouped under the term. These include the creation of Fair Trade products which aim to give producers a 'decent price' for their labour; of anti-sweatshop products, such as clothes produced by American Apparel or No Sweat; local products, as popularized, for example, by the Italian 'slow food' movement and local vegetable box schemes; and consuming less by, for instance, 'downshifting' or swapping goods on Freecycle (Parkins and Craig 2006; Littler and Moor 2008; Thomas 2008; Sassatelli 2009; Soper *et al.* 2009). It can also include consumer 'buycotts' (boycotting a brand deemed 'unethical', like Nestlé or McDonald's, in favour of an 'ethical' brand); consuming organic produce (whether food or t-shirts); supporting 'environmental' or 'green' products, like solar panels and recycled paper; buying non-genetically modified products; and supporting cause-related marketing (defined by the donation of a small proportion of the products' profits to charity, such as the 'pink products' associated with breast cancer charities) (Ross 1997; Klein 2000; Micheletti 2003; King 2008; Esty and Winston 2009). Alongside this veritable cornucopia of consumer practices we have a variety of associated activities including consumer campaigning and activism, such as Baby Milk Action's campaigns against the misleading marketing of formula as a 'superior' substitute for breast milk (Hilton 2003; 2009).[1]

These various practices while nominally ethical are not always compatible and can at times be downright contradictory. Buying ten organic t-shirts from Marks and Spencer or American Apparel is, for instance, an opposite lifestyle practice to deciding to radically downshift your consumption and not buy any new clothes at all. Buying Fair Trade wine from Chile or Australia contradicts the imperative of 'buying local' to save food miles if you live in Europe. Buying a Starbucks/Product RED coffee is directly opposed to Adbusters campaigns which highlight exploitative practices of transnational corporations such as Starbucks. And so on. This indicates that contemporary ethical consumption is no mere simple force for progressive social change, but rather one which is constituted of a battery of different practices which can at times conflict with each other. In this sense, we might say, ethical consumption is increasingly a zone of 'contradictory consumption'.

Making this point alone does not, however, take us particularly far. But while we will come back to *why* the terrain is so contradictory later on, for now it is perhaps more helpful to find ways to try to navigate it by describing some of the key differences between these practices. One useful basic means of doing so is to make a conceptual distinction between 'consumption' and 'consumerism'. Both are complicated words with their own fraught histories and there can at times be considerable overlap in how they are used. However, 'consumption' tends to more readily refer to the general 'using up' of an object, good or service, regardless of what kind of economic or ideological context the consumption is happening in. 'Consumerism', on the other hand, is more often used to refer to the logic of consuming within a particular type of social and political system: consumer capitalism. In these terms, being 'anti-consumerism' means railing 'against' capitalist consumer culture – or more specifically the current mode of 'turbo consumerism' that marks contemporary neoliberalism. Examples of this include arguing against the promotion of commodities on children's TV or the hypocrisy of corporate 'greenwash', campaigning against multinational clothing companies' use of sweatshop labour, or supporting co-operatives. By contrast being 'anti-consumption' means simply advocating consuming less, whatever the economic system (although importantly, strictly speaking, to be actually 'against consumption' is an untenable position, given that we all need to consume to live).

The conceptual distinction between these areas can help us to describe some of the differences between various forms of ethical consumption and their internal complexities. Some activities, for example, fall more clearly into one particular camp. Adbusters are primarily anti-consumerist in outlook, in that their sub-vertisements poke fun at the inanities of contemporary neoliberal consumer culture. The American 'voluntary simplicity' movement has mainly been 'anti-consumption' in its leanings, as it has primarily been concerned with using fewer consumer objects, even though ironically its style and imagery spawned many new 'hippie' commodities and services (Elgin 1981; Frank 1997). Some actions cross into both: *Buy Nothing Christmas* is for some people a tool to critique contemporary neoliberal consumer culture and for others an opportunity to simply buy less stuff. Finally, there are forms like the cause-related marketing campaign Product RED which fall into neither category (Banet-Weiser and Lapandsky 2008). RED is not critical of corporate consumer culture, nor interested in slowing consumption: on the contrary, it seeks to expand the revenues of companies like Armani, Starbucks and American Express through promoting their (quite limited) association with an anti-AIDS charity and to galvanize consumption of their products.

The terms 'consumption' and 'consumerism' can also help explain why 'ethical consumerism' is for many people a tautology, or impossibility; for neoliberal capitalism relies on a structural disparity between rich and poor, and is therefore not itself an 'ethical' system to those whose ethical standards include a belief in socio-economic equity. 'Ethical *consumption*', on the other hand, is a much broader term, encompassing as it does acts of consuming within a wide range of economic systems. However, one notable complication here is that whilst 'consumerism' is dominantly used to refer to the system of consumer capitalism which has emerged since the mid-twentieth century – or to the gradual emergence of a post-Fordist, 'consumer-led' marketplace – the word has another meaning, referring to the consumer movement which emerged alongside it which campaigned for value for money and the comparative testing of consumer goods. This movement is thoroughly documented in Matthew Hilton's work (2003; 2007; 2009). Hilton argues that the submergence of this definition of consumerism represents how its movement 'has been outgunned and defeated in many ways, [as] instead the dominant definition of consumer society promoted by the institutions of global governance has been the impoverished language of choice [which] creates barriers between those who can and cannot participate in consumer society' (Hilton 2009: 249–50).

Hilton's work on consumerism also foregrounds the historical and geographical dimensions of ethical consumption. From the Swadeshi movement, in which Gandhi urged people to 'buy Indian' products to combat British imperialism (an early example of a 'buycott'), through the 'White Label' anti-sweatshop products sold in the US, to the anti-slavery sugar sold in Europe, ethical consumption has both a long, and wide, history, as a number of commentators have highlighted (Frank 2000; Cohen 2003; Hilton 2003; 2007; 2009; Micheletti 2003). One useful schematization of ethical consumption's broader historical landscape is Gabriel and Lang's analysis of four main different consumer 'waves' or stages taking place during the twentieth century in the West: co-operative consumers; 'value for money' consumers, as represented by the magazine *Which?*; Naderism, after Ralph Nader's early legal work from the 1960s which represented little Davids against the Goliaths of big corporations; and the 'alternative consumerism' that emerged as a reaction to the Reagan and Thatcher years, through which ethical consumption as we know it today became a powerful force (1995: 152–72; 2005: 39–53). Meanwhile, study of the *geographies* of ethical consumption is a more recently expanding area, and includes work on the global supply chains between consumer and producer (as in work around the 'fetishized defetishization' of Fair Trade, for example) and the global nature of consumer resistance movements and their local specificities (Varul 2008; Goodman 2009; Hilton 2009).

These varied geographies and histories are a key reason as to why ethical consumption does not have a consistent terminology. The phrase 'political consumerism' for instance has been more widely used in Scandinavia; this term is more capacious in its ability to include boycotts and protests alongside various forms of consumption, reflecting the social-democratic heritage of the area (Micheletti 2003). The sheer variety of these practices and cultural differences in conceptions of consumer practices means that, as the field proliferates, it is increasingly necessary to define what type of 'ethical consumption' is under discussion. In fact, even the term 'ethical consumption' itself is relatively recent in its widespread use, becoming popular over the last few decades alongside the rise of 'organic' and 'green' products and the boom in Fair Trade (Harrison *et al.* 2005; Nicholls and Opal 2005). It is also itself a historically and culturally specific term: it marks one particular moment which has been seized not only by activists attempting to translate egalitarian politics into the field of consumption, but, increasingly, by neoliberal corporations adopting various forms of 'ethical consumption' to attract customers and create profit.

Radical consumption or corporate co-option?

This brings us to the second key question asked by this chapter, of whether ethical consumption is produced primarily through the whitewashing, greenwashing and profit-seeking actions of corporations. Is its 'radical' or 'progressive' impact negligible because of this corporate involvement?

Here it is important to point out that by no means *all* ethical consumption is produced by corporations: there are many co-operatives in existence producing ethical goods and services. These include individual initiatives such as co-operative food shops like Park Slope in Brooklyn in the US, or Infinity Foods in Brighton in the UK. Then there are larger organizations such as The Co-operative Group in the UK (the organizational descendant of the nineteenth-century Rochdale Pioneers, the various components of which include a bank, a chain of convenience stores and funeral parlours) or the many farming co-operatives in France, as championed by Jose Bové and the Confederation Paysanne (Bové and Dufour 2001).

While it is certainly the case that the recent expansion of corporate involvement in this sphere has been substantial, the specific effects depend on which particular segment of 'ethical consumption' we are talking about. Products sold as 'organic' in Europe and the US, for instance, are subject to stringent legal regulations and nothing which fails to meet specific criteria can be legally sold as organic. 'Green products', on the other hand, are a much more ambiguously defined and less tightly legislated area and so are ripe for exploitation. Many corporations are attempting to make promotional capital from 'greening' their image: for example, in the US in 2007, Home Depot reclassified 60,000 of its existing 176,000 lines of products as 'green', often on tenuous and contradictory grounds: 'plastic-handled paintbrushes were called nature-friendly because they were not made of wood. Wood-handled paintbrushes were promoted as better for the planet because they were not made of plastic. An electric chainsaw? Green, because it was not gas-powered' (Krauss 2007: 1). Meanwhile, over in Britain, the Advertising Standards Association ruled that advertisements by car manufacturer Lexus and petrochemical giant Shell should be banned, as they both misled the public with their green claims (ASA 2008: 7–8).

As I have discussed elsewhere, this problem of 'greenwashing' is rapidly increasing both in terms of its sheer quantity and the degree of its complex permutations (Littler 2009a; 2009c). One way of comprehending it is to situate greenwashing in relation to the broader activity through which many corporations have, over the past few decades, steadily increased their interest in the domain of 'corporate social responsibility' or CSR. CSR encompasses a variety of corporate activities – sponsoring charities, cause-related marketing (e.g. supermarkets producing 'school vouchers') and annual audits outlining 'community involvement'. The argument over whether corporations *should* be engaged in broader community activities and in public–private partnerships is a fraught one, and one which does not necessarily neatly map on to left/right political divisions. The influential neoliberal theorist Milton Friedman, for example, continually argued against CSR on the grounds that it detracts from the profit motive; whereas the equally neoliberal marketing guru Philip Kotler has continually argued that it enhances profits (Kotler and Lee 2006). The campaign organization the CORE coalition – which includes a number of non-governmental organizations (NGOs) like Friends of the Earth, Amnesty and Christian Aid – has pointed out at length the intense contradictions of many CSR campaigns and the social damage which has been carried out under its name (Christian Aid 2004; CORE 2009). CORE argues that the term 'corporate social *responsibility*' should be replaced by 'corporate social *accountability*': because corporations need to be held to account *by society*, rather than, for example, handed the power to make social decisions about healthcare and education. As I have argued elsewhere, we might draw from these terms to understand CSR as, above all, *a discursive contest for control over the social* (Littler 2009: 50–69).

A similar logic or set of limitations applies to ethical consumerism, to which CSR is in many ways intimately connected. This is because 'ethical' products and services produced by corporations *can* indeed be of progressive value, but, crucially, only at the whims of corporations themselves; and in addition corporations may hype their claims or use them to hide more exploitative aspects of their practice. (Wal-Mart, for example, is routinely accused of greenwash because it heavily promotes its two 'green stores' in the US while its thousands of other stores remain resolutely 'un-green'; see Clark 2006; Spotts 2006.) The only means through which ethical products produced by corporations can be *relied* upon is if minimum 'ethical' standards are enforced through national and international regulation: through which particular types of substandard, unsustainable or exploitative products – whether fridges pumping out excess CO_2 or computers assembled by children – are banned. In terms of the 'ethics' of equality, any strictly equal mode of production necessitates producing on a co-operative basis. In other words, we might say, it is only when corporate social *accountability* gains steam, and when individual involvements with collective *co-operatives* expand, that consumption will become more genuinely 'radical'.

Ethical consumption and the 'responsibilization' of the individual

But where does this leave the role of the individual in relation to ethical consumption? Can we say that ethical consumption is an individualistic form of politics, a means through which neoliberal governments encourage consumers to become 'responsibilized' amidst the atrophying of wider social safety nets? Or is it a zone of democratic potential, engaging people in places and ways that conventional politics cannot reach?

Academics have argued in both directions. At one end of the spectrum is the argument that the individualization of ethical consumption can be an empowering form of 'productive democracy'.[2] Mica Nava and Ulrich Beck have for example both gestured toward the political possibilities of ethical purchasing (Nava 1992: 195–200; Beck 1997) For Michele Micheletti, ethical consumption 'expands the policymaking process and plays a role in reinventing politics and democracy' (Micheletti 2003: 14). Most recently, the work of Clive Barnett *et al.* into the subjects and spaces of ethical consumption has argued that it 'is a political phenomenon in which everyday consumption practices are reconstituted as the sites for citizenly acts that reach beyond the realm of consumption *per se*' (Barnett *et al.* 2007).

On the other hand, a number of commentators have argued that ethical consumption is not only restrictive but damaging. The area in which these arguments have been most pronounced tends to be in work on governmentality and environmentalism. Tim Forsyth and Zoe Young have for example argued that we are in 'a new green order' where politicians announce that debate over climate change should begin, but that the answers are all sewn up:

> There seems to be a consensus among global elites about where to start (be afraid, be very afraid. . . . but always trust the government), how to address the challenge (change development patterns in the South to 'offset' carbon emissions produced by business as usual in the North), and who is responsible (mainly you and me). Real doubts and arguments are suppressed while market friendly 'solutions' are served up on a nice, glossy plate.
>
> (Forsyth and Young 2007: 29)

These terms are similar to Timothy Luke's analysis of 'green governmentality' in which state environmental policy and discourse is preoccupied with the 'conduct of conduct' of individuals within that system, and George Monbiot's searing critique of 'eco-junk' as a deluded solution to environmental crisis (Luke 1999; Monbiot 2007b). These anti-ethical-consumption narratives argue that people's fears are being channelled into one set of neoliberal solutions. The individual is burdened with an overwhelming, rather than partial responsibility for change – what scholars drawing upon Michel Foucault's work on governmentality call 'responsibilization'. In these terms, ethical consumption is a symptom of a profoundly individualistic society in which individuals are being presented with both the opportunity of and responsibility for tackling a number of deep-rooted social problems – poverty, exploitation, mass industrialization, pollution – through their purchasing decisions in a world in which we are encouraged to 'shop for change'.

Both positions can themselves have different politics to them and degrees of sophistication. Governmentality approaches – with their emphasis on the trans-mission of power through rationalities, mentalities and technologies in everyday life – tend to interpret ethical consumption from a somewhat 'top-down' perspec-tive, whereas 'productive democracy' approaches tend to interpret green products by privileging 'bottom-up' systems of people power. And it is here that we can see both the strength and weaknesses of both positions. The key strength of a 'responsibilization' narrative is its ability to demonstrate how individual acts are encouraged through multiple sites and particular discourses; its danger – in its more reductive incarnations – is of pompously dismissing consumption as little more than false consciousness and providing an account of a relatively hermetic system of neoliberalism without showing an awareness of how this is supported or challenged through a variety of different sites and locations. The key strength of the 'productive democracy' narrative is in recognizing the political poten-tial of the very *enthusiasm* people can bring to ethical consumption; its key danger is in offering a celebratory individualism without locating its analysis in relation to larger political systems.

We might say that there is therefore, as I have argued elsewhere, much to be gained from bringing sophisticated versions of both these approaches together, alongside other relevant tools (Littler 2009: 92–115). There is a need to look at ethical consumption in its particularity, whether as a specific instance or a wider 'subgenre', and to ask what are the specific power dynamics and affective charges in circulation. Only then can we tell whether, and how, the particular type of ethical consumption under discussion is working as a 'lever for change' (Barnett and Soper 2005) in the sense of moving towards more forms of equality – whether environmental, mental or social – or whether it subtly works to entrench further inequalities and forms of exploitation.

Sanctimonious shopping: status pursuit for the middle-classes?

The issue of how different kinds of ethical consumption have their own specific power dynamics and affective resonances brings us to the last issue of this chapter: the question of *who* is buying so-called ethical products and *why*. Is ethical consumption mainly used as a high-end status pursuit for the moneyed classes, a panacea for middle-class guilt?

Many commentators have pointed out that ethical consumption is not a fully or particularly democratic mode of political engagement in that it only 'gives votes' to those people who have enough financial and social capital to buy the products in question. It is not available to everybody. This situation is most pronounced in sectors where there is a significant price mark-up for the 'ethical' goods in question, such as organic food, which tends to be sold at a higher premium than non-organic. This gives rise to ethical consumption being used as a mark of social or cultural distinction: as a form of consumption used to discriminate against the less culturally or financially well endowed. Sharon Zukin, for instance, has written about the geography of alternative consumption practices in the US, and of how places like farmers' markets and organic food work to attract processes of gentrification which can exclude and displace working-class and ethnic minority residents and consumers (Zukin 2008: 724–48).

With the rise of anxieties about both sweatshops and global warming, the concepts of consuming less as a means of saving CO_2 and of the 'hidden costs' of buying cheap commodities have become much more popular. These narratives are important, yet one by-product is that both the working-classes and 'developing countries' can at times only too easily be made scapegoats for the wider problems of contemporary consumerism. For instance, 'The Devil Wears Primark', a UK TV series about sweatshop labour, focused on the labour practice 'behind' the cheap disposable fashion sold in shops like Primark; and in her recent work *The Thrift Book*, the *Sunday Times* columnist India Knight railed against the exploitation of budget stores such as – again – Primark (Knight 2009). While the production and distribution of cheap high street commodities undeniably involves ecological and social exploitation, singling out the poorer end of the market as the place consumers should avoid in order to 'make a difference' undeniably discriminates against working-class people, who want access to goods just as much as middle-class people. As David Bosshardt puts it, 'what the customer gets at Dollar Stores is the feeling of at least minimum empowerment, because Dollar Stores offer a mix of consumer products that even the poorest can afford' (Bosshart 2006: 12). The issue here is that more solidly middle-class high street shops are less often evoked as problematic.

Such scapegoating echoes a longer-standing historical process in which attacks on consumption have been a means of dismissing particular groups of people who are just beginning to obtain more power: whether newly enfranchised white women at the turn of the twentieth century, newly moneyed American teenagers of the mid-twentieth century or newly middle-class Indian and Chinese consumers today (Hebdige 1981; Huyssen 1987; Bowlby 1993). The singling out of the particular consumer traits of such groups can encode classed, gendered and racialized prejudice and anxieties about such groups effectively 'getting above their station' through their erroneous and wayward consumption.

In these terms, ethical consumption functions as a further brand of middle-class distinction, one used to discriminate against the poor, whether 'at home' or overseas. However, it is also equally important to point out that this is by no means always the case. We cannot essentialize ethical consumption as *de facto* middle-class, both because many working-class people embrace it and many middle-class people reject it. In the UK, for instance, large numbers of extremely wealthy middle-class people are not in the least bit concerned about ethical consumption or are either mildly hostile or virulently opposed to it. The Tory MP Anne Widdecombe, for example, notoriously disparaged Fair Trade coffee by saying 'I think conscience coffee tastes ghastly'. It is equally common for articles in mainstream lifestyle media publications to belittle or mock the history of ethical consumption by stating that it 'used to be' worthy/dull/unfashionable 'until recently'. Ethical consumerism is also regularly mocked as ridiculous and abnormal in 'henlit' novels (henlit being chicklit in which the chicks have 'grown up' and had kids) which tend to both feature and be written by wealthy, middle-class women who mock eco-minded and organic-buying mothers (Littler 2009c). Middle-class sneering *at* ethical consumption is therefore just as much a phenomenon as middle-class sneering-*at-others* through ethical consumption.

What is less frequently pointed out in such mainstream media discourse is that there are strong historical associations between many disempowered or more 'marginal' groups and ethical consumption. For instance, there is a long history of women's involvement in critical and political consumption, as the historical work of Michele Micheletti, Dana Frank and Lizabeth Cohen has documented; including, for example, US housewives' boycotts against supermarket labour exploitation and women's centrality within the aforementioned Swadeshi movement in India (Frank 2000; Cohen 2003; Micheletti 2004; Littler 2009b). Likewise, working-class communities were pivotal to the emergence of the co-operative movement and still remain crucial as customer-owner-participants of the Co-operative supermarket in the UK, an organization which also champions Fair Trade produce.

Ethical consumption is therefore not the exclusive province of the middle-classes. However, 'consumerist' modes of ethical consumption tend to be more oriented to the middle-classes than co-operative endeavours, and it is this type of consumption that is used as a badge of distinction and disparagement in numerous ways. One useful language through which these complications can be thought is Felix Guattari's work in *The Three Ecologies*. This emphasizes thinking in terms of social, environmental and mental ecologies and the disjunctions between them. Using this schema, for example, we can describe how particular practices of ethical consumption (like, say, buying organic foods at Wholefoods supermarket in an upper-class area) might embody progressive environmental ecologies (in that they support non-intensive modes of farming and discourage the use of pesticides) but much more unequal social and mental ecologies (in that shopping there becomes a badge of exotic distinction for the rich while the store's non-co-operative hierarchies act to further shore up these inequalities of wealth). Guattari's work also enables us to consider both the affective and emotional dynamics at play and the languages and feelings being mobilized by any particular instance of ethical consumption (which Gay Hawkins' work on waste and recycling discusses so well) alongside the circuits of power and wealth in operation (Hawkins 2006).

To conclude, we can say that there is plenty 'wrong' with ethical consumption. It can, for example, be used to shore up inequalities of wealth; to help corporations mislead the public, and avoid being more thoroughly environmentally or socially 'ethical'; to facilitate snobbery; and to distract people from the thorough, ongoing work which needs to be done to create more equal and environmentally sustainable societies – from tightening up product legislation to facilitating co-operatives to banning corporate exploitation in the field of production, distribution and marketing. However, at the same time, these problems and complications should not blind us to the important fact that can also be plenty 'right' with it. It can help people to 'share the wealth' through consumer co-operatives; it can pressure companies to pay attention to the social and environmental impacts of their products and supply chain; it can offer people an alternative to products produced through exploitation; it can focus our attention on the need for social, psychological and environmental sustainability. This means that, today, exploitation can not only be addressed, and defeated, by consumption labelled as 'ethical', but also produced through it; and so extrapolating the differences between these areas, picking the reasons for these differences apart, and acting on them will be one of the most important ways we might progress as citizens or consumers.

Acknowledgements

Thanks to Sara Hackenberg and Tania Lewis for their helpful feedback during the writing of this chapter.

Notes

1 www.babymilkaction.org/.
2 I borrow this term from Robin Murray, who uses it to describe the political potential of public enthusiasm for recycling (Murray 1999). This is obviously quite a different issue from ethical consumption, mainly as it does not involve buying a service; but the term remains a useful one.

Bibliography

Advertising Standards Authority. (2008) *Environmental Claims in Advertising: Is Green a Grey Area?*. Online. Available HTTP: www.asa.org.uk (accessed 15 July 2009).

Banet-Weiser, S. and Lapandsky, C. (2008) 'RED is the new black: brand culture, consumer citizenship and political possibility', *International Journal of Communication*, 2: 1248–68.

Barnett, C. and Soper, K. (2005) 'Consumers: agents of change?', Interview by Jo Littler for *Soundings*, 31: 147–60.

Barnett, C., Clarke, N., Cloke, P. and Malpass, A. (2007) 'Globalising the consumer: doing politics in an ethical register', *Political Geography*, 26(3): 231–49.

Beck, U. (1997) *The Reinvention of Politics: Rethinking Modernity in the Global Social Order*, Cambridge: Polity Press.

—— (2006) *Cosmopolitan Vision*, trans. C. Cronin, Cambridge: Polity Press.

Boltanski, L. and Chiapello, E. (2006) *The New Spirit of Capitalism*, London: Verso.

Bosshart, D. (2006) *Cheap: The Real Cost of the Global Trend for Bargains, Discounts and Consumer Choice*, London and Philadelphia: Kogan Page.

Bové, J. and Dufour, F. (2001) *The World is Not for Sale: Farmers Against Junk Food*, London: Verso.

Bowlby, R. (1993) *Shopping with Freud*, London: Routledge.

Callon, M. *et al.* (2002) 'The economy of qualities', *Economy and Society*, 31(2): 194–217.

Castree, N. (2006) 'The future of environmentalism', *Soundings*, 34: 11–21.

Christian Aid (2004) *Behind the Mask: The Real Face of Corporate Social Responsibility*, London: Christian Aid.

Clark, A. (2006) 'Is Wal-Mart really going green?', *The Guardian*. Online. Available HTTP: www.guardian.co.uk/environment/2006/nov/06/energy.supermarkets (accessed 6 November 2006).

Cohen, L. (2003) *A Consumers' Republic: The Politics of Mass Consumption in Postwar America*, New York: Vintage.

CORE (2009) *The Corporate Responsibility Coalition*. Online. Available HTTP: www.corporate-responsibility.org (accessed 15 July 2009).

Elgin, D. (1981) *Voluntary Simplicity: Toward a Way of Life that is Outwardly Simple*, New York: Morrow & Co.

Esty, D.C. and Winston, A.S. (2009) *Green to Gold: How Smart Companies Use Environmental Strategy to Innovate, Create Value, and Build Competitive Advantage*, New Jersey: Wiley.

Forsyth, T. and Young, Z. (2007) 'Climate change CO_2lonialism', *Mute*, 2(5): 28–35.

Frank, D. (2000) *Buy American: The Untold Story of Economic Nationalism*, Boston, MA: Beacon Press.

Frank, T. (1997) *The Conquest of Cool: Business Culture, Counterculture and the Rise of Hip Consumerism*, Chicago, IL: University of Chicago Press.

Gabriel, Y. and Lang, T. (1995) *The Unmanageable Consumer: Contemporary Consumption and its Fragmentations*, London: Sage.
—— (2005) 'A brief history of consumer activism', in R. Harrison, D. Shaw and T. Newholm (eds) *The Ethical Consumer*, London: Sage.
Goodman, M. *et al.* (eds) (2009) *Consuming Space: Placing Consumption in Perspective*, Aldershot: Ashgate.
Guattari, F. [1989] (2000) *The Three Ecologies*, trans. I. Pindar and P. Sutton, London: Continuum.
Harrison, R., Shaw, D. and Newholm, T. (eds) (2005) *The Ethical Consumer*, London: Sage.
Hawkins, G. (2006) *The Ethics of Waste: How We Relate to Rubbish*, Maryland: Rowman and Littlefield.
Hebdige, D. (1981) *Subculture: The Meaning of Style*, London: Routledge.
Hilton, M. (2003) *Consumerism in Twentieth-Century Britain: The Search for an Historical Movement*, Cambridge: Cambridge University Press.
—— (2007) 'Consumers and the state since the Second World War', *The Annals of the American Academy of Political and Social Science*, 611: 66–81.
—— (2009) *Prosperity for All*, Ithaca, NY: Cornell University Press.
Huyssen, A. (1987) *After the Great Divide: Modernism, Mass Culture and Postmodernism*, Bloomington, IN: Indiana University Press.
King, S. (2008) *Pink Ribbons, Inc: Breast Cancer and the Politics of Philanthropy*, Minneapolis, MN: University of Minnesota Press.
Klein, N. (2000) *No Logo: Taking Aim at the Brand Bullies*, London: Flamingo.
Knight, I. (2009) *The Thrift Book: Live Well and Spend Less*, London: Penguin.
Kotler, P. and Lee, N. (2006) *Corporate Social Responsibility: Doing the Most Good for Your Company and Your Cause*, Hoboken, NJ: John Wiley and Sons.
Krauss, C. (2007) 'Retailer Looks for Ways to Apply a Green Label', *New York Times* extract in *The Observer*, 8 July: 1–2.
Littler, J. (2006) 'Tacking turbo consumption: an interview with Juliet Schor', *Soundings*, 34: 45–55.
—— (2009a) *Radical Consumption: Shopping for Change in Contemporary Culture*, Buckingham: Open University Press.
—— (2009b) 'Gendering anti-consumerism: alternative genealogies, consumer whores and the role of ressentiment', in K. Soper, M. Ryle and L. Thomas (eds) *The Politics and Pleasures of Consuming Differently*, Basingstoke: Palgrave Macmillan.
—— (forthcoming) 'Good housekeeping: green products and consumer activism', in S. Banet-Weiser and R. Mukherjee (eds) *Commodity Activism*, New York: NYU Press.
Littler, J. and Moor, L. (2008) 'Fourth worlds and Neo-Fordism: American Apparel and the cultural economy of consumer anxiety', *Cultural Studies*, 22(5): 700–23.
Luke, T.W. (1999) 'Environmentality as green governmentality', in É. Darier (ed.) *Discourses of the Environment,* Oxford: Blackwell.
Micheletti, M. (2003) *Political Virtue and Shopping: Individuals, Consumerism and Collective Action*, NY and Basingstoke: Palgrave Macmillan.
—— (2004) 'Why more women? Issues of gender and political consumerism', in M. Micheletti, A. Follesdal and D. Stolle (eds) *Politics, Products and Markets*, Brunswick/London: Transaction Books.
Monbiot, G. (2007a) *Heat: How We Can Stop the Planet Burning*, London: Penguin.
—— (2007b) 'Eco-junk: green consumerism will not save the biosphere'. Online.

Available HTTP: www.monbiot.com/archives/2007/07/24/eco-junk/ (accessed 15 July 2009).

Murray, R. (1999) *Creating Wealth from Waste*, London: Demos.

Nava, M. (1992) *Changing Cultures: Feminism, Youth and Consumerism*, London: Sage.

Nicholls, A. and Opal, C. (2005) *Fair Trade: Market-Driven Ethical Consumption*, London: Sage.

Parkins, W. and Craig, G. (2006) *Slow Living*, Oxford: Berg.

Ross, A. (1997) *No Sweat: Fashion, Free Trade and the Rights of Garment Workers*, London: Verso.

Sassatelli, R. (2007) *Consumer Culture: History, Theory and Politics*, London: Sage.

—— (2009) 'Representing consumers: contesting claims and agendas', in K. Soper, M. Ryle and L. Thomas (eds) *The Politics and Pleasures of Consuming Differently*, Basingstoke: Palgrave Macmillan.

Simms, A. (2005) *Ecological Debt: The Health of the Planet and the Wealth of Nations*, London: Pluto.

Soper, K. (2008) 'Alternative hedonism, cultural theory and the role of aesthetic revisioning', *Cultural Studies*, 22(5): 567–87.

Soper, K., Ryle, M. and Thomas, L. (eds) (2009) *The Politics and Pleasures of Consuming Differently*, Basingstoke: Palgrave Macmillan.

Spotts, G. (2006) *The High Cost of Low Price*, New York: Disinformation Books.

Thomas, L. (2008) 'Alternative realities: downshifting narratives in contemporary lifestyle television', *Cultural Studies*, 22(5): 680–99.

Zick Varul, M. (2008) 'Consuming the Campesino: Fair Trade marketing between recognition and romantic commodification', *Cultural Studies*, 22(5): 654–79.

Zukin, S. (2008) 'Consuming authenticity: from outposts of difference to means of exclusion', *Cultural Studies*, 22(5): 724–48.

3 The simple and the good
Ethical consumption as anti-consumerism

Kim Humphery

The 'shopocalypse', known to most as the global financial crisis, seemed to strike, like all world-shattering events, without warning. In fact, the warnings were many; offered up both by the more sober of economic analysts and by those for whom the consumer marketplace has long been a source of contention. The Reverend Billy, of the US-based Church of Stop Shopping, in adroitly coining the shopocalypse term, insisted that the US had finally spent itself to death in 2008 and that the credit-drunk consumer was at last turning to restraint and perhaps even a renewed sense of social citizenship.[1] In voicing this hope, the Reverend heralded the apparent affirmation of what the American sociologist Juliet Schor has called 'the new politics of consumption', a politics centred on contesting a mentality of consumerism and advocating frugality-oriented lifestyle change (Schor 2000). Talk of a shopping Armageddon in many respects encapsulates the characteristically individualized nature of this opposition. For many recent critics of a so-called 'affluenza' the very act of purchasing or, conversely, the refusal to do so has become at one and the same time the source of and solution to a socially and environmentally damaging Western overconsumption that was bound to implode.[2]

Schor's use of the word 'new' in relation to a contemporary politics of consumption might well be contested on the grounds that the mass market has long been the subject of political and cultural condemnation by Marxist, liberal and conservative critics alike. Nevertheless, Schor's epithet was well chosen. In the affluent West, especially, a swag of books and a sea of websites (and the groups and networks they represent) testifies to the millennial rise of an invigorated critique of consumerism in the global North – and of a range of anti-consumerist political and lifestyle responses to an affluent world seemingly hostage to the commodity and the dollar.

Western public intellectuals – often dealing in the genre of the bestseller polemic – have been particularly active over the past decade or more in exposing the nasty realities of a now (temporarily) abated global commodity binge. North American commentators critical of Western consumerism – from Schor (1999), Lasn (1999), de Graaf *et al.* (2001) and Schwartz (2005), to Frank (1999), Kasser (2002), Barber (2007) and many others – have been joined by critics elsewhere.[3] This recent opposition to an increasingly globalized consumer culture has been characterized in part by an environmentalist ethos. But this contemporary challenge to consumerism and any return to its pre-2008 heights is also social, cultural and emotional in focus. While almost all recent critics have highlighted the need for an environmentally sustainable and globally equitable economic system, many have emphasized also how a culture of consumerism undermines our individual sense of well-being and happiness; contributes to a mentality of overwork, haste and instantaneous gratification; underscores a bland, cultural homogenization of life; and fragments communities and social relationships, robbing us of a sense of civic connectedness and responsibility.

These claims are not novel. They are an echo of a long and still vibrant trajectory of popular critical and social theoretical thinking in relation to commodity capitalism, of which the work of Zygmunt Bauman is perhaps the most prominent of contemporary 'high theory' exemplars. For Bauman (2007), the West has become in 'liquid modern' times a society of consumers characterized by 'a set of existential conditions' through which people unthinkingly embrace consumerist culture. This is a culture that plunges us into an 'economics of deception', a logic that falsely promises happiness through consumptive excess while undermining social bonds and community cohesion in the process.

There is much in, and much to dispute about, these claims, particularly when made by the public intellectual. They are claims also that are characteristic of a literature that has rapidly dated as the world economy has faltered. Ironically, a new politics of consumption has been both confirmed and partially undermined by a global economic downturn. A mentality of commodity acquisition at all costs – stoked by nearly two decades of unregulated economic growth and a market hooked on easy credit – has definitely lost its sheen for governments now picking up the pieces. A consumerist ethos is still with us – and may well be gearing up once again – but the temper of the moment has, it seems, shifted to a grudging recognition of limits. Yet, by the same token, recent anti-consumerist polemic has been so determined to condemn the affluenza of boom-time economies and pathologize the 'mindless consumers' who people them that it has left itself with little to say about overconsumption and lifestyle change in a time of rising unemployment, mortgage defaults, and relative – if temporary – shopper restraint. In many respects, critics have thus been relegated to awkwardly celebrating the recessionary interruption of global hyperconsumerism, and arguing perhaps a little too hopefully that out of the latest crisis of capitalism will come positive long-term change.

These observations serve to position contemporary critique. However, it is not the central intent of this chapter to discuss consumption-oriented commentary and theory. Rather, what I want to do here, albeit briefly, is explore some of the practical and conceptual dimensions of current efforts in the affluent West to contest consumerism. In particular, I want to place 'ethical consumption' in the broader context of a Western anti-consumerist politics, and to unravel how consumption as the performance of a particular moral sensibility relates to other forms of opposing consumerism, especially those focused on substantial lifestyle change.

Anti-consumerism

The internet now showcases the websites of a wide array of political groups and networks critical of Western consumerism and overconsumption. In terms of the Western world alone, these range from well-established environmental organizations and consumer associations to specific campaign groups, centres of research and information, and alternative living networks. Many such organizations and networks simply target consumption – and related issues such as waste – as part of a wider programme of campaigns; others concentrate squarely on critiquing and seeking to transform Western material life.

In the broadest sense, research and education-oriented organizations offer a wealth of information on the negative impacts of high consumption and on how to address issues of environmental and social sustainability. The list of these organizations is long but includes Redefining Progress, the International Society for Ecology and Culture, the New Economics Foundation, the Ethical Consumer Research Association, the Center for the New American Dream, the Worldwatch Institute, the Consumer Citizenship Network, and the Association of Conscious Consumers.[4] Similarly, internationalized advocacy organizations, such as Friends of the Earth, Greenpeace, Slow Food, Adbusters, Consumers International, the Fair Trade Federation and the Association for a Tobin Tax for the Aid of Citizens engage in both a local and a global field of political activity.[5] It is, however, the numerous nodal internet sites – acting as the voice of small groups, regional and national organizations, and alternative living networks – that best articulate a contemporary cultural and lifestyle politics of consumption. These include those targeting particular corporations and retail chains such as Delocator, Sprawl-Busters and Whirl-Mart Ritual Resistance.[6] More general forms of consumption activism and cultural opposition to commercialism are evident in the widely varying activities of groups such as the Church of Stop Shopping, Résistance à l'Aggression Publicitaire, Action Consommation, Food Not Bombs, Consume-HastaMorir and the Associazione per i Consumi Etici ed Alternativi.[7] Finally, a life politics of frugality, simplicity and slowness is purveyed by numerous nationally based groups and information portals such as Freegan Info, the Simple Living Network, and Bilanci di Giustizia.[8]

Collectively, these groups represent not so much a new politics of consumption but a field of activism, advocacy and life practice that is more broadly and usefully conceptualized as a politics of anti-consumerism. Here, consumerism does not designate – as in a more specialized North American or British context – a movement for consumer rights, but is used in the pejorative and more commonly understood sense as referring to a culturally manufactured, socially constructed and economically mandated desire for and preoccupation with the endless acquisition of consumer goods and experiences. As a 'politics' however, anti-consumerism is a little hard to pin down, not least because it constantly looks to a set of political values – ecological balance, social justice, global equity, democratic rights – that move us way beyond overconsumption as the problem to be confronted. Indeed, anti-consumerism is perhaps best conceived not as a coherent movement or theory but as a political current informing, to various degrees, the actions of an array of organizations, networks and individuals.

It is for this reason that contemporary anti-consumerist politics in the West must be identified as involving a number of intertwined strands: from the activism of culture jamming and the civics of ethical consumption, to the life politics of downshifting, slow living and voluntary simplicity and the more community-oriented interventions of local collective initiatives to create or maintain alternative economic practices and to construct or maintain 'sustainable' communities. To a greater or lesser extent a systemic politics of varying dimensions also pervades these responses: from the advocacy of legislative measures to control advertising and impose environmental taxes on consumer goods to more radical calls for the subordination of market imperatives to social and moral goals. These overlapping strands of critique and activism constantly move between macropolitical and micropolitical aims and actions. That is, they focus both on the achievement of abstract goals, such as ecological balance and global justice, and on more immediate aims, such as individual self-fulfilment and the cultivation of an attitude of care towards both others and nature.

Above all, however, it is the micropolitical or, more exactly, a politics of the self, that has shaped the new politics of consumption. Perhaps not surprisingly, contemporary anti-consumerism illustrates very clearly the manner in which a politics of change in the West is now, as Alberto Melucci (1996) has ably theorized, deeply enveloped with individual experience, with the nitty-gritty of everyday life in which questions of personal conduct – but more especially of emotion, feeling, embodiment and selfhood – are central. As a result, much recent anti-consumerist commentary and practice has tended to be framed in terms of advocating for lifestyle change. A contemporary Western literature on consumerism – and much of the new politics of consumption in action – can in many respects be defined as a celebration of alternative ways of achieving life satisfaction, meaning and purpose beyond the realm of consumption. At its least challenging, this involves merely suggesting that people adopt environmentally sustainable behaviours or take personal steps to control their spending. However, this is matched by a much more vigorous and politicized promotion of 'simple' and 'slow' lifestyles.[9] Indeed, Amitai Etzioni, one of the most analytical of recent consumption critics, has suggested that a possible (though as yet limited) shift towards 'simplicity' among Western populations is a rich potential source of reduced consumption and social change. In offering a typology of frugal lifestyles, Etzioni (2003: 8–12) portrays so-called downshifting as a moderate or politics-lite form of voluntary simplicity engaging mostly the well-off, who tone down their consumption to a limited degree. This is contrasted with 'strong simplification' through which people give up both income and socio-economic status in order to pursue a more encompassing form of economic moderation and non-material fulfilment. Finally, 'holistic simplifiers' for Etzioni adopt comprehensive life change informed by a coherent philosophy of frugality and identified with simple living as a broader social movement.

A move from the 'simple' to the 'slow' dovetails easily with Etzioni's schema. Directly associated with the Italian – and now international – Slow Food movement, slow living as a political response to a globalized, corporately controlled consumer culture might be characterized as involving the same Etzionian scale of dedication. As the New Zealand-based writer Wendy Parkins (2004) has usefully argued, the 'slow' in slow living conveys an opposition of varying intensity to the cultural homogeneity, economic globalization and corporate dominance that shapes our lives. Importantly notions of the slow, particularly in relation to Slow Food, also signal a promotion of 'pleasure, taste, authenticity, connectedness, tranquillity and community' as an antidote to neoliberal capitalism (Parkins 2004: 371). In no uncertain terms, this makes for a 'politics of time' that is anti-consumerist, and one that perceptively unmasks the crucial link between forms of exchange and the temporal pace of everyday life. However, contra to more puritan forms of simple living, consumption itself (particularly of locally sourced and traditionally produced goods) is in fact embraced by slow activists as a potential vehicle of both enjoyment and political expression.

Of course, advocacy of the simple and the slow has not gone uncontested, even by those of us who share the concerns of an anti-consumerist politics. As critics have been quick to point out, celebrants of downshifting routinely ignore the extent to which voluntary lifestyle change is heavily dependent on economic security and class status, while the 'personal growth' oriented ethos of down-shifting tends to eclipse broader political concerns. Similarly, the North American consumption activist Michael Maniates (2002) has suggested that while deeper forms of voluntary simplicity offer a constructive alternative to consumerism, the contemporary simple living movement is nevertheless rampantly individualistic, middle-class in nature and nostalgic for a pastoral life. The appeal to slow living is equally problematic. While the Slow Food movement, for example, has become an important global voice on food issues, critics such as Labelle (2004) and Donati (2005) legitimately point out that its focus on gastronomic pleasure, specialized culinary traditions, and a nostalgic celebration of cultural authenticity renders the movement politically amorphous and thoroughly bourgeois in address and appeal. Most notably of all, the simple and the slow as expressions of a politicized life transformation are, and will most likely remain, marginalized forms of social action – notwithstanding the hopeful insistence by some that practices such as voluntary downshifting are widespread. As a consequence, these forms of anti-consumerism rest not only on an individualistic voluntarism but on a perennial vanguardism.

Other chapters in this book take up some of these themes, and my intention here is certainly not to deride the importance of a life politics – of the task of reframing a sense of self and the everyday practices through which we conduct our existence – as a central element of contemporary anti-consumerism. In terms of the present discussion, however, what is of interest is the interconnection or otherwise between a politics of lifestyle alternatives and a politics of the ethical purchase. As Deidre Shaw and Terry Newholm (2002) have argued, deep forms of simple living (and, by implication, slow living as well) can be interpreted as 'radical' modes of ethical consumption, a radicalism demonstrated, Shaw and Newholm insist, precisely by the adoption of an anti-consumerist ethos. What then, we might ask, are the dimensions of ethical consumption itself, particularly if it somehow slips between moderate and radical versions of responsible consumer behaviour only the most extreme of which can be interpreted as anti-consumerism?

The good citizen

A notion of responsible or 'good' consumption, informed by a moral and political conscience in relation to a variety of issues and expressed in the 'mindful' purchase or, alternatively, boycott of goods, is the inescapable bedrock of a contemporary anti-consumerism. While a concern with lifestyle has tended to govern the new politics of consumption, the ethics of consumer choice can be identified as an accompanying dominant thematic of this politics. Indeed, it would be hard to imagine a critique of consumerism that does not invoke notions of responsible consumer choice, even though debate rages on the extent to which such market-based behaviour constitutes an adequate form of political action.

Without doubt ethical consumption – while hardly as yet substantially challenging dominant production and distribution systems – is an increasingly popular way of making a political statement and/or constituting a sense of the moral self. Clearly, an ethos of ethical consumption can be expressed in a number of ways, from purchasing sustainable, organic or cruelty-free commodities to buying Fair Trade goods that guarantee reasonable terms of exchange for small-scale and Third World producers, to investing in ethical shares and to participating in consumer boycotts of particular products. Ample evidence suggests that 'thinking ethically' about consumption has a growing resonance in Western populations, and this point has been well made by the founders of the British *Ethical Consumer* magazine, Mary Rayner, Rob Harrison and Sarah Irving. Indeed, they write of a new wave of 'ethical consumerism' arising in a number of Western countries since the 1980s in part connected with the ascendancy of the global free market and the steady demise of government regulation of corporate activities. In this context, citizens themselves have been drawn into the role of watchdog and regulator in relation to issues of animal welfare, environmental sustainability, and workers' and human rights (Rayner *et al.* 2002).[10] Elsewhere, Harrison and his colleagues Newholm and Shaw have further suggested that as consumption has become a more prominent part of life in the West, the consumer marketplace has necessarily become a field for the expression of political opinion and ethical self-actualization as much as a place of hedonistic desire (Harrison *et al.* 2005).

A more detailed explication of this contention has been offered by the Swedish political scientist Michele Micheletti (2003). A number of writers, Micheletti among them, have explored notions of 'political consumerism' and 'consumer citizenship' in ways that challenge orthodox left and liberal conceptualizations of political action and relate closely to ethical consumption as a political model.

Micheletti in particular argues that Western citizens increasingly act as 'political consumers', taking into account social and ethical issues in their shopping decisions. This remakes, Micheletti insists, our very notion of political action by dissolving the assumed barriers between public and private interests, and between economics and politics. Here, politics takes place as a form of democratic 'responsibility taking' and is characterized by what Micheletti calls 'individual-ized collective action'. Politically driven individual consumption decisions thus express self-interests but also link us to others making similar consumption choices and articulate the collective goals of justice, human rights and environmental sustainability.[11]

Allied to this formulation of consumer activism is the notion of consumer citizenship, a concept energetically invoked by a range of writers, particularly the British philosopher Kate Soper. Soper (2004) has explored the manner in which consumption can be a terrain of civic virtue and responsible action where citizen-consumers can pursue their conceptualizations of the good life in a manner that is nevertheless deeply linked to their citizen concerns for Fair Trade and environmental sustainability. This form of consumption, Soper contends, is more broadly linked to the rise of 'alternative hedonism' within Western nations which serves as a rationale for a gradual shift to ethical and green consumption. Alternative hedonism, for Soper, 'points to the way in which enjoyment of affluent consumption has become compromised by its unpleasant by-products (noise, pollution, stress, health risks, excessive waste, and aesthetic impact on the environment) and has thus prompted revisions in thinking about the good life' (2004: 114). Faced with diminishing returns from a fast-paced and materialistic lifestyle, the pleasures of existence have, for a small but increasing number of people, become empty, leading to an emerging ethos of counter-consumerism whereby pleasure is pursued through the adoption of different levels of, and attitudes towards, consuming.

These are sophisticated, if briefly outlined, arguments, and elsewhere in this book the broad field of ethical consumption is examined in considerably more detail than I have done here. One admirable characteristic of recent work on conscience consumption and consumer citizenship is its explorative nature, and its preparedness to philosophically ground an ethics-based response to overconsumption in an intellectually rigorous manner. This sits in contrast to much of the available literature on downshifting and simple living in particular, which remains largely content to enthusiastically advocate for lifestyle change in an often less than analytical and self-reflexive way.

Yet ethical consumption as a political strategy has found it difficult to escape, perhaps even more so than practices such as downshifting, the charge of shallowness. Its critics, while often recognizing the importance of responsible market behaviour, have portrayed ethical consumption as little more than a 'Bobo politics'.[12] Even more problematically, conscience consumption appears simply to bolster the ideology of sovereign consumer choice, thus commodifying the nature of ethical behaviour and conflating civil protest with tokenistic market-based options.[13] Any counter-insistence that we are witnessing a shift in the terrain of civic action from traditional political arenas to the realm of economic life is suggestive but contentious. As Roberta Sassatelli (2006) usefully observes, ethical consumption is surely better conceived as an activity that *gestures* towards change rather than being a form of political practice that constitutes in and of itself a significant threat to dominant socio-economic structures.

Perhaps, then, Newholm and Shaw are right in contending that ethical consumption can only present a substantial challenge to a world of hyperconsumerism if it is combined with the more avowedly anti-consumerist tenor of simplification. While not necessarily enamoured of simple living as 'an answer' many consumption activists would readily agree that the process of contesting consumerism must be multi-pronged. It must not simply talk of responsible consumer choice, but must suggest that we as individuals engage in altering the way we work and live and, most importantly, that we recognize the need for structural economic and political reform to support this transformation (see Humphery 2009: ch. 3).

I share this activist perspective. I do, however, remain a little uneasy with any assumed continuum between different forms of anti-consumerist response. Equally, I am a little suspicious of the notion that it is possible to name certain responses as somehow automatically more contestational than others. My own work suggests that it is in fact difficult to construct anti-consumerism as a unified and easily interpreted political field, not least because of the way in which responses such as those emphasizing lifestyle change, on the one hand, and those emphasizing ethical consumer choice, on the other, both awkwardly intersect and often simply – and perhaps inevitably – deal in the contradictory.

This is clearly demonstrated when it comes to the manner in which consumption is ostensibly privileged as a site of social change. In opening this chapter I noted the penchant of a contemporary Western discourse of anti-consumerism to view the act of consumption itself as being at the dead-centre of Western social decline while also, somewhat ironically, identifying consumption as a pathway to change. In no uncertain terms, anti-consumerism is an outcome of the end of productivist thinking; it is not the *making* of things it principally looks to but their *purchase or non-purchase*. It is a politics that accepts the realities of Bauman's liquid modernity; we are no longer principally workers but consumers, the site of identity – and struggle – is no longer principally the workplace but the market. Anti-consumerism is thus willingly drawn into and a purveyor of a particular narrative of late-modernity whereby the terrain of consumption and money is seen as a dominating source of social formation and individual consciousness. But, precisely because this terrain *has* now seemingly colonized our everyday life and mental landscape, it becomes a principal field of political identity and action. Oddly, then, the materialistic ideology of Western consumption is thoroughly contested, but how we act *as consumers* is retained as a principal medium of opposition.

This might lead some to count anti-consumerism as hopelessly circular and just plain limited. In many respects it is, at least as articulated in much recent polemic. Consumption appears to eclipse all else as the issue of the moment, and as the only reference point of political action. A contemporary Western anti-consumerism can at times appear a grab bag of concerns and actions, offering only a vague sense of what tackling consumption aims to achieve beyond the 'happiness' of frugality and the individual performance of particular morals. All this undoubtedly makes for an amorphous field of opposition. But what needs also to be recognized is the unfolding nature of this politics, one that constantly touches aims beyond its immediate reference points. As Jo Littler in this collection argues, we need to be careful as to how we interpret the political limits and potential of ethical consumption and, I would add, of other forms of contesting consumer cultures. Anti-consumerism finds itself engaged in a string of conceptual moves. It certainly begins with and privileges a focus on the individual consumer as the locus of responsibility and on the Western self as the agent of personal and social transformation. But it speaks also of broader visions; of a respect for the natural world; of a dedication to global equity; of the preservation of local economies and non-corporate forms of production and trade; of the reinvigoration of forms of democratic governance and policy making; and of the reconnection of people to place and community. Moreover, in its various permutations, a contemporary anti-consumerism in the West is productively drawn – often unintentionally – into unsettling well-worn assumptions about the kinds of action that constitute 'the radical' and 'the oppositional' and that might challenge overconsumption and its myriad ramifications.

This latter point can be very clearly seen in relation to both a life politics and ethical consumption; and it is on this issue that I will end this chapter. On the face of it, advocacy of lifestyle change (at least of the strong variety) seems unques-tionably to constitute a deeper challenge to overconsumption and the logic of consumerism than does an insistence that we 'buy better'. Certainly, transforming one's working and everyday life is a harder task than checking one's purchasing behaviour. Yet, what disturbs this hierarchy of opposition is the differing way in which the connection between 'self' and 'other' is routinely conceptualized in these two dominant forms of contemporary Western consumption politics.

Overwhelmingly, advocacy of simplicity and frugality (and to a lesser extent slowness) rests, as I intimated above, on the promotion of the contented self. This is in one sense strategic; what better way to promote a politics of change, and to recruit people to it, than to offer a promise of individual existential well-being. More so, however, simplicity as a philosophy is deeply inflected with the belief that we can only truly connect with and care about others if we have 'worked on' and 'care for' ourselves. Here, well-being is not simply the aim of social change, it is the wellspring of it. Change begins with the self and *extends to* the other (the latter rightly conceived as fellow human beings, non-human animals, and the natural world). This approach clearly resonates with fragments of contemporary Western populations, and it connects with a more widespread desire for existential equilibrium. It is indeed a potentially powerful form of socio-political dissent as Etzioni contends. However, as both a personal/social change literature and a field of action, simple living – in concentrating on the remaking of the Western self as a form of political intervention – markedly fails in at least two respects. First, a simplicity literature/movement has, to my mind, singly failed to offer a concrete explanation of *how* personal happiness translates into society-wide transformation. Instead of rigorously explicating the processes through which an attention to the self burgeons into a renewed relationship with the other simplicity has tended towards merely asserting, as an act of faith, an automatic connection between the two. Second, in emphasizing states of personhood – of inner being – as the origin of social transformation, simplicity and related philosophies have tended to displace the importance of altruism as a crucial source of change.

It is at this point that ethical consumption offers a partial response. In practical terms consuming responsibly and ethically is indeed less personally and visibly challenging (and more immediately doable) than opting for alternative ways of living. Yet, precisely because ethical consumption is so encased in a thematic of the moral, it is potentially more outward looking than strategies such as downshifting and simplicity.[14] The various threads of an ethical/responsible consumption movement do seem to collectively speak more directly of a broader set of political issues (Fair Trade and global economic reform, environmentalism and animal rights, localization and social obligation) than is immediately tackled by a more 'personal well-being'-oriented discourse of anti-consumerism. At base, ethical consumption does not, in fact privilege the self, but the abstract other, although a performance of self is certainly part and parcel of the ethical purchase (and perhaps, as critics contend, this performance is all the ethical purchase or non-purchase ultimately comes to). Like simplicity, ethical consumption conceives politics as the product, first and foremost, of individual action, but its motivating impulse is precisely the altruism (towards fellow human beings, non-human animals and nature) that simplicity relegates to being a consequence of 'getting the self in good shape'. Which, then, is the more radical, the more oppositional, the more full of potential?

The immediate answer is, as Shaw and Newholm reasonably contend, ethics and frugality rolled into one. But here, too, we hit a problem, not only because questions of personal well-being (what is beneficial for oneself) and individual altruism (what is good for beings and things beyond oneself) often fundamentally conflict, but because a politics of the simple *and* the good constitutes an all too solid edifice of 'individualized collective action', to return to Micheletti's term. Together, the simple and the good can thus constitute a formidable response to a world geared to consumption, but what is also reinforced is the fundamental weakness of both of these dominant forms of 'anti-consumerism': their propensity to sideline the question of structural socio-economic reform brought about through collective effort that is not mediated through individualized acts, but effected through purposeful interconnection and collaboration. In this, the simple and the good speak of a contemporary Western anti-consumerist politics more generally, and of its current need to more dynamically articulate the notions of change with which it works.

Notes

1 See Rev. Billy Bulletin, 'Shopocalypto!', www.revbilly.com. The Rev. Billy (alias Bill Talen) has been a key player in a Western cultural politics of consumption over the past few years. Parodying both the saccharine religiosity of US Christian fundamentalism and the consumer fundamentalism of North American society, the Reverend, along with congregation and choir, regularly blitzes major retail stores offering pavement sermons that promise shoppers salvation from their consumer addiction.

2 The all too overused term 'affluenza' has been playfully defined as 'a painful, contagious, socially transmitted condition of overload, debt, anxiety, and waste resulting from the dogged pursuit of more' in de Graaf, J., Wann, D. and Naylor, T.H. (2001) *Affluenza: The All-Consuming Epidemic*, San Francisco: Berrett-Koehler, 2. Overconsumption has been variously conceptualized but refers essentially to a tendency to consume goods and services at a level over and above that which is necessary to maintain a reasonable standard of living and at a rate that is greater than can be environmentally sustained in terms of resource provision and the handling of waste.

3 See also, from France, Comeliau, C. (2002) *The Impasse of Modernity*, London: Zed Books; from Australia, Hamilton, C. and Denniss, R. (2005) *Affluenza: When Too Much is Never Enough*, Sydney: Allen & Unwin; and from Britain, James (2007) *Affluenza: How to be Successful and Stay Sane*, London: Vermilion.

4 For current information on these groups see Redefining Progress (www.redefining progress.org), Ethical Consumer Research Association (www.ethicalconsumer.org), International Society for Ecology and Culture (www.isec.org.uk), New Economics Foundation (www.neweconomics.org), The Center for the New American Dream (www.newdream.org), Worldwatch Institute (www.worldwatch.org), The Consumer Citizenship Network (www.hihm.no/concit/), and Association of Conscious Consumers (www.tve.hu).

5 For current information on these groups see Slow Food (www.slowfood.com), Adbusters (www.adbusters.org), ATTAC (www.attac.org), Greenpeace (www.green peace.org), Consumers International (www.consumersinternatonal.org), and Fair Trade Federation (www.fairtradefederation.org).

6 For current information see Delocator (www.delocator.net), Sprawl-Busters (www.sprawl-busters.com), and Whirl-Mart Ritual Resistance (www.breathingplanet. net/whirl/).

7 For current information see Résistance à l'Aggression Publicitaire (www.antipub.org), Action Consommation (www.actionconsommation.org), Food Not Bombs (www. foodnotbombs.net), ConsumeHastaMorir (www.consumehastamorir.com), and Associazione per i Consumi Etici ed Alternativi (www.consumietici.it/acea).

8 For current information see Freegan.info (www.freegan.info), The Simple Living Network (www.simpleliving.net), and Bilanci di Giustizia (www.bilancidigiustizia.it).

9 For the definitive history of the simplicity movement in the USA, see Shi, D. (1985) *The Simple Life: Plain Living and High Thinking in America Culture*, New York: Oxford University Press. For the classic advocatory text see Elgin, D. (1993) *Voluntary Simplicity: Towards a Way of Life that is Outwardly Simple, Inwardly Rich*, revised edn., New York: Harper. See also Dominguez, J. and Robin, V. (1999) *Your Money or Your Life: Transforming Your Relationship with Money and Transforming Your Life*, New York: Penguin; and Andrews, C. (1998) *The Circle of Simplicity: Return to the Good Life*, New York: HarperPerrenial. There is a less well developed literature on slow living, but see the excellent discussion of the field by Parkins, W. and Craig, G. (2006) *Slow Living*, Oxford: Berg. See also Petrini, C. (2001) *Slow Food: The Case for Taste*, trans. W. McCuaig, New York: Columbia University Press; and Honoré, C. (2004) *In Praise of Slow: How a World Movement is Challenging the Cult of Speed*, London: Orion.

10 Note here the use of the term 'consumerism' as an effort to invoke a connection with the established movement for consumer rights and responsibilities. As I have already intimated this specialized utilization of the term runs up against the much more usual understanding of consumerism as a form of excess (and, as such, its continued use by consumer advocates and organizations is, I would argue, of dubious value). Similarly, we might note in passing that the often used term 'consumer activism' falls prey to the same confusion. Many contemporary activists do not in fact conceptualize themselves as 'activist consumers', but as forging a critique of consumerist forms of consumption and of the very use of the term 'consumer' to designate oneself as a person.

11 Once again, the use of the term 'consumerism' here, while it draws on a long political tradition, leads I think to an unhelpful conflation of meaning.

12 Bobo refers to bourgeois bohemian (a middle-class high-end consumer who espouses non-materialistic values). The term was coined by David Brooks in his book *Bobos in Paradise: The New Upper Class and How They Got There*, New York: Simon & Schuster, (2000).

13 For a range of critiques of ethical consumption see, for example, Worth, J. (2006) 'Buy now, pay later', *New Internationalist*, November: 2–5; Johnston, J. (2001) 'Consuming global justice: Fair Trade shopping and alternative development', in J. Goodman (ed.) *Protest and Globalization*, Sydney: Pluto Press; Bryant, R.L. and Goodman, M.K. (2004) 'Consuming narratives: the political ecology of "alternative" consumption', *Transactions of the Institute of British Geographers*, NS 29: 344–66; and Guthman, J. (2003) 'Fast food/organic food: reflexive tastes and the making of "yuppie chow"', *Social & Cultural Geography*, 4 (1): 45–58. See also Jo Littler's chapter in this collection.

14 What they both share, however, is a certain *moralism* as well as an entirely unfounded assumption that it is only the politically conscious consumer or frugal liver that invokes moral decision making and ethical considerations in the act of consumption. For an examination of the way in which all consumption decisions in some way invoke a day-to-day ethics of care, concern and altruism see Barnett, C., Cloke, P., Clarke, N. and Malpass, A. (2005) 'Consuming ethics: articulating the subjects and spaces of ethical consumption', *Antipode*, 37(1): 23–45; and Miller, D. (1998) *A Theory of Shopping*, New York: Cornell University Press. This broad issue of the moral in relation to ethical consumption is an important one, though I have not focused on it here. For one of the best recent critiques of political moralizing see Bennett, J. (2002) 'The Moraline Drift' in J. Bennett and M.J. Shapiro (eds) *The Politics of Moralizing*, New York: Routledge: 11–26.

Bibliography

Andrews, C. (1998) *The Circle of Simplicity: Return to the Good Life*, New York: HarperPerennial.

Barber, B. (2007) *Consumed: How Markets Corrupt Children, Infantilize Adults and Swallow Citizens Whole*, New York: Norton.

Barnett, C., Cloke, P., Clarke, N. and Malpass, A. (2005) 'Consuming ethics: articulating the subjects and spaces of ethical consumption', *Antipode*, 37(1): 23–45.

Bauman, Z. (2007) *Consuming Life*, Cambridge: Polity.

Bennett, J. (2002) 'The Moraline Drift', in J. Bennett and M.J. Shapiro (eds) *The Politics of Moralizing*, New York: Routledge.

Bryant, R.L. and Goodman, M.K. (2004) 'Consuming narratives: the political ecology of "alternative" consumption', *Transactions of the Institute of British Geographers*, NS 29: 344–66.

Comeliau, C. (2002) *The Impasse of Modernity*, London: Zed Books.

de Graaf, J., Wann, D. and Naylor, T.H. (2001) *Affluenza: The All-Consuming Epidemic*, San Francisco, CA: Berrett-Koehler.

Dominguez, J. and Robin, V. (1999) *Your Money or Your Life: Transforming Your Relationship with Money and Transforming Your Life*, New York: Penguin.

Donati, K. (2005) 'The pleasure of diversity in slow food's ethics of taste', *Food, Culture & Society*, 8(2): 227–42.

Elgin, D. (1993) *Voluntary Simplicity: Towards a Way of Life that is Outwardly Simple, Inwardly Rich*, revised edn, New York: Harper.

Etzioni, A. (2003) 'Introduction: voluntary simplicity – psychological implications, societal consequences', in D. Doherty and A. Etzioni (eds) *Voluntary Simplicity: Responding to Consumer Culture*, Lanham: Rowman & Littlefield.

Frank, R.H. (1999) *Luxury Fever: Why Money Fails to Satisfy in an Era of Excess*, New York: Free Press.

Guthman, J. (2003) 'Fast food/organic food: reflexive tastes and the making of "yuppie chow"', *Social & Cultural Geography*, 4(1): 45–58.

Hamilton, C. and Denniss, R. (2005) *Affluenza: When Too Much is Never Enough*, Sydney: Allen & Unwin.

Harrison, R., Newholm, T. and Shaw, D. (2005) 'Introduction', in R. Harrison, T. Newholm and D. Shaw (eds) *The Ethical Consumer*, London: Sage.

Honoré, C. (2004) *In Praise of Slow: How a World Movement is Challenging the Cult of Speed*, London: Orion.

Humphery, K. (2009) *Excess: Anti-consumerism in the West*, Cambridge: Polity.

James, O. (2007) *Affluenza: How to be Successful* and *Stay Sane*, London: Vermilion.

Johnston, J. (2001) 'Consuming global justice: Fair Trade shopping and alternative development', in J. Goodman (ed.) *Protest and Globalisation*, Sydney: Pluto Press.

Kasser, T. (2002) *The High Price of Materialism*, Cambridge, MA: MIT Press.

Labelle, L. (2004) 'A recipe for connectedness: bridging production and consumption with slow food', *Food, Culture & Society*, 7(2): 81–96.

Lasn, K. *Culture Jam*, New York: Eagle Books (1999).

Maniates, M. (2002) 'In search of consumptive resistance: the voluntary simplicity movement', in T. Princen, M. Maniates and K. Conca (eds) *Confronting Consumption*, Cambridge, MA: MIT Press.

Melucci, A. (1996) *The Playing Self: Person and Meaning in a Planetary Society*, Cambridge: Cambridge University Press.

Micheletti, M. (2003) *Political Virtue and Shopping: Individuals, Consumerism and Collective Action*, New York: Palgrave Macmillan.

Miller, D. (1998) *A Theory of Shopping*, New York: Cornell University Press.

Parkins, W. (2004) 'Out of time: fast subjects and slow living', *Time & Society*, 13(2/3): 363–82.

Parkins, W. and Craig, G. (2006) *Slow Living*, Oxford: Berg.

Petrini, C. (2001) *Slow Food: The Case for Taste*, trans. W. McCuaig, New York: Columbia University Press.

Rayner, M., Harrison, R. and Irving, S. (2002) 'Ethical consumerism – democracy through the wallet', *Journal of Research for Consumers*, 3. Online. Available HTTP: www.jrconsumers.com/academic_articles (accessed 10 February 2009).

Sassatelli, R. (2006) 'Virtue, responsibility and consumer choice: framing critical consumerism', in J. Brewer and F. Trentmann (eds) *Consuming Cultures, Global Perspectives*, Oxford: Berg.

Schor, J. (1999) *The Overspent American: Why We Want What We Don't Need*, New York: HarperPerennial.

—— (2000) 'The new politics of consumption', in J. Cohen and J. Rogers (eds) *Do Americans Shop Too Much?*, Boston, MA: Beacon Press.

Schwartz, B. (2005) *The Paradox of Choice: Why More is Less*, New York: HarperCollins.

Shaw, D. and Newholm, T. (2002) 'Voluntary simplicity and the ethics of consumption', *Psychology & Marketing*, 19(2): 167–85.

Shi, D. (1985) *The Simple Life: Plain Living and High Thinking in American Culture*, New York: Oxford University Press.

Soper, K. (2004) 'Rethinking the "good life": the consumer as citizen', *Capitalism, Nature, Socialism*, 15(3): 111–17.

Worth, J. (2006) 'Buy now, pay later', *New Internationalist*, November: 2–5.

4   Fair Trade in cyberspace

The commodification of poverty
and the marketing of handicrafts
on the internet

Timothy J. Scrase

1,500 farmers commit mass suicide in India.

(*The Independent* 15 April 2009)

Rich pickings to be had from India's poor.

(*The Australian* 21 October 2009)

The contradictions and inconsistencies of neoliberal capitalism have never been starker. In the context of the global South, since the 1990s the ubiquitous hand of the neoliberal global market has transformed many marginal communities by replacing self-help and co-operative development with 'competitive entre- preneurialism' in which individuals, families and communities of workers compete in the local, and increasingly global, marketplace for a reliable 'customer base'. The globalization of production in the world economy has seen the markets of the global South opened up to worldwide competition and exchange, with the result that many workers have become displaced or exploited in casualized, insecure jobs in manufacturing, tourism or construction or else, in the case of many agricultural workers and farmers, become financially ruined. Artisans and craft workers have not been immune to the effects of these global economic changes, with many losing their traditional jobs leading to unemployment and impoverishment. The Fair Trade movement has been one attempt to counter the negative impacts of the globalized, neoliberal market. Based on content analysis of two major websites devoted to selling Fair Trade goods, particularly handicrafts (Oxfam Australia and Ten Thousand Villages), this chapter provides a critical analysis of the marketing and selling of crafts as an alternative form of income generation for marginal communities. In the context of Fair Trade, we can ask: how are these goods marketed and how do crafts and other goods represent the essence of traditional cultures mediated, as it were, by global economic and cultural forces? And, significantly, how is the purchasing of Fair Trade goods from those in the underdeveloped South a form of 'ethical' consumption? Underpinning the analysis is the notion of the commodification of poverty – the ways marginalized labour, and peoples themselves, are exploited for commercial or charitable gain, thus bringing to bear the contentious and problematic relationship between the globalization of markets, the marketing of third world craft goods in terms of 'fair' trade, and 'ethical' consumption practices more generally.

Fair Trade and ethical consumption

The International Fair Trade Association (hereafter IFAT) describes Fair Trade as:

> a trading partnership, based on dialogue, transparency and respect, that seeks greater equity in international trade. It contributes to sustainable development by offering better trading conditions to, and securing the rights of, marginalized producers and workers – especially in the South.

IFAT prescribes standards in respect of ten areas that Fair Trade organizations must follow in their day-to-day work, and carries out continuous monitoring to ensure these standards are upheld:

1. Creating opportunities for economically disadvantaged producers
2. Transparency and accountability
3. Capacity building
4. Promoting Fair Trade
5. Payment of a fair price
6. Gender equity
7. Working conditions
8. Child labour
9. The environment
10. Trade relations

Fair Trade products can range from tea, coffee and sugar, to gold, sporting equipment and handicrafts. Products, if produced by Fair Trade-approved methods and processes, are given relevant Fair Trade certification, although there are competing certification bodies that have differing rules; for instance the Rainforest Alliance Fair Trade label differs significantly from IFAT certified merchandise. This can create marketing ambiguity and consumer uncertainty especially when alternative terms like 'ethically produced' or 'ethically sourced' are employed to label or explain a product.

Socio-cultural research on Fair Trade has sought to explain it from several standpoints (Nicholls and Opal 2004). One body of literature sees the popularity of Fair Trade in terms of largely middle-class Western consumer dissatisfaction with modern supermarket and department store retailing: a form of commodity fetishism in which blandness, sameness, lack of choice, poor labelling, poor service, and relatively high costs prevail, and so an ethical alternative is sought. Some have described this process as 'ethical selving' (Varul 2008a), a form of morally acceptable consumption that involves purchasing not only Fair Trade, but other goods labelled as green, organic, or animal friendly and the like (see, for example, Varul and Wilson-Kovacs 2008). Indeed, on one of the numerous websites now devoted to critical consumption and anti-corporate globalization, knowmore.org, a list of seventeen standards and labels that they frame as 'positive buying' is provided (see Knowmore.org 2009).

Is the ethical shopper, therefore, a socially conscious, critically engaged global citizen as implied in notions of 'positive buying'? Although relatively few in number, emerging research on Fair Trade consumers tends to see them as either 'hard' (Fair Trade-committed consumer activists) or 'soft' (regular Fair Trade shoppers) consumers. As Varul and Wilson-Kovacs (2008: 9) explain it:

> Two major forms of ethical selving have been identified – both involving a claim to an underlying disposition in a way that allows us to view both as involving 'tastes' in the sense Bourdieu (1979) outlined: as a socially constructed but 'naturalised' power of classification. We called them a 'taste for ethics' and an 'ethical taste,' the former associated with 'true blue' fairtrade supporters and activists, the latter more commonly found in 'mainstreamed' fairtrade shoppers.

In their study of demands for socially responsible products, Becchetti and Rosati found that consumers who were more socially aware and informed about Fair Trade – 'concerned consumers' – were 'ready to pay more for the SR [socially responsible] features of a special kind of products (FT products), aimed at supporting development and inclusion in global markets of commodity producers in distant countries' (Becchetti and Rosati 2005: 21). While consumers thus can be either dedicated or relatively less committed in their support of Fair Trade, undoubtedly Fair Trade itself does little to challenge the 'free' (capitalist) market. Indeed, some have argued that Fair Trade is actually consistent to some degree with free markets in that Fair Trade practices aim to reduce the market disadvantage and increase the competitive levels of marginal producers in the global South in order for them to have equal access in the global trading system (Hayes 2006).

Fair Trade and development

Fair Trade thus can be seen to operate in a complex, globalized commercial environment and, in the context of international aid and development, is not without fault or criticism. Some writers argue that Fair Trade can have important local benefits for some impoverished artisanal or agricultural communities, but does little to tackle broader issues of inequality inherent in global capitalist markets (Manokha 2004). Questions concerning the appropriation of Fair Trade by large commercial interests ('clean-washing'), and of consumer confusion about Fair Trade logos and prices, have been highlighted by Low and Davenport (2005). They go on to explain how notions of 'ethical consumerism' blur the message about trade reform, an inherent goal of Fair Trade. In this context Seyfang (2004) argues that Fair Trade consumerism comes to be seen as an individualized act which pits individuals against global institutions to solve global problems. The complexities and fluctuations of international trade and their impact on Fair Trade agricultural goods were evident when, in the late 1990s, coffee became oversupplied in the international market and both Fair Trade and regular producers (and national economies) suffered, with multinational roasters like Nestlé reaping the benefits as prices were kept down (Lindsey 2004).

Handicrafts and other artisanal goods like silk weaving, dress jewellery and *papier-mâché* have been heavily promoted in recent years in a range of Fair Trade and non-governmental organization (NGO) websites including those of UNICEF, the Red Cross, Aid to Artisans, and Global Exchange. Despite the good will and dedication of these groups and their employees, the effectiveness of the Fair Trade model in many instances remains patchy, however, as artisans are brought into the highly competitive, demand-driven world of global production and consumption where middlemen (the buyers and brokers) dominate. In an earlier study conducted among artisan communities in New Delhi (Scrase 2003a; 2003b) I have argued that Fair Trade, together with NGO support, has been beneficial in some instances where there are properly functioning co-operatives and appropriate training. Artisans, when interviewed, were critical of Fair Trade when it came to the actual promotion of their crafts; they bemoaned the lack of government support and complained about not receiving a fair price for their wares. Artisans were also concerned with increasing competition, particularly the threat posed by mass-produced replicas of their crafts and designs flooding the global handicraft and fashion markets (Scrase 2003b). Why is it that marginal producers like artisans are brought into the world of competitive entrepreneurialism for their survival? Certain crafts are highly desirable, yet the national and global markets for most crafts are fickle and fashion-driven, dominated by the buyers from large department stores in the global North or else powerful local middlemen at the point of production. As Poe and Kyle (2006: 16) found in their study of grass basket makers in Bangladesh: 'The variety of middlemen involved in getting the baskets from the port in Chittagong to the customer in America or Europe absorb from 80% to 90% of the final price.'

Two additional examples serve to illustrate the complexities and contradictions of crafts and Fair Trade in the global marketplace. Esperanza's (2008) ethnographic study of Balinese artisans contracted to produce Native American handicrafts ('dreamcatchers'), Moroccan furniture, and African drums is significant. In the process of 'outsourcing otherness', she convincingly demonstrates the nuanced way powerful middlemen play a crucial role in the production of these commodities by controlling the markets of demand and supply in nuanced ways. For instance, middlemen 'build capital based on their knowledge of "good design" or authenticity, but they also reinforce their cultural capital by creating or controlling the narratives that may help to sell their merchandise better' (Esperanza 2008: 89). Dolan's (2008) study of Fair Trade focuses on the cut-flower industry in Kenya which works under contract for Sainsbury's supermarket chain in the United Kingdom. The normative underpinnings of this industry impose technologies of information gathering, regulation, and surveillance on producer communities. Moreover, she finds that the social relations of production are rarely challenged and embedded hierarchies are maintained. Rather than being a source of liberation, the Fair Trade model followed by the flower growers in Kenya is heavily rule-bound, with endless requirements on quality, quantity and deadlines that are imposed, rather than negotiated, and are often at odds with the local producer community's traditions, values or attitudes. Indeed, her study is revealing in exposing the fact that many flower growers do not know what Fair Trade actually is. Thus, while the UK supermarket consumer lauds the seemingly moral and ethical stance of Sainsbury's in providing Fair Trade produce, the producer remains tied to a bureaucratic quagmire of rules, regulations and demands that are neither fair nor ethical.

Fair Trade, now promoted and advocated by a range of NGOs, operates within the free trade, neoliberal capitalist global market, an arena of competition that has at its core the ideal of an unregulated and open market above all else, and therefore favours those economies already at the apex of the capitalist economic order. Within the sociology of development literature, many critics point out that, in the context of development programmes, neoliberalism becomes normative, imposing new norms for development based around 'rational' market principles and thus regulates and imposes conditions for social progress (see, for example, Mohan and Stokke 2000; Petras 1999). In so doing, the role of 'experts' (development professionals) is legitimized and they come to dominate or impose 'plans' for 'progress and development' (Miraftab 2004). In this revised developmentalist system, in which microcredit plays an increasingly domineering role, the poor become 'accountable' for both the successes and failures of local development agendas and plans which have been imposed on them (Fisher 1997). Effectively, over the past two decades, 'development' has been transformed into a business, a world of competition between small producers and entrepreneurs supported by an array of microfinance schemes, bank loans and privatization agendas promoted by all levels of government and supported by NGOs. Oxfam, for example, epitomized this new approach in its 'make poverty history' campaign in which trade and celebrities, together with a slick marketing promotion, were invoked in a concerted effort to eliminate third world poverty. Yet the 'business' of development, or 'development made sexy' as some have put it (Cameron and Haanstra 2008), is fraught with contradictions. For example, in Australia Oxfam outsources its street donation collections and the private company that runs the service collects 80 to 95 per cent of the first year's donations (of a four-year pledge) regardless of whether the donor withdraws completely or terminates the pledge early (Flitton 2009b: 5).

Where earlier incarnations of Fair Trade were heavily dependent on the development and role of co-operative enterprises, today these idealistic models stand in stark contrast to the individualized, entrepreneurial and competitive models of development now in vogue. Despite the euphoria of the various entrepreneurial development models, social research reveals a trail of development losers and failed projects of microfinance-led reform. Ganguly-Scrase (2008) has shown that such neoliberal reforms and trade liberalization policies have had particularly devastating consequences for largely female Indian garment workers, and Rankin (2001) focuses on the negative consequences of neoliberal policies on women in the global South more generally. Additionally, numerous studies have been critical of microfinance and its providers for various reasons which largely impact on the poor and women (see Fernando 2006).

Two important conclusions can be drawn from the foregoing discussion of Fair Trade. First, that the rise of the Fair Trade movement in the 1990s was 'a conscious attempt to re-regulate a market threatened by deregulation' (deNeve *et al.* 2008: 17) and, as such, it is seen as a political reaction to the localized producer problems caused by neoliberal markets and free trade. Second, notwithstanding the shift of many NGOs to neoliberal development models, that the consolidation and growth in popularity of Fair Trade in the 2000s is the result of both a concerted effort on behalf of NGOs to engage producers in the global South in more meaningful and equitable trade, and a desire by consumers, largely in the global North, to re-engage with the 'origins and social life' of the products they are consuming. The attempts to understand the production processes that go into the making of commodities:

> are the expression of a desire to de-fetishize commodities, to re-think how they are manufactured and traded, and to shift attention onto the workers and resources that produce them. The wish to de-fetishize is a wish to demystify what the market tries hard to keep hidden.
>
> (deNeve *et al.* 2008: 7–8)

This leads us back to the consumer side of Fair Trade once again. The next section analyses the way various products are marketed, principally through the marketing tool emblematic of the new millennium – the internet.

Fair Trade in cyberspace: Oxfam and Ten Thousand Villages

The popularity of third world craft goods and patterns has arisen with the emergence of 'ethic chic', the hybridization of fashion, and a return to 'earthy' and 'natural' forms and colours in interior design. Apart from overseas travel, it is largely by way of catalogues and visits to 'Fair Trade' stores that Western consumers are able to purchase 'authentic' artisanal products. A further forum is internet websites which have become important promoters of artisanal goods from the global South. Yet, with few exceptions, critical studies of Fair Trade marketing and advertising remain a largely under-researched area. Some of the earlier, notable studies focused on crafts made in South and Central America. For instance, in her article 'Selling Guatemala', Hendrickson reveals the various ways handicrafts catalogues construct the 'natural', 'traditional' and even, in some cases, 'primitive' images of Guatemalan life that are used to appeal to consumers. Products have to be tailored to suit the foreign audience, the 'horror' stories of certain communities are toned down, and the fact that the crafts marketed overseas are produced according to strict quality control measures is never revealed (Hendrickson 1996: 118–19). In this context, 'ethnic branding', 'traditional', and 'authentic' thereby become important features in the marketing of crafts. In another notable study from the 1990s, Stephen (1993) focused on the integration and 'ethnicization' of Mexican rugs in the North American consumer markets, showing how the 'branding' of ethnic identity is an important marketing tool despite the revelation that the majority of 'Mexican' rugs were made in India. Authenticity, in its various guises, has become an important delineator in the promotion and marketing of many Fair Trade products, whether or not they are produced in a time-honoured and conventional way, incorporate traditional designs and materials, or represent the 'essence' of the community of artisans producing the goods. Focusing especially on the marketing of handicrafts, Scrase (2009) has found the lines blurred between terms like 'authentic', 'traditional', 'ethnic' and the like, and the claims for equity and fair price for the artisans are often clouded in 'feel-good' rhetoric or notable for their lack of specific financial details regarding contracts.

In the new millennium many artisans find themselves at odds with the demands of the global marketplace. Consider, for example, the case of Northern Thai handicraft artisans producing for the tourist market:

> Viewing commerce as hostile to authenticity, the artisan reluctantly enters any commercial contract, suspicious of being robbed of control over the goods to be produced and afraid of depriving the local tradition of its significance . . . Most of these reluctant artisans, therefore, seem to be blissfully unaware that productive reticence makes one's work more scarce and therefore more valuable. By cultivating their reticence and limiting their participation in the commercial market, the artisans increase the interest of the commercial marketers in their work.
>
> (Wherry 2006: 18–19)

Ironically, for these Thai artisans, it is by *not* mass producing for a large-scale commercialized market that one may reap better financial reward and increased community and personal satisfaction. Yet expanding production and markets is promoted heavily by advocates of Fair Trade which may not necessarily be the best solution for sustainable business.

Oxfam Australia is one of the better-known larger NGOs, which relies heavily on a trusted image, marketing campaigns and transparency to garner financial and political support for its aid and development work in Australia and overseas. Notions such as promoting social justice, working towards a fairer world and being inclusive and consultative are some of the ideological underpinnings of Oxfam's development activities. Apart from government grants and private donations, Oxfam Australia, and Oxfam internationally, raise a proportion of their income from Oxfam retail shops, which are located in major shopping strips and malls, by mail order catalogue and online trading websites such as: www.oxfamshop.org.au. The Oxfam online shopping website is branded Fair Trade: 'Oxfam Shop is a passionate supporter of Fair Trade and deals on a

Fair Trade basis with 85 Fair Trade organisations around the world . . . we are part of a global movement calling for an end to unfair trade practices' (Oxfam Shop 2009). A brief explanation is provided on the website and the World Fair Trade Organization logo is clearly visible, establishing and reaffirming Oxfam's credentials and commitment to Fair Trade principles, as well as providing legitimacy to the alternative trading regime. The website also states that many of Oxfam's overseas producer partners are registered as Fair Trade organizations. A range of other trading principles also guide Oxfam's work with producers including paying them up to 50 per cent of the value of an order in advance. Oxfam does recognize the hazards of retail when it writes: 'Oxfam Shop is a wholly owned subsidiary of Oxfam Australia and although we operate in a fiercely competitive retail environment we are a non-profit organisation' (Oxfam Shop 2009).

Significantly, the online shop has an expanded range of many and varied products, and the website declares that the 'Oxfam Shop is making a difference and so can you by choosing from *our exotic* and exciting range of homewares and gifts' (my emphasis). The gifts to be purchased are listed under categories including 'Oxfam unwrapped', which is an interesting alternative to traditional gift giving as one can purchase a 'gift' (i.e. make a donation) to a community to help build a water tank, or purchase a goat for a village, or help build a school. This form of ethical consumption is becoming popular (see, for instance, www.karmacurrency.com.au), and is clearly well meaning but has also attracted some criticism, especially as the 'gift' is often 'representative' (i.e. the money may be used for other community development programmes) and includes the NGO's costs such as administration fees, publicity and marketing, and lobbying governments for more funds (Flitton 2009a).

An additional concern to note was that, at the time of writing this chapter, Oxfam was having its 2010 January Clearance sale with price mark-downs of up to 50 per cent on some items. This 'charity at a discount' raises the awkward question of whether the discount means a loss of 'profit' for Oxfam, or a loss of income for the producer, the wholesaler, or some other trading arrangement. The notion of a clearance symbolically denotes a 'clearing out' of the goods that did not sell well, or were over-ordered, and does little to dignify the skills and dedication of the artisans who made many of the discounted products. Discounts on prices have the impact of privileging the consumer, who can secure a bargain, and the fact that the nature of the discount arrangements was not revealed somewhat disturbs the feel-good, Fair Trade message that permeates the website.

As mentioned above, the product categories cover a wide range of goods, the majority being handicrafts produced by relatively small-scale enterprises and co-operatives committed in some way to Fair Trade principles. Most items for sale have details of the product, the people who produced it, and may also have links to the NGO, company or co-operative that contracts the making of the goods. The consumer is thus provided assurance that this is a 'legitimate' product, the purchase of which will provide continued livelihood for the producer communities and individuals. As a partner in aid and trade, one's purchase of such goods raises the act of buying to the level of partnership in the aid, development and maintenance of the villages and towns of one's 'fellow' citizens, albeit on a completely uneven playing field.

The 'consumer as partner' ideal is reinforced by the vignettes and stories accompanying many of the items for sale and serve to remind the consumer of how they can make a great difference to the lives of those making the goods. One of the suppliers for Oxfam is 'Mahaguthi – Craft with a Conscience' from Nepal. The stories about these Nepalese artisans' lives are remarkable and serve to teach the consumer, if they bother to check, the various benefits and beneficiaries of their purchases. The stories, too, add an authentic sense to the shopping experience, de-fetishizing the commodity as it were, so that one can become intimately connected to the lives of the producers and communities creating the goods. In this way, Fair Trade shopping becomes a form of 'romantic commodi-fication' (Varul 2008b) where the consumer can dream and imagine themselves in 'other' worlds, helping and assisting the needy for example, or realizing other liberating possibilities. As Varul (2008b: 661) elaborates:

> Other than most mass produced consumer goods, Fair Trade goods by default refer back to remote regions in a highly credible way. Fair Trade can rely on mutually supportive indices of distance and authenticity in connection with the testified existence of the substrates of its imagination.

Oxfam offers an 'ethical' alternative for shopping, but what of the millions of producers who remain cut off from accessing the Fair Trade markets and support of the large and powerful NGOs, or the co-operatives whose products become unfashionable or redundant, or those who do not meet the quality control imposed by the buyers and the fickle consumers? Whether fair or free, ultimately prosperity is achieved by market success and persistent sales, not the feel-good stories that accompany the product.

The Ten Thousand Villages website (www.tenthousandvillages.com) is the second example I will discuss. With strong links to Christian charity – the Mennonite Central Committee (MCC) – the group was initially founded in 1946, and over succeeding years built its profile and international links with artisanal communities so that by 1996 it was incorporated as 'Ten Thousand Villages'. It is one of the world's oldest charitable, Fair Trade organizations. With such a well-established company, and with more than 150 retail outlets, one can expect the website to be professionally designed and informative – and it is. The company is thoroughly committed to Fair Trade principles, and sees as its central value to put artisans first when it comes to dealing with producers, and trade and retailing generally. As they explain: 'Fair trade provides under- and unemployed artisans with an opportunity to earn vital income and improve their quality of life by establishing a sustainable market for their handcrafted products' (TTV 2010a). Similarly to Oxfam Australia's philosophies and trading principles, artisans contracted by Ten Thousand Villages receive up to 50 per cent in cash advances when an order is placed, and payment in full when an order is shipped. In addition, designers work closely with artisans to build traditional skills, and to use natural materials and employ sustainable practices. Trust, reliability and brand quality are all essential features promoted by Ten Thousand Villages.

In addition, the website is very much customer focused. On the gift ideas page (TTV 2010b) they write: 'Finding special *gifts for him*, or unique *gifts for her* can be difficult. Each distinctive item in our collection is handmade by talented artisans around the world [. . .] Browse the ideas below to find the perfect gift that gives twice' (emphasis in original).Throughout the various webpages of their online shop, a commitment is made to satisfying the customer, as well as providing information about the product and the group of artisans that made it. Their dealings with artisans are seemingly professional, rigorous and emphasize quality control and reliability above all else:

> North American customers buy products they need and want to enrich their lives. An ongoing selling relationship with customers is only sustainable if Ten Thousand Villages sells products that meet their needs. Despite all of the other factors we consider in establishing buying relationships, Ten Thousand Villages can only buy from groups that are producing products our customers will buy.
>
> (TTV 2010c)

Thus, it is important to recognize the subtle yet all too clear message that goods need to be in demand and desired by the discerning North American (USA and Canadian) consumer market. It is also worth mentioning that they too, like Oxfam, have a 'clearance' items page where products are offered at a greatly reduced price, and with no refund.

It is notable therefore that both the Oxfam website shop and that of Ten Thousand Villages are similar in terms of website design, product marketing and philosophy. One can also find the same Fair Trade handicraft providers, such as Mahaguthi mentioned earlier, on their various 'items for sale' pages. The quality of the brand and its reputation is all important for both organizations. The Fair Trade difference is promoted heavily, as the following illustrates:

> Here at Ten Thousand Villages Oriental Rugs, we believe in a global economy that is sustainable and fair to everyone involved. This means providing well-made, quality products for our customers and a fair livable income for our artisans. When you purchase a rug through Ten Thousand Villages, you not only acquire a beautiful piece of functional art, you also support lives, culture and education in Pakistan.
>
> (TTV 2010d)

On the same webpage, one can follow four weblinks which provide additional information on: The People Behind the Rugs; Empowering Women; Supporting Schools; and Pakistan Earthquake Relief. Overall it becomes apparent that the central concerns of the Ten Thousand Villages website are, first, the selling of

products to fund development, aid and relief work; second, to present an underlying educative message about self-reliant development in the global South; and
third, to promote Fair Trade principles.

Stereotypes, trust and the 'Fair Trade' brand

The Fair Trade shopping websites of both Oxfam and Ten Thousand Villages are
notable for their similarities, high quality design and, apart from some concerns
noted above, the relatively transparent details of the trading relationships and
products they market. Both websites appeal to those consumers committed to
development justice, and rely heavily on additional information such as stories
about the craft, or the community of artisans, to promote the items. In some
instances additional background information is provided concerning the aid and
development programmes being undertaken in the village, farm or urban
community as a result of one's Fair Trade purchases of particular items. Three
questions emerge from this analysis and can be considered briefly. First, are
stereotypes of producers from the global South perpetuated in Fair Trade
marketing? Second, what is the significance of 'trust' in Fair Trade advertising?
And third, in market terms, how significant is it to maintain the Fair Trade brand
as reliable, high quality and secure?

As mentioned earlier, content analysis studies of Fair Trade websites and
shopping catalogues have found the use of stereotypes such as 'traditional',
'authentic', 'hand-made', 'ethnic' and the like to be commonplace (Hendrickson
1996; Dwyer and Jackson 2003; Scrase, 2003b; 2009). In this vein, a recent
study (Varul's 2008b) has analysed the Traidcraft Spring 2009 catalogue and
advertisements promoting the Fair Trade chocolate company, Divine Chocolate.
The persistence of stereotypes in the selling of authenticity is evident: in the
case of Traidcraft it is 'producer as needy and therefore inferior' (Varul 2008b:
669); for the latter, it is by way of gender stereotyping – using images of 'exotic',
sexualized, young black African women in its revamped advertising campaign.
As the author explains it:

> Divine needs to add symbolic use value to its brand, engage in a consciously
> designed commodity aesthetic in order to push into unchartered mass markets.
> This is the declared aim of the campaign analysed here, which is described in
> a press release as 'a significant step-change in Fairtrade marketing, which is
> fast moving on from its purely activist image'.
>
> (Varul 2008b: 669)

In the case of Divine, Fair Trade is mainstreamed by making use of the very same
tools employed in free trade marketing and brand recognition – social
stereotyping – no matter to what degree this may be at odds with some of the
underlying principles of Fair Trade (such as promoting gender equity and human
rights and dignity). Oxfam and Ten Thousand Villages have also mainstreamed
their activities, and their Fair Trade shops are commercially appealing and

consumer friendly. While significant for the level of product information provided, they nevertheless resort to the stereotypical representation of first world consumer helping third world producer: a form of empowerment charity that goes beyond the mere giving of money for relief, but nonetheless perpetuates a dependent relationship that smoothes over the fundamental inequalities inherent in global trading regimes. For the politically informed consumer, both websites (and the organizations) are appealing. For the not so inquisitive, any of the educative messages remain buried on the extra links and additional webpages.

The second dimension to be considered is that of trust in Fair Trade. A potential consumer, who has never heard of Fair Trade, may be inclined to support it simply by reference to the term 'fair', yet may also remain sceptical that relatively small NGOs, traders and community groups can actually offer a fair deal for producers located thousands of kilometres from their home. An important element to Fair Trade has been the stories of its social and community successes that accompany the marketing of its products. Granville (2009) argues that the stories and vignettes with each product are essential, and that the producers are seen to benefit, particular because Fair Trade prices are often at a premium. As she argues:

> By being confronted with stories of good deeds, consumers with a natural inclination to benevolence can be convinced that the FT [Fair Trade] scheme is beneficial to small producers in developing countries . . . The probability which the FT consumer assigns to FT stories is determined by the strength of the feel-good effect. If that effect is intense, negative stories about FT will have only minor impacts.
>
> (Granville 2009: 24)

It would seem that in the case of the two websites analysed, both organizations are long established, have global recognition and attract committed and dedicated patrons with generally high levels of benevolence, so the trust factor would be high. The products advertised do have accompanying stories of development successes which lead to personal appeal and the perpetuation of a 'feel-good' factor. It is important to mention, though, that the trading failures are not visible on the websites and promotion materials, nor is information about the actual costs and other contract details, as well as final prices paid for the handicrafts, available to the general public. So, within the neoliberal development framework, one maintains a degree of healthy scepticism as to the successes of all Fair Trade contracts.

The third issue to consider is the Fair Trade brand. From its relatively humble, 'alternative' beginnings, the Fair Trade movement has been careful to cultivate brand recognition where companies must strictly adhere to the central Fair Trading principles. Both websites analysed proudly boast of their Fair Trade credentials, with logos clearly visible; make mention on several occasions, their philosophy of Fair Trade and what it means practically for producers; and have links to webpages of other Fair Trade organizations, companies, brands and

products. In thinking about the brand the average consumer may ask: what does
Fair Trade represent? Most consumers, one can reasonably assume, have no
knowledge of the intricacies of the international market for, say, coffee, and so
rely on advertising and personal taste in making their choice. Fair Trade offers
an additional criterion to consider, especially with a prominent logo and a smiling
face of a coffee producer from Kenya or Timor Leste on the packet on the
supermarket shelf. For some, simply the word 'fair' may be enough to incline
them to purchase the coffee; for others, the fact that it may be more expensive
means that they are unwilling to pay the price premium as it seems 'unfair'. Either
way, it would seem to be the case that Fair Trade relies heavily on an educative
principle to go with the brand, and both websites analysed had significant details
about the nature of where and how the goods were produced, and in what ways
these communities will benefit from their purchase. Thus, the Fair Trade brand is
imbued not merely by ethical trading and advertising, but by a higher level of
personalized, self-realized consumption practices.

Conclusion: commodifying poverty in Fair Trade

> Today fussy, capricious, fashion-crazed consumers and vulnerable image-
> oriented, buyer-driven corporate brands are making sweatshops an antithesis
> of productive corporate global development. These children of late capitalist
> niche markets apply the general and developing recipe knowledge of
> capitalism to gradually steer global business towards the path of global social
> responsibility. This pull factor is accompanied by the political consumerist
> push factor. Together the pull factor of capitalism and push factor of social
> justice activism use market logic and niche market competition to broaden
> the global horizon of transnational corporations, consumers, and even
> governments. The global market – just like the capitalistic market of anti-
> slavery centuries ago – is hatching a new wave of humanitarian sensibility.
> This time it goes under the captions of global social justice, triple bottom-
> lining, corporate social responsibility, and no sweat.
>
> (Micheletti and Stolle 2008: 764)

As Micheletti and Stolle point out, humanitarian capitalism, or inclusive
capitalism, is emerging as consumers are, to a degree, beginning to question the
nature of the products they are consuming. Fair Trade is emblematic of this
evolving phenomenon of socially aware consumption and is slowly gaining
momentum in terms of wider market acceptance. Nevertheless, the Fair Trade
regimes of quality control, meeting orders on time, and other criteria may be far
from fair for producers (Dolan 2008). We are reminded that producers under
Fair Trade are vulnerable. While the trade relationships between producers and
buyers are contracted to be more equitable, fundamental problems like gaining
access to large Northern markets and department stores are persistent and
unpredictable. The capricious nature of various global commodities markets is

equally disturbing and can impact on prices dramatically, as can the weather, over-production, and a myriad other factors such as the fickle wants and demands of consumers.

Is Fair Trade shopping a form of counter-hegemonic consumerism? In a critical assessment, Johnson (2002) finds that Fair Trade discourse tends to 'rely on individualistic notions of choice and consumer sovereignty, obscures the structural linkages between core and periphery in a globalised economy, and belies the collective environmental implications of individual free choice in the marketplace' (2002: 55). Significantly, she also points out that Fair Trade discourse, rather than providing or stimulating any serious discussion of structural inequality, instead supports a more liberal, de-politicized vision of cultural difference. In the two websites analysed above, one could concur with this general assessment, although Oxfam Australia does have a number of more critically oriented publications and documents on its organization website (not its shopping website) explaining the world of globalized, unfree trade, Oxfam's general programmes and policies, research reports, and so forth (Oxfam 2009).

The commodification of poverty under Fair Trade persists, nonetheless, in that when it comes down to it, relatively wealthy consumers are enticed to buy various goods in order to help financially struggling producers. One could say, it is the 'commodification of poverty with a conscience' whereby consuming to reduce poverty becomes an educative and empowering experience to learn about the causes of unequal trade and global poverty, tempered, as it were, by the precondition of one actually reading the educative message accompanying the product. In other words, an unequal trading relationship is thereby established and it is up to the consumer to think through the implications of buying, or choosing not to buy, a Fair Trade labelled product. This raises the question of consumer morality under capitalism. How many consumers actually stop to think about and reflect upon the social relations, and complex market arrangements, that produce the goods purchased each day? Fair Trade raises the possibility of critical thinking of trade inequity, albeit contingent upon the personal dispositions and outlook of the individual consumer.

Despite drawbacks, the effectiveness of Fair Trade as a form of ethical consumption is limited, but nevertheless an ideal and alternative worth pursuing. When reflecting on the possibilities of Fair Trade, Sarah Lyon concluded that despite limitations and contradictions, these

> do not necessarily weaken the transformative potential of Fair Trade as a vehicle for economic equality and social justice in the international arena. Overstating the exceptional nature of Fair Trade consumption may potentially weaken this transformative potential.
>
> (Lyon 2006: 461)

In spite of the ideological opposition to Fair Trade by the pro-free market lobby, its lack of government support, and relative lack of consumer knowledge, it remains a fundamental option for those consumers seeking a more equitable and just world in which free markets are controlled and trade is regulated and underpinned by partnership, trust and transparency rather than economic supremacy.

Bibliography

Becchetti, L. and Rosati, F.C. (2005) 'The demand for socially responsible products: empirical evidence from a pilot study on Fair Trade consumers', Palma de Mallorca, Spain: Society for the Study of Economic Inequality, Working paper 2005–04.

Bellman, E. (2009) 'Rich pickings to be had from India's poor', *The Australian*, 21 Oct: 38.

Cameron, J. and Haanstra, A. (2008) 'Development made sexy: how it happened and what it means', *Third World Quarterly*, 29(8): 1475–89.

deNeve, G., Luetchford, P., Pratt, J. and Wood, D.C. (2008) 'Introduction: revealing the hidden hands in global market exchange', in G. deNeve, P. Luetchford, J. Pratt and D.C. Wood (eds) *Hidden Hands in the Market: Ethnographies of Fair Trade, Ethical Consumption, and Corporate Social Responsibility*, Bingley: Emerald JAI Press.

Dolan, C.S. (2008) 'Arbitrating risk through moral values: the case of Kenyan fairtrade', in G. deNeve, P. Luetchford, J. Pratt, and D.C. Wood (eds) *Hidden Hands in the Market: Ethnographies of Fair Trade, Ethical Consumption, and Corporate Social Responsibility*, Bingley: Emerald JAI Press.

Dwyer, C. and Jackson, P. (2003) 'Commodifying difference: selling EASTern fashion', *Environment and Planning D*, 21: 269–91.

Esperanza, J. (2008) 'Outsourcing otherness: crafting and marketing culture in the global handicrafts market', in G. deNeve, P. Luetchford, J. Pratt and D.C. Wood (eds) *Hidden Hands in the Market: Ethnographies of Fair Trade, Ethical Consumption, and Corporate Social Responsibility*, Bingley: Emerald JAI Press.

Fernando, J.L. (ed.) (2006) *Microfinance: Perils and Prospects*, Abingdon: Routledge.

Fisher, W.F. (1997) 'Doing good? The politics and antipolitics of NGO practices', *Annual Review of Anthropology*, 26: 439–64.

Flitton, D. (2009a) 'Foreign aid gifts' misleading message really gets my goat', *The Age*. Online. Available HTTP: www.theage.com.au/opinion/society-and-culture/foreign-aid-gifts-misleading-message-really-gets-my-goat-20091228-lh8k.html (accessed 29 December 2009).

Flitton, D. (with Jamali, D. and Raj, H.) (2009b) 'Charities hand over up to 95% to street marketers', *The Sydney Morning Herald*, 26 Oct: 5.

Ganguly-Scrase, R. (2008) 'Survival in the era of the post-multifiber arrangement: experiences of garment workers in India', *Journal of Third World Studies*, XXV(2): 39–57.

Granville, B. (2009) 'Trust in Fairtrade: the "feel-good" effect', CGR Working Paper 27, Centre for Globalisation Research, School of Business and Management, Queen Mary, University of London (January 2009).

Hayes, M.G. (2006) 'On the efficiency of Fair Trade', *Review of Social Economy*, 64(4): 447–68.

Hendrickson, C. (1996) 'Selling Guatemala: Maya export products in US mail-order catalogues', in D. Howes (ed.) *Cross-cultural Consumption: Global Markets, Local Realities*, London and New York: Routledge.

International Fair Trade Association (IFAT) (2008) Online. Available HTTP: www.ifat.org (accessed 24 October 2008).

Johnson, J. (2002) 'Consuming global justice: Fair Trade shopping and alternative development', in J. Goodman (ed.) *Protest and Globalisation: Prospects for Transnational Solidarity*, Sydney: Pluto Press.

Knowmore.org (2009) Online. Available HTTP: www.knowmore.org/wiki/index.php?title = Ethical_Consumerism (accessed 19 December 2009).

Lindsey, B. (2004) *Grounds for Complaint?: 'Fair Trade' and the Coffee Crisis*, London: Adam Smith Institute.

Low, W. and Davenport, E. (2005) 'Has the medium (roast) become the message? The ethics of marketing Fair Trade in the mainstream', *International Marketing Review*, 22(5): 494–511.

Lyon, S. (2006) 'Evaluating Fair Trade consumption: politics, defetishization and producer participation', *International Journal of Consumer Studies*, 30(5): 452–64.

Manokha, I. (2004) 'Modern slavery and Fair Trade products: buy one and set someone free', in van den Anker, C. (ed), *The Political Economy of New Slavery*, London and New York: Palgrave.

Micheletti, M. and Stolle, D. (2008) 'Fashioning social justice through political consumerism, capitalism, and the internet', *Cultural Studies*, 22(5): 749–69.

Miraftab, F. (2004) 'Making neoliberal governance: the disempowering work of empowerment', *International Planning Studies*, 9(4): 239–59.

Mohan, G. and Stokke, K. (2000) 'Participatory development and empowerment: the dangers of localism', *Third World Quarterly*, 21(2): 247–68.

Nicholls, A. and Opal, C. (2004) *Fair Trade: Market-Driven Ethical Consumption*, London, Thousand Oaks and New Delhi: Sage.

Oxfam (2009) 'Oxfam Australia's Online Resources'. Online. Available HTTP: www.oxfam.org.au/resources/pages/home.php (accessed 2 January 2010).

Oxfam Shop (2009) Online. Available HTTP: www.oxfamshop.org.au (accessed 1 January 2010).

Petras, J. (1999) 'NGOs: in the service of imperialism', *Journal of Contemporary Asia*, 29 (4): 429–40.

Poe, K. and Kyle, S. (2006) 'Fair Trade – is it really better for workers? A case study of Kaisa grass baskets in Bangladesh', Working Paper, Department of Applied Economics and Management, Cornell University, Ithaca, New York.

Rankin, K.N. (2001) 'Governing development: neoliberalism, microcredit and rational economic woman', *Economy and Society*, 30(1): 18–37.

Scrase, T.J. (2003a) 'Precarious production: globalisation and artisan labour in the third world', *Third World Quarterly*, 24 (3): 449–61.

—— (2003b) 'Producing on the margins: Asian artisans in the global economy', in T.J. Scrase, T. Holden and S. Baum (eds) *Globalization, Culture and Inequality in Asia*, Melbourne: Trans Pacific Press.

—— (2010) 'From marginalized artisan to impoverished entrepreneur: the globalization of the trade in crafts and its impact on Indian artisans', in M. Gillan and B. Pokrant (eds) *Trade, Labour and Transformation of Community in Asia*, Basingstoke: Palgrave Macmillan.

Seyfang, G. (2004) 'Eco-warriors in the supermarket?', CSERGE Working Paper EDM 04–07.

Stephen, L. (1993) 'Weaving in the fast lane: class, ethnicity and gender in Zapotec craft commercialization', in J. Nash (ed.) *Crafts in the World Market*, Albany, NY: SUNY Press.

Ten Thousand Villages Online Shop (TTV) (2010a) 'Fair Trade Values'. Online. Available

HTTP: www.tenthousandvillages.com/php/fair.trade/fair.trade.values.php (accessed 3 January 2010).

—— (2010b) 'Gift ideas'. Online. Available HTTP: www.tenthousandvillages.com/catalog/gift_idea.index.php (accessed 3 January 2010).

—— (2010c) 'Artisan partners'. Online. Available HTTP: www.tenthousandvillages.com/php/fair.trade/fair.trade.artisan.php (accessed 3 January 2010).

—— (2010d) 'The Fair Trade difference'. Online. Available HTTP: http://rugs.tenthousandvillages.com/fair_trade_difference (accessed 3 January 2010).

The Independent (2009) '1,500 farmers commit mass suicide in India', *The Independent*. Online. Available HTTP: www.independent.co.uk/news/world/asia/1500-farmers-commit-mass-suicide-in-india-1669018.html (accessed 19 December 2009).

Varul, M.Z. (2008a) 'Ethical selving in cultural context: fair trade consumption as an everyday ethical practice in the UK and Germany', paper presented at the 3e Colloque international sur le commerce equitable (3rd Fair Trade International Symposium), FTIS 2008, Montpellier, France, May 2008.

—— (2008b) 'Consuming the campesino', *Cultural Studies*, 22(5): 654–79.

Varul, M.Z. and Wilson-Kovacs, D. (2008) 'Fair Trade consumerism as an everyday ethical practice – a comparative perspective', An ESRC-Funded Research Project, University of Exeter.

Wherry, F.F. (2006) 'The social sources of authenticity in global handicraft markets: evidence from Northern Thailand', *Journal of Consumer Culture*, 6(1): 5–32.

5 Neoliberalism, the 'obesity epidemic' and the challenge to theory

Michael Gard

How should we understand the 'obesity epidemic'? It is customary and necessary for academic analyses to locate comparatively specific social and cultural phenomena, such as the emergence of the 'obesity epidemic', within broader theoretical frameworks. For example, concepts such as risk and governmentality have been influential among critically minded public health scholars. At the risk of offering a crude gloss, in this chapter I will bundle these ideas up into what I will call the critique of neoliberalism. I do this while acknowledging the hugely diverse and contested meanings scholars assign to the term neoliberalism. In fact, the term is perhaps more contested than many of its current aficionados imagine given its origins in post-Great Depression Germany of the 1930s. Here, neoliberalism was formulated as an antidote to what its adherents called 'vulgar liberalism', their term for unfettered capitalism and what they saw as its inevitably destructive tendencies.

For many contemporary scholars, however, neoliberalism is not so much an antidote to free-market orthodoxies but rather an expression of their growing hegemony. In the context of day-to-day life and personal consumption, the focus of this volume, the critique of neoliberalism holds that individual citizens are increasingly called upon to manage their personal conduct in the interests of the neoliberal state. In the words of one of the editors of this volume:

> A central feature of the neoliberal focus on self-regulation involves the displacement of questions of social responsibility away from government and corporations onto individuals and their lifestyle 'choices', reflecting a growing 'ethicalization of existence' (Rose 1989: 263–64). The centre of political life has shifted, then, towards the private sphere with citizenship increasingly seen as being 'produced by personal acts and values', a shift that Berlant sees as '[d]ownsizing citizenship to a mode of voluntarism' (1997: 5).
>
> (Lewis 2008: 227)

So, to what extent does this explanatory framework adequately account for the emergence of the 'obesity epidemic'? To what extent has a preoccupation with economic efficiency and down-sizing the role of government *produced* widespread concern about obesity? And if not the cause, to what extent do the forces of neoliberalism sanction the reconfiguring of ethical mores such that the 'obesity epidemic' is framed as a problem for individuals, and not governments or corporations, to solve?

Closer to the concerns of this volume, I also want to consider the 'obesity epidemic' in the context of growing anxiety about the nature and ethics of Western patterns of consumption. In other words, to what extent should we understand the 'war on obesity' as a proxy for other concerns about Western over-consumption? In general, my argument in this chapter will be that, in part because of the radically inconclusive state of obesity science, we need to see the 'obesity epidemic' as an arena of ideological contestation in which the forces of neo-liberalism and the critics of consumption are only part of the story. Nonetheless, pervasive anxieties about excessive consumption are shaping both the questions that researchers ask and the anti-obesity public policies being proposed. But while it is important to isolate and render intelligible the discursive threads that con-stitute social phenomena, we must also keep multiple and even antagonistic lines of analysis open if our purpose is to understand both the history and the future of the 'obesity epidemic'.

The war on obesity

The 'obesity epidemic' presents policy makers with a particularly intractable set of problems, many of which are either qualitatively or quantitatively different from the problems associated with other public health concerns such as cigarette smoking. For smoking, we at least have what amounts to a scientific consensus about tobacco's health risks. This provides a relatively clear rationale and concrete goal for policy action: we want fewer people to smoke because smoking is bad for your health. Of course, even given these relatively conducive pre-conditions, anti-smoking policy remains a complex and contested business with different countries and individual jurisdictions approaching the issue in different ways.

In the case of obesity, policy makers do not have the relative luxury of a single target. To name only a few, advocates for curbing television watching, television advertising, computer usage, eating in restaurants and car driving can all be readily found in the obesity science literature as well as those in favour of food labelling, nutrition education in schools, more bicycle paths, taxes on high-calorie foods and government-funded weight loss surgery. Some obesity researchers have naively fantasized about an 'all of government' future in which obesity would be attacked in a coordinated fashion on multiple fronts (for a striking example, see Bonfiglioli *et al.* 2007), while others, such as Peters *et al.* (2002), essentially advocate a war on what they call 'modern life'. Whether or not readers see the idea of an all-out war on obesity as wise or realistic, my point here is to allude to the sheer complexity and singularity of obesity as a public health problem.

To make matters significantly worse, while controversies are a normal part of any empirical exercise, obesity science has produced a series of conflicting and confusing findings about even the most fundamental questions. Neither researchers who study food consumption, nor those who measure physical activity levels, have been able to produce a 'smoking gun' for what appear to be quite consistent, simultaneous and widespread changes in Western body weights (for commentaries on this point see Gard and Wright 2005 and Eisenmann 2006). One consequence of this is that there are some obesity researchers who are actually prepared to suggest that the social environment has played little or no role in increasing obesity rates (Wilkin *et al.* 2006). This is an extraordinary and, admittedly, far from mainstream conclusion. And yet, given the current state of obesity research, it is not a simple view to refute. Likewise, researchers who claim that obesity is actually caused by a virus or, alternatively, is the result of adverse bio-chemical conditions *in utero* tend to dismiss criticisms of their ideas by pointing to the failure of other researchers to produce anything more convincing (for example, see chapter 7 of Vogel 1999; Eisenmann 2006). Looking at US and Canadian data, Eisenmann (2003) has argued that there are no clear signs of increasing inactivity or dietary intake for children and, therefore, higher rates of childhood obesity could be the result of more emotional stress and/or toxins in the environment, perhaps linked to less sleep and poorer mental health. It probably goes without saying that debates about what to do about increasing childhood obesity are likely to take a very different shape if the problem is taken to be the result of stress and depression rather than, say, eating too much junk food or sitting in front of computers.

Beyond the apparently empirical domain, the problem of doing something about population obesity rates is made trickier still by what we might call the cultural politics of obesity and obesity research. Here I am referring to the vested economic and political self-interests and affiliations that shape the positions that people take. Once again, this is hardly a situation peculiar to obesity. Regulating the use of tobacco needed governments with the courage to oppose large corporations as well as to take away some of the pre-existing freedoms of businesses and individuals to buy, sell and advertise tobacco products. Moreover, this had to be done in a situation where some scientists and lobbyists were being paid to misrepresent the state of scientific knowledge.

Policy debate about obesity, though, is perhaps even more coloured by cultural politics although these may not always be as obvious as that which prevailed in the tobacco controversy. In fact, my argument in this chapter is that radical empirical uncertainty in the science of obesity produces a context in which almost any interest group, no matter how extreme or misguided, can point to evidence to support whatever it is they want to say about obesity.

In providing some examples to support this claim below, my intention is to provide some context for the ways in which the 'obesity epidemic' is reshaping what we might call the ethics of consumption. In other words, how and with what justification is the intensified focus on body weight changing the moral dimensions of consuming things like food, technology and exercise?

The scourge of food

At the risk of understatement, obesity researchers have developed an increasingly keen interest in Western culture's relationship with food, particularly but not only over the past fifteen years. Overall, they do not like what they see. However, those who criticize and therefore seek to change Western food consumption face a range of obstacles, not the least of which is the problem of evidence. The inherent imprecision associated with measuring the dietary consumption of large populations increases dramatically when one's focus becomes changes over, say, 50 or 100 years. As a result, it is just as easy to cite researchers who claim that, on average, Westerners are eating the same or fewer calories than they used to (Nicklas *et al.* 2001; Rolland-Cachera and Bellisle 2002; Eisenmann 2003) as it is to find others who say they are eating more (Nestle 2002; Finkelstein *et al.* 2005; Hensrud and Klein 2006). In fact, some researchers write as if increasing energy consumption were simply self-evident, seemingly unaware that, as the following early example from the *British Medical Journal* shows, the opposing view has been put by leading researchers in important journals:

> The prevalence of clinical obesity in Britain has doubled in the past decade. The Health of the Nation initiative has set ambitious targets for reversing the trend in recognition of the serious health burden which will accrue, but efforts to develop prevention and treatment strategies are handicapped by uncertainty as to the aetiology of the problem. It is generally assumed that ready access to highly palatable foods induces excess consumption and that obesity is caused by simple gluttony. There is evidence that a high fat diet does override normal satiety mechanisms. However, average recorded energy intake in Britain has declined substantially as obesity rates have escalated.
>
> (Prentice and Jebb 1995: 437)

In short, my point here is that it is absolutely not the case that on the narrow question of average daily caloric consumption we can point to a majority mainstream view that is being opposed by a pesky radical fringe. Rather, no mainstream view exists.

In earlier research I have shown how some of this confusion is clearly due to a mixture of academic insularity and laziness (Gard and Wright 2005). For example, it is common for obesity researchers to ignore or fail to notice opposing points of view. As a result, there is a tendency to make 'common sense' assertions about, say, the amount that Westerners eat and to support these assertions with academic references that have little or no bearing on the assertion being made.[1] And as a number of contributors to this volume make clear, researchers also live and work in cultural contexts where the discourse of rampant and problematic over-consumption is pervasive.

If the problem were simply one of academic standards we might hold out hope that the 'truth' about Western appetites might yet emerge so long as we can keep obesity researchers on the straight and narrow. The reality, I think, is that obesity researchers are no less or more intelligent or virtuous than those in other fields. Rather, the question of caloric consumption remains intractable because it is not a research problem that lends itself easily to investigation. The empirical problems associated with trying to measure the exact caloric consumption of a single person are well known. Apart from the technical subtleties involved, there is the unresolved (perhaps unresolvable) methodological dilemma that once you attempt to monitor personal value-laden behaviours like eating and drinking, you inevitably change those behaviours, rendering the final measurements at best questionable and at worst meaningless. As the focus of research moves from the individual to a larger sample, by necessity the measures used, such as surveys and recall diaries, become increasingly crude and imprecise. The results of this kind of research must then be extrapolated to entire national populations if we are to say anything about how much the people of a particular nation 'normally' eat and drink. This process of extrapolation, of course, has its own methodological problems and controversies and adds yet another layer of uncertainty.

If we move away from a relatively narrow empirical focus on average daily energy consumption, the broader obesity science community usually glosses over the complexities that I have just described. Speaking at the level of broad generalities rather than empirical specifics, most obesity researchers take it as self-evident that a majority of us are consuming too much food.

In the obesity literature, there are at least two ways in which the over-consumption of food is demonized. First, there is a general and widespread assertion that the 'obesity epidemic' has been caused by the transformation of what we might call Western food cultures. This argument comes in a variety of shapes and sizes. For example, there are those who say that the food we eat today is stuffed with sugar, salt and fat so that we find it hard to say no even when we've had enough (for example, Bouchard and Blair 1999; Dionne and Tremblay 2000). Pi-Sunyer (2003: 859) writes:

> Intake has gone up because in the developed world food is now very abundant, very available, very palatable, and very cheap. At the same time that our buffet table is growing more luxurious year by year, physical activity is declining. Both at work and at play, people do less and less physical exertion each year.

I am often struck by the suggestively emotive language used by some obesity scientists when talking about consumption. Pi-Sunyer invokes here the image of rampant excess ('growing more luxurious') and fully laden 'buffet tables' in every home. And despite – or perhaps because of – the complex underlying science of food consumption discussed above, Pi-Sunyer also seems untroubled in editorializing about the 'developed world' and the lives of the people in it. I would simply emphasize here that the author's almost sneering generalizations about food consumption run counter to the underlying research base which paints a much more complex picture.

Proponents of the over-consumption thesis tend also to argue that food is ubiquitous and that there is simply no escaping temptation. This applies to food itself as well as advertisements that encourage us to consume. There are those who lament the fact that we eat more of our meals in restaurants (Dietz 2001; Dubbert *et al.* 2002; Nestle 2002; Cafaro *et al.* 2006) and a host of nutrition experts who are convinced that it is not so much the amount we eat but the displacement of good foods by bad (Bray and Popkin 1998; Rolland-Cachera and Bellisle 2002). An obvious example of this comes from those who say we eat too many carbohydrates (particularly simple carbohydrates) and that this is out of step with our cultural as well as biological heritage as meat and plant eating hunter-gatherers (McMichael 2002). Taken together, these arguments hold that we have, in a sense, 'dumbed down' our food cultures, moving towards food that is quick to obtain and quick to digest. This line of thinking has spawned a vast array of food gurus, including those who think we need to take more time to enjoy higher quality, more sophisticated food. For example, readers might consult the various tracts of the 'Slow Food' movement or Atrens (2000) who recommends that we need to cultivate our taste for the 'exquisite'.

A second, narrower line of attack on food consumption comes from both popular and scientific commentators who want to implicate the fast-food industry directly for causing the 'obesity epidemic'. Here, in the tradition of other corporate bad guys like 'Big Tobacco', 'Big Oil' and 'Big Pharma', the enemy is 'Big Food', classically the target of Eric Schlosser's (2001) book *Fast Food Nation* and Morgan Spurlock's 2004 film *Super Size Me*. The arguments are not very different in the scientific and scholarly literature where the influence of fast-food companies on obesity levels is regularly taken for granted by researchers. For example, Swinburn (2008) calls the 'obesity epidemic' a case of business success but market failure and, therefore, a situation crying out for strong government action and regulation in many areas of lives, not just food. Elsewhere, in an article titled 'The perils of ignoring history: Big Tobacco played dirty and millions died. How similar is Big Food?' for *The Milbank Quarterly* (Brownell and Warner 2009: 264), the prominent obesity researcher Kelly Brownell muses thus about the future of the food industry:

> Industry stands at a crossroads where one turn would mean fighting change, defending practices like targeting children, forestalling policy changes, and selling as much product as possible no matter the consequences, and the other would require retooling, working with the public health community, selling far fewer harmful products, and promoting healthier options with much greater urgency. Adopting the first option while laying claim to the second was the path taken by the tobacco industry. Is the food industry different, or is history repeating itself, this time with another substance?

Brownell and Warner are at pains to point out that there are many differences between the tobacco and food industries and that these differences partly explain why lawsuits in the US directed against the makers of fast-food have so far been unsuccessful. Interestingly, though, they warn about emerging research into the addictive qualities of substances like sugar and caffeine. Whatever one thinks about the concept or science of addiction, Brownell and Warner are surely correct to suggest that if addiction establishes itself within obesity discourse, debates about the ethics of food consumption are likely to be significantly transformed. After all, as the following editorial from the *New England Journal of Medicine* attests (Ludwig 2007: 2327), the idea that what we eat is largely a matter of corporate behaviour rather than individual responsibility is already widespread:

> Parents must take responsibility for their children's welfare by providing high-quality food, limiting television viewing, and modelling a healthful lifestyle. But why should Mr. and Ms. G.'s efforts to protect their children from life-threatening illness be undermined by massive marketing campaigns from the manufacturers of junk food? Why are their children subjected to the temptation of such food in the school cafeteria and vending machines?

It is worth noting here the way the author seems unable to decide whether modern parents can be trusted to make rational choices about consumption or whether they are simply the passive recipients of corporate propaganda. Notice also the way the author has inserted the idea of 'life-threatening illness' as a given within the ethical choices produced. In other words, whatever choices parents end up making, the author has ramped up the ethical dimension of these choices by casting them as life-or-death decisions.

This tension aside, as with most areas of obesity research, the empirical case against 'junk food' is anything but watertight and the results of studies consistently confound what might seem common sense positions. It is in part for this reason that a long list of predominantly conservative and/or pro-business commentators are able to prosecute the idea that the 'obesity epidemic' is, more than anything else, an issue of personal responsibility (for examples, see Divine 2004; Eberstadt 2003; Fumento 1997).

That capitalism's advocates might emphasize the importance of personal responsibility over corporate behaviour is not surprising. However, once again, the comparison with tobacco is instructive. It is true that a band of scientists, journalists, lobbyists and politicians made systematic attacks on mainstream science, arguing that the existing lung cancer research literature was 'inconclusive'. Despite this, the empirical case against tobacco was clear enough early enough to a critical mass of scientists who worked methodically on the problem until there could be no doubt. The contrast with obesity could not be starker. After a generation of research into the causes of increasing body weight some obesity researchers are now arguing that we should just give up (for example, see Research Update 2009). This confusion has created the perfect conditions for advocates in favour of greater individual responsibility, as well as those inclined to blame obesity on corporate excess and rampant over-consumption, to claim that the science is on *their* side.

Consuming from the couch

An almost identical set of conceptual and methodological problems faces the study of physical activity as faces those who study food consumption. To begin with, generating knowledge about how much physical activity people are doing or not doing must happen in a cultural context that has, in many respects, already made up its mind. Without breaking stride to refer to evidence of any kind, popular science books like Pool's *Fat: Fighting the Obesity Epidemic* announce:

> Our cars, our televisions and computers, leaf blowers, our riding lawn mowers, our self-propelled vacuum cleaners – all of these make it easier for us to get through the day without doing something that might leave us out of breath or cause us to break out in a sweat. And, unlike the situation with calories and fat in our food, there is no sign that things have gotten better over the past two or three decades. Year by year the average American exerts himself less and expends less energy in physical activity, with no sign of turnaround.
>
> (Pool 2001: 163)

Rising childhood obesity levels in the late 1990s and early 2000s were greeted by a frenzied, media-fuelled condemnation of the laziness of modern children. In my own country, Australia, we began the current century with newspaper headlines like 'Poor diet, exercise put young at risk' (Patty 2000) and approached the end of its first decade with 'Teen health at risk from fat, lazy life' (Hall 2008: 11).

Space does not permit a more detailed discussion of historical trends in physical activity. As with food, obesity researchers who do not study activity levels *per se* tend to take the idea that most of us are less active as self-evident, requiring little or no justification. Meanwhile, researchers who study levels of physical activity have used a variety of indirect methods to generate comparisons with the recent and distant past and these data generally fail to support the assumption of increasing sloth, a point that is regularly acknowledged in the literature (Pratt *et al.* 1999; Møller *et al.* 2007).

Is this the end of the matter? It is difficult to know how much stock we should put in physical activity secular trend research because of the crude data used and rough estimates that need to be made. But whatever else we might say, the idea that, for example, teenagers lead 'fatter' and 'lazier' lives than teenagers from generations past is not a scientific claim, but rather one based on nostalgia and stereotypes. Nowhere is this more apparent than if we look at the connection between childhood obesity and technology use.

The idea that technological advancement creates ever more passive and physically inferior human bodies has been with us at least since Victorian times, although an argument could be made that it is one of the founding myths of Western culture. At any rate, twentieth-century anxiety about the physical fitness of Western bodies preceded the idea of an obesity epidemic and, therefore, helped to frame research about it. As early as 1985 leading obesity researchers were pointing the finger of blame at television (Dietz and Gortmaker 1985). This set the scene for 20 years of research into the effects of televisions, video players and computers on the waistlines of adults and children. As with other areas of obesity research, many studies were inconclusive. On the whole, though, researchers have concluded that technology usage, particularly electronic forms of entertainment, have very little causational bearing on people's body weight or the amount of physical activity they do.

The sustained but ultimately unsuccessful empirical campaign to implicate technology in childhood obesity was, among other things, an attack on a particular kind of consumption. In both media reporting and scientific journal articles, spoilt modern children are contrasted with earlier generations who, it is repeatedly claimed, were satisfied with simpler, cheaper and healthier forms of recreation. Currently, not only do obesity researchers demonize the existence of certain forms of technology in the home, they also instruct parents and children on the quantity and ways in which this technology should be consumed. For example, they suggest that television watching should be limited to a certain number of minutes per day and children should not have televisions in their bedrooms.

I have been at pains not to argue that the 'obesity epidemic' has ushered in radically new moral codes. For the most part, bourgeois concerns with self-restraint and leftist suspicion of capital and commerce dominate, more or less, as they have always done. Still, the ease with which obesity researchers dispense advice about how we should conduct ourselves at work, rest and play continues to surprise me. If anything, what the idea of an 'obesity epidemic' has done is to extend the reach of expert advice further and further into the deepest corners of our personal conduct. And if, as many social theorists tell us, consumption is now a central means through which we express ourselves and live our lives, then some obesity warriors want to have a say here too. In an article that links obesity, biodiversity loss and what the authors call over-consumption, Cafaro *et al.* (2006: 556) begin the following quote by talking about agricultural practices, but move with blinding speed to the idea that we must consume less of everything in order to be better people:

> By considering consumption as a key issue in agricultural ethics, we challenge the 'more is better' mentality at the root of many of our agricultural and environmental problems. Wendell Berry, Matsuo Fuoka (1985) and other sustainable agriculturalists teach us that taking a stand against this mentality, saying 'I don't need a bigger farm' (or car, or bank account), may leave more time and resources for cultivating ourselves and our relationships to people and to nature. As philosophers and religious teachers have emphasized, temperance makes us better people and helps create better societies.

The risks of theory

Since at least the early 1990s the concept of risk proved a seductive and generative focus for theorizing social life. For Beck (1992), a world increasingly organized, not around exploiting opportunity, but around avoiding and managing risk represented a qualitative break from the past. For authors such as Petersen (1997), Lupton (1999) and Howell and Ingham (2001) the possible theoretical uses for risk in the fields of health and health promotion were obvious. Lupton argued that Western societies tend to attribute blame with reference to liberal humanist, or what she called neoliberal, notions of free, rational and sovereign individuals. We are, she says, encouraged, sometimes forced, to survey our own health behaviours while governments withdraw from many areas of public welfare. In such a climate, then, blame tends to be individualized rather than connected to wider social networks.

The problem with this line of argument is that it works so long as the author skates across a range of health concerns and never dwells long enough to treat any one area in relative detail. It is true, as I have shown above, that there is a great deal of interest in the behaviour of individuals among many obesity researchers, much of it insultingly condescending. The 'obesity epidemic' has also undoubtedly generated a mountain of media comment that intrudes, hectors and blames individual citizens for both letting themselves go and letting the side down.

What I have tried to show in this chapter, though, is that obesity public policy is a complex, contested and disorganized arena. There are many obesity researchers who regularly and explicitly argue against a focus on individual behaviour and point out how ineffective this approach is in fighting obesity. And far from Lupton's assessment that a preoccupation with risk tends to disconnect health problems from wider social networks, a great deal of obesity research and anti-obesity public policy agitation focuses *precisely* on social networks and the physical and cultural environments in which people live (for a much talked about recent example see Christakis and Fowler 2007).

While some researchers and commentators argue for a war on obesity because of what they see as the unsustainable financial costs being imposed by ill-disciplined individuals, just as many others want to fight obesity by addressing the behaviour of governments and corporations. In other words, in looking at responses to the 'obesity epidemic', the neoliberal mantra of efficiency and personal responsibility is but one of the many voices trying to be heard.

However, there is perhaps a more interesting debate to be had about whether the very existence of the 'obesity epidemic' is evidence of creeping neoliberal ortho-doxies and the rise of the self-governing citizen. With the ethics of consumption in mind, we might ask whether neoliberalism establishes social and political conditions in which raising obesity levels are more likely to be seen as an urgent threat or at least more likely to be exaggerated in terms of health risk.

Once again, though, I think there are reasons to be cautious before leaping on the critique of neoliberalism. For example, authors such as Fitzpatrick (2001) and Le Fanu (2000) see health authorities' interest and intrusion in our personal lives as stemming from the rise of the 'new public health' and its concerns with social disparities in health. That is, they propose that a social disparities focus unavoidably leads to a consideration of personal decisions and behaviours that contribute to these disparities. Along similar although not identical lines, Crawford's (1980) classic paper 'Healthism and the medicalization of everyday life' draws our attention towards social movements that sought to discredit modern, hierarchical, industrial medicine in favour of a more 'holistic' and individually 'empowered' approach to one's health. Crawford's point was, in part, seeing oneself as being 'empowered' also made one much more culpable for one's health.

My point here is that there are many frameworks we might draw from if we wanted to explain why our consumption of food and technology has come to the attention of policy makers and health researchers. Is it creeping governmentality, the management of risk and the vested interests of corporate power? Or is it, instead, a result of the *critique* of corporate power (à la *Super Size Me*) or the product of purportedly socially progressive movements interested in economic and health disparities and the constrained decisions about health and lifestyle that people must make?

One of the problems here is that proponents of the critique of neoliberalism cannot simply point to the existence of anti-obesity social policies as support for their theoretical framework. Authority figures have at most times in history concerned themselves with the intimate behaviours of citizens. More important, though, is that it is quite difficult to show that a public health issue like obesity is being driven by dry concerns with health costs and neoliberal efficiency or the altruistic threads found within modern medicine and leftist social concerns. Which is cause and which is effect? And are people governing themselves more today than in the past or simply in different ways?

I have argued in all my research into obesity that too much has been made of rising body weights. However, in my view it is not at all clear that obesity science's interest in food consumption is of a purely nosey, obtrusive or moralizing kind. The people in this area of study exhibit a wide range of motivations and ideological tendencies. Rather than an example of neoliberal hegemony, the 'obesity epidemic' is a substantial social movement with diverse and complex historical roots. In fact, part of what explains its emergence is the way different ideological and public policy traditions have found themselves all wanting to achieve the same thing, albeit for different reasons. And it is partly because obesity science has delivered so little by way of robust scientific knowledge that no one ideological force has prevailed.

Rather than the 'obesity epidemic' signalling a change in the ethics of consumption, the ethics of consumption is only one of the many battlegrounds upon which debates about obesity are happening. And we should remember also that the ranks of obesity sceptics – those who, like me, have questioned the seriousness of rising obesity – include arch neoliberals from some of the better known right wing think tanks. In other words, the 'obesity epidemic' is not the product of any single ideological enterprise, just as it is not fully explainable via any pre-existing theoretical project.

Note

1 Readers interested in examples of this could consult chapter 6 of Gard and Wright 2005.

Bibliography

Atrens, D. (2000) *The Power of Pleasure*, Sydney: Duffy and Snellgrove.

Beck, U. (1992) *Risk Society*, Sage: London.

Bonfiglioli, C., King, L., Smith, B., Chapman, S. and Holding, S. (2007) 'Obesity in the media: political hot potato or human interest story?', *Australian Journalism Review*, 29(1): 53–61.

Bouchard, C. and Blair, S.N. (1999) 'Introductory comments for the consensus on physical activity and obesity', *Medicine and Science in Sports and Exercise*, 31(11 Suppl): S498–501.

Bray, G.A. and Popkin, B.M. (1998) 'Dietary fat intake does affect obesity!', *American Journal of Clinical Nutrition*, 68(6): 1157–73.

Brownell, K.D. and Warner, K.E. (2009) 'The perils of ignoring history: Big Tobacco played dirty and millions died. How similar is Big Food?', *The Milbank Quarterly*, 87(1): 259–94.

Cafaro, P.J., Primack, R.B. and Zimdahl, R.L. (2006) 'The fat of the land: linking American food overconsumption, obesity, and biodiversity loss', *Journal of Agricultural and Environmental Ethics*, 19(6): 541–61.

Christakis, N.A. and Fowler, J.H. (2007) 'The spread of obesity in a large social network over 32 years', *New England Journal of Medicine*, 357(4): 370–79.

Clark, C.M. (2000) 'Combating sloth as well as gluttony: the role of physical fitness in mortality among men with type 2 diabetes', *Annals of Internal Medicine*, 132(8): 669–70.

Crawford, R. (1980) 'Healthism and the medicalization of everyday life', *International Journal of Health Services*, 10(3): 365–88.

Dietz, W.H. (2001) 'The obesity epidemic in young children: reduce television viewing and promote playing', *British Medical Journal*, 322(7282): 313–14.

Dietz, W.H. and Gortmaker, S.L. (1985) 'Do we fatten our children at the television set? Obesity and television viewing in children and adolescents', *Pediatrics*, 75(5): 807–12.

Dionne, I. and Tremblay, A. (2000) 'Human energy and nutrient balance', in C. Bouchard (ed.) *Physical Activity and Obesity*, Champaign, IL: Human Kinetics.

Divine, M. (2004) 'Dying for another snack', *The Sun-Herald*, 30 May: 15.

Dubbert, P.M., Carithers, T., Sumner, A.E., Barbour, K.A., Clark, B.L., Hall, J.E. and Crook, E.D. (2002) 'Obesity, physical inactivity, and risk for cardiovascular disease', *The American Journal of the Medical Sciences*, 324(3): 116–26.

Eberstadt, M. (2003) 'The child-fat problem', *Policy Review*, February and March: 3–19.

Eisenmann, J.C. (2003) 'Secular trends in variables associated with the metabolic syndrome of North American children and adolescents: a review and synthesis', *American Journal of Human Biology*, 15(6): 786–94.

—— (2006) 'Insight into the causes of the recent secular trend in pediatric obesity: common sense does not always prevail for complex, multi-factorial phenotypes', *Preventive Medicine*, 42(5): 329–35.

Finkelstein, E.A., Ruhm, C. and Kosa, K. (2005) 'Economic causes and consequences of obesity', *Annual Review of Public Health*, 26: 239–57.

Fitzpatrick, M. (2001) *The Tyranny of Health: Doctors and the Regulation of Lifestyle*, London: Routledge.

Fumento, M. (1997) *The Fat of the Land: The Obesity Epidemic and How Overweight Americans Can Help Themselves*, New York: Viking.

Gard, M. and Wright, J. (2001) 'Managing uncertainty: obesity discourses and physical education in a risk society', *Studies in Philosophy and Education*, 20(6): 535–49.

—— (2005) *The Obesity Epidemic: Science, Morality and Ideology*, London: Routledge.

Hall, J. (2008) 'Teen health at risk from fat, lazy life', *The Sun-Herald*, 5 October: 11.

Hensrud, D.D. and Klein, S. (2006) 'Extreme obesity: a new medical crisis in the United States', *Mayo Clinic Proceedings*, 81(10 Suppl): S5–10.

Howell, J. and Ingham, A. (2001) 'From social problem to personal issue: the language of lifestyle', *Cultural Studies*, 15(2): 326–51.

Le Fanu, J. (2000) *The Rise and Fall of Modern Medicine*, New York: Carroll and Graf.

Lewis, T. (2008) 'Transforming citizens? Green politics and ethical consumption on lifestyle television', *Continuum: Journal of Media and Cultural Studies*, 22(2): 227–40.

Ludwig, D.S. (2007) 'Childhood obesity – the shape of things to come', *New England Journal of Medicine*, 357(23): 2325–27.

Ludwig, D.S. and Pollack, H.A. (2009) 'Obesity and the economy: from crisis to opportunity', *Journal of the American Medical Association*, 301(5): 533–35.

Lupton, D. (1999) *Risk*, London, Routledge.

Nicklas, T.A., Baranowski, T., Cullen, K.W. and Berenson, G. (2001) 'Eating patterns, dietary quality and obesity', *Journal of the American College of Nutrition*, 20(6): 599–608.

McMichael, T. (2002) 'Not knowing what makes us tick has made us sick', *The Australian*, 17 September: 9.

Møller, N.C., Wedderkopp, N., Kristensen, P.L., Andersen, L.B. and Froberg, K. (2007) 'Secular trends in cardiorespiratory fitness and body mass index in Danish children: the European Youth Heart Study', *Scandinavian Journal of Medicine and Science in Sports*, 17(4): 331–39.

Nestle, M. (2002) *Food Politics: How the Food Industry Influences Nutrition and Health*, Berkeley, CA: University of California Press.

Patty, A. (2000) 'Poor diet, exercise put young at risk', *Daily Telegraph*, 2 August: 19.

Peters, J.C., Wyatt, H.R., Donahoo, W.T. and Hill, J.O. (2002) 'From instinct to intellect: the challenge of maintaining healthy weight in the modern world', *Obesity Reviews*, 3(2): 69–74.

Petersen, A. (1997) 'Risk, governance and the new public health', in A.R. Petersen and R. Bunton (eds) *Foucault, Health and Medicine*, London: Routledge.

Pi-Sunyer, X. (2003) 'A clinical view of the obesity problem', *Science*, 299(5608): 859–60.

Pool, R. (2001) *Fat: Fighting the Obesity Epidemic*, New York: Oxford University Press.

Pratt, M., Macera, C.A. and Blanton, C. (1999) 'Levels of physical activity and inactivity in children and adults in the United States: current evidence and research issues', *Medicine and Science in Sports and Exercise*, 31(11): S526–33.

Prentice, A.M. and Jebb, S.A. (1995) 'Obesity in Britain: gluttony or sloth?', *British Medical Journal*, 311(7002): 437–39.

Research Update (2009) 'New direction needed for obesity research', Deakin health expert claims. Online. Available HTTP: www.gsdm.com.au/newsletters/deakin/june09/16.html (accessed 12 June 2009).

Rolland-Cachera, M.F. and Bellisle, F. (2002) 'Nutrition', in W. Burniat, T. Cole, I. Lissau and E. Poskitt (eds) *Child and Adolescent Obesity: Causes and Consequences, Prevention and Management*, Cambridge: Cambridge University Press.

Rosmond, R. (2004) 'Aetiology of obesity: a striving after wind', *Obesity Reviews*, 5(4): 177–81.

Schlosser, E. (2001) *Fast Food Nation: What the All-American Meal is Doing to the World*, London: Allen Lane.

Swinburn, B.A. (2008) 'Obesity prevention: the role of policies, laws and regulations', *Australia and New Zealand Health Policy*, 5(12): doi:10.1186/1743-8462-5-12.

Vogel, S. (1999) *The Skinny on Fat: Our Obsession with Weight Control*, New York: W.H. Freeman and Company.

Wilkin, T.J., Mallam, K.M., Metcalf, B.S., Jeffrey, A.N. and Voss, L.D. (2006) 'Variation in physical activity lies with the child, not his environment: evidence for an "activitystat" in young children (EarlyBird 16)', *International Journal of Obesity*, 30(7): 1050–55.

Part 3

Commodities and materiality

6 Placing alternative consumption

Commodity fetishism in Borough Fine Foods Market, London

Benjamin Coles and Philip Crang

Setting out stalls

> It's 6:30am on Saturday morning in Borough Market. Vans and lorries containing the day's foods compete with each other for parking along the streets adjacent to the market halls. They are anxious to have their goods off-loaded before Southwark Council's parking wardens begin writing tickets. Other market vendors are wheeling out display cabinets and unpacking meat lockers that are stored on site. While game animals are on the floor waiting to be hung, one of the workers at Furness, a fishmonger and game seller, is building the stall's display of fish and seafood, propping open a shark's mouth, wrapping an octopus around a piece of driftwood and attaching salmon heads to the sides of the cage. Some vendors are pulling tarps off the wooden boxes and wine casks that make up the 'architecture' of their pitches, while others assemble prefabricated wooden stalls. One vegetable seller is wheeling an old wooden wheelbarrow with wobbly wheels and peeling green paint down the passageway while chatting to traders who write out chalk signs that describe what they are selling and something about where it comes from.
>
> (Field Notes: 16 June 2007)

Ethical consumption does not exist in the abstract. It may invoke ideas of overarching principles in order to challenge the predominant mores of consumer culture, but since it is a form of consumption itself it is, of course, also thoroughly culturally implicated. In this chapter our focus is on a specific facet of this ethical consumer culture: how ethical consumption takes and makes place. This 'cultural geographic' approach emphasizes where ethical consumption happens and the geographical imaginations that it fosters. Here, we illustrate that approach by drawing upon a 'topography' – a piece of place writing – focused on Borough Market in London, England, and based on ethnographic research in the market by one of us, Ben, spread over a little more than two years (Coles 2010). Borough Market is a self-styled 'good' food market located in and among the railway arches near London Bridge Station, next to the South Bank of the River Thames. Energized by the belief that 'everyone has the right to eat well' (see www.boroughmarket.org.uk), Borough Market sells foodstuffs that are positioned as better quality, more ethical, and otherwise 'alternative' to those which are available from more mainstream retailers such as supermarkets. As a result, Borough Market is prominent within, and in many ways iconic of, a wider trend of contemporary consumer culture marked by the emergence of 'alternative' consumption spaces, and in particular, alternative forms of food consumption. These spaces present themselves as somehow different to, and better than, mainstream retailers and by extension, mainstream systems of commodity provision. Specifically, Borough Market places particular emphasis on matters of provenance, and is thereby positioned within various 'alternative food systems and initiatives' (AFIs) that individually stress specific types of food production/ consumption practices and ethics: organic, Fair Trade, local and farm-sourced, among others (Murdoch and Miele 2004; Maye *et al.* 2007).

Our general argument is that the dynamics of place and place-making play a central role in these 'alternative' forms of consumption. More particularly, three concerns animate our approach to ethical consumption. First, we are interested in consumption as a placed activity. Geographers have long argued that place-making is a fundamental human activity, akin to the use of language, and hence central to human endeavours and our relations with each other and non-humans (Sack 2003). More specifically, a welter of writings on retail spaces – from shopping malls and centres, to department stores, supermarkets, and home shopping – has made the case that consumption is both undertaken within and fashioned by distinctive settings (Goss 1993; Falk and Campbell 1997; Miller *et al.* 1998). In turn, consumption has been understood as something more than the purchase of a commodity, involving a range of other relationships with goods (such as browsing, gazing, appraising) and with the other things and people that make up retail space (such as the sociality generated by proximity with these others) (Shields 1992). What is true for consumption in general is true for ethical consumption more particularly.

Second, because consumption operates as a genre of cultural practice manifested through places, it is not a purified activity. It has been widely noted how oppositions between 'alternative' and 'mainstream' consumption are being broken down as alternative consumption discourses are appropriated more widely (Jackson *et al.* 2007), but our argument here is a broader one. Ethical consumption operates in real world settings, outside of sealed realms of both ethical reasoning and economic calculation. The ethics of ethical consumption are thereby entangled with a range of other impulses, and the 'ethical' qualities that such commodities are seen as possessing operate within wider spaces of 'qualification' (Callon *et al.* 2002; Harvey *et al.* 2004). Conceptually, a range of work has framed ethical consumption through the lens of lifestyle in order to explore how concerns with, for example, the well-being of the planet can be conjoined with concerns for the self in alternative consumption discourses (Binkley 2003). More prosaic clues exist as to this entanglement, too. Take, for example, the semantic leakiness around the notion of 'good food'. Food can be made and judged 'good', or 'better' than the industrialized norm, in a number of ways: as ethically good, as enacting improved relations between consumers and other people, living beings and environments; but also as having some premium value, as being 'special'; as tasting good, as more pleasurable, with better material qualities and sensory affects; and as healthy, as good for us in its effects upon our bodies and minds. Specific manifestations of 'goodness' tend to shuttle across and knit together these meanings. So, for example, organic foods are defined and regulated according to their relations to the land, but in consumption are also encountered through their ingestion, both in claims for organic fresh produce as tasting different and/or better than non-organic equivalents and in evaluations of healthy diets. It is for this reason that we frame this chapter in relation to 'alternative' rather than specifically 'ethical' consumption. To put it somewhat crudely, we are sceptical that a purely ethical consumption operates in cultures and sites of consumption, but instead see it as operating through the production of various kinds of 'alternative' and 'better' spaces and qualities. It is for this reason too that Borough Market intrigues: as a place that represents a different kind of food consumption from that provided by the UK's contemporary norm, the supermarket; or, as one leading market trader expressed the ethos of the market, as a place that is defined as better than 'that supermarket shite'.

Third, this chapter frames ethical consumption in relation to the politics of the commodity form, and specifically in relation to a 'double commodity fetish' (Cook and Crang 1996). A common conception of ethical consumption is as critique of commodity fetishism. Here, the magical, fetishistic qualities of commodities are attributed to their masking of their own origins (Jhally 1990). It is this that produces the commodity form's ability to be seen as the source rather than the outcome of the social production of value. As consumers we usually know little about where the goods we consume come from, of exactly what they are composed, under what conditions they came to be, and how they reached us. This disconnection of consumers from commodity production and provision, it is argued, opens up the space for commodity enchantment through the mythical imaginations of advertising and branding operations. In turn, that enchantment is both opposed to, and troubled by, realistic knowledge of provenance. Thus, famously, Nike's expensive and carefully engineered associations of its brand and products with forces of empowerment and self-realization are punctured in the 'sign wars' and 'culture jamming' that see Nike associated with production conditions in 'The Third World' (Goldman and Papson 1998; Stabile 2000; Peretti with Micheletti 2004).

A reconnection of consumers to commodity origins – framed variously in terms of tracing, discovering, provenance – thus becomes a *leitmotiv* of ethical consumption (Kneafsey *et al.* 2008). Often related to a particular conception of an ethical life as based upon responsibility for the consequences of our actions, such reconnection depends upon knowledge, and more specifically upon geographical knowledge (Sack 1992; see also Chopra and Kundu 2008; Cook *et al.* 2007; Miller 2003). We need to know where commodities come from, and of what and how they are composed, in order to take ethical responsibility for and through our consumption of them. Such a framing of ethical consumption has prompted various critical responses. One has been to question the role of knowledge, at least in terms of informed evaluation by consumers, in ethical action more generally and ethical consumption in particular. A focus on what consumers know can overlook the importance of other factors in shaping ethical consumption practices, notably individual biographies and wider identifications with ethical values and causes forged outside of consumer cultures (Barnett *et al.* 2005). It also runs the risk of a fixation on individual consumers and their choices rather than collective action or infrastructures of commodity provision and consumption habits (Littler *et al.* 2005; Clarke *et al.* 2007). Another line of critique has been to consider critically what, somewhat inelegantly, might be termed the fetishistic character of the de-fetishization of commodities (Binkley 2008). Here emphasis is put on the rhetorical nature of any unveiling of commodity origins, and the role of ethical marketing discourses in producing material and symbolic use values for ethical commodities (Goodman 2004; Wright 2004; Zick Varul 2008). Mediating such critiques is recognition that geographical knowledge of commodities is always re-presentational. It may be experienced as revelatory, as something previously unknown or unconsidered, but in fact such knowledge is never simply an unveiling, rather a creative performance of reconnection (Cook *et al.* 2000).

Set in Borough Market, London, this chapter explores the role of this particular place in performing an ethics of connected consumption. It does so through two interrelated discussions. First, we focus on the 'placing' of consumption in Borough Market. It may seem unremarkable to claim that the things bought and consumed at Borough Market are experienced as coming from Borough Market, but like all retail spaces that location performs a distinctive material semiotic and sensescape, in this case one that 'places' alternative foods within distinctive geographical discourses and imaginaries which are not tied to their specific origins and travels. Second, we focus more on the 'displacements' of Borough Market. Here our emphasis is less topographic and more topological, as we explore how other places are folded into Borough Market through processes of discovery, material transformation and translation. Together these two themes emphasize the mutual constitution of alternative foods and their geographies.

Placing

The good foods found in Borough Market are encountered not in isolation, but in place. The market itself, constituted by distinctive material textures and sensory experiences, plays an important role in the appreciation of the goods within it. Its location, between and under the railway lines; its architecture; its assortment of material displays, as old wheelbarrows, push carts and tables are used to display produce; the crowds, noise and sense of activity; all of these are vital to the feel and meanings of the market. That sense of place translates into a particular sort of packaging of the goods for sale, a packaging that presents a sense of where these goods are from and hence what qualities they have; a distinctive visual material culture that produces an alternative commodity fetish.

In illustration, let us consider some of Borough Market's bread. Bread at Borough Market is usually sold with some information about its origins: through the deployment of both regulated and unregulated product descriptors (for instance organic, artisanal); and through the provision of more specific information (for instance about flour suppliers or the biography and ethics of a particular baker). However, the appreciation of bread's qualities is recognized to be a more corporeal, less purely cognitive practice. In part this is about the qualities that are there in the consumption of the bread itself: how it looks, smells, tastes. Certainly, getting customers to engage with the bread itself is crucial, as baker Johnny emphasizes:

> Samples are important because they show that we're different and better than anyone else. The difference between our products and another's is in the taste. That's where all of those production things we were talking about come through. You can tell a customer about better cropping, organic fertilizer, all of that, but at the end of the day, it's taste that matters to them. That's why they'll spend the extra money and if the taste isn't there, and the quality, then they won't come back. Taste is what this market's all about.
>
> (Personal Interview,
> Johnny: 10 February 2007)

But it also involves a wider material array, as the following field note suggests:

> I'm with Matt Jones, one of the owners, and head baker, of Flour Power City Bakery. We are in an office above his Bakery near Deptford, in industrial south-east London. Matt produces (in his words) 'good bread . . . rustic, down-to-earth bread using only organic flour, salt, yeast and water. You don't need anything else.' While waiting for Matt to arrive, a receptionist, explaining that I was at a commercial food production site, asked me to sign a form authored by the public health department stating that I didn't have any communicable diseases and hadn't been on a farm. After the interview, we don protective clothing, white jackets and hairnets, and wash our hands before entering Matt's bakery downstairs. A big room with large, commercial ovens, steel work-surfaces, and storage areas for 50kg sacks of flour and other ingredients, the bakery is accessed through a steel door and is separated from the ancillary rooms by interlocking plastic strips. The bakery is very clean (flour not withstanding), and workers, dressed like us, handle finished goods with latex gloves. Finished products are stored in stackable plastic crates, in which they are delivered to various retail spaces. Once reaching Borough market the goods are unloaded and stacked in wicker baskets placed on wooden tables. Handwritten signs label each type of product. The tables stand next to a demonstration bakery, made of reclaimed brick – 'in order to match the buildings across the street' I am told – that houses a bread oven, work surface, mixers, and is topped by windows and countertops through which bakers interact with customers. One of the employees tells me it's a 'demonstration bakery made up to look like an artisan bakery'. A vinyl

laminate sign carries the company's logo and includes an image of a hand-painted chalkboard sign. This sign jars: a sign of a sign, marking a site at which an artisan bakery represents itself as an artisan bakery.

(Field Notes: 20 February 2007)

Wicker, not plastic; wooden tables, not stainless steel; and, to Ben's notable surprise, chalkboard *and* vinyl. The materials staging this display of bread are designed to contribute to its artisanal, rustic quality, and contrast notably with the materials of its safe, hygienic production. Returning to the quotation included in the preceding field note, whilst Matt Jones accurately presents his bread's ingredients as only 'organic flour, salt, yeast and water' it seems that in order to present 'good bread . . . rustic, down-to-earth bread' you do in fact need something else, something more, a 'material practice' (Thrift 2008) that differentiates Borough Market's foods from the industrialized mainstream of the supermarkets.

This material differentiation from supermarkets is not limited to the immediate display of Borough Market's foods. The wider feel of the place matters. Consider, for example, the role of the market's 'climate'. Largely undercover, but not closed off from the elements and the wider environment, the market stages a very different architectural event compared with the British supermarket. In consequence, the rustic product displays of wicker, wood, chalk and board (and so on) constitute not just a themed pastiche but interventions in a distinctively hybrid urban nature.

> Drips and puddles abound at Borough Market because its passages, and the stalls themselves, are hosed down with water at the end of each day. Rainwater also collects in the arches and seeps through, a creeping damp from above. Water collects easily in the gutters and near the drains, where it mixes with whatever else is on the floor and nearby streets. These types of organic mixings are as much a part of Borough Market as the goods it sells, and they provide a valuable component to the material culture that brackets their sale. The puddle and small rivulet of what one might call 'water' is disconcerting, especially as it escapes its own space and mixes with mine – I remember a drip that fell into my coffee. The lines between outside and inside, as well as between production and consumption, are blurry at Borough Market. Its surfaces are anything but sterile. Unlike other retail places, there is little attempt at Borough Market to keep these front and back spaces rigidly separate. Rubbish is removed to the back, and outside, but it still manages to seep through to the front, especially if the weather is right. The physical structure of the market is open to these possible encounters. A bread seller tells me that Borough Market is kept scruffy around the edges. The market is designed to feel lived in, real; here, drips happen.
>
> (Field Notes: October 2006)

The market is not, then, a hermetic packaging of its products. It is a theatre within which affects can be produced. This is partly about rhythm and kinaesthetics:

'Borough Market is about movement and activity', according to a bread seller, 'it's real, organic'. The market is also a place that actively engages the senses, as the following field note reflects:

> It's lunchtime on a warm Friday in the spring. I'm in the thick of it, trying to shuffle through the throng, getting bashed, bashing, annoying everyone around me as I stick out my elbows to make room for a photo. The air is thick with food smells, filled with the sounds of people, sticky with sweat as bodies collide. I can almost taste the market and feel its excitement.
>
> (Field Notes: 18 May 2007)

In the official narrative of Borough Market, the market is explicitly presented in theatrical terms. As opera singer Kevin Loe elaborates:

> There are a number of people who sing at Turnips [one of the market's green grocers]. Most are friends of mine who started after I did. Borough Market is like a theatre. The stallholders are the performers, the customers the audience. People like to come and be part of the show. You'd never get the same kind of exchange in the aisles of a supermarket . . . I have a large voice, it carries far . . . London is a bit of a drab city, but the market brings it to life.
>
> (Kevin Loe, cited in Dean *et al.* 2006: 45)

Borough Market is also a place of touches. These textures and sensations are experienced closer to the body than the other senses, and as a mode of active sensing touching helps to shape the market's economy. Whilst in some instances touching can impinge upon the flow of capital within the market, as when one feels that there are too many people close to you and so you need to leave, or when one judges that a fish is too squishy to be fresh, most of these haptic sensations reproduce the market as a space of alternative consumption. Staging encounters, prompting events, mediating various kinds of touch between subjects and objects, are necessarily imprecise, however. These material, affective practices provide forces that energize this space of consumption, but the results are not pre-determined, and are sometimes elusive. In one of his favourite anecdotes, illustrating his wider sense that the market has become too much of 'an experience' and too little about sales, wine and French rural food merchant Christoph remarks that:

> This place has gotten out of hand. We used to have samples out because that's how we sold our products . . . We let customers taste the difference, you know taste before they buy. But now, tourists come here just to eat. They don't buy, just walk around eating free samples . . . and they expect it. I was talking to a customer once, and had my sandwich sort of behind the till. I turned around and found someone eating it, telling me how good it was, my lunch!
>
> (Personal Interview,
> Christoph: 27 September 2007)

More enigmatically, sometimes something is happening, some sort of 'ordinary affect' is being relayed (Stewart 2007), but it is not certain what:

> I'm watching a family. Their child, a toddler, reaches out to touch the fur of a dead rabbit hanging from one of the cages. Mom rushes over to stop him and says something I can't hear. She turns back to dad. The toddler runs back, this time going after a deer dripping blood from where the head used to be. Mom rushes over again to stop him, dragging the boy off by the arm. Again says something I can't hear. They all walk away, Mom has her child by the arm, the boy keeps looking back towards the dead animals.
>
> (Field Notes: January 2007)

In conclusion, the ethical consumption done at Borough Market does not operate within 'an intellectualized and abstract system of knowledge', but is 'a practical-moral and contextually specific activity' (Miller *et al.* 1998: 6). Goods are encountered and appreciated in place. Place is central to the aesthetics of alternative consumption (Murdoch and Miele 2004). In this particular place, that involves in part an extended geography of 'packaging', where the material fabric of the market – constituted across scales ranging from signage, to stalls, to architecture, to forms of sociality, to location – is experienced as surrounding commodities, adding layers to them, framing how we view them, providing additional 'knowledge' about them. Indeed, in this sense Borough Market could be seen as akin to a themed environment, a place that participates in the sign-economy of the alternative and ethical, helping to constitute the senses of heritage, rurality, urbanity and so forth that matter to alternative cultures of consumption. However, as we've gestured towards, the market could also be viewed in more theatrical, performative terms, as a geography of encounter and mediation of subject–object relations. In the market people and things touch each other. In that vein, it is the character of the mediation between people and things that is crucial to the experienced 'alternative' qualities of market consumption. Borough Market, for example, performs its foods as more 'authentic' and 'real', as having simpler, more natural qualities, through the sense of their more direct, less distanced presence. If Borough Market 'packages' its foods, this is not the supermarket's material culture of product packaging, but an environmental staging, a performing of product through the scenography and direction of a theatrical place.

Displacing

Using the case of Borough Market we have argued, then, that alternative consumption involves a differentiation from mainstream consumption, and that retail places play an important role in such differentiation. At Borough Market, the ethical qualities of its foods are entangled with, and somewhat swamped by, a wider staging of the market's qualities, a broader sense of place. Borough

Market is not therefore simply a mask, veiling the true origins of the foods sold within it by confining consumers' geographical imaginations to this bounded place, for the market's qualities include a sense of connection to wider worlds of food production. Borough Market presents itself, and consumption within it, as having a more 'extroverted sense of place' (Massey 1991), in which its own distinctiveness as a place of consumption emerges from its relations with other places, especially of food production. Thus other places are folded into Borough Market. Consumption in Borough Market is constituted in the here and now through senses of the there and then. Its assembled quality, its 'intersection of numerous actor-networks' (Miller *et al.* 1998: 6), is not simply hidden, but creatively presented. In that sense, the market not only places ethical consumption in a particular setting, but also helps to constitute its 'displaced' quality, by which we mean its reach beyond the parochial, its sense of the movements of things and people that bring it into being (Crang 1996). We now turn more directly to what we might call these 'aesthetics of displacement'.

We have already alluded to a number of ways and material forms through which other places are folded into this particular site on London's South Bank. First, Borough Market's foods are often cast as not just from but of various other places, their distinctive qualities related to their geographical origins and 'terroirs', whether these are legally recognized as 'geographical indications' or not (for wider considerations see Berard and Marchenay 2006; Coombe 2005; Moran 1993). Second, the material presentation of foods through predominantly artisanal and rustic aesthetics displaces contemporary London. Third, marketing materials, in the form of visual displays and information leaflets, that emphasize the provenance of foods bring other landscapes and their agricultural practices into the heart of the city. And fourth, vendors themselves perform identities from elsewhere and/or enact convincing connections between here and there. Thus, the presence of Cumbrian meat in Borough is described in a field note as follows:

> Farmer Sharp's stall provides Cumbrian meat. This is laid out according to type – lamb, mutton, beef, veal – and it is all displayed, under glass, in a refrigeration case. Rams' horns rest on top of the glass-case, along with a set of cards that offer preparation and cooking tips as well as different recipe ideas for the Farmer Sharp's products. Behind the counter, employees, wearing peaked caps, woolen shirts and braces, work at cutting meat, serving customers and keeping the stall tidy. The entire stall is set up below a giant poster advertisement for Farmer Sharp's Herdwick Lamb and Mutton, its claims for the distinctive taste and eating quality of Herdwick sheep maturing on the heather and grasses of the Lake District Fells accompanied with a visage of Farmer Sharp gazing down on his stall and the market.
>
> (Field Notes: 23 August 2007)

Borough Market's principal coffee retailer, Monmouth Coffee, further illustrates these geographies of displacement, in this case with respect to transnational and global networks of provision. Monmouth Coffee roasts and retails quality, speciality coffees. The company's mission statement illustrates something of its quality conventions and their basis in networks of provision:

> We roast coffee from single farms, estates and cooperatives around the coffee growing world. We travel to coffee producing countries looking for coffees that reflect the flavour profile that each area is known for, as well as unique coffees that challenge our expectations. When we taste a coffee that we like, we want to know where it comes from and who grows, picks and processes it. We then look to establish a relationship with the grower and exporter of that coffee. We believe that where such a relationship exists, quality, quantity and price requirements can be discussed in an open and equal way. We see this as sustainable, fair and equal trade.

This mission statement is published in Monmouth's 'Coffee Lists' newsletter, available in store and online. A range of other news items and features present the provision of Monmouth coffees to consumers, and further illustrate how the global reach of Borough Market is framed. To take just one example, headed as a 'visit to origin' the following is an account of a trip to Colombia, published in the July 2008 issue of Coffee Lists:

> Looking out of the window on the flight from Bogota to Neiva we could see that the rainy season had arrived in Colombia. The waters of the Magdalena River were overflowing with muddy water from the rain in the hills above. Arriving in Neiva from Bogota is like getting out of a fridge and into a frying pan. It is hot and humid and it is always a relief to get onto the road for the three and a half hour drive to Pitalito. This was a brief but intense and positive visit to see the farmers of Quebradon. We met with the board members on the first day and discussed the previous crop and the upcoming mitaca crop. The next day we drove up into the hills of Palestina for a meeting at the local school with all of the farmers in the group. The group has established its own cupping (tasting) laboratory and with the help of Rodrigo Junior (son of board member Rodrigo Sanchez Valderrama) and Claudia (daughter of board member Felix Samboni) the farmers are learning about their own coffees and how changes in the picking and processing can affect the flavour of the final cup. This is incredibly important for the development of the coffee quality. It is difficult for farmers to improve the quality of their coffee if they do not understand how changes in processing can impact on the final cup. We are sending Quebradon a sample of Octavio Rueda's micro-lot so that Rodrigo Junior and Claudia can roast and sample the coffee with the members of the group. For some farmers this will be the first time they will be able to taste their own coffee.
>
> (Monmouth Coffee,
> Coffee Lists Newsletter: July 2008)

In this account, Monmouth's Quebradon coffee is cast as relating consumers and producers through Monmouth's careful mediation. In part, this mediation separates and distances, as Colombia and the UK are differentiated through the familiar discourses of exoticized travel. On the other hand, the narrative also explicitly promotes the knitting together and refashioning of these places, as consumers in London learn something about producers in Colombia, and producers in Colombia learn to see and taste coffee like roasters and consumers in London. Of course, this mediation operates at various levels of intensity, and beyond the newsletter Monmouth customers at Borough Market are more likely to experience just a glancing touch upon these highly charged networks of connection. The following field note recounts the presence of Quebradon in Monmouth's market stall, on one July morning:

> When it is my turn in the queue, I tell the sales assistant that 'I would like to buy some coffee, but that I don't know what I want or even where to begin . . . but the last time I really bought coffee and thought about it was when I purchased some Wild Ethiopian . . . or something like that; I quite liked that.' She responds by telling me 'No problem [with not knowing where to begin] but unfortunately we've sold out of that Ethiopian. What do you like and how do you make coffee?' I tell her that I like 'that full coffee flavour, if that makes sense, oh and I use a cafeteria [often called a *French Press* or *Press Pot*].' She smiles and says, 'All right, I suggest this one', before pointing out a coffee from Colombia called 'Cooperativa Quebradon, Huila,' with a 'medium roast'. The assistant tells me that 'It is citrusy, with flavours of lemon, and it is bright. In fact, it's one of my favourites and works very well with the press pot. Sometimes the others get sort of lost in them, but this one is good. Nice fruit and lemons.' She then points me to the tasting notes where I can read more about Quebradon and tells me to 'Come back soon and tell me what you think'.
>
> (Field Notes: 24 July 2008)

Thus in both marketing materials and retail encounter the origins of a Monmouth coffee are presented. Together, these accounts say something about the presence of other places, in this case the municipality of Palestina, near Huila, Colombia, in Borough Market. For us, it illustrates various 'aesthetics of displacement', different senses of how Borough Market's culture of consumption is made through the presence of other places and people. Most obviously, this involves an *opening up* of place through consumption. Borough Market presents a world of flavours. Its good foods are made both through its connection to other places and through concerns for what goes on there and for how those foods come to be here, in Borough Market. The Monmouth coffee drinker is positioned as connected to, and with interests in, elsewhere. Such concerns are, as we discussed in the early part of this chapter, central to the geographies of ethical consumption and its commodity forms. They are also, clearly, implicated in other consuming desires: for difference; for tastes that 'work' and please; for the self-satisfactions of knowledgeable discrimination. The consumer is understood to care about coffee growing in Palestina for many reasons. Monmouth Coffee offers to negotiate those multiple concerns.

However, at the same time as this place of consumption is fashioned as open, as not closed off to other places, it also *localizes* and bounds. This is true in two senses. First, the global flavours available in Monmouth are placed, framed in relation to areally defined flavour profiles. The cosmopolitan consumer is positioned as selecting from a diverse range of localities (the Ethiopian or the Colombian?) (see Hannerz 1996). The world is fashioned as a diverse range of placed goods, to be consumed in order to make the consumer's own place in the world richer, more textured, more diverse and complex. Secondly, Borough Market also localizes alternative consumption within its own boundaries. Here is where 'good' food resides, outside are the mainstream wastelands of 'bad' food. Thus is the somewhat rigid dichotomization of good and bad consumption (Guthman 2003) enacted through the place marketing of alternative retail spaces like Borough Market. Thus too is goodness located within wider urban geographies and sociologies of consumption, a location that can displace in other ways, as Sharon Zukin's narrations of New York and its gentrifications have shown. For alternative consumption's performance of difference from mainstream consumer culture feeds into wider dynamics of urban redevelopment and its symbolic economies, such that the diversity performed within the market can operate as a safe, pleasurable engagement with difference that pushes aside more awkward complexities, encounters and places within the city (Zukin 2008; 2010).

The narratives of Monmouth Coffee speak, then, to the fashioning of Borough Market as both an open and bounded place. They also represent the mobilities through which other places come to be there. Distinct emphases on this movement coexist. On the one hand, there is the sense of Borough Market as a place of *discovery*. The consumer can discover new or diverse tastes and products because the Market and its retailers have discovered new or diverse producers. In both cases, this facilitates a heroic subject-position, one in which a world of difference exists, invites exploration and rewards skilled navigation and a successfully channelled spirit of adventure. On the other hand, there is also an explicit recognition that products at Borough Market do not simply await discovery, but emerge from interactions between producers, providers and consumers. Thus, for Monmouth, their coffees are *emergent*, not just sold. This is true materially and in terms of taste, through Monmouth's role as both a roaster and a buyer discussing 'quality' and 'requirements' with coffee growers. Chiming with wider discourses of ethical consumption governance, Monmouth presents this as a 'relationship' in which negotiations are 'open and equal'. Nonetheless, it is clear that it is this governance, these interactions, which regulate quality, that produce the 'good(s)'. Moreover, at stake here is the articulation of, and translation between, different notions of 'goodness'. The relationships that produce Monmouth's Quebradon coffee are cast in terms of fairness, sustainability and equality; but the character of those relationships is also seen as enabling the successful delivery of tastes that work for Monmouth's customers, so that this Colombian coffee becomes 'good in the press pot'.

In summary, then, in Borough Market we see the associations between alternative consumption and a cosmopolitan sensibility. We also get an insight into how these associations are produced through the 'displaced' character of this place, its presencing of other places. In part this presence involves a geographical imagination in which other different places are discovered, their distinctive products collected, and that array of difference then made available for consumption. But important too is a sense of geographical entanglement, of implication with and in other places, rather than simply a distanced consumption. This includes the kinds of responsibility emphasized by those who frame ethical consumption as a fundamentally geographical practice (Sack 1992). Perhaps more prominent, though, is a sense of governance, of a concern for the successful organization of displacement, and in particular the articulation of the varying good qualities of the market's good foods.

Conclusion

This chapter has reflected on the relations between ethical consumption and place, through a case study of Borough Market in London. Our general argument has been that ethical consumption is enacted through place and that, in consequence, the ethics of consumption are a matter not just of the relations between consumers and commodities but of the places where they come together. By way of conclusion, we outline briefly three more specific aspects to this argument, each of which forms part of an agenda for better understanding the placing of ethical consumption.

First, Borough Market illustrates how place is central to the enmeshing of the ethics of consumption with other cultural economies of quality, including senses of the good other than the ethical. Borough Market is concerned with 'good food' in the broadest sense. Ethical and political sentiments are bound up with identity constructions, culturally coded experiences of urban space and eating, corporeal pleasures, and affecting moments. Retail spaces are crucial sites for this location of the ethical within such wider formations of alternative consumption. They shape how ethical consumption is entangled with other commercial and consumer impulses. Such entanglements, and the places that stage them, cannot just be dismissed as a corruption or co-option of a pure, ideal ethical consumption, but need to be taken seriously in order to consider critically ethical consumption's actually existent forms.

Second, place is a prime means through which the de-fetishization of commodities occurs. As we set out in the opening part of the chapter, many accounts of ethical consumption have emphasized the critique of the commodity fetish through greater awareness about the origins of the goods we consume. Places foster geographical imaginations, and different places of consumption can be seen as making these geographical imaginations in better or worse forms. The geographer Robert Sack has set out a wider argument for a 'geographical guide to the good and the real', arguing that 'it is good to create places that increase our awareness of reality and increase the variety and complexity of that reality' (Sack 2003: ix). For Sack, many places of consumer culture – he attends in particular malls and advertising sign-economies – are profoundly problematic in these terms, as their fantastic, imaginary geographies mask the reality of commodity biographies and flatten cultural and geographical difference into ersatz simulations and familiar stereotypes and motifs (1992). Likewise, for Sack, places of alternative consumption can be considered as 'good places', or at least better places, if they increase awareness, variety and complexity. Borough Market certainly enacts its goodness in relation to these criteria, with its privileging of provenance emphasizing both the making of diverse commodity worlds and consumer awareness of how these diverse things come to be. Borough Market illustrates, then, how claims to the good are enacted through the very fabric of retail space and the social theatre it stages.

Third, however, Borough Market also exemplifies the fetishistic character of this de-fetishization. Alternative consumption spaces represent and perform commodity geographies. Clearly this performance involves something more (and less) than the unveiling of commodities, something more (and less) than the revelation of their social and geographical reality. Building on a body of work considering the representation of commodity origins within ethical consumption, we have argued that Borough Market illustrates the role of retail places in this fetish of de-fetishization. Concerns have included the necessary deployment of commodity aesthetics including forms of advertising, branding and retail display and theatre; how a distinctive fashioning of such forms is central to the making of alternative consumption; and the relations between ethical concerns and other interests in commodity origins, that is with other cultural investments in provenance, such as tastes for authenticity. More particularly, through an interrelated analysis of Borough Market's processes of 'placing' (the performance of place-specific encounters of objects and subjects) and 'displacing' (the folding in of 'other' places to 'this' place) we have sought both to draw out the complex representations of commodity origins within alternative consumer cultures, and to suggest the need for a wider interest in the places within which ethical consumption is done.

Bibliography

Barnett, C., Cloke, P., Clarke, N. and Malpass, A. (2005) 'Consuming ethics: articulating the subjects and spaces of ethical consumption', *Antipode*, 37: 23–45.

Berard, L. and Marchenay, P. (2006) 'Local products and geographical indications: taking account of local knowledge and biodiversity', *International Social Science Journal*, 58(1): 109–16.

Binkley, S. (2003) 'The seers of Menlo Park: the discourse of heroic consumption in the "Whole Earth Catalog"', *Journal of Consumer Culture*, 3(3): 283–313.

—— (2008) 'Liquid consumption. Anti-consumerism and the fetishized de-fetishization of commodities', *Cultural Studies*, 22(5): 599–623.

Callon, M., Meadel, C. and Rabeharisoa, V. (2002) 'The economy of qualities', *Economy and Society*, 31(2): 194–217.

Chopra, A. and Kundu, A. (2008) 'The Fair Tracing project: digital tracing technology and Indian coffee', *Contemporary South Asia*, 16(2): 217–30.

Clarke, N., Barnett, C., Cloke, P. and Malpass, A. (2007) 'Globalising the consumer: ethical consumerism and new repertoires of public action', *Political Geography*, 26: 231–49.

Coles, B. (2010) 'Placing alternative consumption: a topography of Borough Market, London', Unpublished PhD Thesis, Royal Holloway, University of London.

Cook, I. *et al.* (2000) 'Social sculpture and connective aesthetics: Shelley Sacks's "Exchange Values"', *Ecumene: A Journal of Cultural Geographies*, 7(3): 337–43.

Cook, I. and Crang, P. (1996) 'The world on a plate: culinary culture, displacement and geographical knowledge', *Journal of Material Culture*, 1: 131–53.

Cook, I., Evans, J., Griffiths, H., Morris, R. and Wrathmell, S. (2007) 'It's more than just what it is: defetishizing commodities, expanding fields, mobilizing change . . . ', *Geoforum*, 38: 1113–26.

Coombe, R.J. (2005) 'Legal claims to culture in and against the market: neoliberalism and the global proliferation of meaningful difference', *Law, Culture and the Humanities*, 1(1): 35–52.

Crang, P. (1996) 'Displacement, consumption and identity', *Environment and Planning A*, 28(1): 47–67.

Dean, P., Dillon, S., Green, H., Murphy, D., French, J. and de Thample, R. (2006) *The Borough Market Book*, London: Civic Books.

Falk, P. and Campbell, C. (eds) (1997) *The Shopping Experience*, London: Sage.

Goldman, R. and Papson, S. (1998) *Nike Culture*, London: Sage.

Goodman, M.K. (2004) 'Reading Fair Trade: political ecological imaginary and the moral economy of Fair Trade foods', *Political Geography*, 23(7): 891–915.

Goss, J. (1993) 'The magic of the mall: an analysis of form, function and meaning in the contemporary retail built environment', *Annals of the Association of American Geographers*, 83(1): 18–47.

Guthman, J. (2003) 'Fast food/organic food: reflexive tastes and the making of "yuppie chow"', *Social and Cultural Geography*, 4(1): 45–58.

Hannerz, U. (1996) 'Cosmopolitans and locals', in *Transnational Connections: Culture, People, Places*, London: Routledge.

Harvey, M., McKeekin, A. and Warde, A. (eds) (2004) *Qualities of Food*, Manchester: Manchester University Press.

Jackson, P., Russell, P. and Ward, N. (2007) 'The appropriation of "alternative" discourses by "mainstream" food retailers', in D. Maye, L. Holloway and M. Kneafsey (eds) *Alternative Food Geographies: Representation and Practice*, Oxford: Elsevier.

Jhally, S. (1990) *The Codes of Advertising: Fetishism and the Political Economy of Meaning in the Consumer Society*, London: Routledge.

Kneafsey, M., Cox, R., Holloway, L., Dowler, E., Venn, L. and Tuomainen, H. (2008) *Reconnecting Consumers, Producers and Food. Exploring Alternatives*, Oxford: Berg.

Littler, J., Barnett, C. and Soper, K. (2005) 'Consumers: agents of change?', *Soundings*, 31: 147–60.

Massey, D. (1991) 'A global sense of place', *Marxism Today*, June: 24–29.

Maye, D., Holloway, L. and Kneafsey, M. (eds) (2007) *Alternative Food Geographies: Representation and Practice*, Oxford: Elsevier.

Miller, D. (2003) 'Could the internet de-fetishise the commodity?', *Environment and Planning D: Society and Space*, 21(3): 359–72.

Miller, D., Jackson, P., Thrift, N., Holbrook, B. and Rowlands, M. (1998) *Shopping, Place and Identity*, London: Routledge.

Moran, W. (1993) 'Rural space as intellectual property', *Political Geography*, 12(3): 263–77.

Murdoch, J. and Miele, M. (2004) 'A new aesthetic of food? Relational reflexivity in the "alternative" food movement', in M. Harvey, A. McKeekin and A. Warde (eds) *Qualities of Food*, Manchester: Manchester University Press.

Peretti, J. with Micheletti, M. (2004) 'The Nike sweatshop email: political consumerism, internet and culture jamming', in M. Micheletti, A. Follesdal and D. Stolle (eds) *Politics, Products and Markets. Exploring Political Consumerism, Past and Present*, Piscataway, NJ: Transaction Publishers.

Sack, R. (1992) *Place, Modernity and the Consumer's World*, Baltimore, MD: The Johns Hopkins University Press.

—— (2003) *A Geographical Guide to the Real and the Good*, New York: Routledge.

Shields, R. (1992) 'The individual, consumption cultures and the fate of community', in R. Shields (ed.) *Lifestyle Shopping. The Subject of Consumption*, London: Routledge.

Stabile, C.A. (2000) 'Nike, social responsibility and the hidden abode of production', *Critical Studies in Media Communication*, 17(2): 186–204.

Stewart, K. (2007) *Ordinary Affects*, London: Duke University Press.

Thrift, N. (2008) 'The material practice of glamour', *Journal of Cultural Economy*, 1(1): 9–23.

Varul, M. Z. (2008) 'Consuming the campesino. Fair trade marketing between recognition and romantic commodification', *Cultural Studies*, 22(5): 654–79.

Wright, C. (2004) 'Consuming lives, consuming landscapes: interpreting advertisements for Cafedirect coffees', *Journal of International Development*, 16(5): 665–80.

Zukin, S. (2008) 'Consuming authenticity. From outposts of difference to means of exclusion', *Cultural Studies*, 22(5): 724–48.

—— (2010) *Naked City: The Death and Life of Authentic Urban Places*, New York: Oxford University Press.

7 Feeding the world

Towards a messy ethics of eating

Elspeth Probyn

Introduction

As the essays in this book attest, the ethics of consumption are hard to figure. As individual consumers, we are faced with so many choices that it is hard to know what to do. We may, with good reason, question what our individual acts can do in the bigger picture of dwindling natural resources. While governments around the world have recently woken up to the economic facts of the depletion of oil, water and land – hastily summarized under the rubric of 'global warming' – what we as individuals can do seems so small. The structural and historical backdrop to our current plight is so vast that surely any individual act is meaningless. Because of this schism responses tend to be framed in moralistic terms. Ideas about what is 'good' or 'bad' are laid out in black and white terms, which often posit 'us' versus 'them'. The composition of who constitutes 'them' or 'us' varies – on the one hand, big business, fast food chains, and on the other alternative food networks, and local farmers' markets – but this framing does not encourage a careful sense of ethical action. As we will see in this chapter, trying to elaborate ethical ways of being in the world are much more difficult than following moral codes of conduct.

The French sociologist of food Claude Fischler argues that eating now goes to the very core of subjectivity. While the modes of identity formation and eating are varied (for instance, elsewhere I have interrogated how eating plays into colonial networks of governance, Probyn 2000), the current situation exacerbates the connection between eating and one's self. Playing on the well-known aphorism, he argues that 'if I am what I eat, and I don't know what I eat, how do I know who or what I am?' (2009 cited in Raoult-Wack and Bricas 2002: 332; Fischler 1990). With colleagues, Fischler has investigated how the connection with food permeates wider national differences, arguing that for instance 'Americans attach moral dimensions to eating . . . more than the French' (Rozin *et al.* 1999: 179). Based on a systematic comparison of different nation-states, they found that Americans are encouraged to frame eating in strict terms of 'freedom' and responsibility. Here 'freedom' is understood as an individual's right to buy foods free from sugar, fat, carbohydrates and now a number of more specialized foods, such as 'gluten-free'. In broad terms this plays out in a reification of choice, which isolates the individual in his or her eating, and oscillates between a climate of blame, with media advertising as a prime target, and a narrow sense of individual choice. This contrasts starkly with the French tradition of eating together, which Rozin, Fischler and others argue fosters a climate of contractual responsibility. In national attitudes, Americans tend to position eating as a way of 'engineering the self', whereas it is argued that Europeans favour a more communal or commensal (literally eating together) view of the self in society.[1]

Nowhere is the conundrum of individual action versus global catastrophe more acute than in the arena of food. In the past decade the face of food consumption has changed dramatically. The range of foodstuffs available to Western consumers would have been unthinkable as recently as a generation ago. 'Exotic' produce has been domesticated, and the ability to consistently procure fresh produce has scrambled previous notions of seasonality. We benefit from technological advances but we are rarely forced to be cognizant of their wider implications. In the past several decades we have seen a major restructuring of the global food supply system. The balance of power has shifted from the food manufacturers, such as Nestlé or Kraft, to mega retail chains, such as Wal-Mart, Tesco and Aldi. Sourcing of produce has diversified so immensely that it often becomes very difficult to know where any particular product has come from at any given time. This complexity renders the logics of previous political strategies much less evident. For instance, the boycotting of products, which was one quite powerful way for individuals to protest against conditions of labour in distinct national regimes, relied on being able to identify key players – such as Dole – and central places of supply – such as grapes from Chile (under Pinochet's regime), or apples from South Africa (during Apartheid). Thankfully those political regimes no longer exist (although to what extent food boycotts aided their respective demise is a moot point). But the increasing sophistication of 'just-in-time' supply chains and the huge diversification of the provenance of produce means that a boycott of goods is much less feasible today than it was only a decade or two ago.

Food facts

In his sobering book *The End of Food* (2008), Paul Roberts outlines some of the challenges that we face globally in terms of radically addressing questions of food security. For many the concept of 'food security' has become a more useful notion than sustainability because it emphasizes the multiple levels that need to be 'secure' in global terms: for example, labour conditions, environmental issues, bio-diversity, etc. Roberts succinctly maps out the background against which any response to food security must be placed. In the West we have benefited from a history of technological advances, government policies and big retail ruthlessness, which has resulted in remarkably cheap and available food. In the West the cost of food has continually dropped in the past several decades thanks to the mass production of cheap protein (beef, chicken and pork), and the monocultures of grain and corn that underpin this economy. Thanks to the ferocious might of the American food lobbies, the past several decades have seen the US government pouring huge amounts of money into subsidizing farmers, which has produced a continual oversupply of food in the USA. Against any tenet of free trade or neoliberalism, subsidies and 'deficiency payments' mean that food produced in the USA is produced under cost. For instance, corn, milk and sugar are respectively sold for thirty-two per cent, thirty-nine per cent and fifty-six per cent of what it actually costs to produce (Roberts 2008: 135). This is without calculating the external costs or externalities.

In traditional economic theory externalities are all those costs that producers do not have to – and therefore do not – include in their costings. Michel Callon, a sociologist of economics and markets, explains:

> Economists invented the notion of externality to denote all the connections, relations and effects which agents do not take into account in their calculations when entering into a market transaction. If, for example, a chemicals plant pollutes the river into which it pumps its toxic products, it produces a negative externality.
>
> (1999: 187)

His example is a fairly obvious one about the external costs not included in food pricing. But as we will see there are many others. As many now recognize, the changing nature of the food system has distorted food markets massively. It has led to the conversion of over-supply into over-consumption, whereby the West's plates have been systematically 'supersized'. Concentrated animal feeding operations (CAFOs) transformed husbandry into a Fordist factory line, whereby animals are pumped with hormones, and genetically trained to grow big quick. Some meat, such as pork, is pumped with water that adds as much as thirty per cent weight. With the grace of state governments in the US these CAFOs move to wherever regulations are the most lax and the easy supply of grain is most efficient and cheap.

Unnatural food

As an example, trans fats are one of the more insidious effects and products of globalized industrial agribusiness. The vast majority of trans fats are industrially created as a side effect of the hydrogenation of plant oils – a process developed in the early 1900s and first commercialized as Crisco in 1911. The goal of hydrogenation is to add hydrogen atoms to unsaturated fats, making them more saturated. These more saturated fats have a higher melting point making them attractive for baking. Their reduced tendency for oxidation means that they will last seemingly forever. Trans fats have no good nutritional value and add to the accumulation of 'bad' cholesterol (Cameron-Smith and Sinclair 2006: 293). Why would we want to eat something that is so devoid of goodness and so divorced from its natural state? The answer is the taste and profit. Because of their high fat saturation they melt in the mouth, allowing for that smooth 'mouth feel' that we have grown to love.

Soybean is the main crop used to produce trans fats. Much of it comes from that vast region in the Midwestern states of America and the Prairie provinces of Canada; formerly considered to be breadbaskets growing wheat, they're now global providers of trans fats and high-fructose corn syrup (HFCS). Seventy per cent of agricultural land in the Midwest of the US is now given over to single crop corn or soybean. Since WWII there has been a steady and all-encompassing move away from family-run farms to huge industrialized enterprises, many indentured to Monsanto. The corn is processed as syrup for the huge soft drinks market. In her book *Animal, Vegetable, Miracle* Barbara Kingsolver describes the interconnection of government subsidies, mega agribusiness and science: 'the US consumption of "added fats" has increased by one-third since 1975, and our consumption of HFCS is up by 1000 per cent' (Kingsolver *et al.* 2007: 14–15). Her conclusion about the resulting obesity is succinct: 'Obesity is generally viewed as a failure of personal resolve, with no acknowledgement of the genuine conspiracy in this historical scheme' (Kingsolver *et al.* 2007: 15. Individual bodies are entangled with, and inseparable from, historical contexts of consumption.

In the West, thanks to websites such as Ban Trans Fat (www.bantransfats. com), the problem of trans fats has become more evident (Ban Trans Fat 2008). McDonald's has a rather chequered policy of not using trans fats in some countries – Australia and Denmark – but using them in others, most notably those where there is little attention paid to anything but the end cost of food. The Ban Trans Fat group sued Kraft because of the high level of trans fat in Oreo cookies. In the group's discussion of the case they quote Michael Mudd, Kraft senior vice-president for corporate affairs: 'You can make a cookie without trans fat but what you're trading off is the unique taste and texture that people have come to expect.' For Kraft it's not their problem – it's our tastes that are to blame (Ban Trans Fat 2008). But as our awareness shifts, 'trans-fat free' becomes a selling point.

In general, it is the poor and overwhelmingly those in the developing world who continue to eat trans fats. According to Dariush Mozaffarian, from the Harvard Medical School and Harvard School of Public Health,

> The current evidence suggests that, compared with Western nations, the intake of trans fats from partially hydrogenated oils may be much higher in developing countries, typically because partially hydrogenated oils represent the cheapest (and often subsidized) choice of fat for cooking.
>
> (Mozaffarian 2006)

While the contexts of development around the world are so very different that it is hard to lump them together as 'developing countries', two major thematics stand out. With the increased global circulation of cheap and poor-quality food basics, locally developed agriculture is collapsing. Local farmers simply cannot compete. The only way they can survive is by exporting their specialized crops to overseas markets (Dolan and Humphrey 2000). The destruction of these local economies can only lead to increased migration into the cities. While global migration or flow of the poor is one of the defining political and demographic features of today's world, internal migration from villages to cities is equally important.

There is, of course, no one simple line that connects all the different factors. Nonetheless the West's, and particularly America's and increasingly the UK's, hunger for ever cheaper food is being felt around the world. The deforestation of huge tracts of land in Brazil is a well-publicized fact, and the easy culprit is McDonald's. However McDonald's has stopped sourcing beef from deforested rainforest. But it is not only the production of cattle that causes the damage. Brazil has a burgeoning economy of single-crop farming, most often soybeans and corn. These are exported to the factory farms around the world. The situation becomes even more dramatic when one counts the 'externalities', which as previously mentioned are the hidden costs of why we have never eaten so cheaply (Spencer 2005).

In addition, global structural changes are creating whole new classes in different parts of the world. Peasants become the urban dispossessed and the poor. In places like China or India there are the new, massively numerous – if still proportionally small – middle classes, with aspirational hungers for Western food lifestyles. An astounding finding from the Chinese Health Ministry is that Chinese urban boys aged six are now 2.5 inches taller and 6.6 pounds heavier than was the average thirty years ago. On average six-year-old boys in Beijing and Shanghai now measure and weigh nearly the same as American boys (MacLeod 2007). Economic expansion means that meat is much more commonly available and eaten than was the case earlier, and cattle are produced in industrialized feedlots rather than raised in the traditional manner. In China, as elsewhere, lingering ideas link prosperity and fat, as in the saying 'a fat child is a healthy child'. A story from *USA Today* cites a Beijing businessman at a McDonald's with his daughter happily eating a hamburger: he comments, 'our daughter will definitely be taller than us. She has eaten better than my wife and I. When I grew up, in winter all we had to eat was cabbage' (MacLeod 2007). We need to remember that this man may well have experienced mass starvation at first hand. Who would blame him for wanting his child to be taller and bigger than his generation?

The entry of mega entities such as Wal-Mart into food retail at the end of the 1980s completes the transformation of food into a commodity. As Roberts puts it, 'the success of the modern food system . . . is to make food behave like any other consumer product' (2008: xiv). Big retail investment in the 'orchestration of freight logistics and growing' paved the way for centralization of food, which has devastated previous regional lines of food distribution. This has affected the possibility of creating regional markets for food structurally, so that produce isn't shipped to and fro from hubs that are often thousands of miles away from either point of sale or production sites. The investment in transport systems is ultimately paid for by suppliers, who have, over the past several years, been forced to pay the cost of cheap supermarket food. Roberts calculates that slotting fees charged by the top retailers in the US for placement of products amounts to some $USD16 billion, costs which come entirely from suppliers.

The mammoth oversupply in American food, in tandem with the government policies which help produce the situation, has of course had a tremendous impact on the rest of the world. In George W. Bush's words:

> I want America to feed the world. I want our great nation that's a land of great, efficient producers to make sure people don't go hungry. And it starts with having an administration committed to knocking down barriers to trade, and we are.
>
> (cited in Roberts 2008: 171)

Here the tragedy of the thirty-six million deaths from hunger each year (in Kofi Annan's reckoning in the Global Humanitarian Forum 2009) is matched by the patently false depiction of US agri-business as a 'free market'. With the acceptance of GATT, NAFTA and the latest WTO arrangements, there is no industry more protected than American agriculture. The hopes of the Green Revolution, which was to end world hunger through technology and mono-crops in the developing nations in the 1970s and 1980s, are as dead as the soil they grew in. The 'revolution', which promoted the wholesale growth of crops like maize in Kenya, was based on unfeasible conditions and its limited success was due to a huge increase in fertilizer use. When the oil crisis hit in the 1980s, the costs of petroleum-based fertilizer soared, thereby unveiling the unsustainability of the Green Revolution. At the same time the artificially low cost of American grain skewed any level playing ground. In1986 John Block, the then US Secretary of Agriculture, declared that:

> The idea that developing countries should feed themselves is an anachronism from a bygone era. They could better ensure their food security by relying on U.S. agricultural products, which are available in most cases at lower cost.
>
> (Roberts 2008: 130)

Good and bad eaters

This sketch of events demonstrates that the ethics of eating is a minefield. Against most of the well-intentioned plans, the actualities of global food production unfortunately stack up, perpetuating what Roberts defines as 'simplistic solutions to an external complex problem' (Roberts 2008: 285). As with other simplistic solutions to complex and difficult problems (from sexual abstinence as protection from HIV to the 'war' on terror) there is often a large kernel of moralism at the heart of the debates. Indeed food and eating may have overtaken sexuality as the province of moralism and prohibition.

Julie Guthman's work has done much to complicate the feel-good politics of food especially as it is promoted in northern California, the mecca of foodie activism. Guthman's argument does much to advance a more reflective ethics of food (Goodman and DuPuis 2002). Her main point of intervention is to problematize some of the assumptions that underlie arguments of 'good food', which as she points out often posit who is a good eater/person and who is not. As with my argument above, Guthman draws together questions about obesity and the often-privileged politics of local and organic food. In an article intriguingly entitled, 'Can't stomach it: How Michael Pollan *et al.* made me want to eat cheetos' (Guthman 2007), Guthman takes aim at the ways in which proponents of better eating such as Pollan and others 'turn our gaze, perhaps inadvertently, from an ethically suspect farm policy to the fat body'. As she says, 'these authors seem unaware of how obesity messages work as admonishment' (Guthman 2007: 77). Rather than considering how an amalgamation of bad government policy, global retail pressures and unequal distribution of funding is creating a situation whereby people in developing countries are suffering from the medical consequences of obesity, the good food arguments individualize and damn the over-weight, and more often than not the poor. The underlying assumption that slips in is that if people are fat they have decided not to eat well. This is, of course, a very American mode of individuating what are often structural problems. As Guthman bitingly puts it:

> The messianic quality and self-satisfaction is not accidental. In describing his ability . . . to conceive, procure, prepare and (perhaps) serve his version of the perfect meal, Pollan affirms himself as a super-subject while relegating others to objects of education, intervention, or just plain scorn.
>
> (Guthman 2007: 78)

Along with many others, Pollan's suggestions for action tend to be individualized. 'Shake the hand that feeds you' (Pollan 2008: 160), 'look the farmer in the eye' are familiar catch cries of much of the so-called alternative food movement. However, as Guthman points out, this avoids tackling the increasingly rotten roots of the modern food system, from government policy to systemic farm labour inequities to the inequalities between the global North and South.

For other researchers a narrow focus on the local can result in 'a conflation of spatial relations with social ones' (Hinrichs 2000: 301). In her study of 'embeddedness and local food systems', Clare Hinrichs closely interrogates the idea that face-to-face transactions between producers and consumers automatically results in 'a counter-point to transnational corporations', and queries the idea that the local 'promises human connection' (2000: 298). The concept of embeddedness has become central to much research on networks especially within rural and agricultural sociology. Originating in Karl Polanyi's work in the 1950s, the focus is on 'human economy [as] embedded and enmeshed in institutions, economic *and* non-economic' (Polanyi 1957: 250). This was then further extended by Mark Granovetter's (1985) attention to the imbrications of social and economic networks. While the emphasis on the human side of networks was undeniably important, for many this has led to an over-evaluation of the role of the small-scale and therefore the supposedly more human aspect of food production and

consumption. As Holloway and Kneafsey put it, 'the valorization of the local
. . . may be less about the radical affirmation of an ethic of community or care
and more to do with . . . a conservative celebration of the local as the supposed
repository of specific meanings and values' (2000: 294). In Michael Winter's
pithy conclusion the turn to the local is 'simplistic' and encourages an 'emerging
defensive localism' (2003: 26).

However, for many, organic 'local' farming has become the most prevalent
way to promote ethical eating. This overlooks how fast and the extent to which
organic has moved from alternative to mainstream, with large supermarket chains
now offering organic produce sections. In her history of organic in the West, and
especially in California and the US, Guthman (2003) traces the not always
innocent origins of the burgeoning market of organic food. She pinpoints one
particular product – salad mix or mesclun – that 'gave a jump start to the
California organic sector [and] became what is likely the largest in the world in
terms of crop value' (Guthman 2003: 47). Of course with little nutritional value,
salad mix is hardly going to feed the world in a better way – as many of us fondly
hoped would be the result of alternative eating. Although mainly associated with
the 1960s counter-culture, Guthman argues that the real take-off for organic
happened later and was propelled by restaurants and cashed-up business people.
Far from being the food of hippies, organic became known to the producers at
least as 'yuppie chow'.

Back to roots

In an open letter published a few days before the American elections of 2008,
Michael Pollan addressed the president-elect and the man he hoped would be the
'farmer-in-chief'. He wrote that it's time to get back to what he calls 'resolarizing
the American farm': a return to the principles that sunshine, soil and water are
the basis for growing things. It's a call to remember age-old practices: that cows
should eat grass, that their manure should go back into the earth, and that crops
need to be rotated so as not to deplete the nutrition in the soil. Pollan realizes his
proposal will cause an enormous shake-up in the current state-of-play:

> To grow sufficient amounts of food using sunlight will require more people
> growing food – millions more. This suggests that sustainable agriculture will
> be easier to implement in the developing world, where large rural populations
> remain, than in the West, where they don't.
>
> (Pollan 2006)

Much of our organic produce now comes from the global South, a fact that is
greeted with alarm by many. However, the history of organic farming practices in
the West demonstrates that many of our ideas about organic or sustainable
farming came first from the South and moved to the North. For instance,
F.H. King's 1911 book *Farmers of Forty Centuries* was entirely based on his
admiration for what he called 'the permanent agriculture' of China, Korea, and
Japan (King 1911). His successor, Albert Howard, one of the forefathers of the

modern organic movement, was inspired by the traditions of East Asian farmers. Howard was an English scientist who worked in agricultural development in India for twenty-six years. He was awestruck about what he found there:

> In the agriculture of Asia we find ourselves confronted with a system of peasant farming which, in the essentials, soon became stabilized. What is happening today in the small fields of India and China took place many centuries ago. The agricultural practices of the Orient have passed the supreme test – they are almost as permanent as those of the primeval forest, of the prairie, or of the ocean.
>
> (Howard 1943)

In our present moment of environmental turmoil we often forget that the late 1930s and '40s were a time of huge change in farming as the British and American public became aware of the dangers of how nature could boomerang when thwarted. One notable counter-strategy was the idea of 'trash farming', advanced by an iconoclastic American farmer. In 1943, Edward Faulkner published *Plowman's Folly* where he explained his ideas about how to reverse the damages to the soil that he blamed on chemical pesticides and over-ploughing (Beeman 1992: 96). Faulkner's conception of trash farming saw soil as a living system of capillaries. When conventional ploughs are used the soil mass is violently broken apart, disrupting the capillary connections through which water seeps. Faulkner's answer was taken from Asian farming practices. Eschewing the plough, he recommended disc-rotoring the crop residue, or trash, into the soil. The result was a 'trashy' surface soil scattered with debris and 'teeming with organic matter' (Beeman 1992: 96).

Statistics from the UN Food and Agricultural Organization show a massively skewed division of farming labour worldwide. This is also changing the supply of produce within developing nations and the role of these nations as suppliers (Weatherspoon and Reardon 2003; Dolan and Humphrey 2000). Agriculture occupies sixty per cent of the population of developing countries while in developed countries it is one to two per cent of the population (Scialabba 2007). As the West wakes up to carbon fears and reacts in near hysteria about food miles, the question of organic from afar further complicates the picture of what we eat and where it comes from. The UK Soil Association is threatening to withdraw its precious organic certification from countries like Kenya because of the carbon costs of air freighting produce to Western supermarkets. Many have pointed out the bias in these figures:

> Kenyan producers emphasize that carbon emissions for all airfreighted food to Britain represent about 1 per cent of total emissions, and organic food a tiny percentage of that. They point out that, according to World Bank figures, a Briton emits an average 9.4 tonnes of CO_2 compared with an African's 0.3 tonnes.
>
> (Clayton 2007)

Embargos on importing organic produce from the developing world is profoundly unfair. As Elijah Koinange, the secretary of the Kenynan organization, puts it: 'You know, we only ever stopped organic farming because of chemicals and other fertilizers which came from your countries, and you told us they were good' (Clayton 2007). The Food and Agriculture Organization (FAO) points to the advantages of organic farming in the developing world: organic farms provide more than thirty per cent more jobs per hectare than non-organic farms and, thus, create employment opportunities. This ratio is further increased if on-farm processing and direct marketing are considered (CWFS 2007). The FAO concludes that: 'The challenges facing agriculture – old challenges such as increasing world population and new challenges such as high climate variability – are equally characterized by globalization of energy flows, be they ecological, economic or societal' (CWFS 2007).

Ethical eating

What is to be done? In this chapter I have traced out some of what I think are the key factors that must be included in any plan to try to think and eat ethically. These include paying attention to: government policies of large and powerful nations, especially but not only the USA; a history of agriculture that foregrounds the role of Asia in propounding sustainable forms of farming; the impact of the decisions of the North on the global South and the latter's key role in providing sustenance for developing nations and for the supermarkets of the West; and the rise of unnatural foodstuffs and the concomitant effects on the health of everyone living on the planet, which disproportionably hurt the poor. These are the factors that should be at the heart of our discussions about how to eat ethically. The ethics of food production and consumption cannot be resolved by simplistic and narrowly focused actions. Against historical ideas imported from the East to the West about organic as the complex interrelationships of living things, and the interconnections of living things, increasingly consumers are offered 'organic' as a 'solution' to ethical questions of place, and eating. Ethical eating cannot be allowed to slip into morality, bought in recyclable packages. When simplistic solutions are used as a short cut across all the complexities of eating they should leave a bad taste in your mouth.

Part of the problem is the human tendency to look for 'solutions'. Years ago when I decided that a vegetarian diet would be most suitable as the means through which to distribute protein worldwide I included eating fish in my diet. My reasoning was that the world is made up of some ninety per cent water, and that it should be used as a resource for providing cheap protein. In the intervening years however the sorry state of fish farming has become evident with some salmon farms producing as much waste (in terms of fish faeces) as mid-sized towns. In addition to this problem, often the farmed fish escape and further damage bio-diversity by mating with wild fish. So much for a neat solution. However if we drill deeper into the question of farmed fish we will find fascinating experiments whereby fish such as the famed Southern Blue Fin tuna are now being successfully bred on land.[2] This small example, which rose out of a collaboration between Japanese aquaculture researchers, local Australian fishers (in the Eyre Peninsula – an isolated spot in South Australia), Federal and State government, global demand coupled with respect for the tuna, and the technology that rendered it possible, raises the ways in which human appetites, technology, globalization, the local and sustainability interconnect in complicated ways.

At the outset of this chapter I raised the question of what we as individuals can hope to achieve in our endeavours to act ethically. I may have further complicated this question by raising the many factors that contribute to non-ethical and unsustainable practices in the production and consumption of food. While I maintain that these are integral to any plan of action, they may also seem so insurmountable that we may be tempted to give up trying. This, however, is not an option. One way of charting your own course through this minefield is to remember the question of externalities. Being mindful of the human, social, and ecological costs associated with one's everyday food consumption practices is a start. Trying to avoid those that come at too high a cost may give us an idea of what not to do. Following through on practices that come with a smaller global price tag may help us all a little bit. This means that we all need to do our homework in order to know the backdrop against which our individual actions are performed. This will also help keep us modest, honest and focused about what we can do and what is to be done.

Notes

1   This division closely echoes Foucault's argument that a distinction between the care of the self and knowing the self has long been an element of Western society. These arguments were central to the last two volumes of his *History of Sexuality* (1986, 1988), which Luther Martin sums up as 'two differently situated technologies of the Hellenistic self', one focused on self-disclosure with the concomitant requirement of confession, and the other on self-discovery or the care of the self (Martin 1988: 60). Foucault famously elaborated the role of sexuality and 'the practices by which individuals were led to focus their attention on themselves, to decipher, to recognize, and acknowledge themselves as subjects of desire' (1986: 5). It is quite possible to argue that food and eating has taken on the weight of the injunction for self-regulation that sexuality played in the nineteenth and twentieth centuries (Probyn 2000). In either case, the ethics that Foucault put forward arose out of his thinking about the Ancient Greeks' practices of the regimen, wherein the self became a sort of project constituted through 'techniques which permit individuals to affect, by their own means, a certain number of operations on their own bodies . . . so as to transform themselves, modify themselves' (1988: 367). It is notable that the regimen was constituted by reflections on what you ate, and where, your sexual practices, and most centrally all understood as integral to the community of selves (Probyn 1993).
2   For a view of this largely successful attempt to render the tuna fish industry sustainable see the clip (www.youtube.com/watch?v=VwXGrJHGAX8). As a blog comment from Brazil puts it, 'amazing work, maybe you will be the reason I will have sushi with my children' (accessed 1 December 2009).

Bibliography

Ban Trans Fats (2008) Online. Available HTTP: www.bantransfats.com (accessed 13 August 2008).

Beeman, R. (1992) 'The trash farmer: Edward Faulkner and the origins of the sustainable agriculture in the United States, 1943–53', *Journal of Sustainable Agriculture*, IV(1): 91–102.

Callon, M. (1999) 'Actor-Network Theory – the market test', in J. Law and J. Hassard (eds) *Actor Network Theory and After*, Boston, MA: Blackwell Publishers.

Cameron-Smith, D. and Sinclair, A.J. (2006) 'Letter: trans fats in Australian fast foods', *EMJA*, CLXXXV/5.

Clayton, J. (2007) 'Organic farmers face ruin as rich nations agonize over food miles', *Times Online*. Online. Available HTTP: www.timesonline.co.uk/tol/life_and_style/food_and_drink/real_food/article2182994.ece (accessed 8 January 2009).

Committee on World Food Security (CWFS) (2007) 'Assessment of the world food security situation'. Online. Available HTTP: www.fao.org/unfao/bodies/cfs/cfs33/index_en.htm (accessed 8 January 2009).

Dolan, C. and Humphrey, J. (2000) 'Governance and trade in fresh vegetables: the impact of UK supermarkets on the African horticulture industry', *Journal of Development Studies*, 37(2): 147–76.

Eurofood (2000), 'Hain Food buys Celestial Seasonings'. Online. Available HTTP: http://findarticles.com/p/articles/mi_m0DQA/is_/ai_61576617 (accessed 8 January 2009).

Fischler, C. (1990) *L'homnivore*, Paris: Odile Jacob.

—— (2009) 'The meanings of eating', presented at the University of Adelaide.

Foucault, M. (1986) *The Use of Pleasure. The History of Sexuality Volume 2*, trans. R. Hurley, New York: Vintage Books.

—— (1988) *The Care of the Self. The History of Sexuality Volume 3*, trans. R. Hurley, New York: Vintage Books.

Global Humanitarian Forum (2009) Online. Available HTTP: www. globalpolicy. org/social-and-economic-policy/the-environment/climate-change/47871.html (accessed 12 October 2009).

Goodman, D. and DuPuis, M.E. (2002) 'Knowing and growing food: beyond the production-consumption debate in the sociology of agriculture,' *Sociologia Ruralis*, 42(1): 5–22.

Granovetter, M. (1985) 'Economic action and social structure: the problem of embeddedness', *American Journal of Sociology*, 91: 481–510.

Guthman, J. (2003) 'Fast food/organic food: reflexive tastes and the making of "yuppie chow"', *Social & Cultural Geography*, 4(1): 45–58.

—— (2007) 'Can't stomach it: how Michael Pollan *et al.* made me want to eat cheetos', *Gastronomica*, 7(3): 75–79.

Heckman, J. (2007) 'A history of organic farming – transitions from Sir Albert Howard's war in the soil to the USDA National Organic Program'. Online. Available HTTP: www.westonaprice.org/farming/history-organic-farming.htm (accessed 11 November 2008).

Heinz (2008) Online. Available HTTP: www.heinz.com (accessed 11 November 2008).

Hinrichs, C. (2000) 'Embeddedness and local food systems: notes on two types of direct agricultural market', *Journal of Rural Studies*, 16: 295–303.

Holloway, L. and Kneafsey, M. (2000) 'Reading the space of the farmers' market: a case study from the United Kingdom', *Sociologia Ruralis*, 40: 329–41.

Howard, A. (1943) *An Agricultural Testament*, Oxford: Oxford University Press.

Howard, P. (2008) 'Organic industry structure'. Online. Available HTTP: www.msu.edu/ ~howardp/organicindustry.html (accessed 8 January 2009).

King F.H. (1911) *Farmers of Forty Centuries, Permanent Agriculture in China, Korea, and Japan*, Emmaus, Penn.: Rodale Press, 1990.

Kingsolver, B., Hoop, S.L. and Kingsolver, C. (2007) *Animal, Vegetable, Miracle: Our Year of Seasonal Eating*, London: Zed Books.

MacLeod, C. (2007) 'Obesity of China's kids stuns officials', *USA Today*. Online. Available HTTP: www.usatoday.com/news/world/2007-01-08-chinese-obesity_x.htm (accessed 1 September 2007).

Martin, L.M. (1988) 'Technologies of the self and self-knowledge in the Syrian Thomas tradition', in L.M. Martin, H. Gutman and P.H. Hutton (eds) *Technologies of the Self*, Amherst, MA: University of Massachusetts Press.

Mozaffarian, D. (2006) 'The danger of trans fats'. Online. Available HTTP: www.project-syndicate.org/commentary/mozaffarian1 (accessed 1 September 2007).

Polanyi, K. (1957) 'The economy as instituted process', in K. Polanyi, C.M. Arensberg and H.W. Pearson (eds) *Trade and markets in the early empires*, Glenco, IL: Free Press.

Pollan, M. (2006) 'My 2nd letter to Whole Foods'. Online. Available HTTP: www.michaelpollan.com/article.php?id = 83 (accessed 11 November 2008).

—— (2008) *In Defence of Food: The Myth of Nutrition and the Pleasures of Eating*, London: Allen Lane.

Probyn, E. (1993) 'Technologizing the self: Foucault and "le souci du soi"', in her *Sexing the Self: Gendered Positions in Cultural Studies*, London: Routledge.

—— (2000) *Carnal Appetites: FoodSexIdentities*, London: Routledge.

Raoult-Wack, A. and Bricas, N. (2002) 'Ethical issues related to the food sector evolution in developing countries: about sustainability and equity', *Journal of Agricultural and Environmental Ethics*, 15: 325–34.

Roberts, P. (2008) *The End of Food: The Coming Crisis in the World Food Industry*, London: Bloomsbury.

Rozin, P., Fischler, C., Imada, S., Sarubun, A. and Wrzesbiewski, A. (1999) 'Attitudes to food and the role of eating in life in the U.S.A., Japan, Flemish Belgium and France: possible implications for the diet-health debate', *Appetite*, 33(2): 163–80.

Scialabba, N.E. (2007) 'Organic agriculture and food security', Food and Agriculture Organization of the United Nations. Online. Available HTTP: ftp://ftp.fao.org/paia/ organicag/ofs/OFS-2007-5.pdf (accessed 8 January 2009).

Shiva, V. (2002) 'In praise of cowdung'. Online. Available HTTP: www.cqs.com/ cowdung.htm (accessed 11 November 2008).

Spencer, M. (2005) 'Foodmania', *The Observer*. Online. Available HTTP: http:// observer.guardian.co.uk/foodmonthly/story/0,1546291,00.html (accessed 1 September 2007).

Weatherspoon, D.D. and Reardon, T. (2003) 'The rise of supermarkets in Africa: implications for agrifood systems and the rural poor', *Development Policy Review*, May 2003, 21(3): 333–55.

Winter, M. (2003) 'Embeddedness, the new food economy and defensive localism', *Journal of Rural Studies*, 19: 23–32.

8 Drinking to live

The work of ethically branded bottled water

Emily Potter

Introduction

The phenomenal growth of bottled water markets around the world has been one of the most notable success stories of the modern beverage industry. The 1980s and 1990s represent the heyday of bottled water, with the market expanding during this time from a largely boutique concern comprising mainly European mineral waters, to a multi-product, multi-billion dollar industry. Today, bottled water sales total sixty billion US dollars worldwide. Local brands, imported brands, still and sparkling varieties, and flavoured and 'enhanced' bottled waters jostle on refrigerator shelves, giving traditionally dominant soft drinks a run for their money. And despite a recent high-profile 'backlash' against bottled water in some Western countries, markets continue to boom across the world. Bottled water is the fastest growing segment of the US beverage industry, while in Asia and Australasia the bottled water market has increased by more than five hundred per cent since 1994 (Wanctin 2006). It is estimated that 154 billion litres of bottled water are now consumed globally each year.

A niche, but increasingly prominent, sub-market of the bottled water industry is ethically branded bottled water. As this chapter will discuss, this bottled water product takes one of two forms: either as a 'grassroots' brand solely established and marketed through its ethical credentials (what I will refer to as 'not-for-profit ethical water' brands, a tag under which many of these brands self-identify), or as a corporate owned bottled water product that, for certain periods of time, attaches itself to ethical activities as a manifestation of cause-related marketing. These forms may appear to have significant overlap – and indeed, in part, this is what this chapter will be arguing. Both types of bottled water call on consumers to consider the ethical value of the product, and are branded in terms of social and environmental responsibility. Each also invites the consumer to undertake ethical self-fashioning and to connect to broad and often distant networks of 'good works' through their beverage choice. However, it is necessary to distinguish between the two, as the claims of each product seek to position their version of ethically branded bottled water in distinct ways. While the legitimacy of the 'not-for-profit' claim is open to debate and contested interpretations, especially when the brands sold under this banner operate within a market economy, I use this term here as a way of distinguishing those bottled waters that badge themselves entirely through altruistic purpose.

This chapter will go on to discuss the operations of both kinds of products, their conditions of emergence and their strategies for both enrolling consumers and positioning themselves as crucial technologies in global water provision and futures. It will engage with criticism of ethically branded bottled waters that sees such brand strategies as representing cynical or naïve attempts to redeem and retain the popularity of an environmentally and socially irresponsible product. While this charge has some traction in the context of cause-related marketing campaigns for well-known bottled water brands, I will argue that it is inadequate for fully understanding the work of ethically branded bottled water products, especially those which identify as 'not-for-profit' commercial beverages. Moreover, the chapter will contend, reading the ethical branding of bottled water, in whatever form, strictly in terms of capitalistic profit motives is to narrowly interpret the neoliberal cultures within which these bottled water brands are produced and consumed.

In a move away from these critiques, the chapter seeks to situate the rise of ethically branded bottled water within the context of emergent forms of governmentality, under which the water producer becomes a deliberate and conscious player in what Nikolas Rose calls 'the administration of life' (2006: 57). Drawing upon theories of the biopolitical and neoliberal governmentality, in which human life itself – 'sheer life' (Collier and Lakoff 2005: 25) – is subject to governmental practice, and where non-state actors increasingly participate in the regulation and production of civic life, it will argue that ethical brands of bottled water function as technologies in the project of ensuring human well-being. It is the context of a crisis or an 'emergency', especially, which licenses the activities of these products: an emergency widely interpreted as occasioned by the failings (both threatened and realized) of elected state representatives to adequately provide water to their population, thus legitimizing the interventions of private entities into the sustainment of life. I will draw on Agamben's theory of the 'state of exception' (2005) as a means of understanding this invocation of emergency as initiating new roles for, and markets in, bottled water products. In terms of questions of ethical consumption, ethically branded bottled waters offer a particularly productive case study through which to gain insight into the participation of consumption practices in the emergence and operations of biopolitical cultures and governmental forms.

The rise of ethically branded bottled water and neoliberal governmentality

The range and popularity of ethically branded bottled water have echoed the rates of growth previously seen throughout the bottled water market at large. While during 2008, sectors of the global bottled water market slowed from their previous exponential rise, sales volume of these ethically branded products bucked the trend, and even doubled in the UK market. The UK has proved a particular success story for not-for-profit ethical water, with a variety of brands establishing themselves in prominent retail contexts across the country. These include One Water, Belu Water, Frank Water, Thirst Aid Water and Thirsty Planet. All of these donate a percentage of their sales to clean water projects in Africa and Asia, though other ethical water brands in the UK focus on different causes, such as the AIDS-targeted Hot Water. The US and Australia have also seen not-for-profit ethical waters enter into the bottled water market: Ethos Water, sold through Starbucks in the United States and established in 2001, provided the model for Give Water (also US-based), which, like Ethos, provides a portion of sales to charitable causes. Unlike Ethos however, which also directs its philanthropy to clean water projects in the Global South, Give Water supports local charities across a range of causes. Thankyou Water is a relatively new entrant to the Australian bottled water market, where the UK One Water also recently launched its product. Like One Water, Thankyou Water channels the entirety of its profits to clean water projects in Africa and Asia.

As I have indicated, it is important to distinguish between the ethical branding of bottled water as the sole rationale for a product and as a cause-related marketing (CRM) initiative that attaches to pre-existing and market dominant brands. Not-for-profit ethical waters are generally marketed through a 'grassroots' narrative, although they tend to enjoy the investment and patronage of established business and cultural elites. Further, their market share is very small compared with that of the big bottled water brands which, around the world, are owned by some of the largest multinational food and beverage corporations. As the environmental and social consequences of bottled water have more widely circulated, and a 'backlash' against these products has gained pace in certain quarters – something that I will discuss in more detail later – many of these companies have sought to promote the health and well-being contributions and environmentally responsible aspects of bottled water production and consumption. Marketing strategies frequently frame the bottle as contributing to the crucial task of 'personal hydration', as well as providing a much healthier alternative (as 'zero calorie' products) to other beverages on the market, particularly soft drinks, and emphasize the water conservation strategies of the company, or the recyclable nature of the PET plastic bottles used. Other strategies employed by large bottled water manufacturers have involved CRM campaigns that explicitly position their bottled water products – in concert with consumers – as agents of social change.

CRM campaigns around bottled water gained traction during the 2000s, as CRM in general and discourses of corporate social responsibility (CSR) found increased ubiquity. However, as scholars of CSR have noted, the drive to associate private capital with charitable causes is not new (Frankental 2001: 20), particularly as public unease with the size, facelessness and shareholder culture of corporations (where corporations are legally responsible only to the welfare of shareholders) has heightened. Yet the pre-eminence of neoliberalism and its manifestation through the 1980s and 1990s in waves of privatization and public–private 'partnerships' brought private capital into very public arrangements of civic practice that positioned corporations as social stakeholders. In this context, corporations and other non-government actors drawn into regimes of governance encountered rising expectations for them to meet both social – and with the prominence of green concerns during this period – environmental responsibilities.

Corporations have not been alone in this. Implicated in the emergence of new post-welfarist state forms is the individualization of the social realm, within which the responsibilization of individuals to account for and cultivate their own ethical dispositions has seen a radical shift in the terms of citizenship, or belonging within a civic body. Both corporate and individual philanthropy have thus been foregrounded as elected governments retreat from welfare provision, giving primacy to consumption-based practices of 'giving'. '[Citizenship] in the contemporary moment', argues King, '[is] less about the exercising of rights and the fulfilment of obligations and more about fulfilling one's political responsibilities through socially sanctioned consumption and responsible choice' (2006: 73). Ethical products, in particular, promise to realize this cohabitation of individual and corporate responsibility towards the civic realm. For both producers and consumers, the value of their investment in the ethical product is tied to their enrolment in neoliberal paradigms of civil service and the demonstration of this participation through modes of voluntary self-regulation. Consumers targeted by ethical goods are routinely invited to work on themselves as ethical subjects through their consumption of the product and simultaneously to monitor corporate behaviour as producers make their practices open to public scrutiny by way of 'sustainability reports' and other devices.

By associating a company's products with a certain ethical issue, cause-related marketing works to build brand loyalty, appealing to consumer desire to fulfil their ethical responsibilities while also ensuring the corporation's own participation in regimes of social and environmental care. As Starbucks entrepreneur Howard Schultz puts it, 'the consumer has begun . . . to perform an audit on what a company stands for in terms of its culture, its practice and the way it interacts with the people it serves' (Harrison 2003: 3). Ethical products are thus participants in what Callon *et al.* term 'the economy of qualities' – the process by which goods are 'qualified', or rendered desirable and useful, by producers and consumers (2002: 197). 'The characteristics of a good', Callon *et al.* explain, 'are not properties which already exist and on which information simply has to be produced so that everyone can be aware of them.' Rather, their qualities must be generated and revealed through various strategies of calculation, accountability and audit (198). Consequently – and as part of the corporation's role within new systems of governance – networks of auditing services, international framework agreements, consultants, new marketing practices and the collaboration of non-governmental organization (NGO) partners are crucial devices for the project of delivering and measuring corporate social responsibility. Indeed, as Andrew Crane explains, NGOs are now super brands in their own right, thus providing valuable capacity for corporate partners. In Europe especially, Crane relates, NGOs 'enjoy a much higher degree of trust (forty-eight per cent) than either government (thirty-six per cent) or business (thirty-two per cent)' (2005: 227).

The marketing of ethically branded bottled water

In recent years, the belief that consumption is a means by which individuals pursue 'meaning in their lives', and 'connect' to broader social networks, has come to influence marketing strategies across Western economies (King 2006: 11). Variously this consumer imperative is interpreted as a result of social alienation in the wake of neoliberal change, and as a manifestation of an invigorated consumer–citizen culture. For both producers and consumers, then, the benefits – both economic and socio-political – of 'altruistic' practice are very much a part of ethical marketing discourse. 'Values are an asset' writes consultant Chris Arnold. 'Brands that come top of many surveys live and breathe some form of ethics' (2009: 21,17). Cause-related marketing campaigns around bottled water evidence this, as they both attach ethical credentials to the company at hand, and offer to consumers the capacity to ethically fashion themselves through their purchase. Subtextually, it can be argued, they also offer to 'offset' any environmental or social concerns that consumers might have regarding the product, although bottled water is never explicitly positioned in these terms.

Popular bottled water brands that have attached themselves to ethical causes are the internationally marketed Volvic water (owned by Danone), and the various bottled water products belonging to Australian company Coca-Cola Amatil (CCA). Volvic's '1 for 10 Litres' campaign, slated to run between 2008 and 2010, promises to provide ten litres of potable drinking water to communities in Ghana, Malawi, Mali, Zambia, Ethiopia and Niger for every litre of Volvic natural mineral water and Volvic 'Touch of Fruit' flavoured bottled water sold. This will be achieved through the donation of funds towards building wells and community education programmes on water management, to be delivered by World Vision. More complex is CCA's portfolio of CRM initiatives attached to its bottled waters in Australia, New Zealand, Papua New Guinea (PNG), South Korea, New Guinea, Fiji and Indonesia. These include Nature's Own bottled water, sold in PNG, which raises funds for HIV/AIDs research through the National AIDS Council of PNG, and New Zealand's carbonated flavoured water brand, L&P, that sponsors the Prostate Cancer Foundation of New Zealand.

In Australia, CCA's signature bottled water is Mount Franklin, launched in 1989, which dominates market share, particularly among women, who are its targeted demographic. Forty-three per cent of Australian women identify Mount Franklin as their favourite bottled water brand. In line with other bottled water producers, CCA has striven to associate Mount Franklin with health, well-being and environmental sustainability, and a variety of CRM campaigns have put the brand to work in this way. One of its most high-profile campaigns, an alliance with the Australian National Breast Cancer Foundation (NBCF), was initiated in 2007 and continues to run. Different strategies have been employed by Mount Franklin during this campaign, such as financial donations to the NBCF, awareness-raising initiatives, and 'positivity' programmes for breast cancer sufferers and survivors. All of these enrol the consumer as actively involved in the philanthropic process, both as its co-constituent and as its potential target. The 'Well of Positivity' website that operated through 2007 invited consumers to leave a message of support for those affected by breast cancer. CCA pledged to donate $1 to the NBCF for each message left, up to a total of $250,000. Meanwhile, the 'Pink Lid' campaign, which runs each year in October – breast cancer awareness month – is framed by CCA as a mode of community service: explains Director of Media and Public Affairs, Sally Loane, 'You walk into any supermarket and you see this wall of pink [lids] and immediately women think "it's breast cancer month, I had better have a mammogram"' (2009).

Mount Franklin's 2007–08 'Buy me, plant a tree' campaign similarly sought to 'enable' consumers. According to Loane, CCA's customers want to 'help the environment' but are unsure of how to do so – 'they might switch off a few lights but they don't necessarily go out there and plant a tree' (2009). During this campaign, consumers of Mount Franklin were invited to visit the CCA website and enter the barcode of their bottle: on doing so, consumers would have a tree planted in their name. Such a discourse of ethical enablement and of working on the self implies a form of individual auditing that mirrors the companies' own attempts to model themselves as responsible citizens.

It is a discourse very much employed, too, by brands of not-for-profit ethical water that seek to differentiate themselves from the large corporate producers of bottled water. The purchase of ethically branded products is strategically situated as part of a set of ethical calculations that a consumer undertakes in neoliberal regimes of self-monitored conduct where the question of 'how to live?' is put at stake (Collier and Lakoff 2005: 33). Aihwa Ong describes this as characteristic of new citizenship forms, in which 'the security of citizens, their well-being and quality of life, are increasingly dependent on their own capacities as free individuals to confront globalized insecurities by making calculations and investments in their lives' (2006: 501). While these not-for-profit ethical water brands routinely describe their practice in contrast to the interests of big business, they commonly draw attention to the very personal ways in which their products came to be, thus emphasizing the individualized ethical awakening embodied in these bottled water products.

For brands such as Frank Water, One Water, Give Water and Thankyou Water, for instance, narratives of a transformative event experienced by the product's (always youthful, thus conveying energy and cultural change) founder/s are key to the marketing of these products. On the website of each, and in media coverage and other PR materials that accompany the bottles, are prominently placed stories of the product's origins, usually involving its founder's realization that while drinking water is plentiful in the West, it is a scarce resource for many millions around the globe. For Katie Alcott, a trip to India and a case of dysentery in her twenties was her inspiration to launch Frank Water, 'a water bottle brand that would fund clean water projects where they were most needed' (Frank Water 2009). Similarly, One Water founder and CEO Duncan Goose started his bottled water initiative 'after seeing [developing countries' water] conditions first hand . . . while on a two-year motorbike voyage around the world' (Asher 2009).

Routinely positioned by its ethical credentials as a tool for individual civic participation, the ethically branded water bottle can be seen as an active device of what Kersty Hobson calls 'techno-ethics' – a 'form of anti-consumption consumption' (2006: 331) – where the consumer in concert with this technology undertakes the social and individual work of a 'sustainable citizen' (317). 'Drink Give. Do Good' announces the Give Water website. Despite the language of action employed here, implicit in this 'consumer-led' philanthropy is the lack of *extra* work required by the bottled water drinker. In the act of choosing (and buying) the bottle alone, the ethical work is undertaken. Duncan Goose explains, again in relation to One's launch in Australia: 'We are not asking people to give money or trying to grow the Australian bottled water market, we are just asking current buyers to make an educated purchase and simply choose One in the knowledge that as they drink water, so does Africa and Asia' (Palmer 2009). Ben Lewis of Give Water expresses a similar sentiment: 'Our goal is to turn consumers into philanthropists without changing anything in their daily lives' (Give Water 2009). Thus the language of consumer enablement is shared by the CRM endeavours of large-scale bottled water manufacturers and the makers of not-for-profit ethical waters.

Moreover, while the individual grassroots narrative is a key device for the branding of not-for-profit ethical water, both these products rely upon similar networks of expertise, cultural status and association. For each, statistical data, sites of concern such as impoverished African villages or medical research, new technologies, celebrity endorsements and the participation of other crucial actors such as NGOs and business sponsors, are assembled in order to produce or 'stabilize' (Barry and Slater 2002: 181) the bottled water product and to secure its market. One Water in the UK, for example, prominently displays the celebrity endorsement of its products on its website and in its advertising campaigns. Hollywood star Mischa Barton, and UK actors David Tennant and Claire Goose, sister of One Water founder Duncan Goose, call on bottled water consumers to 'Switch for Africa', while Duncan Goose himself has become a celebrity, voted ITV's Greatest Living Briton in 2007. In Australia, Thankyou Water is endorsed by pro surfer Mick Fanning and celebrity chef Donna Hay, and has been supported by companies such as packaging manufacturer Visy, which donated 30,000 PET plastic bottles to the initiative. Thankyou Water also hired a 'social media advisor' to enable their product promotion through social networking technology – something that CCA, too, is experimenting with in the latest iteration of its breast cancer campaign, inviting Twitterers to turn their avatars pink in support of the cause.

Active in these assemblages, too, for all forms of ethically branded bottled water, is the water bottle itself as a *material* technology that is employed in deliberate ways. The pink lids of Mount Franklin are echoed by the four differently coloured labels of Give Water products, which allow the consumer to choose – much like Kerekere, the café cited in the introduction to this book – which cause their purchase will benefit. As a review of Give Water explains, '[s]ales of blue bottles support children's causes; pink bottles support breast cancer research; green bottles support environmental causes; and orange bottles support muscular-disorders research. "Consumers want choice," the entrepreneur [behind Give Water, Ben Lewis] says. "They want to choose how they give back, and they want to give back locally'" (Sussman 2009). Consumer choice consequently entails ethical as well as commercial decisions. Moreover, these material features of the ethically branded water bottle invoke the very material concerns to which it seeks to connect: the pink lids of Mount Franklin bottles, for example, that trigger a woman's awareness of the need for a breast check. Not-for-profit brands targeting clean water projects similarly materialize the link between the product purchased by the consumer and the 'good work' that this purchase will do. This link is water. The images and information attached to these brands elide the privately purchased and consumed containerized water (in general, a luxury item in the West) with the public water infrastructure that will be provided to poorly resourced communities in the global South. All water is thus put on an equal footing, as a common denominator of life.

It is from this premise, of water as a marker of what Collier and Lakoff term 'sheer life' (2005: 25) – the bottom line for human well-being – that ethically branded bottled water finds its further and more complex rationale. Again, this is a provenance shared by not-for-profit ethical waters and their corporate counterparts. Threaded through discourses of individualized 'self-realization' (Pringle and Thompson 1999: xxii) and responsibilized consumption around these bottled water products is the context of 'the emergency' in which the bottle is mobilized by new state actors in an articulated project of sustaining life. The critique of ethically branded bottled water as a strategy of redemption amidst a growing bottled water backlash is consequently an insufficient frame for understanding the logic of these products. This is what I now go on to discuss, before returning to 'the emergency' as a legitimizing context not just for ethically branded bottled water markets, but for the participation of their producers in contemporary governmental practice.

Bottled water backlash

A high-profile turn against bottled water in affluent Western countries is frequently cited as the reason for the rise of ethically branded water, particularly the linking of ethical associations to already existing bottled water brands. As bottled water has gained market share so too has it accrued negative press for being both environmentally and socially unsound. The PET plastic bottles used to containerize water since the late 1980s are a particular source of concern, drawing on fossil fuels and generating hundreds of millions of wasted bottles every year which pollute water ways as well as contributing hugely to landfill. The plastic 'nurdles' (plastic resin beads) that form the basis of PET plastic bottles have gained much publicity for ending up along coastlines and in the stomachs of fish and birds. Bottled water is also criticized for consuming vast amounts of energy in its bottling and transportation process. Brands sold worldwide such as Fiji Water, Volvic and Evian accrue many 'water miles' in the movement of a single bottle from source to consumer. Additionally, bottled water has come under fire for generating distrust in public water supplies, particularly in light of marketing campaigns emphasizing the health benefits and reliable nature of bottled water.

As a result bottled water has fallen out of favour in certain circles. While the consumption of bottled water, particularly of European and other imported brands, as well as 'high-end' products such as the US Bling H20 bottled water (sold in a Swarovski crystal-encrusted bottle and retailing at close to US$40), was once particularly associated with social status and taste, the fashion conscious have now turned against the bottle. *Time* magazine proclaimed 'The War on Bottled Water' as number four on its list of the top ten food trends of 2008: wrote columnist John Cloud, 'bottled water is now unforgivably '90s' (Cloud 2009). Campaigns against bottled water have been endorsed by high-profile figures such as one-time London Mayor Ken Livingstone, US celebrity chefs Mario Batali and Alice Waters, and actress Sarah Jessica Parker, who 'lapped up kudos for sipping a glass of New York tap water in aid of a UN fundraiser' (Polaris 2009a). At the more everyday end of the spectrum, too, reusable bottles like the Sigg aluminium bottle have risen in popularity due to their environmentally friendly nature, and local community groups which campaign for the return of publicly available water to public city spaces have sprung up

A recent spate of well-publicized bottled water bans has also contributed to this shift. In the US, San Francisco city prohibited the purchase of bottled water by its own departments and agencies in 2007. Similarly, municipalities in the UK, Australia and Canada have also phased out internal bottled water purchasing. Cities such as New York, Salt Lake City and London have run campaigns promoting the quality of their tap water, while in Canada 'bottled water free zones' have been set up across universities and colleges (Polaris 2009b). Australia has seen the first instance anywhere in the world of a water bottle ban across an entire town in the small regional community of Bundanoon, New South Wales. Taking effect in mid 2009, Bundanoon's ban was seen as sparking 'off a worldwide debate about the social and environmental effects of bottled water that has put the beverage industry on the defensive' (Foley 2009).

According to bottled water campaigners, such strategies have succeeded in reducing global bottled water consumption. The Polaris Institute, a Canadian NGO that monitors and agitates against the bottled water industry, relayed in February 2009 that Nestlé, which owns seventy bottled water brands across the world, had announced a 1.6 per cent drop in sales of this product during the previous year (Polaris 2009b). According to the Polaris Institute, global sales of bottled water have consistently fallen since 2003. In the UK market, a reduction in bottled water sales has also been noted, with segment analyst Zenith International reporting a decrease of 3.5 per cent across the UK in 2007 (Merrett 2008).

Yet a correlation between these statistics and the bottled water backlash is not straightforward. Zenith also report that, in this year, 'poor summer weather was identified as [a] key reason for [the] overall . . . decline in UK sales volumes', while the 'global financial crisis' of 2008 has also been cited as a reason for this. Moreover, Zenith sees cause for continued optimism in the strength of this product.

'Despite such a disappointing summer', they continued, 'the role of bottled water in emergency situations and the surge in ethical waters highlighted new areas of consumer resonance' (Merrett 2008). This reference to 'emergency situations' – specifically, as I will explain, situations in which human life is put at risk by the inadequacies of the state – flags a key rationale for bottled water manufacturers in general, and one that ethically branded bottled water has particularly attached to: the role of bottled water in sustaining and administering life.

The emergency and the administration of life

Criticisms of ethically branded bottled waters as redemptive exercises in 'green-washing', 'blue-washing' or 'pink-washing' – depending on which ethical cause the brand addresses – fail to account for the significance of neoliberal govern-mentality and its enrolment of non-governmental actors in political practice, and thus tend to read its attention to public and environmental health concerns as solely opportunistic. Yet, private capital cannot be disentangled from the state and its commitment to secure the well-being of its population which, as Foucault argues, is the biopolitical object of modern governmental practice. Governmentality in this understanding, writes Judith Butler, is a 'mode of power concerned with the maintenance and control of bodies and persons, the production and regulation of persons and populations, and the circulation of goods insofar as they maintain and restrict the life of the population' (2006: 52). Given this, it is productive to consider the rise of ethically branded bottled water not as a technique for redeeming shaky markets, but rather more broadly as a means for initiating and expanding new markets in the service of life.

These 'diverse logics of the market' for which profit maximization cannot fully account (Bakker 2009: 1783) are certainly shadowed by some very public concerns raised over the privatization and corporatization of water. Water activists routinely oppose the marketization of water provision through the argument that water, as a fundamental need of human beings and a freely available resource, should not be owned by any one entity or individual. 'The necessity of water to life is why, under customary laws, the right to water has been accepted as natural, social fact', writes Vandana Shiva (2002: 21). Water's privatization, whether through containerized water production, or through corporations moving into the management and provision of public water supplies, is therefore regarded by its opponents as antithetical to every individual's claim to clean, accessible water. For these critics, water provision is considered to be the ultimate responsibility of the state. Shiva, for example, describes the encroachment of private capital on established traditions of water rights as a 'clash of cultures: a culture that sees water as sacred and treats its provision as a duty for the preservation of life and another that sees water as a commodity, and its ownership and trade as fundamental corporate rights' (2002: x). Yet the task of providing water to those in need (as Zenith suggests bottled water is doing), and thus ensuring the right to water, is exactly what the producers of ethically branded bottled water also claim.

Zenith is not alone in referring to bottled water as an emergency technology: bottled water manufacturers and advocates commonly frame the product in these terms. In a media release titled 'Bottled water companies support Australians in time of emergency', the Australasian Bottled Water Institute – a lobby group representing bottled water producers in Australia and New Zealand – claims that 'bottled water is a vital part of Australia's natural disaster and terrorism emergency response'. 'Australia's bottled water companies have already donated more than $2 million in product to community agencies and emergency services during Victoria's bushfire crisis [of February 2009] . . . The effect of bush fires on municipal supplies means that Victorians will continue for some time yet to rely on bottled water for their personal consumption and the industry is committed to meeting this need' (Gentile 2009). Sally Loane from CCA similarly positions the company's water bottle products, in a defence against anti-bottle water movements: 'I think people have got to sit back and think, well, it's actually something that we need in Australia. We [are] sign[ed] up with [the] government's . . . emergency response plans, which means that in the event of contamination or something happening to the dams or the water supplies, we are then able to supply the populace with bottled water. We do that all the time' (Staight 2008).

While on the one hand, this discourse of emergency appears a strategic move to situate the bottle as a crucial technology on a par with, and even superior to (for its implied reliability), municipal water supplies – given the criticism of bottled water as a superfluous product in developed countries especially, where tap water is largely of consistently good quality – it also invites further reflection. Loane's reference to CCA's integration with state emergency response strategies speaks clearly of the corporation's contemporary role in biopolitical practice. Given the multiplicity of actors in neoliberal systems of governance, the state's responsibility to 'optimize [the] capabilities' of its population (Bull 2007) – understood by political theorists such as Martha Nussbaum as its central role – is consequently diffused, as private interests become simultaneously defined as 'agents of development' (Sadler and Lloyd 2009: 616).

Agamben's theory of the emergency, or crisis situation, as triggering new manifestations of sovereign power is a useful frame for thinking through the interventions of water bottle producers in the administration of life. Here, biopolitics is played out in the declaration of the 'state of exception', under which usual law is suspended and the 'bare life' of citizens (akin to Collier and Lakoff's 'sheer life') excised from their previous political rights, is centralized as a site for the operations of sovereign power. While Agamben's concern is particularly the production of the biopolitical body through sovereign power – what Bull calls 'the true awfulness of sovereignty and our abjection before it' (2004) – his attention to the governmental forms that are initiated by the state of exception, and its origins in the emergency, point to sovereignty as a practice rather than a stable point of authority or, as Butler puts it, a 'unified locus for state power' (2006: 53). Thus, for Rabinow and Rose, reflecting on the implications of Agamben's theory, 'sovereign power is no longer confined to those who are explicitly agents of the state – it apparently extends to those who have authority over aspects of human vital existence' (2006: 202).

This is something that not-for-profit ethical water brands also assert – their role in modes of sovereign power where the state is perceived as inadequate or failed, and in need of non-governmental enterprise. The language of crisis or emergency peppers the rhetoric of these bottled water producers, providing further entanglement with the ethically branded corporate waters from which they seek to distinguish themselves. It is a matter of interest that both anti-bottled water campaigners and not-for-profit ethical water companies cite the same or similar statistics concerning the poor water conditions of many communities in the global South, indicating the interventions of both in the politics of life. '1.1 billion people in the world . . . don't have access to safe drinking water', states the Polaris Institute. 'Yet in the self-indulgent West, we're mired in an argument over our precious bottled H_2O' (Polaris 2009a). This kind of moralism is crucial to the marketing of not-for-profit ethical waters and all employ it to a greater or lesser extent. The One website puts the problem in these terms: 'One billion people without clean water, two million deaths each year, but did you know that the bigger problem is actually that people spend an average of five hours a day walking to collect water? . . . Imagine what your day would be like if you spent five hours walking to your local shop for a drink?' (One Water 2006); while Thankyou Water reports its alignment with the UN's 'Water for Life Decade' initiative, naming its mission as 'funding solutions to the developing world's water crisis and in turn reaching out to those who cannot reach out for themselves' (Thankyou Water 2009).

Conclusion

Implied in these claims of not-for-profit ethical water brands is the insufficiency of the state to supply adequate and accessible water to its populations, and although none of these companies seeks to address this issue through the supply of bottled water in the locations it targets, the bottle is employed within its markets as a device through which the water crises of the global South can be addressed. The bottle of not-for-profit ethical water, just like the 'ethical' CRM initiatives of corporate-owned bottled waters, is thus firmly situated as a participant in governmental strategies, both domestic and global. Furthermore, in these arrangements of consumer and producer intervention into the biopolitical realm, bottled water is normalized as a technology of water provision and as an agent for the securitization of sheer life; as Duncan Goose affirms, 'people have recognized that water is water; why wouldn't you opt to buy a brand that changes people's lives?' (Fry 2007).

The rise of ethically branded bottled water has witnessed a proliferation of products striving to differentiate themselves as agents of social change, mobilizing the bottle of water to ethico-political ends. However, in their strategies, logic and enrolment in neoliberal governmentality, 'grassroots' not-for-profit ethical waters and ethically branded bottled water owned by large corporations can claim no moral high ground over the other. Indeed, to talk in such terms is to overlook the complex operations of neoliberal cultures in which these products participate, and through which the ethical brand can be understood as an active force. Foucault's articulation of the biopolitical agenda of modern governmental practice, within which the responsibility of the state to ensure life is now diffused among a host of non-state actors, and Agamben's insight into the role of the 'emergency' in generating and legitimating new forms of sovereign power, offer instructive means of contextualizing the rise of ethically branded bottled water in ways that give meaning to these products beyond conventional commodity logic. Both forms of ethically branded bottled water discussed in this chapter are situated within local and global arrangements of personal and civic administration, where the ethical project of managing the self connects to broader social and political programmes. If the 'ethicalization of existence' (Rose 1989: 263–64) puts the question of how to live at stake, then there are a host of actors who contribute to its answer. As a technology of intervention and provision in global water futures, ethically branded bottled water makes its claim to life as an always-vulnerable entity to be sustained by the 'good work' of ethically oriented production and consumption.

Bibliography

Agamben, G. (1998) *Homo Sacer: Sovereign Power and Bare Life*, trans. D. Heller-Roazin, Stanford, CA: Stanford University Press.

—— (2005) *State of Exception*, trans. K. Attell, Chicago and London: University of Chicago Press.

Arnold, C. (2009) *Ethical Marketing and the New Consumer*, Chichester: John Wiley.

Asher, J. (2009) '"Ethical" bottled water takes a playful turn', *Nine MSN News*, 15 January. Online. Available HTTP: http://news.ninemsn.com.au/national/719186/ethical-bottled-water-brand-takes-playful-turn (accessed 24 August 2009).

Bakker, K. (2009) 'Neoliberal nature, ecological fixes, and the pitfalls of comparative research', *Environment and Planning A*, 41: 1781–87.

Barry, A. and Slater, D. (2002) 'Introduction: the technological economy', *Economy and Society*, 31(2): 175–93.

Bull, M. (2004) 'States don't really mind their citizens dying (provided they don't all do it at once): they just don't like anyone else to kill them', *London Review of Books*, 16 December. Online. Available HTTP: http://www.lrb.co.uk/v26/n24/malcolm-bull/states-dont-really-mind-their-citizens-dying-provided-they-dont-all-do-it-at-once-they-just-dont-like-anyone-else-to-kill-them (accessed 22 October 2009).

—— (2007) 'Vectors of the Biopolitical', *New Left Review*, 45. Online. Available HTTP: www.newleftreview.org/?view = 2667 (accessed 4 January 2009).

Butler, J. (2006) *Precarious Life: The Powers of Mourning and Violence*, London and New York: Verso.

Callon, M., Méadel, C. and Rabeharissoa, V. (2002) 'The economy of qualities', *Economy and Society*, 31(2): 194–217.

Cloud, J. (2009) 'The war on bottled water: top ten food trends', *Time*, 18 February. Online. Available HTTP: www.time.com/time/specials/2008/top10/article/0,30583, 1855948_1864255_1864271,00.html (accessed 20 January 2010).

Collier, S.J. and Lakoff, A. (2005) 'On regimes of living', in A. Ong and S.J. Collier (eds) *Global Assemblages: Technology, Politics, and Ethics as Anthropological Problems*, Malden, MA: Blackwell.

Crane, A. (2005) 'Meeting the ethical gaze: challenges for orienting the ethical market', in R. Harrison, T. Newholm and D. Shaw (eds) *The Ethical Consumer*, London and Thousand Oaks, CA: Sage.

Foley, M. (2009) 'Small Australian town stands up for the tap', *New York Times*, 15 July. Online. Available HTTP: www.nytimes.com/2009/07/16/world/asia/16iht-water.html (accessed 30 July 2009).

Frank Water. (2009) Online. Available HTTP: www.frankwater.com (accessed 12 September 2009).

Frankental, P. (2001) 'Corporate social responsibility – a PR invention?', *Corporate Communications: An International Journal*, 6(1): 18–23.

Fry, C. (2007) 'Springs and roundabouts', *The Guardian*, 22 March. Online. Available HTTP: www.guardian.co.uk/environment/2007/mar/22/water (accessed 24 August 2009).

Gentile, T. (2009) 'Bottled water companies support Australians in time of emergency', *Australasian Bottled Water Institute*, 13 February. Online. Available HTTP: www.bottledwater.org.au/lib/pdf/MR-BushFiresDonations-130209.pdf (accessed 8 October 2009).

Give Water. (2009) Online. Available HTTP: www.drinkgive.com (accessed 10 September 2009).

Harrison, R. (2003) 'Corporate social responsibility and the consumer movement', *Consumer Policy Review*, 13(4): 127–31.

Hobson, K. (2006) 'Bins, bulbs, and shower-timers: on the techno-ethics of sustainable living', *Place and Environment*, 9(3): 317–36.

King, S. (2006) *Pink Ribbons, Inc.: Breast Cancer and the Politics of Philanthropy*, Minneapolis and London: University of Minnesota Press.

Lee, J. (2009) '"Ethical" water flows into the spin cycle', *The Sydney Morning Herald*, 15 January. Online. Available HTTP: www.smh.com.au/news/environment/water-issues/ethical-water-flows-into-the-spin-cycle/2009/01/14/1231608794639.html (accessed 24 August 2009).

Loane, S. (2009) Interview with Emily Potter. CCA Headquarters, Sydney, 10 July.

Merrett, N. (2008) '"Ethical" water brands may boost flagging UK sales', *Beverage Daily*, 8 April. Online. Available HTTP: www.beveragedaily.com/Industry-Markets/Ethical-water-brands-may-boost-flagging-UK-sales (accessed 2 February 2009).

One Water. (2006) Online. Available HTTP: www.onedifference.org (accessed 14 July 2009).

Ong, A. (2006) 'Mutations in citizenship', *Theory, Culture and Society*, 23(2–3): 499–505.

Palmer, D. (2009) 'Ethical water brand to donate all profits to clean water projects', *Australian Food News*, 14 January. Online: Available HTTP: www.ausfoodnews.com.au/ 2009/01/14/ethical-water-brand-to-donate-all-profits-to-clean-water-projects.html (accessed 8 March 2009).

Polaris Institute. (2008) 'Pulling heart strings for profit: how the bottled water industry is fighting the backlash', 13 March. Online. Available HTTP: www.polarisinstitute.org/pulling_heart_strings_for_profit_how_the_bottled_water_industry_is_fighting_the_backlash (accessed 8 March 2009).

—— (2009a) 'The Story of EAU', 23 March. Online. Available HTTP: www.insidethebottle.org/story-eau (accessed 13 May 2009).

—— (2009b) '2008 bottled water profits down, bottled water bans up', 19 February. Online. Available HTTP: www.insidethebottle.org/2008-bottled-water-profits-down-bottled-water-bans (accessed 13 May 2009).

Pringle, H. and Thompson, M. (1999) *Brand Spirit: How Cause Related Marketing Builds Brands*, Chichester and New York: Wiley.

Rabinow, P. and Rose, N. (2006) 'Biopower today', *BioSocieties*, 1: 195–217.

Rose, N. (1989) *Governing the Soul: The Shaping of the Private Self*, London and New York: Routledge.

—— (2006) *The Politics of Life Itself: Biomedicine, Power, and Subjectivity in the Twenty-First Century*, Princeton, NJ: Princeton University Press.

Ross, A. (2009) 'Bottler of a fund-raiser', *The Age*, 4 August. Online. Available HTTP: www.theage.com.au/news/entertainment/epicure/bottler-of-a-1fundraiser/ 2009/08/03/ 1249152550769.html (accessed 7 September 2009).

Sadler, D. and Lloyd, S. (2009) 'Neo-liberalizing corporate social responsibility: a political economy of corporate citizenship', *Geoforum* 40 (4): 613–22.

Shiva, V. (2002) *Water Wars: Privatization, Pollution and Profit*, Cambridge, MA: South End Press.

Staight, K. (2008) 'Hope springs eternal', *Australian Broadcasting Corporation*, 21 September. Online. Available HTTP: www.abc.net.au/landline/content/2008/ s2369117.htm (accessed 24 April 2009).

Sussman, B. (2009) 'University of Pennsylvania: bottled water you can feel good about', *Inc. Magazine*, 1 March. Online. Available HTTP: www.inc.com/magazine/20090301/ university-of-pennsylvania-bottled-water.html (accessed 20 July 2009).

Thankyou Water. (2009) Online. Available HTTP: www.thankyouwater.org (accessed 3 August 2009).

Wanctin, L. (2006) *Have You Bottled It? How Drinking Tap Water Can Help Save You and the Planet*, London: Sustain.

9 Ethical consumption, sustainable production and wine

Paul Starr

Save Miguel

The global cork industry, especially the flow of cork into wine bottle closures, is dominated by Portuguese producers. Companies such as Amorim have seen their market share of the wine closures market erode in recent decades due to the success of alternate 'technical' closures, such as screwcaps. The key problem that drove the switch to technical closures is the failure rate for corks, which can contaminate wine with trichloanisole (TCA, cork taint), allow ingress of oxygen enough to oxidize and spoil wines, change the flavour of wines (particularly white wines) and sometimes be a vector for mould taints. There is little scientific consensus on failure rates for cork-sealed wines, but it is likely that somewhere between 2 per cent and 10 per cent of all cork-sealed wines will be negatively impacted by their closure and not present to the consumer the quality intended by the producer. Cost savings to producers have also driven uptake of alternatives, but the key factor has been product quality from the producer side, translating into cost reductions (including to retailers) and consumer protection from faulty products.

The cork industry has taken many different approaches to downplaying or correcting product quality issues, or attacking the alternate closures. One recent approach has involved a viral marketing campaign. Social networking and other sites were seeded with mystery teasers about the need to 'Save Miguel'. A YouTube video, starring American comic Rob Schneider, continued the mystery as Rob travelled to Portugal on a quest to find out who Miguel was and why he needed saving. The video eventually reveals that Miguel, who works hard and provides many good things for many good people, as well as protecting the environment, is actually a Portuguese cork oak tree. Ending with a cringe-worthy parody of the lack of snob value in opening a screwcapped bottle for a special occasion, the campaign did generate press attention about the cork industry, albeit much of it negative.

What was particularly interesting about Save Miguel, and a prior collaboration between the cork industry and the World Wildlife Fund on cork forest conservation (asking consumers to stop buying screwcaps to save the environment), was that the underlying problems with cork closures (product spoilage, lack of consumer protection) were elided. Instead, a sustainable production and consumption argument (including the social values of the cork landscapes) was advanced *against* the ethical production and consumption framing used by cork critics. That said, the campaign also makes an ethical plea to the audience – 'Save Miguel' or let him die, clearly an invitation to make the ethical, life-affirming choice of avoiding screwcapped wines.

While this campaign is an example of an argumentative sidestep – a reframing – it helps bring out how wine is a product to think about as a way of under-standing contemporary debates on ethical consumption, including how this may or may not be the same as sustainable consumption. This chapter uses a focus on Australian wine, including its standing in key international markets, as a way to tease out some of the relationships between ethics and sustainability in discourses of consumption and production.[1]

To begin with, wine is a field of considerable ethical and sustainability concern. Wine is an internationally traded commodity product that is the subject of intersecting debates about sustainable consumption and production issues such as food miles, carbon footprints, materials choice, production practices, water security and the implications of climate change. There is also a significant *social* sustainability debate within and about wine, specifically about social respon-sibility, especially as regards the private and public consequences of alcohol consumption.

Wine in the United Kingdom

In the United Kingdom, Australian wine has been a success story until very recent times. Wine, and alcohol more broadly, however is currently the subject of intense debate in the UK. The debate is dominated by social factors – anti-social behaviour, violence and public health issues. Environmental sustainability issues are significant too, but less so than the social impacts of alcohol pricing, avail-ability and consumption. The main environmental issues in play in debates about wine supply chains (and much of the UK debate is targeted at retailers, rather than producers) are about food miles and product carbon footprints, including a focus on wine packaging (DEFRA 2009).

Major UK retail chains have been leaders globally in developing compacts and tools to address sustainability issues throughout their supply chains.[2] In the case of wine, there are increasing requirements for producers wishing to access UK retail shelf space that they be able to quantify (not just describe) the carbon footprints for their products and operations. This includes many aspects of the product life cycle, from the vineyard, through wine making, packaging, transport and international shipping.

UK retailers have been less able to lead on the social side of wine consumption debates. Partly because they are retailers, and targeted by public health advocates and activist campaigns for alcohol retail practices in general, UK retailers have been unable to differentiate in their responses between the different types of alcohol they sell. For example, retailers have generally had to contest the broad anti-alcohol backlash in the UK in total, rather than being able to give ground on some products (such as high-strength beer, volume spirits and ready-to-drinks) while holding the line for products with different consumption and risk profiles, such as wine or light beer.

Wine in Australia

Australian public debate about the ethics and sustainability aspects of wine looks like a completely different set of conversations to those happening in the UK. The Australian debates are about sustainable production, occasionally sustainable consumption and production, but only rarely are they framed in ethical consumption terms, or as social issues.

This applies more generally to debates about food and wine in Australia, where predominantly social perspectives, such as those evidenced in Rebecca Huntley's *Eating between the Lines: Food and Equality in Australia*, are rare (Huntley 2008). For Huntley, her starting point is in social analysis, and is that food is an issue of class difference – a failure of social equality. Starting from here, she tries to make sense of phenomena such as the rise of farmer's markets, or time use preferences of families (spend time cooking or use that time for something else), as issues of social inequality. While at times class analysis and equity issues are germane to these trends, they are usually not major causal factors in the Australian context – something Huntley is unable to reconcile in her analysis. In the end, her book reads quite strangely, seeming to miss the point by focusing on issues such as social equity and class, rather the economic, industrial, cultural and environmental aspects of these debates.

Environmental aspects dominate social issues in Australian wine debates.[3] The major environmental issue for Australian wine at present is water, either in its own right, or in combination with climate change. The core (in volume terms) of Australian wine production takes place in the Murray Darling Basin regions such as the Riverina and the Riverland, and these are the areas hardest hit by restrictions in available water allocations and a hotter, drier climate. Food miles and carbon footprints of Australian wine are primarily raised in public debate by producers, such as Yalumba, which are leading on these issues (and to a degree are required to do so in order to maintain and grow positions in international markets such as the UK where these are significant concerns).[4]

Whereas UK retailers are the target of campaigns, advocacy and activism on ethical consumption and alcohol issues, Australian retailers experience less of this pressure than do producers and producer bodies. Primarily this is because Australia is a significant producer of alcoholic products, rather than being predominantly a retail supply chain. For example, recent debates in Australia about teenage drinking and the tax treatment of alco-pops (ready mixed, or ready-to-drink products, usually containing a mix of carbonated, sweet beverage and distilled alcohol) did not focus on the ethical consumption issues, or the choices made by retailers, but instead focused on the behaviour of distiller-packer producers who used differences in the tax regimes to aggressively grow their market share and sales via lower prices.

The history of Australian wine innovation also helps explain part of the current problems being encountered by the industry. Australia has been a world-leader in technical research, in the development of wine science and wine technology, in professional, science-based wine education, and in applying a range of extension and knowledge transfer approaches in order to spread new practices throughout the industry. But this success has created a bind. Much of it is replicable by competitors, especially when key science is published in the scientific literature (such as on fault-identification, post-bottling chemistry and closure choice, or the importance of pH to wine stability over time). Indeed, many Australian competitive advantages were actively shared around the world via Australian 'flying winemakers' consulting in many wine-producing countries and regions from the 1970s on. There are competing producers, such as in South America, who are able to replicate those innovations, while having lower labour and other input costs.

But there is another consequence of having a history of innovation as part of 'Brand Australia' in the current context of climate change. In key export markets such as the UK and the US, tastes and preferences have shifted away from wines perceived to be over-ripe and too alcoholic, exactly the kinds of wines that can result from very hot, or compressed vintages, or decisions to leave fruit on the vine chasing richer flavours. This consumer shift from high-alcohol, blockbuster wines risks stranding Australian wine regions and producers, especially under conditions of climate change where hotter, shorter vintages, with less available water, become more normal. It is difficult for Australian wine, built on ceaseless inquiry and technical innovation, to mount a successful defence of high-alcohol wines as something that is just the product of the seasons. The history of intellectual and technical innovation in Australian wine produces a reasonable expectation in the minds of opinion-makers and informed consumers that the industry should be able to innovate its way out of high-alcohol wines, even where these higher alcohol levels are part-product of a warming world.

Supply chains, value chains

Professor Andrew Fearne was recently 'Thinker in Residence' in Adelaide, a programme sponsored by the South Australian Government. During this residency, Professor Fearne looked at issues and opportunities confronting the food and wine industries. His approach is less standard industry supply chain analysis and more what he refers to as 'value chains' (Fearne 2009). The definition used for this is:

> Sustainable value chains are those in which collaborative relationships facilitate the effective flow of information, to enable rational decision-making and effective resource allocation, for the benefit of the value chain as a whole. Value chains can only be sustainable if chain members are in tune with and responsive to the needs of their customers, the wants of final

consumers and the complex interaction between what they do, how they do it and the natural environment within which they operate.

(Fearne 2009: 5)

As this indicates, Fearne's definition of sustainable value chains is a shift away from past models of linear, supply chain thinking. Multiple points in value chains send and receive market signals, and sustainability includes attunement and responsiveness to multiple signals, including from final consumers. While the environment is important as a point of distinction between supply chain and value chain thinking, the most significant difference is described by Fearne as a 'paradigm shift in thinking (from supply "push" to demand "pull"), and a collaborative re-allocation of resources and responsibilities amongst all stakeholders in the value chain' (Fearne 2009: 5).

Fearne makes five recommendations for realizing sustainable value chains for food and wine production in South Australia. The first is to develop 'thought leadership' through awareness-raising and education about the principles and practices of sustainable value chains. The second is to set up an open-access service for collecting and disseminating integrated market intelligence and consumer insight. Third is to draft a holistic food policy; fourth is to review and reform education and training; and fifth is to set up regional co-innovation clusters (co-innovation being a coinage to refer to collaborative approaches to innovation).

Value chain thinking can offer a pathway to more inclusive, less linear analysis, of how supply chains, consumer and producer behaviours, and cultures of consumption work. However, as both the definitions Fearne uses and the recommendation on market intelligence and consumer insight indicate, consumer sovereignty is a foundational assumption of value chain thinking. The challenge for producers is to understand and respond to consumer values, beliefs, preferences, desires and behaviours. The extent to which 'upstream' points in supply chains can define, describe and delimit the consumer is elided.

There is a consequence of this for understanding how things have gotten to the current point. The Australian wine industry has successfully assisted in producing certain cultures of wine preference and consumption in key markets. Producers, importers and key critics in markets such as the US, or alliances between producers and supermarket buyers in the UK, have built taste segments and markets for blockbuster South Australian red wines (US) and reliable-value 'sunshine in a bottle' ripe wines (UK) at key, low price-points (Catchpole 2009). While the value chain recommendations made for food and wine in South Australia in Fearne's work make sense, they do not recognize that part of the challenge for the industry is its past successes with creating consumer preference and consumer demand.

Another international wine commentator brought to Adelaide to research and write about great vineyard sites and the future of the industry is Andrew Jefford. Resident in Adelaide through 2009 and into 2010, Jefford (the author of major books on French vineyards and wine) takes a different approach to diagnosing what's wrong with Australian wine, and prescribing solutions. One of his key points, though perhaps lacking in detailed evidence from market research, is that many international consumers approach the purchase and use of wine as a decision about an agricultural, cultural, even artisanal product, rather than an industrial beverage like beer, milk or fruit juice (Jefford 2009).[5] For Jefford, the self-identification of Australian wine as the Australian wine *industry* runs counter to the kind of consumption-positioning you would need to make available if your product was to be seen as cultural, from agriculture, and perhaps artisanal.

There is much more to Jefford's analysis than this, and his work is still in progress, but the point about wine as an industrial or agricultural (horticultural, viticultural) product is a useful supplement to the critique of value chain thinking as making the consumer sovereign at the expense of recognizing the consumption fashioning that producers, their trade representatives, and governments have achieved. The sovereign consumer, originator of choice in the market, often appears in current ethical consumption (and some sustainable consumption) discourses in a form little different from nineteenth-century political economy.[6] This can have real consequences for how supply, or value, chains, can work and be understood.

Discourses of ethical consumption often focus on individual choices, on occasions of choice, conceived of as problems. The problem is making the ethical (right) choice between two or more consumption options – as a discrete choice, not an instance within a pattern of consumptive choices, habits and behaviours. This is discretion and discernment, one choice at a time. The dynamic almost inevitably becomes one of good behaviour/bad behaviour, right choice/wrong choice, ethical/unethical. It is a choice problem, rather than being about aggregated impact, total cost, potential benefit and the complete footprint of bundled consumption choices.

While the discourses of ethical consumption may help to link discrete consumption choices to broader political issues and processes (such as vegetarian discourses of meat consumption linking to critiques of agribusiness), they can elide some of the diversity, even cross-purposes, of how notions of ethical consumption are used by consumers. Though sustainable consumption has a link to the rough consensus of the sustainable development literature that sustainability is about preserving the environmental, social, cultural and economic opportunities of future generations (fairness over time), ethical consumption can encompass complete bans on alcohol, gambling, cigarettes, drugs in general, certain types of revealing clothing, and cultural products containing profanity, or from different religions. Clearly, only some conceptions of 'ethical consumption' fall into this territory, but it is worth noting the diversity of approaches to 'ethical consumption' have less of a consensus as to what is ethical, what is moral, than the literatures and practices of sustainable consumption may have for what is sustainable, or at least 'less unsustainable'.[7]

What is often in play in discourses of ethical consumption, which we also see in Andrew Fearne's work on value chains, is the desire to recognize and empower a sovereign consumer, or a consumer whose sovereignty is being suppressed by restricted access to opportunities to make choices and hold to ethical routines. The recognition that ethical consumption is best understood as a politics, rather than just the signalling of human demand, is not really a recognition of the complex roles of producers, governments and others in production and consumption choice-making. Instead, it is often seen in ethical consumption discourse as a politics of mobilization and representation. It is the sovereign consumer asserting their political rights as a citizen in a market democracy.

While this helps if the objective is to think about consumption as a politics and as a pathway to 'global justice', it can also be a dead-end. Accepting the defining frame of market democracy and the sovereign consumer-citizen can make it harder to take alternate pathways to understanding the issues and problems such as those facing Australian wine. Some ethical consumption approaches, for example, would not permit the recognition of Andrew Jefford's argument about producer and consumer non-industrial wine behaviours and preferences. They would sit poorly, as what Jefford is suggesting is that some wine decisions are made in a pastoral, rather than market-rational, frame, and that this positioning is available to at least a part of Australian wine. That consumers sometimes choose to relinquish their rational-sovereign, market-democratic role, and make preference decisions on non-market, even irrational, grounds, is not always a matter of a sovereign misled or suborned.

Economics, as a discipline, is still getting to grips with these consumer and producer choices and behaviours that seem to exist separately to how sovereign consumers in rational market democracies should operate. For example, theories of choice and market behaviour have for many years accepted that the reputation of actors and agents in markets can be a key factor in decision-making (often as a short-cut to avoid information costs). However, only some consumer choices that refer to reputation do so with reference to the reputation of a single firm alone. Firm reputation has been extensively studied, within and without economics, but consumers often make decisions on consumption choices based on more collective ideas of reputation.

For example, a UK supermarket consumer at Tesco or Safeway, looking at an instore promotion and discount for an Australian wine brand such as Yalumba's Oxford Landing, will often be thinking about both the reputation of the brand and the reputation of the collective category in which the brand can be located – such as 'Australian wine'. For economics, understanding how 'French cheese', 'Japanese cars', 'Italian shoes', 'Parma ham' or 'Australian wine' play out as categories of collective reputation is quite a new field of research. In particular, the mechanisms for how collective (or group) reputations are built or lost are only just beginning to receive attention (Castriota and Delmastro 2009).

While economists are only just turning their critical attention to the study of how collective reputation works, thinkers about wine cultures, production and consumption have already been engaging in this analysis. Perspectives such as those of Andrew Fearne and Andrew Jefford differ markedly, to the point of disagreement on fundamentals such as whether wine production and consumption should be seen as an 'industry' or not, or if consumer decisions should be approached within or without a market-democratic, sovereign consumer frame. Within the Australian 'industry' itself, including commentators, researchers and other stakeholders, there is also a diversity of approaches to understanding what is wrong and what might be done about it. That said, there is considerable agreement that the problem involves a sense of having built a successful collective reputation, which has dominated market and non-market sentiment, and then ossified while the world changed around it.

There is a diversity of responses as well as approaches to understanding the problem of Australian wine. Government-backed industry strategies attempt to avoid discrimination, arguing that we can repeat many of our past successes by doing similar things (smart production, badging reliable quality and value, export market penetration) a bit better, a bit more, or for different markets (especially China), while perhaps trying a few new things as well (such as telling the stories of high-quality Australian wine, or marketing along the lines of regional diversity). Other approaches have more focus.

The First Families of Australian Wine is one new example of a response to the problems facing Australian wine that is explicitly about differentiation and building an alternate collective reputation. Building on international examples of family-owned, medium-sized, wine companies marketing collaboratively, twelve family wine businesses have funded a joint initiative to differentiate and highlight their heritage, environmental commitments, diversity and product quality. The initiative, explained via a website and extensive promotional events in key markets, attempts to tell a producer story of difference, quality and history, although it is not specifically engaging with key end-market concerns, such as the social consequences of alcohol consumption in the UK.[8]

The most extensive critique to date of the First Families of Australian Wine concept has been written by industry analyst Tony Keys. Keys notes that the First Families concept had been launched ahead of working out the strategy for exactly what it is they will do and how they will do it (Keys 2009). While it is accurate to note that the First Families grouping did not start with a business plan, detailed market research and a complete strategic agenda for market and consumer change, the concept does address many of the key criticisms levelled at Australian wine – sameness rather than diversity, value rather than quality, an entry point product rather than a destination product, wine of method rather than wine of place, industrial rather than agricultural, a technocracy rather than a heritage and history. Initiatives such as this and the recent Landmark Australia tasting tutorials that brought key wine professionals and opinion leaders from major export markets to learn about the history, diversity and quality of Australian wine also show a recognition of how important are the points of information provision and opinion formation before the end consumer in these supply chains is reached.

Conclusion

Australian wine is a good subject for thinking about the ethics and sustainability of production and consumption. Debates such as those about wine closures illustrate how sustainability arguments (cork forests, cork communities, heritage of cork landscapes) can be mobilized as a counter to ethical consumption arguments (product quality, consumer protection) and vice versa.

The key point is that there are consequences from taking a focus on either ethical consumption or sustainable consumption. Sustainable consumption is not always the best discourse or lens to use, but can help sometimes to avoid the good/bad binaries associated with ethical consumption. Ethical consumption approaches (and discourses) can often drive the users/participants into positions of flagging consumption and production choices as either ethical (good) or unethical (bad). At least some of the time, sustainable consumption approaches start with an acknowledgement of footprint, of environmental impact, couching decision-making in a context of size of footprint, kind and extent of impact, consequences of choices, and these consequences as part of a pattern of choices and impacts, with total patterns (themselves not static) recognized as the main game. The sum total of a string of individual, ethical, consumptive choices can still be unsustainable.

Rather than give up on the notion and use of ethical consumption completely, we can opt for care and nuance. Work such as Rebecca Huntley's book on food, class and social exclusion shows the consequences of a too-blinkered adherence to consumption ethics as the focus. The same import of care goes for sustainable consumption (and sustainable production) as a focal lens – borne out by the experience of the Australian wine 'industry' attempting to inject sustainable production stories into international debates about ethical consumption and wondering why things were not working out. For Australian wine, responses such as the First Families initiative cannot afford just to tell stories of sustainable production. The slide in reputation of Australian wine is caught up in ethical debates, as well as questions of sustainability, and correcting that slide will require an address to questions in the ethical frame, including the social responsibility of high-alcohol wines. Doing both ethics and sustainability is what is required. Doing just one runs the risk of missing the consumer conversation, or, as with the cork industry's Save Miguel campaign, attempting to greenwash legitimate consumer protection concerns.

Notes

1   Wine, and alcohol in general, is an interesting product category for thinking about ethics, sustainability, market democracy and consumer sovereignty for an additional reason that is not the focus of this article. It is one of a few legal products whose consumption can impair the capacity of a consumer to make informed, sovereign choices about further consumption.
2   For examples of leading initiatives in product supply chain sustainability, see the publications of the Waste Reduction and Packaging (WRAP) Programme, www.wrap.org.uk/.

3 As the country is a large wine producer and exporter, public debates in Australia about wine are often led by economic and financial matters (including industry consolidation, prices and oversupply), then environmental considerations, then cultural issues, and only then would social or ethical issues appear.
4 It is perhaps indicative of the focus on water and the lack of deep industry debate on food miles and carbon footprints that these latter concepts are not being mobilized by producers to contest the inroads being made into Australian domestic consumption by imported wines, including New Zealand sauvignon blanc.
5 For many pieces of writing produced during his stay in Australia, see Andrew Jefford's blog site at www.andrewjefford.com/blog including his addresses to the AGM of the Australian Wine and Brandy Corporation and at the National Wine Centre.
6 For an introduction to the history of market, or economic, democracy, see Thomas Frank, *One Market Under God: Extreme Capitalism, Market Populism and the End of Economic Democracy*, London: Vintage, 2002.
7 I am not arguing here for any kind of conceptual superiority of 'sustainable consumption' over 'ethical consumption' – the point is to flag the diversity, even incompatibility, of different understandings of what 'ethical' may mean in the consumption of goods and services. It is also important to stress how 'ethical consumption' writing and acting often locate themselves at the scale of discrete choices (individual or group) about consumption, whereas the notion of a consumption footprint is often fundamental to sustainable consumption (starting at the aggregation of impact and opportunity, rather than the point of discrete choices).
8 For more details about the First Families of Australian Wine initiative, see http:// www.australiasfirstfamiliesofwine.com/au/.

Bibliography

Barnett, C., *et al.* (2007) *The Subjects and Spaces of Ethical Consumption: Doing Politics in an Ethical Register*. Available HTTP: www.consume.bbk.ac.uk (accessed 26 November 2009).

Castriota, S. and Delmastro, M. (2009) 'The economics of collective reputation: minimum quality standards, vertical differentiation and optimal group size', *AAWE Working Paper No. 50 Economics*, American Association of Wine Economists, November. Available HTTP: www.wine-economics.org (accessed 26 November 2009).

Catchpole, A. (ed.) (2009) 'Australia', *Harpers Wine & Spirit*, October.

Department for Environment, Food and Rural Affairs (2009) *Making the Most of Packaging: A Strategy for a Low Carbon Economy*, London: DEFRA.

Fearne, A. (2009) *Sustainable Food and Wine Value Chains*, State of South Australia: Adelaide.

Frank, T. (2002) *One Market Under God: Extreme Capitalism, Market Populism and the End of Economic Democracy*, London: Vintage.

Huntley, R. (2008) *Eating Between the Lines: Food and Equality in Australia*, Melbourne: Black Inc.

Jefford, A. (2009) *Andrew Jefford Blog*. Available HTTP: www.andrewjefford.com/blog (accessed 18 December 2009).

Keys, T. (2009) 'Future for Australia's First Families of Wine not Clear as Yet', *Australian and New Zealand Wine Industry Journal*, 24(5): 65–71.

10 Eco-ethical electronic consumption in the smart-design economy

Richard Maxwell and Toby Miller

The ecological crisis reveals the urgent moral need for a new solidarity, especially in relations between the developing nations and those that are highly industrialized
Pope John Paul II (1990)

I think the economic logic behind dumping a load of toxic waste in the lowest wage country is impeccable and we should face up to that – Larry Summers
(cited in *The Economist* 1992)

This chapter addresses ethical consumption and electronics.[1] We explain the value of international political economy (IPE) to understand the topic. Then we examine the use of technology to make consumption environmentally friendly, through computer-based consumer applications and a redesigned electricity grid. Finally, we address information and communication technologies (ICTs) and electronic waste (e-waste).

Let's begin with some numbers to illustrate the centrality of electricity and electronics to consumer ethics. About 2.5 per cent of the world's greenhouse-gas emissions result from the electricity consumed by personal computers, data monitors, printers, fixed and mobile telecommunications, televisions, local-area networks and server farms (data centres with servers, storage machines, network gadgetry, power supplies, and cooling technology). That's about the same as aviation, if the energy required for ICT manufacture is included. Server farms alone use 1.5 per cent of the US electricity supply, at a cost of US$4.5 billion. The energy required to run them keeps going up. British data disclose that in the 1980s, 400–800 watts per square metre was typical; during the heyday of the dotcoms, it was 750–1000 watts per square metre; and 1000–1200 watts per square metre between 2004 and 2006. Today, 1500–2000 watts per square metre is the norm, and the number of power stations being built around the world is also increasing – by 150 per cent a year (Corbett and Turco 2006; Gartner 2007; Wald 2007; Parsley 2008; ITU 2009: 4).

According to the International Energy Agency (IEA), ICTs accounted for about 15 per cent of global residential electricity consumption in 2009. Over 5.5

billion devices need external power supplies, including two billion TV sets and a billion personal computers, in addition to cell-phone services, which are utilized by half the world's population (up from 145 million in 1996 to around four billion in 2009, with International Mobile Telecommunications-2000 [AKA 3G] cell phones necessitating higher frequencies and greater power use than their predecessors). About 40 per cent of US homes have video-gaming consoles, which collectively consume electricity at the same annual rate as San Diego, the ninth-largest city in the country (ITU 2009: 5; Mouawad and Galbraith 2009: 1). Residential energy use by electronic equipment in the Global South is growing at twice the rate of consumption in the Global North. If these trends continue without governments and manufacturers taking action to improve energy efficiency, the IEA estimates that electricity consumption by electronic equipment will rise to 30 per cent of global demand by 2022, and 45 per cent by 2030 (The Climate Group 2008: 18–23; IEA 2009: 21).

We are told that ICTs are crucial to democracy, economic efficiency, and pleasure. A dual discourse of virtue holds that ICTs will save the two 'ecos' (the economy and ecology) as per Barack Obama's 'Green New Deal' (ITU 2009: 2, 5, and 2008: 67–84; Jones 2008; Houghton 2009). Consumption in the smart-design[2] technological economy is meant to counter pollution and waste. But we need to be aware that such consumption moves in a circuit from geopolitics, on to the grid, and then to devices connected to it, whether they are Google's million server farms or the three hours of TV a day that 2.5 billion people around the world watch (Thussu 2007: 593; Hancock 2009; for Google's account of itself and its consumers, see googleblog.blogspot.com/search/label/green). And that's before we consider e-waste.

Greenpeace estimates that between twenty and fifty million tons of e-waste is generated each year, 75 per cent of which is 'disappeared' via inadequate recycling that exposes the world to dangerous toxins (Rydh 2003; Grossman 2006; Williams 2008; see images under 'China' at edwardburtynsky.com). In addition, there are risks of radiation poisoning by TVs, computer monitors, cell phones, laptops, telecommunication and electrical towers, electronic games, and power lines (Cox 2007; Brigden *et al.* 2008; Lean 2008). Satellites discharge toxic chemicals and nuclear waste, wildlife is poisoned by toxic emissions, communication towers and wires kill up to fifty million birds annually in the US, and media-related nanotechnology emits toxic byproducts that remain poorly understood at the atomic scale (Avatar Environmental 2004; Broad 2007; crnano.org; Schoenfeld 2007).

International political economy

In addition to cultural studies' traditional association of consumption with subcultural resistance – whether via popular culture, anti-war activism, extra-legal recreational drug use, anti-globalization movements, or alternatives to traditional lifestyles – we must forge a new blend of purchase and politics, of fun and foreign policy. This runs counter to a series of myths in neo-classical economics: that consumption is sovereign, labour is irrelevant, technologies – including electronics – are sublime, the economy works because of entrepreneurs and executives, meritocracy is real and omnipresent, and collective action by progressives is wrong (Miller 2004; 2008). The seeming displacement of *meta-récits* such as Marxism within some cultural studies may ironically mirror capitalism's preference for microeconomic research, privileging the firm and the consumer as units of analysis over attempts to understand *cui bono* issues (Shah *et al.* 2007). An IPE approach highlights political processes and economic structures. Recent work has shown that when the analysis of political economy is alienated from green consumption, it becomes difficult to comprehend the scale at which an ecological ethics of consumption must intervene (Conca *et al.* 2001; de Pelsmacker *et al.* 2005; Stolle *et al.* 2005; Carducci 2006; Migone 2007; Connolly and Prothero 2008; Mazar and Zhong forthcoming).

ICT consumption, undertaken in the cause of information and entertainment, is unsustainable because of its perilous environmental impact. So how are the concrete relations of ICTs mystified? And how does this relate to ethical consumption? As our greatest ethnographer of shopping noted, commodities originate 'outside us' (Marx 1987: 43), but are quickly internalized. Wooing consumers by appearing attractive in ways that borrow from romantic love and totemic worship, they rapidly reverse that relationship. We end up learning about romance and community from commodities, which seem to become part of us through the double-sided nature of advertising and 'the good life' of luxury. Transcendence and human solidarity are articulated to objects, and commodities dominate the human and natural landscape. The corollary is the simultaneous triumph and emptiness of signs as sources and measures of value in a way that conceals the work of their creation, and their post-purchase existence. Designated with human characteristics (beauty, taste, serenity, and so on) they compensate for the absence of these qualities in everyday capitalism.

Commodity dreams are created and fuelled by multinational marketers keen to stoke the fires of aesthetic and autotelic desire, as when Apple refers to the iMac as a 'modern art installation' (cited in Schaefer and Durham 2007: 44) or advertises 'Do-It-Yourself Parts for iBook' (apple.com/se/support/ibook/diy) even though the company is notorious for sealing off its products from inspection and transformation. So we see an aestheticization of commodities to make them appealing that also hides their conditions of production and discourages a concern with their ultimate fate once they have been discarded by consumers, despite the fact that the process can actually play upon mythologies that suggest consumers are also creators. This co-creation myth invokes the sovereign consumer who is free as a bird at the same time as it wagers that the co-creation myth will govern consumer conduct in keeping with manufacturers' business interests, and sustain the balance of power between management, labour, and the environment firmly in favour of corporations (Miller 1993; Zwick *et al.* 2008).

Ethical consumption is difficult when components with distinct production histories are bundled together. Electronic devices may be manufactured all over the planet, making it difficult to track their individual and composite production histories – unlike consumer action against such merchandise as sporting apparel. The lack of unionization in globally dispersed electronics manufacturing poses a tremendous challenge to political organization and consumer activism (Monbiot 2003: 56–58; Ferus-Comelo 2008). In addition, iPod batteries are made to last a year, iPhones can be recharged a finite number of times, and most established iPod sleeves and holders do not fit new versions, because built-in obsolescence designed by Apple requires consumers to buy replacement technology. This compulsory repetition is seemingly undertaken each time as a novelty, governed by what Walter Benjamin called, in his awkward but occasionally illuminating prose, 'the ever-always-the-same' of 'mass-production', cloaked in 'a hitherto unheard-of significance' (1985: 48). Only after continual pressure from Greenpeace and other non-governmental watchdog groups (not consumers) did Apple begin to green its business model. Until 2009, Apple had no plans to protect iPod production workers (who work in at least four different countries) from mercury, lead, and flame retardant (Nimpuno *et al.* 2009).

IPE can help us see that the culture industries are *environmental participants* as well as signifying agents of information and pleasure. ICTs are not just things to be read; they are not just coefficients of political and economic power; and they are not just industrial objects. Rather, they are all these things – hybrid monsters, coevally subject to rhetoric, status, and technology: to text, power, and science; all at once, but in contingent ways (Latour 1993). Working with such insights, progressive activists have mixed the pleasures of consumption with an appreciation of its political-economic and cultural implications (think of Greenpeace, culture jammers, or AdBusters).[3] For Marx also said that while a 'commodity appears, at first sight, a very trivial thing, and easily understood . . . it is, in reality, a very queer thing' (1987: 76). And queering that thing can disclose each device's history, and our place in it. While delivering versions of this paper to twenty-something activists and artists from Latin America, Asia, Europe, and the US, we were struck by their scepticism about the worth of ethical consumption versus legislative action. They avowed that, from a political-economic perspective, the biggest problems of eco-ethical consumption do not begin at home, and hence cannot be addressed at one site. The example below makes the point.

At a 2009 meeting in India with government and business leaders, the US Secretary of State, Hillary Rodham Clinton, outlined her country's plan to foment ecologically sound consumption on a global scale. Clinton spoke of 'the challenge' for international environmental policy to recognize 'the different needs and responsibilities of developed and developing countries alike'. Nation-states must not ignore the global ecological crisis: 'The times we live in demand nothing less than a total commitment,' she said. 'The statistics are there for everyone to see.' Clinton went on to identify an ethical dilemma at the base of US policy. On the one hand, 'The United States and other countries that have been the biggest historic emitters of greenhouse gases should shoulder the biggest burden for cleaning up the environment and reducing our carbon footprint'. On the other hand, developing countries should not give up their dreams of emulating

US industrial production and consumption: 'The United States does not and will not do anything that would limit India's economic progress,' but will work collaboratively to 'devise a plan that will dramatically change the way we produce, consume, and conserve energy' in order to 'develop sustainably' and 'eradicate poverty' (Clinton 2009).

Clinton gave her speech at India's ITC Green Centre, one of the largest buildings in the world to receive a top rating from the US Green Building Council for Leadership in Energy and Environmental Design (LEED). Built for the second-largest cigarette maker in India, the ITC Green Centre is known for its green construction – and corporate green-washing (Landler 2009). With that backdrop, Clinton described the sustainable society the US would like to see: one where 'the private sector can play a role, along with government' in an 'innovative and entrepreneurial spirit' to create 'smart design', with green buildings modelling the 'smart design of whole communities' to renovate entire nations (Clinton 2009). This smart-design economy was welcome, provided that its political-economic arrangements suited the US government and 'private sector' and rejected China's example of locking out solar and wind technology from the West to favour national producers (Bradsher 2009).

We have outlined Clinton's policy announcement and its setting in some detail to establish the need for a multi-sited, political-economic approach to consumption – one that considers the entire life-cycle of products and services as they make their way across the globe, such that table-top decisions made by political élites, work arrangements imposed in manufacturing plants, and recycling waste generated by electronics are all germane to decisions made by consumers (Lebel and Lorek 2008). Understanding and enacting ethical consumption requires studying up, down, and sideways, borrowing Laura Nader's renowned formulation calling for an ethnography of the powerful (1972) and George Marcus' endorsement of multi-sited analysis that looks at where products begin, live, and expire (1995).

In the case of ICTs, representations of production and post-consumption (work, chemical and raw-material inputs, and exploitation) are generally displaced by representations of text and consumption (leisure, style, and equality). These two, delineable, phases of truth and lies become indistinct when underlying reality is lost. Signs start to refer to themselves, with no residual need of correspondence to the real (Baudrillard 1988). In embracing simulation, 'human needs, relationships and fears, the deepest recesses of the human psyche, become mere means for the expansion of the commodity universe' (McChesney and Foster 2003: 1).

We are aware of the risk that IPE can concur with Kant's gendered derision of consumption when he called for '*man's emergence from his self-incurred immaturity*', independent of religious, governmental, or commercial direction (1991: 54). But we see great value in Heidegger's account of how public opinion is, literally, manufactured as the production, distribution, and destruction of physical meaning, in a way that provides for the occlusion of its own processes of production, distribution and after-life.

The forester who measures the felled timber in the woods and who to all appearances walks the forest path in the same way his grandfather did is today ordered by the industry that produces commercial woods, whether he knows it or not. He is made subordinate to the orderability of cellulose, which for its part is challenged forth by the need for paper, which is then delivered to newspapers and illustrated magazines. The latter, in their turn, set public opinion to swallowing what is printed, so that a set configuration of opinion becomes available on demand.

(1977: 299)

As the forester's work is subsumed into modern pulp and paper production, labour and environment disarticulate from one other. Paper mills and printing presses are hailed as 'revolutionary': newspapers, magazines, books, and fine paper become signs of progress and intellectual life that seem to bear no relation to his role, or to their own environmental aftershocks. The lesson is that without a moral obligation to worker and forest, we become 'devices of our devices' in a world where commodity signs and preconfigured opinions urge us to 'settle mindlessly into the convenience that devices may offer us' (Introna 2005; Sirowy 2008). Drawing on these IPE insights, we'll now look at two instances of corporate and governmental initiatives that herald ethical consumption, but warrant close critical inspection.

Wal-Mart

In the same week that Clinton visited India, Wal-Mart announced a new environmental strategy. The largest retailer in the world, it tops the *Fortune 500*, with 2008 sales that were a third of India's Gross Domestic Product. The company boasts its own television network, broadcast over three thousand stores in the US. One hundred and forty corporations advertise on its six channels, and the model is being emulated in China, Brazil, and Britain (*The Economist* 2008). As a commentator for Harvard Business Publishing noted, 'once Wal-Mart is involved, everything gets much, much larger' (Winston 2009). That was certainly the view of twenty-first-century demonstrators, who protested vigorously when the company gained entry to Indian markets, leading to more carefully orchestrated arrivals in the nation's retail sector just prior to Clinton's tour. And it has led to productive debates about an exploitative employer that appeals to poor consumers worldwide because of its convenience and pricing[4] (Gentleman 2007; Bellman 2009; Gereffi and Christian 2009).

Wal-Mart's new 'Sustainability Product Index' adds an electronic twist to ethical consumption in the smart-design economy. Its three-stage plan will assess suppliers' green characteristics, build a free and open database on the life-cycle of materials used in the products it sells, and enable consumers to make choices based on the environmental impact of the products they buy. Wal-Mart will not set performance standards that could pressure suppliers and their products to be greener – the existing plan does not rank companies, or list champions chosen for their greenness. The Index will, however, generate information about supplier companies and, eventually, product contents, so that green-conscious consumers can factor in the environmental footprint associated with making a purchase at Wal-Mart, thinking about pollution at the same time as price, availability, and satisfaction. If consumers favour green products, the market will force suppliers to mend their dirty ways. Carrefour (France) and Tesco (Britain), the second- and third-largest retailers in the world, are also pursuing environmental strategies as part of their corporate-responsibility efforts. Neither has proposed providing customers with an index like Wal-Mart's. Instead, they seek to reduce greenhouse emissions in their logistics and stores while supporting sustainable fisheries and low-impact, wood-based materials – a much further-reaching commitment.

The toxicity of components, workplace hazards, and other issues related to labour and environmental justice are absent from Wal-Mart's assessment of sustainability. There are already numerous databases that provide life-cycle assessments (LCAs) of products' chemical and other contents, as well as websites like GoodGuide.com that help consumers identify the green credentials of producers and products. But if Wal-Mart's Index develops as the prognosticators claim, it could expand the possibilities of ethical consumption in three areas. First, it plans to build the database with the participation of non-government organizations, university researchers, and government agencies, along with its usual business partners. Second, unlike most LCA databases, which are often privately held by corporations and vended at vast cost, Wal-Mart plans to open its database to free public access. Finally, because of the firm's domination of the retail market, a Sustainability Product Index could expose the internal operations and environmental impact of most consumer-goods manufacturers. And if it creates an alliance with other big-box retailers, as some reports claim, the Index could have wider application (Makower 2009; Winston 2009; Wal-Mart 2009a).[5]

That said, Wal-Mart is a watchword for the exploitation of human and other resources (ironically, the company once hosted Clinton on its board) (Featherstone 2004; Quinn 2005). Also, Wal-Mart's Index recapitulates the myths of green consumption and market efficiency in balancing green supply and demand. Consistent with Clinton's vision of the smart-design economy, Wal-Mart represents a 'private sector' that empowers consumers to make green choices, sustaining economic growth and/as environmental sustainability. Wal-Mart depicts itself as a leader in green business strategies, as if governmental policy had played no role in changing the rules by which such mega-retailers must operate. It is hard to find mention in Wal-Mart's own documentation of the political process that shaped its makeover; but if we dig enough (Wal-Mart 2009b), we find explicit references to the European Union's Restrictions on the Use of Certain Hazardous Substances in Electrical and Electronic Equipment (RoHS), adopted in 2003 – three years before Wal-Mart set out to green itself. The RoHS Directive limits the use in consumer goods of carcinogenic metals and compounds (lead, mercury, cadmium, and hexavalent chromium), and fire retardants that endanger humans and wildlife (polybrominated byphenyls and polybrominated diphenyl ethers). So once we get beyond the rhetoric of Wal-Mart's Sustainability Index, the catalyst for change turns out to be political intervention and green governance in the world's biggest economy. The retailer's commitment to eco-ethical consumption in fact indicates that big-box retailers are 'private-sector' participants in public policy. Similar ties between corporations and the state apply to the electricity that powers green electronic initiatives, and other techniques of ethical consumption.

The grid

There is a link between attempts to fight the economic crisis and the fight against global warming, through publicly funded programmes that shift investment to renewable sources of energy generation (solar, wind, biomass, etc.) and reduce energy consumption by retrofitting buildings (Pollin *et al.* 2009). The smart-design economy sees ethical consumption moving to the forefront of electronic consumption, greening inputs and production processes, and disposing of electronic gadgets responsibly. But the largest-scale activity has been in reducing the electricity consumption that powers consumer and business electronic systems (TV, radio, the internet, music, telephony computing, and other appliances). ICT firms are at the centre of the smart-design economy, offering services that claim to reduce energy consumption. New technologies are creating a 'smart grid' that meters, analyses, regulates, and charges for electricity usage in homes and office buildings via Internet Protocols (IPs) that can alert grid operators instantaneously to fluctuations in demand from networks and appliances.

Utility customers who use smart-grid metering to reduce consumption turn off air conditioning during peak times, or power some appliances down while others run at lower rates, and their electronics are automatically plugged and unplugged from the grid as needed. This marginally reduces their living standards due to a greener relation to the environment. But such new means of ethical consumption are circumscribed by the corporate-welfare orientation of the smart-design economy, because the largest private firms use public funding to broaden their expertise and deepen their hold on emerging computerized energy-management systems. These shifts are about technological fixes for technologically caused problems. They are not radical changes in lifestyle by either companies or people.

For despite its professed love of *laissez-faire*, the corporate world is not above receiving *largesse* from governments. The US Department of Energy (DOE) has funded private utilities and other businesses like IBM, Cisco, and General Electric (GE) to implement and study pilot programmes for smart-grid projects (US Department of Energy n.d.). IBM positions itself 'as a strategic advisor to Washington's top policymakers and bureaucrats' on the need for a national 'smart infrastructure' (McDougall 2009). GE and Google, *inter alia*, are lobbying Congress for investment in the smart grid (Glader 2009). Cisco and IBM are building a smart grid for Amsterdam to reduce greenhouse gas emissions (GreenBiz.com 2009c). By late 2009, GE's supposedly 'green' business was contending for some of the US$400 billion in 'economic stimulus' allocated to alternative energy projects by numerous governments around the world. For example, it hoped to grab subsidies for a new industrial battery factory in New

York State. The backdrop is that GE holds the record for polychlorinated biphenyls dumped into US waterways (Maxwell and Miller 2008; GreenBiz.com 2009b). Cisco and GE are building a smart grid in parts of Miami (GreenBiz.com 2009a). Google has marketed software for the computerized smart grid, while GE offers a metering system for it, along with hardware and services to create and run a green home. Its 'ecoimagination' brand earned US$17 billion in 2008 (Glader 2009). Part of that revenue came from the hundreds of millions of dollars GE received from municipalities, the DOE, and the US Department of Defense to develop smart-grid systems (Guevarra 2009).

An effective smart grid promises to lower electricity usage and reduce emissions, but what eventualities await commercial energy producers whose business will suffer from lowering demand? The answer offers another example of what happens when 'private-sector' interests dominate the smart-design economy. Metering the grid between customers and central systems through IPs allows system managers to track fluctuations of supply and demand moment to moment. This is important for balancing the load and saving energy. But commercial-energy producers in the US see another value in this technology. They plan to use research data from smart-grid pilot programmes on fluctuations in consumption as evidence to convince regulators to approve real-time price fluctuations. Lower demand will mean lower rates, and peak prices will follow peak usage (Simon 2009). It looks as though energy producers are willing to accept the social gains of smart design only if it makes money.

Smart-grid technology promises to reduce both cost and global warming. But flexibility in pricing poses problems for consumers who might otherwise feel comfortable with smart design. Commercial utilities want to use regulation to make back this money from customers, via a bogus 'green' rationale for fluctuating rates: that they encourage conservation and keep inessential energy use down during peak demand (Simon 2009).

US commercial utilities aren't alone in resisting change or seeking regulation to help them. In France, the main energy producer (majority-owned by the state) has faced declining profits as a result of eco-ethical consumption combined with smart-grid metering. Regulators have approved a system to compensate the utility for its losses by taxing smart-grid company revenues. Consumer advocates see this as an unjustified reward for energy producers that will ultimately be paid by consumers in higher rates for smart-metering services (Jolly 2009).

In both the US and French cases, declining profits for energy producers in a smart-design economy seem assured. But as envisioned by the US and its satellites Britain and Australia, the 'private sector' still holds the ultimate place of respect in a smart-design economy: the market-oriented model has a deep foothold in the political economy that shapes emerging energy-management systems. Despite its avowed commitment to *laissez-faire*, there has been no resistance from the so-called private sector to public subsidies, beneficial regulation, publicly funded research and development, or pilot projects for smart-grid technology. Such corporate welfare *should* bring a recognition by beneficiaries of their indebtedness to a mixed-economy model, and the legitimacy of democratic control of their activities. Yet corporate-welfare recipients will not tolerate taxpayers claiming the status of stakeholders in their business. To recognize taxpayers as investors would mean they were owed a return on investment. The 'private sector' pretends instead that it imagined, paid for, and created the technology, the applications, and the markets.

In the foreseeable future, rewards for eco-ethical action through taxpayer investment and ecologically sound living will be externalized as the price of services charged by energy companies to green consumers, with social gains, public investment, and internal cost savings welcomed by the energy business – on condition that profit continues to grow as per the pre-green era.

Conclusion

While we were drafting this chapter, Greenpeace took a major protest action against Hewlett-Packard (HP), a leading manufacturer of printing technology, because the company had postponed from 2009 to 2011 its commitment to phase out brominated flame retardants and polyvinyl-chloride plastics, which can release dioxin when burned and may cause cancer. Activists 'decorated' the multinational's global headquarters in Palo Alto (see Figures 10.1 and 10.2).

Climbing atop the corporation's home, they painted an 11,500 square-foot message on the roof (with safe, children's paint). In addition to the *graffiti*, automated phone calls from William Shatner to employees protested against HP's failure to abide by its undertakings. His phone message spoke directly to workers from a consumer's perspective that was also an activist's one. He even perorated politely: 'wishing you an enjoyable day' (Frey 2009).

Greenpeace's direct, spectacular action definitely makes the commodity queer, as per Dr Marx, and draws on many forms of direct action to do so. At one level, it deploys the power of celebrity culture, with a *Star Trek* hero as its pitchman (in a highly ironized way, because Shatner parodies his own *persona* as a lapsed Shakespearian, ageing idol, and ponderous spoken-word performer). At another level, the action borrows from political spectacle by trespassing in order to deface the bland but seemingly secure property of a powerful corporation, demonstrating street-level (and higher!) activism. Finally, it utilizes the discourse of consumerism to avow the right of users to materials that are safe for all.

Figures 10.1 and 10.2 Greenpeace's rooftop sign at Hewlett-Packard's headquarters in Palo Alto

This is ethical consumption at play: developing the politics of spectacle, but eluding the search for expressive totality so common in identity politics by drawing on IPE and multi-sited knowledge (Carducci 2006; Muldoon 2006). That involves tracking the life of each commodity sign – establishing its eclectic, electronic legacy via design, manufacture, electricity, use, disposal, and recycling. We think that's a model for analysis and activism alike.

Acknowledgements

Thanks to Tania Lewis and an anonymous reviewer for comments on earlier drafts.

Notes

1   To stay abreast of these issues, readers may care to visit the blog greencitizenship. blogspot.com.
2   'Smart design' appears across hundreds of thousands of web pages. Navigating them will give you fascinating insight into how commerce and art marry – to corporate advantage.
3   See the chapters by Lewis and Potter, Humphrey, and Littler in this volume for a further discussion of anti-consumerist activism and politically organized consumer movements.
4   We might also mention the protests against the company's infiltration of Teotihuacán (Vidal 2004).
5   Big-box retailers are generally understood to be 'large retail stores operated by national or multinational chains. Big-box stores have been criticized for their labour market practices, their contribution to the trade deficit and many other things. On the other hand, they are popular shopping venues and have been a boon to consumers because they offer expansive product lines at low prices' (Haltiwanger *et al.* 2009).

Bibliography

Avatar Environmental (AE) (2004) 'Avian/Communication Tower Collisions', prepared for Federal Communications Commission, submitted 30 September 2004, West Chester, PA.

Baudrillard, J. (1988) *Selected Writings*, in M. Poster (ed.) Stanford, CA: Stanford University Press.

Bellman, E. (2009) 'Wal-Mart exports big-box concept to India', 28 May, *Wall Street Journal*. Online. Available HTTP: http://online.wsj.com/article/SB1243466972772 60377.html (accessed 30 May 2009).

Benjamin, W. (1985) 'Central Park', trans. L. Spencer with M. Harrington, *New German Critique*, 34: 32–58.

Bradsher, K. (2009) 'China builds high wall to guard energy industry', *New York Times*, 14 July: B1.

Brigden, K., Santillo, D. and Johnston, P. (2008) *Playing Dirty: Analysis of Hazardous Chemicals and Materials in Games Console Components*, Amsterdam: Greenpeace.

Broad, W.J. (2007) 'NASA forced to steer clear of junk in cluttered space', *New York Times*, 31 July: F4.

Carducci, V. (2006) 'Culture jamming: a sociological perspective', *Journal of Consumer Culture*, 6(1): 116–38.

Climate Group, The (2008) *Smart2020: Enabling the Low Carbon Economy in the Information Age*, Global Sustainability Initiative.

Clinton, H.R. (2009) 'Remarks following ITC Green Building Tour and discussion', 19 July, Mumbai and New Delhi. Online. Available HTTP: www.state.gov/secretary/rm/2009a/july/126206.htm (accessed 25 July 2009).

Conca, K., Princen, T. and Maniates, M.F. (2001) 'Confronting consumption', *Global Environmental Politics*, 1(3): 1–10.

Connolly, J. and Prothero, A. (2008) 'Green consumption: life-politics, risk and consumption', *Journal of Consumer Culture*, 8(1): 117–45.

Corbett, C.J. and Turco, R.P. (2006) *Sustainability in the Motion Picture Industry*, November, Integrated Waste Management Board of the State of California. Online. Available HTTP: http://personal.anderson.ucla.edu/charles.corbett/papers/mpisreport.pdf (accessed 2 December 2006).

Cox, S. (2007) 'Are your cell phone and laptop bad for your health?', 31 July, *AlterNet*. Online. Available HTTP: www.alternet.org/healthwellness/58354/?page = 1 (accessed 12 August 2007).

de Pelsmacker, P., Driesen, L. and Rayp, G. (2005) 'Do consumers care about ethics? Willingness to pay for Fair-Trade coffee', *Journal of Consumer Affairs*, 39(2): 363–85.

The Economist (1992) 'Let them eat pollution', 8 February, *The Economist*: 66.

—— (2008) 'How not to annoy your customers', 5 January, *The Economist*: 54.

Featherstone, L. (2004) *Selling Women Short: The Landmark Battle for Workers' Rights at Wal-Mart*, New York: Basic Books.

Ferus-Comelo, A. (2008) 'Mission impossible? Raising labor standards in the ICT sector', *Labor Studies Journal*, 33(2): 141–62.

Frey, M. (2009) 'Finger painting for a good cause', 28 July, *Greenpeace.org*. Online. Available HTTP: http://members.greenpeace.org/blog/greenpeaceusa_blog/2009/07/28/finger_painting_for_a_good_cause (accessed 20 August 2009).

Gartner (2007) 'Gartner estimates ICT industry accounts for 2 percent of global CO_2 emissions', 26 April. Online. Available HTTP: http://gartner.com/it/page.jsp?id = 503867&format (accessed 4 May 2007).

Gentleman, A. (2007) 'Indians protest Wal-Mart's wholesale entry', *New York Times*, 9 August. Online. Available HTTP: www.nytimes.com/2007/08/09/business/world business/09iht-walmart.4.7061818.html (accessed 11 August 2007).

Gereffi, G. and Christian, M. (2009) 'The impacts of Wal-Mart: the rise and consequence of the world's dominant retailer', *Annual Review of Sociology*, 35: 573–91.

Glader, P. (2009) 'GE says "green" business revenue grew 21%', *Wall St Journal*, 27 May. Online. Available HTTP: http://online.wsj.com/article/SB124339691665357611.html#articleTabs%3Darticle (accessed 28 May 2009).

GreenBiz.com (2009a) 'GE, Cisco and others team with Miami for $200M smart grid project', 20 April. Online. Available HTTP: www.greenbiz.com/news/2009/04/20/ge-cisco-miami-smart-grid (accessed 22 April 2009).

—— (2009b) 'General Electric to power up new battery plant in upstate New York', 12 May. Online. HTTP: www.greenbiz.com/news/2009/05/12/ge-battery-plant (accessed 17 May 2009).

—— (2009c) 'IBM and Cisco to help Amsterdam become a "smart city",' 14 July. Online. Available HTTP: http://greenbiz.com/news/2009/07/14/ibm-cisco-amsterdam-smart-city#/nl/home (accessed 29 July 2009).

Grossman, E. (2006) *High Tech Trash: Digital Devices, Hidden Toxics, and Human Health*, Washington: Island Press.

Guevarra, L. (2009) 'DOD enlists GE for $2M project to make military base a smart microgrid model', 8 July, *GreenBiz.com*. Online. Available HTTP: www.greenbiz.com/news/2009/07/09/dod-enlists-ge-for-microgrid-model (accessed 19 July 2009).

Haltiwanger, J., Jarmin, R. and Krizan, C.J. (2009) *Mom-and-Pop Meet Big-Box: Complements or Substitutes?*, United States Census Bureau, Center for Economic Statistics, CES 09–34.

Hancock, S. (2009) 'Iceland new home of server farms?', *BBC News*, 10 October. Online. Available HTTP: http://news.bbc.co.uk/go/pr/fr/-/2/hi/programmes/click_online/829 7237.stm (accessed 1 December 2009).

Heidegger, M. (1977) *Basic Writings from Being and Time (1927) to The Task of Thinking (1964)*, trans. J. Stambaugh, J.G. Gray, D.F. Krell, J. Sallis, F.A. Capuzzi, A. Hofstadter, W.B. Barton, Jr., V. Deutsch, W. Lovitt, F.D. Wieck and D.F. Krell New York: Harper & Row.

Houghton, J. (2009) 'ICT and the environment in developing countries: opportunities and developments', paper prepared for the Organization for Economic Cooperation and Development.

International Energy Agency (IEA) (2009) *Gadgets and Gigawatts: Policies for Energy Efficient Electronics – Executive Summary*, Paris: Organization for Economic Cooperation and Development.

International Telecommunication Union (ITU) (2008) *ICTs for Environment: Guidelines for Developing Countries, with a Focus on Climate Change*, Geneva: ICT Applications and Cybersecurity Division Policies and Strategies Department, ITU Telecommunication Development Sector.

—— (2009) *ITU Symposium on ICTs and Climate Change*, hosted by CTIC, Quito, Ecuador, 8–10 July 2009: ITU Background Report.

Introna, L. (2005) 'Phenomenological Approaches to Ethics and Information Technology', *Stanford Encyclopedia of Philosophy*. Online. Available HTTP: http://plato.stanford.edu/entries/ethics-it-phenomenology/ (accessed 23 January 2009).

Jolly, D. (2009) 'France resists a power-monitoring business', *New York Times*, 22 July: B2.

Jones, V. (2008) *The Green-Collar Economy: How One Solution Can Fix Our Two Biggest Problems*, New York: HarperOne.

Kant, I. (1991) *Political Writings*, 2nd edn, trans. H.B. Nisbet, H. Reiss (ed.), Cambridge: Cambridge University Press.

Landler, M. (2009) 'Meeting shows U.S.–India split on emissions', *New York Times*, 20 July: A6.

Latour, B. (1993) *We Have Never Been Modern*, trans. C. Porter, Cambridge, MA: Harvard University Press.

Lean, G. (2008) 'Mobile phones "more dangerous than smoking"', *The Independent*, 30 March. Online. Available HTTP: http://independent.co.uk/life-style/health-and-wellbeing/health-news (accessed 2 April 2008).

Lebel, L. and Lorek, S. (2008) 'Enabling sustainable production-consumption systems', *Annual Review of Environment and Resources*, 33: 241–75.

McChesney, R.W. and Foster, J.B. (2003) 'The commercial tidal wave', *Monthly Review*, 54(10): 1–16.

McDougall, P. (2009) 'IBM's green shoots: government, healthcare, India', *Information Week*, 20 July. Online. Available HTTP: www.informationweek.com/blog/main/archives/2009/07/ibms_green_shoo.html;jsessionid=543FTGYCLUVHEQSNDLPSK HSCJUNN2JVN (accessed 2 September 2009).

Makower, J. (2009) 'Wal-Mart's Sustainability Index: the hype and the reality', *GreenBiz.com*, 16 July. Online. Available HTTP: http://greenbiz.com/blog/2009/07/16/Wal-Mart-sustainability-index (accessed 29 July 2009).

Marcus, G. (1995) 'Ethnography in/of the world system: the emergence of multi-sited ethnography', *Annual Review of Anthropology*, 24: 95–117.

Markillie, P. (2005) 'Crowned at last', *The Economist*, 2 April: 3–6.

Marx, K. (1987) *Capital: A Critique of Political Economy. Volume 1: The Process of Capitalist Production*, trans. S. Moore, E. Aveling and F. Engels, New York: International Publishers.

Maxwell, R. and Miller, T. (2008) 'Ecological ethics and media technology', *International Journal of Communication* 2, Feature: 331–53.

Mazar, N. and Zhong, C. (forthcoming) 'Do green products make us better people?', *Psychological Science*. doi:10.1177/0956797610363538.

Migone, A. (2007) 'Hedonistic consumerism: patterns of consumption in contemporary capitalism', *Review of Radical Political Economics*, 39(2): 173–200.

Miller, T. (1993) *The Well-Tempered Self: Citizenship, Culture, and the Postmodern Subject*, Baltimore, MD: The Johns Hopkins University Press.

—— (2004) 'A view from a fossil: the new economy, creativity and consumption – two or three things I don't believe in', *International Journal of Cultural Studies*, 7(1): 55–65.

—— (2008) '"Step away from the croissant": media studies 3.0', in D. Hesmondhalgh and J. Toynbee (eds) *The Media and Social Theory*, London: Routledge.

Monbiot, George (2003) *The Age of Consent: A Manifesto for a New World Order*, London: Flamingo.

Mouawad, J. and K. Galbraith (2009) 'Plugged in age feeds hunger for electricity', *New York Times*, 20 September: A1.

Muldoon, A. (2006) 'Where the green is: examining the paradox of environmentally conscious consumption', *Electronic Green Journal*, 1(23), article 3.

Nader, L. (1972) 'Up the anthropologist – perspectives gained from studying up', in D.H. Hymes (ed.) *Reinventing Anthropology*, New York: Pantheon Books.

News Corporation (n.d.) '0 by 2010', *NewsCorp*. Online. Available HTTP: newscorp.com/energy/index.html (accessed 9 August 2009).

Nimpuno, N., McPherson, A. and Sadique, T. (2009) *Greening Consumer Electronics – Moving away from Chlorine and Bromine*, Göteborg and Montreal: ChemSec (the International Chemical Secretariat) and Clean Production Action.

Parsley, D. (2008) 'Server farms: where the internet lives', *Building*, 11.

Pollin, R., James Heintz, J. and Garrett-Peltier, H. (2009) *The Economic Benefits of Investing in Clean Energy*, Amherst: Center for American Progress and Political Economy Research Institute of the University of Massachusetts.

Pope John Paul II (1990) 'Peace with God the Creator, peace with all of creation', 1 January, Message of His Holiness for the Celebration of the World Day of Peace. The Papal Archive. The Holy See. Online. Available HTTP: www.vatican.va/holy_father/john_paul_ii/messages/peace/documents/hf_jp-ii_mes_19891208_xxiii-world-day-for-peace_en.html (accessed 30 March 2009).

Quinn, B. (2005) *How Wal-Mart is Destroying America (and the World)*, 3rd edn, New York: Random House.

Rydh, C.J. (2003) *Environmental Assessment of Battery Systems: Critical Issues for Established and Emerging Technologies*, Göteborg: Department of Environmental Systems Analysis, Chalmers University of Technology.

Schaefer, P.D. and Durham, M.G. (2007) 'On the social implications of invisibility: the iMac G5 and the effacement of the technological object', *Critical Studies in Media Communication*, 24(1): 39–56.

Schoenfeld, A. (2007) 'Everyday items, complex chemistry', *New York Times*, 22 December: C9.

Shah, D.V., McLeod, D.M., Friedland, L. and Nelson, M.R. (2007) 'The politics of consumption/the consumption of politics', *Annals of the American Academy of Political and Social Science*, 611: 6–15.

Simon, S. (2009) 'The more you know . . . ', *Wall Street Journal*, 9 February: R4.

Sirowy, B. (2008) 'Understanding the information society: the potentials of phenomenological approach [sic]', in Frank Eckardt (ed.) *Media and Urban Space: Understanding, Investigating, and Approaching Mediacity*, Berlin: Frank & Timme GmbH.

Stolle, D., Hooghe, M. and Micheletti, M. (2005) 'Politics in the supermarket: political consumerism as a form of political participation', *International Political Science Review*, 26(3): 245–69.

Thussu, D.K. (2007) 'The "Murdochization" of news? The case of Star TV in India', *Media, Culture & Society*, 29(4): 593–611.

US Department of Energy (n.d.) 'Federal Smart-Grid Taskforce'. Online. Available HTTP: www.oe.energy.gov/smartgrid_taskforce.htm (accessed 11 August 2009).

Vidal, M. (2004) 'Comenzó a operar ayer el Wal-Mart de Teotihuacán', *El Universal*, 5 November.

Wald, M.L. (7 November 2007) 'Taming the guzzlers that power the World Wide Web', *New York Times*, 7 November: H7.

Wal-Mart (2009a) 'Sustainability milestone meeting – July 16, 2009'. Online. Available HTTP: http://Wal-Martstores.com/Sustainability/9264.aspx?p = 9191 (accessed 15 August 2009).

—— (2009b) 'Wal-Mart 2009 Sustainability Report – Electronics. Online. Available HTTP: http://walmartstores.com/sites/sustainabilityreport/2009/en_sp_electronics.html (accessed 15 August 2009).

Williams, M. (2008) 'Greenpeace says e-waste from US stopped in Hong Kong', *PC World*, 15 June.

Winston, A. (2009) 'How the Wal-Mart eco-ratings will save money', *Harvard Business Publishing*, 17 July. Online. Available HTTP: http://blogs.harvardbusiness.org/winston/2009/07/how-the-Wal-Mart-ecoratings-wil.html (accessed 21 September 2009).

Zwick, D., Bonsu, S.K. and Darmody, A. (2008) 'Putting consumers to work: "Co-Creation" and new marketing governmentality', *Journal of Consumer Culture*, 8(2): 163–96.

11 The ethics of second-hand consumption

Adrian Franklin

Introduction

Over the past forty years the shame and stigma associated with second-hand consumption has given way to a more confident and exuberant championing of second-hand shopping as an ethical alternative to unregulated and uncontrolled 'consumerism'. This chapter will begin by setting out what is known of the scale and growth of the second-hand market. It will then consider the extent to which this growth is a response to environmentalism and the ethical consumer movement. It will be argued that although these have had an impact they do not explain the complex origins of this market growth, particularly the social, aesthetic, political and moral contexts out of which second-hand consumption has emerged. A more complex theoretical and historical account will be constructed using the works of Walter Benjamin (1955), Zygmunt Bauman (2000), Wolfgang Welsch (1997), David Ley (1996) and Barbara Kirshenblatt-Gimblett (1998) as well as some recent ethnographic studies of collecting, particularly the works of Russell Belk *et al.* (1991), Nicky Gregson and Louise Crewe (2003), Alison Clark (2000) and others. This account will be structured around four distinct if overlapping cultural shifts: first, the 'anti-modern' counter-cultural movements of the 1970s that addressed the liquefaction of tradition and culture and the arrival of what can be called a disposable modernity; second, an 'aestheticization process' that relates to powerful trends in art, design, manu-facturing and consumption that aroused a curiosity for the archaeology of modernity; third, the routinization of collecting in modernity and its association with memory, conservation and preservation; and, lastly the use of second-hand objects in the generation of 'cool' and its material performance through 'stylistic arrhythmia'.

The growth of second-hand consumption

Globally second-hand consumption has grown considerably in the past forty years. While it has always been significant in some markets such as motor vehicles ($100 billion per annum in the US alone), its importance in sectors such as clothing, household goods, books and furniture is now well established. In the US, for example, the size of the second-hand merchandise store market was US$ 4.1 billion in 2003, with second-hand clothes sales totalling $1 billion, garage sales $1 billion, and the second-hand book market worth $0.2 million. These data do not include the dramatic fillip to second-hand markets that occurred after the arrival of internet auction sites beginning with eBay in 1995. By 2003 eBay alone was responsible for auctioning 16 million items per week and provided an income to 68,000 new traders around the world. While we can trace the new-found enthusiasm for second-hand markets to important developments in Western cultures, the growth of these markets has been even more profound in many third world countries. So, for example, 95 per cent of Ghanaians wear second-hand clothing, much of it sourced from Europe. This market now supplies 60 per cent of Ghana's clothing needs and employs over 150,000 people (Wallop 2008). It has become so important that several African countries have tried to protect domestic industries by banning European and American imports.

Although significant and still growing, the second-hand markets of Western industrial countries began to grow strongly in the late 1960s and especially after the 1970s. Up until then there were junk shops, which often sold what we would consider to be antiques and collectables as well as reusable household goods while 'thrift shops' specialized in second-hand clothes. Buying from either, but particularly the latter, carried a considerable stigma that limited them to small, typically discreet, backstreet operations. Often they catered not only to the poor but to the genteel middle classes, 'embarrassed by circumstances' (Franklin 2008). In the post-war economic boom of the 1950s, styles and technologies changed rapidly in consumer markets and buying new became normative. Prices were falling in real terms but, crucially, consumer aspirations were heavily weighted towards new, future-orientated and innovative products. However, in the late 1960s, partly as a new countercultural turn began, objects with histories, pasts and previous use no longer seemed quite so uninteresting, passé or socially staining. A fascination with the past, past styles (art deco experienced a second life, for example) and cultural eclecticism began to spread.

In the 1960s the very first charity shops on the other hand shifted the motive for buying second-hand from 'desperate need' to 'charitable generosity' and in this they followed in the footsteps of the popular jumble sales that had always raised money among local communities in order to fund church-based activities and other worthy causes. Despite some auspicious beginnings, particularly strong support from celebrity donors and enthusiasm from the general public (Franklin 2008), charity shops continued to be a relatively obscure market until the 1970s when the number of new stores opening began to rise steeply, and continued to rise strongly through the 1980s and 1990s (Gregson and Crewe 2003: 21). In the UK for example there were 3,200 charity shops in 1990 but by 1999 they had grown to 6,500. Takings grew from £130 million to £350 million and charity shops became established High Street retailers.

In the mid-1960s garage sales also became popular, with Ratcliffe (1966) noting that they had become a 'growing American phenomenon' while by 1974 *US News* commented that 'garage sales were sweeping the US'. Garage sale fever hit Australia around the same time and the passion for them has never abated. From the 1970s onwards Britain also began to see more second-hand flea markets start up; the Rotary organization for instance held occasional giant markets in regional centres and, inspired by these, the car boot phenomenon took a hold across the nation, becoming the single most popular weekend leisure activity by the 1990s (Gregson and Crewe 1997).

Likewise internet auction sites were first established in the US in the mid-1990s and spread rapidly to become a global element in the expansion of second-hand goods. In 1999 there were 2.5 million listings at any one time and this grew to 4 million by 2000. By February 2005 there were almost 20 million items listed in one day and by 2007 total sales claimed by eBay amounted to nearly US$60 billion (eBay 2008). Critically, internet-based second-hand markets removed the buyer and seller from public exposure and censure, thus removing any remaining misgivings about using second-hand goods.

It is likely that the overall impact of the internet has been to increase second-hand consumption still further because it became a far more reliable means of locating less predictable supplies of used goods. Some 71.8 million active users bought and sold merchandise on eBay in 2005 and around 50 per cent of all internet users browse eBay at least once a month (Black 2007: 16; Franklin 2008: 10). According to Wallop (2008), the average British household has £450 worth of unused goods it can sell at any one time and clearly goods such as unwanted gifts or outdated (but still valuable) clothes and technologies (that might not have been donated to charity) can be disposed of very easily via the internet.

Ethical consumption?

This dramatic growth in second-hand sales has been variously linked to the movement for ethical consumption. Indeed, one of the indicators chosen by the *Ethical Consumerism Report*, published annually by the Co-op Bank, was 'buying for reuse' and more recently 'buying reused clothing'. The politically conscious middle class ethical consumer is associated with the growth of second-hand markets and linked, according to Sassatelli (2007: 189), to other forms of ethical consumption such as farmers' markets, box schemes and organic foods. Equally, Alison Clarke (2000: 99) found that 'nearly new sales [of children's clothes] represent part of a broader move towards ethical forms of consumption, in which goods are recycled and the alienation of conventional retail outlets countered'.

There are good reasons why growing second-hand markets might be linked to an emerging ethics of consumption. While there has always been the injunction not to waste, not to take more than you properly need, the complementary injunction to reuse what others throw away is relatively new. The second half of the twentieth century has seen goods became superseded/redundant while still having much use value left in them (Franklin 2008). Saved by the maxim that 'you never know when they might come in handy', such items began to fill homes, sheds, garages and under-stories of the modern home, giving such spaces a historically novel 'cluttered' look – until they were liberated by a trip to the local waste disposal. One way to see the rise of second-hand markets is to date it to when the ethic of reuse, or the practice of continuing to use what is useful, was first asserted by the environmental movement. However, while reuse was certainly part of the language of environmentalism and many no doubt practised it, it took more than just environmental concerns to build such massive global markets. An equally politicized pitch for reuse came from critics of capitalism, from the late 1960s countercultures to the anti-capitalism/ globalization movements. Several themes can be identified here.

First, was the widespread reaction to the idea of built-in obsolescence, that manufacturers deliberately made things that would become quickly obsolete, forcing more frequent purchase of new goods. This suggested the figure of the designer/producer as dupers of the general public, and as acting against their interests. This was a particularly unmodern association, given that modernity, in the shape of Fordism, was predicated on how capitalist expansion benefits the ordinary worker and narrows the gap between what the wealthy and the modest household could consume. Of course, this critique only half worked. While consumers realized that the transistors they bought in the early 1960s did not last as long as the old valve sets, they were recompensed by new utility, such as portability, lightness, better sound quality and dropping prices.

Second, and related, was the ubiquitous critique of the fashion industry, that did not so much build in obsolescence as institutionalize it very effectively through annual shifts in taste (Miles 1998). The fashion industry could be made to seem the only interested party in this deception, for who would willingly agree to such arbitrary and wasteful calculations? However, we should not forget that the aesthetic, symbolic and social significance of clothing is at least as important as function and that there are more agencies at work in shifting aesthetic values and taste than the fashion industry alone which locates fashions in very specific and highly variable social contexts. This suggests that before a woman of the 1970s would willingly or acceptably wear second-hand clothes designed for the 1940s, or even 1960s, something other than an appeal to common sense, use-value or a sense of social or ecological justice had to happen. They were not reusable until their aesthetic specificity was detached from the temporal and social contexts that gave rise to them. In a powerful sense it was the fashion industry (or a rogue element of it that emerged in the 1970s) itself that negotiated this shift by declaring all styles and mixes of styles simultaneously, or at least potentially, fashionable, making fashion styles more diverse and more the exercise of individual choice (Ewen and Ewen 1982). Only this removed the stigma attached to second-hand clothes because it simultaneously re-badged/recoded them as 'period', 'vintage' or 'classic' (Palmer and Clark 2005) but also cool (Kirshenblatt-Gimblett 1998 and see below section on 'stylish arrhythmia'). As Gregson and Crewe (2003: 11) contend: '"Distinction" too figures . . . [W]hat is being sought through "second-hand" frequently bears a marked similarity to the practices that shape designer purchasing and consumption in the first cycle: difference, taste and individuality.'

The ethical implications of consuming goods that were produced under working conditions not permitted or below standards normative in the West must also be considered. Various forms of response took place from international political interventions, Fair Trade schemes, and trade boycotts with 'reuse' becoming yet another form of resistance. By 2007, for example, *The Ethical Consumer* (2007) claimed that in the UK 'ethical clothing' sales had increased by 79 per cent over the previous year.

While buying new from appropriate sources was perceived as one option, and buying second-hand was another, much second-hand clothing on sale is as ethically tainted as when it was new, and, given that many young women sell clothes in order to restock their own wardrobes, its resale would solve nothing. According to Gregson and Crewe (2003) second-hand markets tend to increase net levels of consumption by folding money back into circulation through second-hand buying and selling strategies. When Gregson and Crewe began their research on second-hand markets they anticipated that 'second-hand goods and their consumers might be seen and see themselves as part of an alternative critical consumer culture . . . Instead, consumption through the second-hand market turns out to be shaped by many of the same motivations that shape consumer culture generally. We see here how thrift – saving money by working at consumption – is a primary imperative. About capturing relative value through "the bargain" – as much as, if not more than the good – that constitutes value' (2003: 11).

Analysing the second-hand revolution

If the emergence of new and substantial markets for second-hand consumption cannot be associated purely with the ethics of environmentalism or the critiques of capitalism noted above, what other processes were at work? I will now consider a number of related and contributing causes of the second-hand revolution that related to broader trends in the culture and politics of the 1970s.

The anti-modernist critique of liquid and disposable modernity

Aside from the arrival of environmentalism as a critique of modernity, the 1970s consolidated several other strands of criticism, the most obvious being doubts and anxieties surrounding the modern fixation on improvement, progress and the future. While these aspects were the foundation of modern appeal, delivering more ethical distributions of life chances through democratizing institutions and improving human well-being, they came at a cost. As Bauman (2000) argues, modernity also destroys former ways of doing things, traditions, pasts and even cultures it deems backward or outdated (see also Berman 1988) with the shift to a liquid form engendering a permanent state of flexibility and change (Berman 1988; Bauman 2000). Under 'solid modernity' various sorts of past and culture were annihilated; under liquid modernity certainty, continuity and security were rendered obsolete. Beginning in the late 1960s and gaining strength in the 1970s, however a number of counter-modernity movements instituted a remarkable anti-modern turn and this frequently found expression in consuming, reviving, reusing and reappraising older objects.

The impact of mass education and the expansion of higher education in the post-1945 period built the foundation for a compelling critique of suburban living as a standardized, monotonous, and privatized form of cultural decline, accompanied by various domestic tyrannies. The case against the suburb centred on cultural quietude and the stifling character of nuclear family life in which younger adults had little space of their own. However, higher education removed an entire generation of students from the suburb to the low-quality, high-density, private rented inner city world that their families had deserted (a large number were from working class origins) a generation before. According to Ley (1996), this experience deepened these students' developing cultural critique of modernity through a range of new consumer practices pioneered by so-called 'hippy culture'. Against the intolerance of modernist legislators, hippy or alternative culture embraced a greater diversity of other non-Western cultures and introduced an institutional air of *tolerance*. Aside from their interest in pre-modern/industrial ways of living, hippy culture also adopted historic forms of consumption, particularly the household-focused, self-provisioning crafts of medieval Europe (pottery, weaving, dyeing, basket making, bread-making, brewing, etc.).

In the UK, beginning with an experiment in Camden Lock, London, older, hard-to-let former industrial and warehouse buildings and yards began to be reused for a range of new craft producers and retailers. Lacking opportunities to sell in mainstream high streets these hippy businesses created and sold through new informal flea markets. However, the experience of using older buildings and cheaper urban space developed into a more generalized aesthetic that ran counter to the modernizing impulse.

Ley (1996) argues that this hippy alternative experiment provided the model for what later became known as gentrification. While a practical expedient, the availability of cheaper older housing that needed renovation turned into an aesthetic appreciation of historic houses, particularly Georgian and Victorian terraced housing – and beyond that, to a generalized fascination with the past and its material cultures. Renovation opposed the modernization of these properties and involved finding and reusing period fireplaces, tiles, doors, gates, plaster moulds and fittings. Often, supplies of these came from demolition programmes or the modernization of older buildings elsewhere. Markets for second-hand building supplies grew and renovation yards were added to the growing list of alternative consumer businesses. Over time the ethic of reuse and the restoration of historic houses turned into an aesthetic of 'heritage', the notion that the past should not be liquefied but preserved.

Once unleashed, the heritage ethic and aesthetic knew no bounds: there were no objects, no matter how humble, that did not deserve to be championed by heritage groups and preserved for posterity. This movement was particularly important since it identified the relatively absent material history of ordinary working class culture, particularly its industrial settings and artefacts, tools, dwellings and everyday domestic material culture. People began to sift through old tip sites and recover bottles, ceramic remains and other commercial containers and these industrial archaeologies formed the basis of new heritage museums, often specializing in the industries of specific towns and villages (Urry 1990; MacDonald 1997). While these museum objects were not circulating in second-hand markets, they encouraged a viewing public to see them as important and interesting, as opposed to merely superseded technologies, and this fuelled new passions for collecting, as we shall see.

The normative practices of sourcing second-hand items and the re-aestheticization of older styles of consumer objects combined with the great success of new flea markets to create an entirely new consumer phenomenon: second-hand consumption as a *pleasurable leisure form* (see the ethnographic work of Maisel 1976; Gregson and Crewe 2003). Camden Lock Sunday Market became one of London's leading tourist destinations, in common with prominent flea markets elsewhere, and this then created the necessary conditions for second-hand markets and exchange to blossom still further. In the UK, the US and Australia this resulted in the car boot/garage sale phenomenon of the 1990s.

Thus while environmental objectives were consistent with the values of alternative, hippy sub-cultures, much more than this was at work in the creation of a second-hand ethos. This sub-culture found a fertile space in former nineteenth-century industrial precincts and there they established a strong foothold in the heart of most cities. Their experiments, such as at Camden Lock, created an exciting new feel through their markets and their taste for consuming the exotic, whether from other cultures or their own past. They encouraged more people to reinhabit the inner city, but not as renters of its crumbling architecture but as restorers, heritage enthusiasts and active fossickers among its layers of archaeology.

The aestheticization of everyday life

For Zygmunt Bauman (1998; 2000) consumer connoisseurship is a defining quality of individual competence in contemporary societies; this means that *taste* is the arbiter of consumption practices rather than newness or merely the ability to buy new. Increasingly, consumer taste has come to require a heightened awareness of aesthetic quality rather than new fashion alone and this is no longer confined to social elites but is widely generalized. Wolfgang Welsch (1997), for example, has identified what he calls an 'aestheticization process' as a key characteristic of late modernity. This involves the mantling of aesthetic content on to more and more surfaces of modern life, from taps to door handles. The aestheticization of everyday life relates in important ways to the *democratization* of art and design.

Design and design schools have had a profound influence over consumption by trying to improve and extend the place of art and design in all levels of society. Design has its origins in the high cultural world of art as opposed to crafts and the rising influence of design can be traced through a process of democratization that began, in Britain as elsewhere, with the internationally orientated Arts and

Crafts movement at the end of the nineteenth century and the Industrial Design movement at the beginning of the twentieth. While early work concentrated on making improved design and aesthetic content available to more people in the routines of production and consumption processes, from the 1970s onwards it became increasingly common for both the designer and the style of design to feature in the description of any good. This in turn was highlighted by the consumer choice movement, and particularly through *Which? Magazine* (and its variants), since one of their stock comparators was 'design quality' (Young 2007). Once a discourse on design and aesthetics entered the process of consumer choice it became very apparent that contemporary design had historic influences in terms both of its style, design orientation and manufacture, opening up the market to re-issues of 'classic' designs and of course the desirability of 'originals'. From the 1980s onwards consumer style guides began to appear as this now desirable knowledge on design, designers, periods and manufacturers was researched and published for the first time (e.g. Jackson 1997; 1998). Once design connoisseurship arrived alongside a proliferation of styles and style fusions there was no longer a singular fashionable look but a multiplicity of styles and as knowledge of these deepened, consumers became more willing to buy 'period', 'retro', 'vintage' and more generally 'twentieth century modern'.

Here then is yet another quite distinct foundation for the growth of second-hand consumption. As Gregson and Crewe (2003: 11) argue: 'For many then, consumption through the second-hand arena is "clever" consumption, a set of practices which reveal and display heightened consumption knowledge/s and skills, and which encode the extent of investment in consumption.' So, if 'good taste' came to require a working knowledge of, or expertise in, historic goods and design as well as their purchase and display in living spaces, then the consumer was liberated from the High Street and set loose in the auction houses, markets, charity shops and car boot sales.

The routinization of collecting in modernity

Recent studies have shown that around one-third of all Americans or sixty-three per cent of American households are collectors with an average of 2.6 collections per household (Schiffer *et al.* 1981; Belk *et al.* 1988; Pearce 1995). What began as the treasure-trove hobby of princes and kings in early modern Europe (whose collections became the foundations for the modern museum) was emulated by middle class amateurs of the nineteenth and early twentieth centuries and then 'recommended' to working class cultures as a self-improving leisure option (particularly by church and chapel organizations). According to Belk *et al.* (1991: 188) collecting accelerated in the remaining part of the twentieth century.

As collecting became a recognized and respected procedure of scientific enquiry and a distinct style of pedagogy, it was further entrenched as a commercially successful marketing strategy. By the mid-twentieth century therefore, collections and collecting had become an entrenched element of modern cultures and children in particular were exposed to it in numerous ways. Schools were and continue to be the principal demographic of museums everywhere and without them many would fail. Through museum collections children were exposed to what was considered valuable and important. Museums taught the elementary notion of objects belonging in classes; that objects belong to evolutionary pathways; that human-made objects demonstrate both characteristics that are universal to all cultures and those that are culturally specific. In addition, children were the main target of merchandise collectables such as cigarette and tea cards, cereal toys and Smurfs (given away with petrol purchases). The idea here was to build brand loyalty as well as use children as leverage on parents' purchasing. Children were encouraged to begin their own collections through schools and youth organizations such as cubs and scouts.

For collecting to become the mass leisure form it did among both children and adults required not only the proliferation of things to collect (which modern manufacturing made possible) but also for those things to acquire meaning and desirability after their first purchase. A large proportion of collected things are second-hand objects and studies of collecting behaviour demonstrate how collecting these also connects to specific qualities of late modern society.

Earlier collecting genres focused on highly collective objects (stamps, coins, bird's eggs, fossils and minerals, for example) of national or regional significance. By comparison, collecting in the later twentieth century became more individualized and collections often related to the biography of the individual or were totemic of their fluid and unfolding character, a point made by Gregson and Crewe (2003) in relation to their observation that collectors make frequent and quite drastic changes to what they collect. The significance of older objects in these strategies illustrates a key connection between contemporary collecting and second-hand objects. Several scholars have noticed that objects chosen for collections frequently have a connection with the collector's childhood (Forty 1986; Bloom 1989). Such objects may invoke fond memories, nostalgia for better times, or, very commonly, collecting may satisfy previously unfulfilled desires to have these objects as children or younger adults. So, for example, a young teenager in the 1970s might only expect to buy or receive a handful of vinyl records per year, perhaps predominantly at Christmas and birthdays. In their 30s and 40s, however, with more disposable income, they have the opportunity to buy hundreds if not thousands of the records they craved as second-hand objects, and their aura, this time as 'collectables', is augmented by their 'rarity', 'value' and 'condition' (Franklin 2008).

Dannefer (1980) shows how this works the same way with second-hand cars. These become 'vintage' and desirable when the high school kids, who craved them when they were new, reach their 40s. While unfulfilled childhood desires, nostalgia for 'golden' pasts and rising values are all motivations for collecting, there is an important overarching motivation that was first described by sociologist Walter Benjamin (1955).

Walter Benjamin argued that the significance of collecting to modern cultures is that it prevents the liquefying, fragmenting and discarding tendencies of modernity from inflicting permanent damage and loss. Left to itself modernity might eliminate periods, objects and sensibilities in its onward march into better times. However Benjamin said that collecting is a form of *memory*, holding still in an aestheticized manner, the look, the feel, the technology, the actual materiality and culture of times past *through its objects*. A return to loved childhood objects might never occur to anyone whose life and world had not changed in any meaningful way. Imagine if the same records were still being sold and freely available; if the technology to play them remained unchanged and if the songs on them were still sung and were never superseded by new styles? There would be no sense of loss, no possible reason to collate and conserve; no way that such objects could register the passage of time or restore a 'golden' era.

This may also explain why there is such a strong moral and conservational dimension to the collecting impulse – and more than just a whiff of the sacred. As a moral quest, collected objects *ought* not to be forgotten for this is to forget people and cultures. Collecting can be viewed as a technology for organizing and protecting memories from disappearing and since our very identities are wrapped up and materialized around memories of our past, collecting is a way of protecting not so much the objects as the people who do the collecting and the audiences who visit and admire them.

There is an even more direct connection between the identity-constructing, memory-preserving nature of second-hand objects and the contemporary efflorescence of collecting that relates to economic change, specifically the shift from manufacturing to service/information economies that has characterized most Western economies. Objects with compelling histories of design and manufacture compare favourably with those currently on sale *new*. The vast majority of things around us are produced overseas by people we do not know, in towns and regions we have never heard of, and under conditions that we might well disapprove of. The marks, back stamps and labels that once described the geography and society of our own modern world have been replaced by the anonymous ciphers of global producers, saying as *little as possible* so as to avoid whatever discrimination exists in faraway markets. Equally, such is the complexity of many objects and the myriad origins of their various parts that it becomes impossible to talk about them as produced 'anywhere' or by 'anyone'. By comparison, collecting restores to the collector and their audiences a more coherent and relevant material culture that speaks very directly to them, the details of its provenance (back stamps, signatures, model numbers, etc.) being as important as its form or function.

The extension of 'cool' and 'stylistic arrhythmia'

In discussing contemporary theoretical work on the recent fascination with second-hand goods, particularly those with kitsch credentials, Kirshenblatt-Gimblett (1998) argues that there is an expressive, radical appeal involved in the act of appropriating what others have rejected:

How is it that objects that attracted slaves to fashion in their first life can be tokens of rebellion in their afterlives? Walter Benjamin noted that the outmoded is a source of revolutionary energy, precisely because to pick it up again, after it has been discarded is a potentially radical gesture . . . What some fads lacked in exclusivity during their first life they gain the next time round through the recoding operation that consumers (low riders, punks) produce – through what Umberto Eco calls semiological guerrilla warfare.

(Kirshenblatt-Gimblett 1998: 274)

In her essay on kitsch and taste Kirshenblatt-Giblett refers to 'stylish arrhythmia', literally a stylishness or coolness that derives its edge from being 'out'. 'What's out for the mainstream is cool for the sub-culture, except that some rejects are cooler than others' (Kirshenblatt-Gimblett 1998: 274).

According to Gregson and Crewe many second-hand shoppers derive at least some of their pleasure from the subversive nature of shopping in these second-hand markets where price, relations between seller and shopper and performance are all subverted within a carnivalesque space. Retro goods become radical or cool to the degree that they represent a better past, the past of heroic, democratizing modernism. Gregson and Crewe (2003: 147) were struck by 'why the 1960s loomed so large in the memories of second-hand shoppers'. Their respondents suggest that 'the sixties represented . . . a time of progressiveness in fashion and design, of quality, innovation and excitement'. It represents a challenge to the notion of aesthetic judgement because it elevated the everyday and the commonplace, and highlighted and celebrated the cultural nature of ordinary lifeworlds. Former street advertising posters for cheap French aperitifs can replace works of art vying for the same domestic space – and cost a lot more.

Conclusion

While it may seem as though the proliferation of second-hand markets is intimately connected with new environmental movements for ethical consumption, this paper has argued that the connection is at best tenuous. On the other hand the paper has discerned a powerful ethical motivation that underlies the remarkable efflorescence of second-hand objects dating from the late 1960s. The desire to resist the liquefying tendencies of modernity in favour of preserving links to a variety of pasts and the antecedents of class, ethnic and regional cultures has its origins in the counter cultures that secured a unique and powerful position at the heart of modern societies everywhere. Much of this cultural work has remained buried beneath the more controversial topic of gentrification but it seems clear enough that gentrification itself has had an important counter-cultural specificity and that through gentrification a new aesthetic movement focusing on everyday material culture appeared, or at least expanded massively, growing beyond the gentrifiers and gentrified districts to become mainstream. In explaining this I engaged with the sociological, spatial and technological specifications of Welsch's 'aestheticization process', and singled out the sociological work of Bauman, Benjamin, and Kirshenblatt-Gimblett whose work can be employed to understand the links between social change and second-hand consumption change. Benjamin provides the crucial link between the elements of retaining, preserving and collecting common to second-hand consumption and the experience of modernity. Older objects and their collection become important sources of memory in societies characterized by rapid social change and disposability. Kirshenblatt-Gimblett refines this idea by showing how disposal and reuse becomes constitutive of cultural boundaries and how the recoding of some people's rubbish as valued commodities can constitute what is 'in' and cool for others: a refinement on processes of distinction-making. Bauman makes it possible to understand the essential similarities of first- and second-hand goods, linking them to both notions of desire, individualism and identity. In liquid modernity where choices and styles proliferate, the long-standing opposition between the new and the superseded, what is fashionable and acceptable (and what is not) could no longer hold sway. Critically however, consumerism and connoisseurship became people's defining qualities and hence it was their aesthetic judgement that became more important that their purchasing power alone. Hence it was the aesthetic qualities of an object rather than its age that determined its desirability. In an increasingly aestheticized world, an object's provenance and aesthetic quality and design history held more influence than its mere novelty and this too propelled second-hand consumption from the outer edges to the mainstream of contemporary societies.

Bibliography

Bauman, Z. (1992) *Intimations of Postmodernity*, London: Routledge.
—— (1993) *Postmodern Ethics*, Oxford: Blackwell.
—— (1998) *Work, Consumerism and the New Poor*, Philadelphia, PA: Open University Press.
—— (2000) *Liquid Modernity*, Cambridge: Polity Press.
Belk, R.W., Wallendorf, M., Sherry, J.F. and Holbrook, M.B. (1991) 'Collecting in a consumer culture', in R. Belk, M. Wallendorf, J. Sherry and M. Holbrook (eds) *Highways and Buyways: Naturalistic Research from the Consumer Behaviour Odyssey*, Provo, UT: Association of Consumer Research.
Belk, R.W., Wallendorf, M., Sherry, J.F., Holbrook, M.B. and Roberts, M. (1988) 'Collectors and collecting', *Advances in Consumer Research*, 15: 548–53.
Benjamin, W. (1955) 'Unpacking my library: a talk about book collecting', in Hannah Arendt (ed.) *Illuminations*, New York: Brace and World.
Berman, M. (1988) *All That is Solid Melts into Air*, Harmondsworth: Penguin.
Black, G. (2007) 'A comparison of the characteristics of eBay consumers and eBay nonconsumers', *Journal of Direct Data and Digital Marketing Practice*, 9: 16–29. doi:10.1057/palgrave.dddmp.4350066.
Bloom, J.D. (1989) 'Cardboard images of the past: baseball card collecting and fragmented historical memory', paper presented at American Studies Association Conference, Toronto.
Clarke, A. (2000) 'Mother swapping': the trafficking of nearly new children's wear', in P. Jackson, M. Lowe, D. Miller and F. Mort (eds) *Commercial Cultures*, Oxford: Berg.

Co-op Bank plc (2008) *Ethical Consumerism Report 2008*, Manchester: Co-op Bank plc.

Dannefer, D. (1980) 'Rationality and passion in private experience: modern consciousness and the social world of old-car collectors', *Social Problems*, 27, April: 392–412.

eBay (2008) 'About eBay'. Online. Available HTTP: http://news.ebay.com/about.cfm (accessed 12 April 2008).

Ewen, S. and Ewen, E. (1982) *Channels of Desire*, New York: McGraw-Hill.

Forty, A. (1986) *Objects of Desire – Design and Society since 1750*, London: Thames and Hudson.

Franklin, A.S. (2008) *A Collector's Year*, Sydney: University of New South Wales Press.

—— (2010) *City Life*, London: Sage.

Gregson, N. and Crewe, L. (1997) 'Excluded spaces of regulation: car-boot sales as an enterprise culture out of control?', *Environment and Planning A*, 29: 1717–37.

—— (2003) *Second-Hand Cultures*, Oxford: Berg.

Jackson, L. (1997) *Austerity to Affluence: British Art and Design 1945–62*, London: Merrell Holberton.

—— (1998) *The Sixties*, London: Phaidon.

Kirshenblatt-Gimblett, B. (1998) *Destination Culture – Tourism, Museums and Heritage*, Berkeley, CA: University of California Press.

Ley, D. (1996) *The New Middle Classes and the Remaking of the Central City*, Oxford: Oxford University Press.

MacDonald, S. (1997) 'A people's story: heritage identity and authenticity', in C. Rojek and J. Urry (eds) *Touring Cultures*, London: Routledge.

Maisel, R. (1976) 'The flea market as action scene', *Urban Life*, 24: 488–505.

Miles, S. (1998) *Consumerism as a Way of Life*, London: Sage.

Palmer, A. and Clark, H. (2005) *Old Clothes, New Looks*, Oxford: Berg.

Pearce, S. (1995) *On Collecting*, London: Routledge.

Raban, R. (1974) *Soft City*, London: Harvill Press.

Ratcliffe, J. (1966) 'How to turn discards into dollars – a look at a growing American phenomenon – the "house sale"', *Reader's Digest*, 89, August: 25–28.

Sassatelli, R. (2007) *Consumer Culture – History, Theory and Politics*, London: Sage.

Schiffer, M., Downing, T. and McCarthy, M. (1981) 'Waste not, want not: an ethnoarchaeological study of reuse in Tuscon, Arizona', in M. Gould and M. Schiffer (eds) *Modern Material Culture*, New York: Academic Books.

The Ethical Consumer (2007) 'Ethical Consumerism Report 2007'. Online. Available HTTP: www.ethicalconsumer.org/ShoppingEthically/UKethicalmarket2007.aspx (accessed 22 November 2007).

Thomas, V.M. (2003) 'Demand and dematerialization impacts of second-hand markets reuse or more use?', *Journal of Industrial Ecology*, 7(2): 65–78.

Urry, J. (1990) *The Tourist Gaze*, London: Sage.

US News (1974) 'Why garages sales are sweeping US', 77: 45–50.

Wallop, H. (2008) 'Credit crunch: charity shops hit as people sell second-hand goods on eBay', *Daily Telegraph* (UK). Online. Available HTTP: www.telegraph.co.uk/finance/newsbysector/retailandconsumer/3531436/Credit-crunch-charity-shops-hit-as-people-sell-second-hand-goods-on-eBay.html (accessed 27 November 2008).

Welsch, W. (1997) *Undoing Aesthetics*, London: Sage.

Young, T. (2007) 'My father – the man who started *Which?*', in *Which? Magazine 50 Years 1957–2007*. Accessed 28/7/10, http://www.which.co.uk.

12 Is green the new black?

Exploring ethical fashion consumption

Chris Gibson and Elyse Stanes

Introduction

Everybody needs clothing for warmth and protection; but clothing is much more than body covering. This chapter contrasts arguments from the neo-Marxist Frankfurt School and poststructuralist/feminist cultural studies to understand and problematize the ethics of clothing consumption as *fashion*. Clothing is a basic manufacturing industry, one which drove the industrial revolution to meet the essential human need to be covered. But fashion is also a *cultural* industry, promoting particular forms of consumption as social practices, because fashion is central to the production of self-identities, a way of marking the body with meaning. Most people own more clothing than is necessary, replace perfectly useable items with changes in season and trends, and wash clothing more often than is needed. These behaviours can exacerbate problems of unsustainable production methods (such as the production of water and energy intensive cottons) and have fuelled industrial systems (such as 'fast fashion' and the international outsourcing of garment construction to pieceworkers with poor labour conditions and protections) that have in turn drawn criticisms from unions, environmentalists and consumer lobby groups (Micheletti *et al.* 2004). Counter-discourses of 'ethical' and 'green' fashion have recently emerged in response – everything from the promotion of organic fabrics to second-hand shopping, Fair Trade textiles and 'clothes swaps'. Indeed, ethical fashion has itself become *the* new trend – if the title of a recent book is anything to go by, green appears to be 'the new black' (Blanchard 2007).

But will transforming the consumption of fashion towards more ethical ends be as simple as convincing people to buy different items of clothing? In this chapter we explore fashion and ethical consumption, reviewing literature on the fashion industry (and critiques therein) and attempts to redress ethical problems through alternative production methods and new consumer behaviours. Initially we overview ethical concerns relating to production (including workers' rights), and consumer campaigns of different persuasions (including anti-sweat shop movements). Later discussion then focuses especially on environmental critiques of fashion production and consumption. This focus – albeit partial – is timely because of intensified concern over climate change and carbon impacts of high-consumption lifestyles (Hobson 2003). We discuss critiques of fashion as an unsustainable industry and various proposals for producing and consuming fashion more sustainably. Initiatives branded as 'green' by fashion houses, manufacturers and environmental groups are contrasted against a range of everyday social practices undertaken by consumers – illuminating constraints, contradictions and opportunities. We argue that corporate-backed attempts to produce fashion more sustainably offer some potential to reduce carbon emissions, but they are problematic in that they 'mainstream' sustainability without challenging the fundamental, growth/consumption-orientated industrial system which has spawned the problems of climate change. Fashion branded as 'sustainable' becomes a new moral economy 'ultimately constrained by the size of niche markets' (Bassett 2010: 45; see also Beard 2008) – while leaving intact the holy grail of more sales and consumption. Against this, we contrast other pertinent dimensions of sustainability and the ethics of consumption – the everyday, non-market, hidden, domestic, and identity-forming aspects of fashion – that exist beyond green branding, but are critical to a more substantial, alternative ethics of fashion consumption.

Fashion – an industry, and a culture of consumption

Meanings for clothing have long since surpassed primary utilitarian needs: from 'traditional' dress and costumes to fashion in urban subcultures, it is clear that cultural differences and expressions are enabled via clothing (McRobbie 1999). In all but the poorest of places clothing choices are informed at some level by considerations of appearance.

Academic analysis of fashion reflects broad distinctions between neo-Marxist positions (heavily influenced by the thinking of Frankfurt School theorist Theodor Adorno), and cultural studies' interpretations of identity, meaning and agency. We consider briefly each of these interpretations. Analysis of fashion as a form of cultural capitalism emphasizes industrial structures and fashion cycles (thus implying that consumers are 'slaves to fashion', mere passive recipients of what the industry tells them to purchase); whereas analysis of fashion as a sphere for cultural meaning focuses on fashion as a catalyst of identity construction, self-expression and creativity.

Neo-Marxist analyses of the fashion industry have emphasized the global organization of the clothing industry, with particular attention to systems of production, manufacturing and advertising (Scott 2002; Doeringer and Crean 2006), and the celebritization of fashion. Fashion is a form of cultural capitalism, thus subject to similar critiques as for capitalism more broadly – from exploitation of low-wage workers (usually women), to the mass deception of the general public through advertising (Adorno 1975; McRobbie 1997). Fashion as means to class distinction (whether the function of clothing's formality in Victorian England to present-day couture brands) can also inform a Bourdieuian critique of the maintenance of bourgeois power (Crane 2000).

From a radical feminist perspective, fashion remains intricately connected to the beauty myth and systems of gendered coding of the body. Although the possibility of liberation is always ever-present (through creative use of fashion to construct challenging self-identities; see Budgeon and Currie 1995), fashion production and celebrity marketing can disempower women and preserve patriarchy. Predictable consumer behaviours are seen as key to industrial structure. Because clothing has become fashion (an industry that changes seasonally), demand is highly price-elastic (Hassler 2003). Larger quantities of clothing are purchased more often if prices fall – a 'truth' of fashion marketing evident when, for instance, consumers squabble over sale items in large department stores during clearance sales (Schor 2005). This logic has led to changes in the geographical organization of the industry. With trade liberalization and advances in transportation, capitalists have increasingly manufactured consumer goods in the third world, for the Western world, for dramatically lower costs. This has been particularly the case with fashion, with labour costs replacing fabric as the most costly input in the 1970s (Weil and DeWeese 2004). The global structure of the fashion industry and the production of clothing increasingly contribute to low wages, excessive working hours, poor job security and disregard for union rights. As retailers continue to compete based on price elasticity, contractors and trading companies seek ever-cheaper means of production. This in turn perpetuates downward pressure on labour prices.

Union agitation and social concern has encouraged some movement on legislation to protect human rights and working conditions – and brought about a particular kind of consumption driven by ethical concerns (Shaw *et al.* 2007). In the early 1990s exposure of labour abuse by brands such as Nike and Gap created pressure from consumers, media and non-government organizations for compliance-driven regulation of clothing work. Campaigns against Nike and Gap led to the introduction of codes of conduct and the setting out of minimum levels of workers' rights, which have since infused the broader Fair Trade agenda (Fletcher 2008). From a neo-Marxist critique, a particular form of ethical fashion consumption has emerged, focusing on items made under decent working conditions, and largely dependent on truth in labelling by brands.

Parallel to neo-Marxist critiques are ideas of fashion as self-expression and catalyst for performing identity. For centuries, clothing has created identity performances through its capacity to communicate, assert self-identity and reveal socio-economic worth or status (Crane 2000). People use dress to evaluate their own characteristics and abilities against those surrounding them; through fashion people develop a self-image which they present to others (Fletcher 1991). The accessibility of fashion facilitates individualism and diversification of taste cultures.

For some, shopping and buying are the activities that create pleasure, while the actual consumption of goods is secondary and may not take place at all. Increasingly known in popular culture as 'retail therapy', shopping has become an end in itself (Hamilton *et al.* 2005). A fashion cycle central to the organizational logic of the clothing and footwear industries is a key element of this fulfilment.

Whether mass deception or means to self-identification, the idea of buying new clothes at every season is now widely accepted, regardless of need (Slater 2000). In the West, very few people own just enough clothing to get by – over-consumption of clothing has become normalized. For these reasons, fashion has been strongly critiqued as giving rise to unethical production and consumption practices, and in particular, for being environmentally unsustainable. It is this latter theme – environmental sustainability – to which we turn in the remainder of our chapter.

Critiques of fashion as unsustainable

Concerns about environmental sustainability are the newest challenge for the fashion industry, emerging in the wake of feminist critiques in the 1960s and union critiques of sweat shop labour in the 1990s, and as the science of fashion material sustainability, production and energy use is better understood. Even more nascent are debates about fashion *consumption* and its implications for sustainability. Whereas a stock of scientific knowledge on the sustainability of fashion production is slowly building (see below), sustainability is only a recent insertion to debates about ethical consumption of fashion more generally. This is not to say that sustainability concerns about fashion have been ignored previously: for decades champions of 'alternative' fibres such as hemp have critiqued environmental impacts of mainstream clothing production, and politic-ally active environmentalists have chosen to buy second-hand clothes and minimize clothing ownership (giving rise to unique second-hand clothing subcultures associated with a broadly left-wing, environmentally conscious, student/activist demographic). What is new is the extent to which 'green' issues in fashion have become mainstream, evidenced in new marketing techniques, discussions of sustainable fashion in popular magazines and television pro-grammes. The rapid rise in publicity surrounding 'green' fashion demands a corresponding intensification in academic analysis, but scholars have responded only belatedly, and intermittently.

Before we consider consumption of fashion in more depth, it is worth survey-ing the stock of scientific knowledge on what makes fashion 'unsustainable' in the first place. This is necessary because later in this chapter we discuss contradictions in the ethical consumption of fashion, and challenges to popular ideas of what constitutes sustainable fashion consumption. Consumption that appears to be 'sustainable' may not be quite so, weighed against knowledge of the various environmental impacts of fashion. Where academic writing and more commonly non-academic 'grey' literature on the fashion industry has discussed environmental impacts and sustainability, five main themes emerge: production and manufacturing, distribution, use, waste and the social ethics of fashion sustainability.

Production of fibres and textiles is most commonly criticized for large consumption of energy and water, and volumes of waste created. However, measurable impacts of fabric and textile production differ greatly depending on fibre type, and growth and harvest methods employed. Less than half of all textiles produced across the globe annually are natural fibres. Of this, cotton dominates, with up to twenty-four million tons produced each year, equivalent to roughly forty per cent of total world textile production. Cotton production appears to cause the most environmental damage, requiring the use of fertilizers and pesticides which contribute to soil contamination (Paakunainen 1995).

The amount of water needed to irrigate cotton crops also varies according to the climate of growth: for instance, in Israel cotton production requires 7,000 litres of water per kilogram, while in Sudan the figure is more like 29,000 litres (Fletcher 2008). Impacts of high water use include leeching of fertilizers and chemicals, soil erosion and adverse changes in water balance (i.e. imbalances in volumes of water in different stages of the water cycle from groundwater to rivers and in the atmosphere, created through extraction and use) (Slater 2000). Accompanying this is the sheer amount of energy consumed during cotton processing, ginning, balling and dyeing, and the highly variable quality of cotton used in fabric construction. Few clothing items made of cotton last (and in particular, children's clothing is known to be made from the poorest quality cotton; see Edwards-Jones 2006), thus fuelling even more rapid production and continued need for growth in cotton farming.

In the past fifteen years, demand for human-made synthetic textiles has doubled (Claudio 2007). In highest demand are acrylic, polyester and nylon. Unlike natural fibres, the main environmental impacts from synthetic textiles relate to energy consumed in production and the emission of chemical particulates, including nitrogen oxides, hydrocarbons, sulphur oxides and carbon monoxides (Laursen *et al.* 1997). The biodegradability of manufactured fibres has also been subject to critique, because toxic by-products are unable to be broken down organically.

Environmental damage caused by the transportation of textiles and completed garments has worsened as commodity chains in the fashion sector globalize. Distribution of raw materials, fibres, wholesale material and finished clothing contributes to air pollution, CO_2 build-up, and thus to climate change. This has been exacerbated with the global contracting of raw materials, out-sourcing various parts of garment construction across international borders, and the increasingly transnational corporatization of fashion marketing and retail.

Just how damaging this shifting geography of fashion production is, however, remains debatable. The critique of globalization (and attendant CO_2 impacts of transportation) implies that local production of fashion is more sustainable. Indeed, several fashion houses have followed this line, including Zara, based in Spain, and American Apparel, based in Los Angeles, US – both of which purposely source products from local suppliers. Despite comparatively higher costs for locally made clothing (with local labour unions more active than in third world countries), these labels have reduced transport costs and market their products through appeals to localism and ethical consumption. What is less apparent is that focusing on local fashion production has enabled other kinds of market advantages: an enhanced ability to respond quickly to changing local consumer preferences, and an ability to avoid discounting on end-of-season stock by organizing clothing production into smaller units rather than single large-scale global productions (Allwood *et al.* 2005).

Moreover (and in an interesting parallel to food production – see Saunders *et al.* 2006), the localization of production alone is unlikely to transform total environmental impacts of fashion because transportation is only one – and certainly not the statistically most significant – factor. Allwood *et al.* (2005) estimated that the transportation of a conventional cotton shirt accounted for eight per cent of its total environmental cost. In addition, as already discussed in the case of cotton, environmental impacts of raw material production vary substantially from place to place – thus making differences in distances of trade and CO_2 impacts drawn from transport comparatively insignificant. Cotton clothing might well score better environmentally if raw materials were produced in a few climatically suitable locations and then transported globally, than if production were localized everywhere. In parallel to other commodities such as food, critical attention needs to be directed towards 'localization' campaigns, for they may only address one (statistically small) component of total environmental impact.

A picture is now starting to emerge regarding household *consumption* of clothing and its environmental impacts. The consensus seems to be that the most profound environmental impacts from the lifecycle of clothing do not come from the production of fibres, or the way that clothing is distributed, or even the manner in which clothing is disposed; rather it is a range of consumption-related activities: the amount of clothing purchased and discarded before its utility is exhausted; and the way that the garment is washed and cared for while in use. If fashion is to become more sustainable, and thus more ethical, then consumption is what appears to matter most.

Environmental impacts of the consumption of clothing invariably escalate as clothing is discarded more quickly, long before the fabrics are worn or the item has lost its shape. In a time of rapid consumer purchasing and discarding, the lifetime of clothing may be less than one season (Slater 2000). Low apparel prices (a result of globalization and poor labour conditions) coupled with the price-elastic nature of demand have enabled 'fast fashion' cycles (more rapid than the usual four seasons) and 'excessive accumulation' (Schore 2005) of garments by consumers. Low prices encourage consumers to shop more often, and commensurately the number of items purchased annually is growing. Allwood *et al.* (2005) analysed the demand for low-cost disposable clothing in the United Kingdom and found that over four years, the number of garments purchased had increased by more than one-third per person. In the US, the average household will spend $US 1,760 on clothing annually. In Australia close to A$15 billion is spent each year on clothing and accessories (ABS 2008). Hamilton *et al.* (2005) estimate that approximately A$1.7 billion dollars is spent annually in Australia on clothing that is not worn. Fast fashion enables shops to change product lines every month if desirable, thus maximizing sales as consumers are tempted by more frequent updates in item availability, and resulting in a higher overall amount of consumption of clothing.

As a larger stock of clothing makes its way through various stages of reuse and recycling to landfill, chemicals used in the production of clothing will contaminate the environment. The United States Environmental Protection Agency (EPA) Office of Solid Waste estimated that Americans throw away thirty kilograms (sixty-eight pounds) of clothing and textiles per person per year (Claudio 2007). In the UK, the amount of clothing and textile waste created annually is nearly forty kilograms per person (Allwood *et al.* 2005). Barely a quarter of this waste is reclaimed; half of this is used by material recovery firms, and the other half incinerated. The other three-quarters of waste textiles are committed to landfill (Fletcher 2008), where textile waste is responsible for toxic chemical leeching and groundwater pollution. Compounding this is the wide-spread practice in the fashion industry of discarding excess stock not sold in each season's run, rather than donating it to charity shops or re-circulating it for consumption in poor countries (a practice stemming from corporate desires to protect brand integrity; see Edwards-Jones 2006: 105).

Critical to making fashion more sustainable is breaking the link between rapid fashion cycles, increases in the overall stock of clothing produced and consumed, and perpetuation of wasteful disposal practices.

Also significant are fashion consumption behaviours after the clothes have been bought: wearing, washing, drying, and mending. Research from the Netherlands showed that an average piece remains in a person's wardrobe for three years and five months, is on the body for forty-four days, and during this time is worn on average between 2.4 and 3.1 days between washing (Uitdenbogerd *et al.* 1998). The process of washing and drying in the household uses as much as eighty-two per cent of total energy use within the clothing lifecycle (Fletcher 2008). Figures from both Australia and the US indicate that over eighty-five per cent of house-holds use top load washing machines, a process that usually requires 151 litres of water. In comparison, front load washing machines avoid immersing clothing in a tub of water and can reduce water use by twenty-sixty per cent (Easter 2007). Across the US, more than 35 billion loads of washing are run annually (Easter 2007).

Meanwhile, practices of mending clothes (and thus extending their lifecycle) vary enormously through time, from place to place, and among demographic groups: whereas socks were once darned for longer life they are now thrown away once holes develop; ill-fitting clothes bought on a whim are often discarded rather than being altered at home; mending skills common in the Great Depression and World Wars have faded (or are seen as antiquated by younger generations); and education systems that presumed sewing was 'women's work' have spawned whole generations of men without skills who consequently refuse to mend clothing. If consumption matters most, then the most significant environmental concerns involve 'invisible' behaviours such as washing, drying and mending.

Sustainable fashion: a new form of ethical consumption?

There is a burgeoning 'grey' literature – popular non-fiction books (Blanchard 2007), magazine articles (*The Environmental Magazine*, *G* magazine) and industry reports by governments and non-governmental organizations (e.g. Allwood *et al.* 2005; *War on Want* 2006) – on 'green' fashion and how clothing can be consumed more sustainably. Such publications discuss improved production processes, and disseminate particular educational 'messages' about consuming fashion more sustainably. Underpinning them all is a strong sense that one's individual ethical position vis-à-vis sustainability, the environment and/or climate change should subsequently inform decisions made to consume fashion in particular ways.

The most common recommendation – and certainly the most publicized in recent years – is the development and promotion of more sustainably produced fibres. New fibres are available that use a variety of natural plant resources in the production of textiles, such as bamboo, jute and flax, usually marketed with overt reference to their 'greener' means of production. They have emerged in response to social and environmental concerns, but account for a relatively small proportion of the current market. A concern is whether such fibres can dominate mainstream production competing against fast fashion production using low-cost cotton (Beard 2008).

Recycled fibres are a low-impact alternative to other virgin fibre sources as they reduce required resources and chemicals, if the fibre is not overdyed (Fletcher 2008). The process of recycling clothing has remained unchanged for two hundred years: fibres are extracted mechanically using a carding machine and formed into yarn by linking much shorter strands (Fletcher 2008). This process is possible for both natural and synthetic fibres, although it is energy intensive compared with repairing clothing, or purchasing second-hand items.

Reuse of clothing includes sale through charity shops and online auction sites, clothes swapping and the redistribution of clothing through charity organizations. According to Laursen *et al.* (1997) the energy used to collect, sort and resell second-hand clothing is between ten and twenty times less than that needed to make a new item of clothing. Charity shops ('op-shops' in Australia) and vintage stores have burgeoned. The original intent of charity shops was to provide for those less fortunate. Since the 1980s second-hand and vintage clothing has become charismatic. At any time, some form of second-hand clothing (usually iconic in a particular period of fashion – flared jeans from the 1960s, disco shirts from the 1970s, Dr Martens boots from the early 1980s) is popularized in fashion, driving the re-incorporation of retro fashion elements into mainstream design.

Vintage and charity shops have thus come to occupy a particular position in the wider fashion industry: they are not merely repositories for old clothes – but rather act as an 'alternative' resource for the mainstream fashion industry to mine for reminders of previous styles and retro looks. Comparatively wealthy, fashion savvy consumers thus regularly turn to charity shops or vintage clothing stores. Among aficionados, shopping for second-hand clothing is viewed as an experience, a way of finding unique treasures of the past to mix with contemporary fashions. Charities are now well aware of this, developing more sophisticated marketing, floor plans and links to the vintage and designer scenes, as well as trumpeting their contributions to sustainability (beyond their original charity function). As described by Neville Barrett, General Manager of Salvation Army Stores Australia: 'Last year we started *Fashion with a Conscience* because we believe that the world is going to run out of resources for fashion . . . the younger generation is more aware of the needs of the community, more savvy, more concerned about the future . . . Where there's an opportunity to merchandize goods to have a particular value, it makes sense for us to do that' (cited in Lam 2009: 6).

The resale of clothing has also been popularized through online auction sites. Clothes and shoes make up eleven per cent of items sold on eBay, second only to antiques/collectables (Blanchard 2007). Online auctions extend the lifetime of garments (but through transport also adding to its ecological footprint), and enable the creation of international and highly specific cultures of second-hand clothing and footwear swapping and collecting, such as with cowboy boots, Panama hats and Hawaiian shirts. Cashing-in on the marketing appeal of sustainability, eBay recently set up a site for the resale of ethical goods.

Less obvious (and certainly rarely marketed as 'green') is the practice recommended in grey literature of choosing well-made 'classic' items of clothing – those items that will last and remain 'chic' despite the cycle of trends – rather than those that are likely to date quickly. On balance, buying 'classic' high-quality items reduces environmental damage through lower overall consumption of clothing. Realistically, wardrobe selections do not need to be changed with seasons, but rather need to be diversified to meet the whims of weather (Blanchard 2007). Certain items – often conservative in appearance – will last longer and seem less out of date than others, considered to be 'timeless' pieces.

Making a return in the grey literature on fashion sustainability is the idea to 'make do and mend' – which was a mantra for an entire generation who lived through the depression and austere war years. Originally, the incentive was simple economic expediency. During times of war clothing was repaired in order to extend its lifecycle: trousers and jackets were patched, worn textiles that could not be used for repairs became rags or dusters. Clothing was transformed and recreated through mending and repair, and use of recycled curtains and waste fabric cut-offs. Blanchard's book (2007) promotes the re-discovery of making do and mending, dedicating an entire chapter to 'do-it-yourself (DIY) style'. This message promotes money-saving and extending the lifecycle of clothing.

Likewise, there are a number of recommendations made in the grey literature regarding the use and care of clothing. The first of these is washing temperature. Richter (2005) concludes in a report for the US Department of Energy that approximately fifty per cent of all energy consumed in the laundry process is used for heating hot water. The fashion industry has to some extent responded to this: care instructions now often recommend the use of cold water on the premise that fabrics may shrink or lose colour in a warmer wash (Easter 2007).

A more straightforward recommendation is to increase the load size of laundry and decrease the frequency of wash loads, thereby reducing the amount of detergent and water used per cycle. Choosing fibres and fabrics that resist soil and odour also reduces the amount of washing needed. Some labels such as Nudie Jeans, based in Sweden, now recommend to consumers that they wash jeans rarely, in order to preserve the denim. Washing instructions for their jeans require that consumers do not wash them for at least six months in order to create a worn look that adapts to body shape.

Complicating ethical consumption of fashion is that the simple act of drying clothing has become a battleground. The use of tumble dryers is increasingly pervasive, and yet adds massively to energy use. In the US, where dryer use has increased most markedly, millions of residents are denied the 'right to dry' on outside lines by community and homeowner associations concerned with the aesthetic appeal of communal dwellings. Communities are now launching campaigns aimed at state and federal legislators to introduce 'right to dry' legislation. Laws seeking to overturn clothes-line bans are now pending in Connecticut, Vermont and Colorado (Rosenthal 2008). Far from being passive consumers, in some places residents have become activists in local planning politics seeking to repeal laws that prevent more sustainable consumption of clothing.

Dressed in green?

Further debate has emerged on whether elements of 'green washing' have crept into fashion marketing, and whether regulators should introduce eco-labelling schemes for fashion in the same manner as for food (Nimon and Beghin 1999). Clothing items are increasingly marketed as 'eco-friendly' or 'sustainable', and celebrities have been recruited to lend their credibility to green fashion (notably Natalie Portman, who licenses her name to a vegan shoe label). Where accreditation systems exist, an eco-fashion item can be assessed on the energy, water and carbon impacts of its full lifecycle (Claudio 2007). Until recently, eco-fashion was restricted to high end hiking, adventure and sportswear. Now mainstream brands such as Levi's and H&M market lines as 'eco'. Statistics from the Organic Trade Association in the US in 2006 estimate that the sale of organic cotton had grown twenty-six per cent on the previous year. In 2004, Wal-Mart, America's largest retailer, began selling organic cotton shirts in some stores and, at present is the world's largest buyer of organic cotton. In the UK, Marks and Spencer has recently created a new sales marketing plan to 'work with our customers and our suppliers to combat climate change, reduce waste, safeguard natural resources, trade ethically and build a healthier nation' (Marks and Spencer 2009). The growth in sales of eco-fashion suggests that consumer tastes in fashion purchasing are changing and that there is a market for clothing that appeals to environmentally conscious sentiments.

Questions remain about the science of eco-clothing products (such as the extent to which gains are offset by other problems); the extent to which marketing eco-clothing merely ghettoizes ecologically sustainable clothing production into a high-cost niche (Beard 2008); and whether what is instead required is industry-wide environmental regulation.

Cultural resources for sustainable fashion consumption

Critiques of the fashion industry as unethical make clear a link between consumptive lifestyles and the lack of sustainability. A problem stems from the fact that advocates of sustainable consumer behaviour assume certain characteristics behind existing consumption patterns and motivations for the purchase of new clothing (see Blanchard 2007). Where recommendations have been made about improving sustainability via consumer behaviour, the focus relies on new practices such as swapping or borrowing clothing, purchasing classic items, purchasing fewer items and shopping online. But these recommendations are made without a clear understanding of the capacity, adaptability and suitability of these ideas for consumers of different backgrounds and persuasions.

What remains rare is research that explores everyday consumption practices to understand *why* people consume fashion; how aware people are about environmental problems associated with clothing; what problems relating to sustainability might stem from cultural values and practices; and whether people already possess cultural resources that could open up constructive avenues for sustainability campaigns (see Hobson 2003). It is often said that sustainability needs cultural change, but what kind of change and how radical it should be is unclear. The marketing of eco-fashion implies that favouring items made from new sustainable materials is sufficient, but in other quarters the requisite cultural change is portrayed as requiring utter transformation of lifestyle and economy. Alternatively, there is evidence that cultural behaviours and attitudes already present in society can be leveraged without the need of radical socio-economic change, or having to surrender to the marketing dictates of a barely different 'green' capitalism. There are cultural meanings and practices embedded in daily life that provide opportunities for more ethical forms of consumption, without people necessarily recognizing the environmental importance attached to them. Ethnographic research is therefore essential to understanding consumption and the culture of fashion – and also how cultural resources might vary geographically.

In this manner, one author (Stanes 2008) used a qualitative framework to explore cultural resources for sustainability in fashion consumption. Everyday fashion consumption practices were examined among a select group of Generation Y Australians. Findings were that consumers carry out a range of behaviours within their personal lives that translate into sustainable practices. Forty per cent of young people who responded to a survey regularly purchased second-hand clothing ('op-shopping'). Crucially, even though purchasing second-hand clothing has sustainability benefits, young people's op-shopping was not especially informed by environmental concerns. For those who op-shopped, its pleasures were related to the experience of shopping and the thrill of finding something unique. Yet others were turned off by the perceived disorder and chaos of second-hand stores. Searching for good-quality second-hand clothing can be unsatisfying when nothing suitable is found (Pears 2006). As one of Stanes' (2008) Generation Y research participants observed:

> Op-shops frustrate me because there is too much stuff packed into one tiny little area. I'm the kind of person who gets really flustered and frustrated if I have to sort through everything to find something. I really gave the op-shop thing a run for maybe 6 months. I just couldn't do it.

In contrast, privately operated vintage clothing shops have increased in popularity, stocking second-hand clothing, usually well-looked-after pieces with either 'classic' or 'retro' appeal. Vintage clothing shops are laid out like new clothing retail stores and will charge a higher price for garments than charity shops. Their growth augments (and yet also complicates) the story of second-hand shopping scenes as cultural resources for sustainability: vintage shops encourage reuse and recycling, but also bite into the non-profit market and shift emphasis from the 'thrill of the hunt' for the obscure hidden treasure, towards a more predictable, reliable commodity-format mode of purchasing.

Somewhat subtle cultural resources around fashion consumption include grassroots cultures of clothes swapping and lending. Borrowing and lending clothing expands one's wardrobe without increasing overall consumption levels. Clothes swapping has become a way of discarding unwanted clothes while also encouraging more sustainable fashion consumption, and formed the basis of new kinds of social events. Katie Pears (2006) has actively used the clothes swap party as a way to promote the sustainable re-consumption of clothing. Pears (2006) hypothesized that clothing exchanges would appeal to young adults who were willing to experiment with consumption of their fashion garments as they actively sought out new experiences. Also notable has been the emergence of clothing swap websites (such as www.swapstyle.com and www.whatsmineisyours.com) and clothes leasing websites (www.dressedup.com.au). Clothing swaps, websites and exchange events are potential cultural resources because they fit into participants' existing lifestyles and bring pleasure, rather than being simply a response to the guilt of over-consumption (Pears 2006). This contrasts with Ha-Brookshire and Hodges' (2009) finding that propensity to donate clothing to charity shops is connected to feelings of guilt brought about by buying more new clothing, and having to find space in wardrobes for new items. A subtle, but potentially illuminating, difference thus exists between cultures of clothes swapping and the traditional charity shop system, with the latter now muddied by a more contradictory ethics of over-consumption, guilt and donation.

In Stanes' (2008) research, gender was the significant variable influencing swapping and sharing behaviour. Females were actively involved in clothes swap parties and undertook the act of borrowing and lending clothes with friends, family and room-mates in the normal course of weekly events (especially when going out on the weekend):

> Me and my house mate, we share a lot of things. Pants and shoes we can't share, but we share a lot of jackets and pretty, going-out tops. When I used to live at home, I used to share with my sister a lot. Even though my sister and I live an hour apart now, occasionally she'll call up and say 'next time you come up can you bring this, and I'll give you this' and we'll exchange.

In contrast, men rarely lent or shared clothing of any type, unless it was in extreme circumstances. For one of Stanes' male participants: 'I absolutely do not want, not need, [am] not in to sharing . . . I would not feel comfortable with people wearing my clothes or wearing somebody else's clothes.'

Different kinds of consumers (and their acts of consumption) constitute cultural resources for more ethical consumption. In Stanes' (2008) findings, those consumers deeply positioned within the fashion cycle (fashion enthusiasts, or more cynically, 'slaves to fashion') actively consumed clothing based on season, trend or occasion. They were responsible for higher overall rates of clothing consumption. Yet they were more likely to pay attention to and enthusiastically embrace new ethical recommendations around fashion – from buying alternative textiles to cotton, to purchasing clothing second-hand and participating in clothes swap parties. They were also actively aware of clothes swap parties, fashion rental websites, the popularity surrounding vintage and second-hand clothing and also the 'hype' behind new sustainable and organic fibres in the retail market place. Those consumers most bound up in the fashion cycle (i.e. the most susceptible to cultural consumption as mass deception, as Adorno might put it) are also those most likely to alter behaviour or to enact agency in shifting clothing use towards a newer, more sustainable self-identity.

Conversely, a different set of contradictory trends emerged relating to those who eschewed fashion, or shopped for clothing's utility over appearance. Those who were indifferent towards fashion and clothing (found in Stanes' research to be usually men) consumed fewer clothes in total – because they were not interested in changing fashions (or in Adorno-esque language, were not deceived by the culture industry's insistence on the continual replacement of perfectly useable pieces with new ones). As a result, fewer clothes were consumed (one participant claimed that they 'only rotate around three shirts') and energy, resource use and waste were reduced. Clothes were often well worn and the maximum potential was gleaned out of the garment. Yet at the same time, 'fashion cynics' were also the most likely to buy new clothing solely based on price considerations (when it was purchased). They were the least likely to consider new eco-fabrics, and the most likely to buy poorly made pieces that were cheap (thus further fuelling the fast-fashion industry, and forms of production that are more environmentally damaging). 'Fashion cynics' were also the least likely to buy second-hand clothes, or to mend old items if they tore or lost buttons. It seems that behaviours, proclivities and practices exist throughout different consumer groups that can be seen as cultural resources for more sustainable, ethical forms of consumption, but these intermingle with other behavioural traits and practices that limit the potential for cultural change.

Conclusion

A clearer picture is emerging of the biophysical impacts of clothing production, distribution and care. Several alternatives have appeared and been promoted by the green movement (and by the fashion industry itself) in the hope that fashion production can become more sustainable (and therefore, more ethical). Yet how we use clothes is not straightforward; what might constitute ethical fashion consumption is opaque. At the crux is a debate about how fashion is consumed, and the agency that consumers enact amidst the influence of peers, media sources, marketers and fashion capitalism itself. Post-Marxist analysis of fashion as a form of cultural capitalism emphasizes industrial sophistication and suggests that consumers sheepishly follow what the industry tells them to purchase; whereas poststructuralist and some feminist readings of fashion focus on fashion as objects of material culture that circulate through social and cultural networks, giving rise to discourses, subject identities, self-expression and creativity. In light of this tension, we sought here to tease out complex and contradictory stories of the ethics of fashion.

Some putatively 'sustainable' consumption practices have been promoted by manufacturers and marketers and adopted seamlessly by consumers; others less so. The position inspired by Adorno – that fashion consumers will buy what they are told to buy, and thus what is required for sustainability is industry-wide regulation – is somewhat borne out in statistics on the growth of the organic cotton trade and the increasing popularity of other 'green' textiles. Certainly the conscription of celebrity in support of eco-fashion initiatives suggests that a neo-Marxist reading of fashion as a system of mass deception remains pertinent – even if the celebritization of fashion becomes directed towards such 'positive' goals as sustainability.

However, while adapting existing marketing tactics to more ethically produced clothing has proved easy, other consumption-related issues remain contradictory. With the rise of vintage fashion and eBay, more people buy clothing second-hand (though frequently with no intent to consume in any more 'ethical' manner). At the same time, however, fewer people know how to make or mend their own clothes (a practice which would expand the lifespan of items and thus reduce overall consumption levels). Sustainability campaigns have surfaced from within the fashion industry, and yet problematic messages normalizing over-consumption of fashion persist in fashion magazines. If anything, fashion cycles continue to speed up based on knowledge of how consumers purchase clothing (tempted by its 'newness' on the shelves). As Edwards-Jones cynically describes in her 'insider' account of the fashion industry, 'In the end we'll be making a dress [line of production] a week, shoving it on a celeb, and getting it into the shops. How depressing is that?'

The link between fashion consumption and self-identity also complicates theoretical interpretation of ethical consumption. Some 'fashion conscious' consumers shop for clothing as 'retail therapy' or even to feed an 'addiction'; such people could be considered over-consumers or 'slaves to fashion'. Yet they appear more likely to buy sustainable and Fair Trade items, to buy vintage, and to mend clothes because they are already aware of fashion and care about clothing. Those most enmeshed in fashion capitalism are often the most critical of the unethical practices supporting it. Conversely, others (often men) buy far less clothing because of a general apathy towards fashion. They are less likely to transform preferences and behaviours, motivated instead by lowest cost, and are less critical of capitalist marketing and production systems. Yet at the same time, consumer cynicism towards fashion could be constructive (in the sense of supporting efforts to lower overall levels of consumption), and as a deeper resistance to the very idea of a compulsory fashion cycle. Our conclusion is that clothing – at once a basic necessity in life and a luxurious indulgence – encapsulates the contradictions of ethical consumption. There is no simple manual to consuming fashion ethically. Instead, fashion consumption needs to be rethought as a social practice intricately woven into cultural capitalism, ever-globalizing networks of the circulation of material objects, and everyday culture. In each of these moments and places of fashion, ethical questions are apparent and made more complex.

Bibliography

Adorno, T. (1975) 'Culture industry reconsidered', *New German Critique*, 6: 14.

Allwood, J.M., Laursen, S.E., Rodriguez, C.M. and Bocken, N.M.P. (2005) *Well Dressed? The Present and Future Sustainability of Clothing and Textiles in the United Kingdom*, University of Cambridge Institute for Manufacturing.

Australian Bureau of Statistics (2008) 2008 Yearbook Australia, Cat. no. 1301.0, viewed 20 July 2009. Online. Available HTTP: www.ausstats.abs.gov.au/Ausstats/subscriber.nsf/0/8D6ED0E197FE38A6CA2573E7000EC2AD/$File/13010_2008.pdf (accessed 10 May 2010).

Bassett, T.J. (2010) 'Slim pickings: fair-trade cotton in West Africa', *Geoforum*, 41: 44–55.

Beard, N.D. (2008) 'Branding of ethical fashion and the consumer: a luxury niche or mass-market reality?', *Fashion Theory: The Journal of Dress, Body & Culture*, 12(4): 447–68.

Blanchard, T. (2007) *Green is the New Black*, London: Hodder and Stoughton.

Budgeon, S. and Currie, D.H. (1995) 'From feminism to post feminism: women's liberation in fashion magazines', *Women's Studies International Forum*, 18(2): 173–86.

Claudio, L. (2007) 'Waste couture; environmental impact of the clothing industry', *Environmental Health Perspective*, 115(9): 449–54.

Crane, D. (2000) *Fashion and its Social Agendas: Class, Gender and Identity in Clothing*, Chicago: University of Chicago Press.

Doeringer, P. and Crean, S. (2006) 'Can fast fashion save the US apparel industry?', *Socio-Economic Review*, 4(3): 353–77.

Easter, E.P. (2007) 'The environmental impact of laundry', in Earth Pledge (ed.) *Future Fashion White Papers*, New Jersey: Greg Barber Co.

Edwards-Jones, I. (2006) *Fashion Babylon*, London: Bantam Press.

Fletcher, K. (2008) *Sustainable Fashion and Textiles: Design Journeys*, London: Earthscan.

Fletcher, R. (1991) 'The messages of material behaviour: a preliminary discussion of non-verbal meaning', in I. Hodder (ed.) *The Meaning of Things: Material Culture and Symbolic Expression*, London: Routledge.

Ha-Brookshire, J.E. and Hodges, N.N. (2009) 'Socially responsible consumer behavior? Exploring used clothing donation behavior', *Clothing and Textiles Research Journal*, 27(3): 179–96.

Hamilton, C., Dennis, R. and Baker, D. (2005) *Wasteful Consumption in Australia*, Canberra: The Australia Institute. Online. Available HTTP: www.tai.org.au/documents/dp_fulltext/DP77.pdf (accessed 20 August 2008).

Hassler, M. (2003) 'The global clothing production system: commodity chains and business networks', *Global Networks*, 3(4): 513–31.

Hobson, K. (2003) 'Thinking habits into action: the role of knowledge and process in questioning household consumption practices', *Local Environment*, 8(1): 95–112.

Lam, L. (2009) 'Shops spot an opportunity', *Inner West Courier*, 23 July: 6.

Laursen, S.E., Hansen, J., Bagh, J., Jensen, O.K. and Werther, I. (1997) *Environmental Assessment of Textiles: Lifecycle Screening of Textiles Containing Cotton, Wool, Viscose, Polyester or Acrylic Fibres*, Ministry of Environment and Energy and Danish Environmental Protection Agency.

Marks and Spencer (2009) Online. Available HTTP: http://plana.marksandspencer.com/about (accessed 2 July 2009).

McRobbie, A. (1997) 'Bridging the gap: feminism, fashion and consumption', *Feminist Review*, 55: 73–89.

—— (1999) *In the Culture Society: Art, Fashion and Popular Music*, London: Routledge.

Micheletti, M., Føllesdal, A. and Stolle, D. (eds) (2004) *Politics, Products, and Markets: Exploring Political Consumerism Past and Present*, New Jersey: Transaction Publishers.

Nimon, W. and Beghin, J. (1999) 'Are Eco-labels valuable? Evidence from the apparel industry', *American Journal of Agricultural Economics*, 81(4): 801–813.

Paakkunainen, R. (1995) *Textiles and the Environment*, Denmark: European Design Centre.

Pears, K. (2006) 'Fashion re-consumption; developing a sustainable fashion consumption practice influenced by sustainability and consumption theory', unpublished thesis, RMIT, Melbourne.

Richter, T. (2005) 'Energy efficient laundry processes', *GE Global Research*. Online. Available HTTP: www.osti.gov/bridge/servlets/purl/842014-FdebHg/native/ (accessed 5 September 2008).

Rosenthal, E. (2008) 'A line in the yard: the battle over the right to dry outside', *New York Times*, 12 April. Online. Available HTTP: www.nytimes.com/2008/04/17/world/americas/17clothesline.html (accessed 23 June 2009).

Saunders, C.M., Barber, A. and Taylor, G. (2006) *Food Miles – Comparative Energy/Emissions Performance of New Zealand's Agriculture Industry*, AERU Research Report No. 285.

Schor, J.B. (2005) 'Prices and quantities: unsustainable consumption and the global economy', *Ecological Economics*, 55(3): 309–20.

Scott, A.J. (2002) 'Competitive dynamics of southern California's clothing industry: the widening global connection and its ramifications', *Urban Studies*, 39(8): 1287–306.

Shaw, D., Shiu, E., Hassan, L., Bekin, C. and Hogg, G. (2007) *Intending to be Ethical: An Examination of Consumer Choice in Sweatshop Avoidance*, Orlando, FL: Association for Consumer Research.

Slater, K. (2000) *Environmental Impact of Textiles: Production, Processes and Protection*, Cambridge: Woodland Publishing.

Stanes, E.R. (2008) 'Is green the new black? Questions of sustainability within the fashion industry', unpublished thesis, University of Wollongong.

Uitdenbogerd, D.E., Brouwer, N.M. and Groot-Marcus, J.P. (1998) *Domestic Energy Saving Potentials for Food and Textiles,* Wageningen, Netherlands: Wageningen Agricultural University.

War on Want (2006) 'Fashion victims: the true cost of cheap clothes at Primark, Asda and Tesco'. Online. Available HTTP: www.waronwant.org/Fashion+Victims+13593.twl (accessed 16 September 2008).

Weil, S. and DeWeese, G. (2004) *Western Shirts: A Classic American Fashion*, Layton, UT: Gibbs Smith.

Part 4

Practices, sites and representations

13 Slow living and the temporalities of sustainable consumption

Wendy Parkins and Geoffrey Craig

> Growing your own vegetables is a bit like making your own fridge or whittling a car. Possible, but stupid.
>
> (A.A. Gill 2008)

Introduction

In late 2008, *The Times* television critic and food writer A.A. Gill launched a broad attack on self-sufficiency, home vegetable gardens, organic food and any alternative practices of consumption outside the mainstream of Western consumer capitalism. The catalyst for this broadside was the television chef and presenter Hugh Fearnley-Whittingstall's new series, *River Cottage Autumn*. Fearnley-Whittingstall, Gill charged, was responsible for perpetuating an unrealistic and simplistic philosophy of sustainability and ethical consumption. At the heart of Gill's critique was an assumption that to grow your own vegetables would be a waste of time, that better alternatives are easily available, and that to persist with such a pastime is sheer indulgence – a 'Marie Antoinette' game, as he put it – for the privileged few who have the luxury of time and money to play at kitchen gardening. In short, Gill's charge was that ethical consumption – in the form of domestic attempts at sustainability – was *un*ethical. In this chapter, we want to think through Gill's critique to explore how sustainable consumption, as a particular manifestation of ethical consumption, is bound up with a certain approach to, and understanding of, time. What is 'stupid' about spending time growing your own vegetables? Why would it constitute a *waste* of time? And what then does this imply about the 'proper' way to consume time in late-modern societies?

In an earlier study (Parkins and Craig 2006), we considered the importance of time in the practice of what we called 'slow living' which we defined as an attempt to live at a slower pace in reaction against the acceleration of just about everything (Gleick 1999) and as a critical response to an over-scheduled and time-poor mode of everyday life. Slow living does not represent a retreat from the world but a reflexive engagement with the temporal, spatial and social complexities of contemporary global existence. Slow living is captured in a range of practices that invest everyday life with meaning and pleasure through a mindful use of time. This investment in time is prompted by, and in turn facilitates, a greater consciousness of a self that is not a solipsistic entity but one who is open to otherness. Against the flow of fast life, slow living reminds us that everyday hospitality, ethical relationships, and the social relations that inform and sustain communities require time.

We also argued that the values of slow living are particularly evident in the sensory and convivial pleasures of food consumption where there is a regard for the individuals and social networks involved in the production and distribution of that food. The Slow Food movement, for instance, seeks to respond ethically to what it calls the 'connections between plate and planet' while also stressing the pleasures of food and conviviality. Slow living, then, is partly characterized by the individual use of consumption practices to help facilitate the reconnection of food consumers and producers. As with ethical consumption more generally, this reconnection can take the form of support for a local food culture or for more distant food producers who engage in environmentally sustainable farming practices and who are marginalized by global agro-food networks. However, contrary to the tenor of much discussion of ethical consumption where an emphasis on the *ethical* presages a distrust of consumption *per se*, we associated slow living with the celebration of the sensory pleasures of food consumption, while distinguishing it from practices of over-consumption or connoisseurship (Parkins and Craig 2006: 124).

In this chapter we will build on our earlier work on slow living by highlighting the fundamental importance of *slowness* to ethical consumption and sustainable living. Ethical consumption, we argue, is premised on an alternative approach to the consumption of time – how we use time, how we value time, how we measure time. Forms of ethical consumption, such as home vegetable gardens, recycling and ethical investment, require individuals to invest time in their mundane practices and to acknowledge the value of slowness where it is allied with environmental sustainability and social justice. More profoundly, the practices of sustainable living, manifested in changing modes of food production and consumption, transportation, and energy generation, require a slowness which carries with it a more acute consciousness of a sense of place and the rhythms of everyday life, including weather patterns and seasonality. What we want to examine in this chapter is the degree to which ethical consumption choices connected to sustainability and the lifestyles to which they give rise may be seen as another example of the conjunction of pleasure and ethics characteristic of slow living. In this way, we will also argue that in order to better understand the practices of ethical consumption, and sustainable living more generally, we need to acknowledge the emotional, sensory and material dimensions associated with such activities.

Focusing on sustainable consumption as one aspect of ethical consumption, we will follow Gill's lead and base our discussion on a consideration of recent television programmes which present viewers with displays of sustainable consumption as a lifestyle – Britain's *River Cottage Autumn* and New Zealand's

Off the Radar. These popular programmes are examples of an emerging genre of green lifestyle television where individuals return to the land in order to live in a more sustainable manner, reconnect with a place-based community, and derive greater pleasure and meaning from their everyday lives. Central to both programmes is a focus on seasonality, the sustainable production and consumption of food, and the pleasures associated with slow living. Of course, such programmes may well be seen as instances of the commodification of sustainable consumption, packaged for urban dwellers who can only aspire to a way of life where a community gathers to feast on the bounty of the land, produced and prepared with patience and attention in bucolic surroundings. In other words, we do not approach these programmes naïvely, as if they are somehow outside contemporary consumer capitalism. We are also aware of their status *as texts*, informed by a particular televisual political economy and temporality. We want nonetheless to emphasize the value of these programmes for depicting what the temporality of sustainable living might *look* like and as testimony of the appeal such lifestyles hold for late-modern consumers.

Gill's contention that domestic practices of sustainability are unrealistic in a complex society is perhaps itself naïve in its assumption that those who are committed to ethical consumption are not well aware of the complexities, if not the contradictions, that impinge on all our consumption choices in late-modern capitalism. Ethical consumption is in fact premised on the acknowledgement of the complexities – and the inequities – of current social arrangements concerning the production, distribution and consumption of (in this case) food. Indeed, a significant factor in the complexity of late-modern societies is not just that they have given rise to a huge variety of 'things' to consume but the ways in which to consume them. When consumer choice can run the gamut from choosing to commute daily in gas-guzzling 4WD vehicles to choosing to go off the power grid and generate one's own electricity, decisions to consume ethically require a negotiation of possibly competing factors such as cost, convenience and environmental outcomes. Gill's assumption that ethical consumption is the exclusive domain of the economically privileged means that he can only see organic or sustainable production as unethical and those who advocate it as sanctimonious and 'small-minded'. He perpetuates stereotypical portrayals of *faux* peasants (and their 'appalling' hand-knitted jerseys) in order to dismiss the concept of sustainable living *tout court* as a fantasy solution to the anxieties of contemporary life. Instead, we will argue that sustainable consumption is often marked by a sometimes inconsistent negotiation of everyday practices, arising from a desire for a different experience of time as well as an ethical impulse to live sustainably.

Time in ethical consumption and sustainable living

Uses of time are, of course, central to all cultural formations. If the triumph of consumer culture has been marked by the collapse of time into money, it has been argued that post-materialist movements have not yet effectively challenged this equation because they have not successfully addressed the 'poverty of desire' that can arise from increased leisure time (Cross 1993: 9). We believe, however, that the variety of practices and movements encapsulated in the concept of slow living represents a promising and renewed attempt to mobilize alternative practices of consumption bound up with different uses of time in the remaking, or at least the renegotiation, of contemporary Western existence. More particularly, we are interested here in the way in which green lifestyle television programmes not only represent a different sense of temporality but also seek to address this 'poverty of desire' through a portrayal of the pleasures and values associated with alternative ways of inhabiting and consuming time.

Ethical consumption, alternative food networks, and forms of sustainable living are more often associated with particular *spatial* dynamics involving a privileging of local places that can potentially yield different economies and social relations. Such activities, however, are also informed by the valuing of a different temporality. However widespread popular forms of ethical consumption may have become, the practice of consuming ethically requires greater time in contrast to the quick and easy convenience of conventional consumption. The very sense of acting ethically – giving regard to the welfare of others – requires time and a certain form of slowness that enhances attention and is at odds with the temporalities associated with a 'drive-thru' culture. Equally, sustainability is fundamentally informed by a temporal dimension, given it entails an ongoing, cyclical and productive relationship between humans and their environment. In this sense, sustainability carries with it a sense of a commitment both to the future (Ehrenfeld 2008: 53) and to the past, in contrast to the preoccupation with the present, the 'now', in the form of the exploitation of available time that informs contemporary global capitalism. In contrast to industrial agriculture that works to the temporal dictates of maximum efficiency and market demand, employing technology to by-pass the natural limitations of climate or landscape, sustainable agriculture is more attuned to the temporality of the seasons. Sustainable farming practices are made possible by, and cannot be disconnected from, the slowness of their food production and a particular orientation to time. The time taken to ripen a cheese or grow an animal to maturity is antithetical to the exigencies of industrialized forms of farm production. It is the patience and the process of working with the land rather than exploiting it as quickly as possible for the greatest gain that marks out sustainable production from the marketplace orthodoxies of agricultural production.

Dominant conceptions of time in contemporary capitalism establish a binary whereby the time not allocated to (paid) work is classified as 'free' time. Alternatively, the time of sustainable living is not 'empty' or 'wasted' time, nor a time that is experienced in a singular, uniform sense: it is a form and experience of time subject to considerable variations of rhythm, duration and speed, often dictated by seasonal demands, and co-existing with quieter moments, driven by a recognition that productivity requires the 'passing of time'. Of course, we should not be too quick to establish a mutually exclusive binary between dominant experiences of time in contemporary capitalism and an alternative time of sustainable living. One does not even need to step outside the home – whether in the city or the country – to encounter competing temporal values and regimes. As anyone who has been the primary carer for an infant knows, for instance, the temporalities of daily modern life are infinitely variable, due to the need to juggle the competing demands of others (such as the infant's need for sleep, play and nurture) with the social, personal or economic needs of the self. For most Western subjects who seek, to varying degrees, a change of lifestyle associated with forms of ethical consumption and sustainable living, however, they must involve themselves in increasingly complex negotiations of time as they oscillate between the temporal demands of different aspects of daily life in conjunction with an ethical framework that privileges sustainability.

Critiques of the impracticalities of sustainable consumption have highlighted the difficulties of these temporal negotiations, often over-determined by economic necessities. The high profile achieved by Julie Critchlow, for instance, the so-called 'burger mum' who became the public face of opposition to Jamie Oliver's healthy school dinners campaign in the UK (and subsequently inspired his next series, *Jamie's Ministry of Food*), is an example of the vehemence with which alternative practices of consumption can be rejected as impractical and elitist for people who have kids to feed and no time to cook. Following May and Thrift's (2001) conceptualization of *timespace*, however, we would argue that such reactions reflect a crisis in the management of time that is a consequence of the uneven and heterogeneous production of time (and space) in post-traditional Western capitalism. Such reactions assume, that is, a link between economic limitations and time impoverishment that would have seemed surprising to, say, working-class families in earlier generations where the management of scant resources *required* an investment of time to ameliorate limited income. In late modernity, the democratization of leisure has outstripped the achievement of economic equalities with the result that the expectation that time will be spent in the provision of food can be dismissed as an imposition of elitist, class-specific values. Time poverty – or its perception – has ironically become an experience of time shared across the socio-economic spectrum but is, we would suggest, a polysemous concept to signify a more nebulous dissatisfaction with the quality of everyday life, understood in varying ways by varying social groups, classes or individuals.

As media debates about class and home-cooking also imply, however, the valuing and use of time differs according to subject position, inflected by class, ethnicity or sexuality as well as income, and is closely connected with a broader understanding of time associated with life narratives. Recent work on 'queer time' and 'queer temporalities' has further explored the understanding of temporality in late-modern culture by emphasizing the way that different subjects and sub-cultures inhabit or experience time in the form of non-normative life narratives. As Judith Halberstam puts it, 'Queer subcultures produce alternative temporalities by allowing their participants to believe that their futures can be imagined according to logics that lie outside of those paradigmatic markers of life experience – namely, birth, marriage, reproduction, and death' (2005: 2). Different forms of life narrative are also bound up with different modes of consumption. One need only think of the normative forms of consumption linked with heteronormative life narratives (the purchase of engagement rings or 'family cars', for instance) to see how time and consumption are indissolubly linked to assumptions about what constitutes 'the good life' in the Western capitalist imaginary.

The valuation of a different sense of time that occurs in forms of ethical consumption and sustainable living, then, is an example of a different investment in the meaning of time, as well as its use. It derives from a conscious valuing of the *quality* of time and the enhanced social and personal pleasures and opportunities that are associated with such a different orientation towards time. It may also lead subjects to question, qualify or reject the normative life narratives that seem to pre-suppose certain consumption choices and patterns. A widespread disenchantment with the ever-growing work-culture of contemporary capitalism has been manifested in a range of responses, from calls for a greater 'work–life' balance where people are able to spend more time with family and engage in recreational and civic activities, to a repudiation of the concept of a 'career path' as the primary marker of a 'successful' life narrative. We have previously described how slow living marks an attempt to make *space* for an enhanced experience of embodied and sensory pleasures through an investment of *time* and this is also evident in forms of ethical consumption and sustainable living that are grounded in the material pleasures of food and a sense of ethical obligation to place, the environment, or a specific community of food producers (Parkins and Craig 2006; 2009). This conjunction of the pleasure and ethics of slow living – in which time for food production and consumption is inextricably bound up with a desire for an enhancement of social relations in everyday life – is made explicit in the recent green lifestyle programmes which we will consider in more detail in the following section.

River Cottage and *Off the Radar*

In *River Cottage Autumn* (Channel 4) and *Off the Radar* (TVNZ), sustainable consumption is chiefly depicted through the production and consumption of food in ways consistent with our concept of slow living. The popularity of these programmes, and others like them, derives from a complex and interrelated number of factors including a concern for environmentalism, the pleasures associated with the cooking and tasting of food, and a physical retreat from the pressures of urban living and a rediscovery of community. We believe that implicit in all these factors is a particular sense of time that is perceived to be lacking in urbanized forms of everyday life. In this section we will consider the appeal of this alternative understanding and experience of time and ask: what is the significance of this desire for a different experience of time connected to sustainable consumption? And how is this different sense of time embodied and represented in these programmes?

The season-based series *River Cottage Autumn* began the latest cycle of programmes presented by eccentric British celebrity chef Hugh Fearnley-

Whittingstall, and culminated in *River Cottage Summer*, which screened in the European summer of 2009. Filmed at Fearnley-Whittingstall's River Cottage – now not only a farm in Devon but a cooking school and a café, as well as a farmshop in Axminster – the programme no longer focuses on a solitary Fearnley-Whittingstall attempting to live self-sufficiently in a small and isolated cottage (as in the original *River Cottage* series) but features a range of gardeners, chefs, livestock handlers and butchers. The inclusion of the expanding business operation of River Cottage is represented not as a contradiction of Fearnley-Whittingstall's philosophy of sustainability but as a testimony of the viability and achievability of such practices. The programme also includes segments filmed beyond 'River Cottage HQ', as Fearnley-Whittingstall profiles other attempts by individuals, voluntary organizations or local government initiatives to implement sustainable production and consumption throughout England. An ongoing focus of attention is also the development of an urban smallholding in suburban Bristol, undertaken on reclaimed land by local residents, as an experiment in the establishment and evolution of sustainable consumption in a non-rural location. Over the course of the series, this smallholding develops from a relatively modest undertaking to supply the residents with eggs and vegetables to include more ambitious projects such as raising pigs and goats for meat and cheese production. The thread connecting all aspects of *River Cottage Autumn* is the emphasis on the growing, harvesting, cooking and consumption of seasonal food.

Off the Radar, a thirteen-part New Zealand television series which screened in 2009, depicted the comedian Te Radar attempting to live sustainably on a five-acre block of land about an hour's drive north of Auckland over the course of a year. Much of the success of the programme – it reached number one in the ratings in New Zealand – was arguably due to the fact that it presented Te Radar's experiment in slow living as a difficult challenge where there was a constant negotiation of the respective pleasures of sustainable living and modern consumer culture. *Off the Radar*'s appealing ambivalence towards sustainability is manifested in the comedic persona of the programme host who is presented in the title sequence as a naïve urban subject – literally sipping a latte – who is whisked away from the city and ends up looking bemused while holding a chicken and a pitchfork. Unlike the established infrastructure of River Cottage, *Off the Radar* begins with the host simply pitching a tent in the middle of the paddock before scavenging among rusted remains in a farm shed and he maintains a relatively spartan existence throughout the series. In the opening episode Te Radar invokes a Gill-like perspective when he discloses that his previous attempts to grow food only resulted in a lot of cherry tomatoes: 'And cherry tomatoes cannot a man sustain,' he quips. Despite his initial confession that he 'has never really been sustainable', however, Te Radar's early comic attempts to establish himself on the land are balanced by the revelation that he grew up on a dairy farm and his subsequent display of some practical skills (such as an aptitude with a rifle, shooting wild turkeys on his property). Despite the presenter's residual skills (not unrepresentative in a country which has historically been so closely linked with and reliant on agriculture), *Off the Radar* nevertheless represents the sheer difficulty, even at times the absurdity, of sustainable consumption co-existing with its pleasures and rewards in a way that eschews easy solutions to the dilemmas of late-modern consumption. Posed as an experiment, sustainability is depicted as desirable and in some sense attainable but never as a fully-achieved goal.

In both *River Cottage* and *Off the Radar*, sustainable consumption is closely tied to temporality: the length of the working day, the passing of the seasons, and the lifecycle of plants and animals determine not only the activities but the duration of labour and the levels of attention or physical vigour required by the tasks at hand. The temporality of both leisure and labour is recalibrated by the adoption of sustainable consumption: in both programmes, social events connected to harvest or hunting are featured, and seasonal changes of weather and hours of daylight influence the way time is spent when work is over. From the longeurs of fishing to the opportunistic impulse of scavenging by the roadside, the lifestyle of sustainable consumption depicted in these programmes requires an alternative approach to time from the more routinized and instrumentalized schedules of daily life, or the speed and instantaneity associated with urban modernity. When Te Radar is packing his jeep before he departs from the city, one object he decides he must have in his new lifestyle is his 'sitting chair', declaring: 'I reckon while I'm waiting for things to grow there's going to be a lot of time for sitting.' What may seem like the utopian promise of extended leisure represented by the 'sitting chair' in fact represents some of the paradoxes of sustainable living whereby time sovereignty – often cited as the holy grail of modern subjects – is replaced by a deference to the temporalities of food production. 'Sitting', as a form of waiting, is not the same as doing nothing but implies a relinquishing both of the kind of control to which the autonomous subject might aspire and the valuing of speed as the most efficient way of achieving desired goals.

In place of the positive values accorded to speed and autonomy, these programmes emphasize physical agency through the tangibility and embodiment of work. As Te Radar puts it: 'I love getting up early in the morning, having that whole day stretching in front of you, and what I really love is that sense of achievement when you can look back at the end of the day and you've done something that you can actually see.' Similarly, Fearnley-Whittingstall reminds us: 'Most of us have forgotten what seasonality looks, smells and tastes like.' The materiality of work accomplished, or food produced, is closely associated with a heightened awareness of sensory pleasure. The pleasures associated with sustainable living, that is, extend from the multi-sensory stimulation involved in cooking – Fearnley-Whittingstall enthuses that 'for me, one of the joys of cooking is the different sensations on your fingertips, as you handle different ingredients' – through to the hard labour of farm work, such as building fences, or the finer motor skills of culinary or gardening expertise. In both cases, there is a sense of time as an embodied experience – it can be measured by the visual and physical evidence of the day's work (the field furrowed, the fence built) or by the taste of the newly ripe and harvested produce ('the taste of a strawberry warm from the sun means summer').

Of course, such programmes generally provide favourable representations of sustainable consumption but they also portray consumption as a multi-faceted sensory experience, both pleasurable and otherwise, in ways which draw attention to the disparities between the uniformity and homogeneity often associated with modern industrialized food production and the vagaries of sustainable production. The depiction of animal butchery, for instance, is followed by ambivalent responses to the consumption of cooked offal, a process perhaps sensationalized further on *River Cottage Autumn* where the butcher's apprentice happens to be a vegetarian. Modern habits of food consumption are also, however, represented as a form of sensory deprivation or a diminution of sensory experience as when, during an episode of *River Cottage Spring*, a teenage girl who lives on junk food and confesses to never eating vegetables, dry retches after eating a nasturtium leaf.

While there is a plenitude of different sensory pleasures that are displayed in these programmes, the focus on seasonality also promotes the idea of deferred gratification – the pleasures of eating asparagus, for example, are aligned with, if not enhanced by, an appreciation of its limited seasonal availability. In stark contrast to the '24/7' culture of contemporary consumption and uniform production, sustainable consumption in *River Cottage Autumn* and *Off the Radar* insists on the indissoluble connection between time and consumption which requires the agency of the subject, whether as consumer or producer. The rigours or deprivations of sustainable living co-exist with its pleasures and opportunities, as when a sleep-deprived Fearnley-Whittingstall complains about monitoring his pregnant ewes throughout the early hours of the morning during lambing season. As the programme hosts are shown responding to the vagaries of rural and seasonal life, that is, they not only represent the producer but also model an alternative approach to consumption linked to sustainability. An active consumer is shown to be the *sine qua non* of sustainable consumption: the ability to improvise, to adapt to the availability or absence of particular products, and to acquire new skills to maximize the use of available resources, distinguish this kind of consumer from both the implied passive consumer at the mercy of dominant modes of consumption and the connoisseur whose knowledge is solely intellectual and detached from the spaces and practices of production.

In these programmes, the sustainable consumer also differs from mainstream consumers by the emphasis on communities of production and consumption and the sharing of resources (both intellectual and material). Perhaps unlike much of the focus on contemporary forms of ethical consumption, which often posit an individualized consuming subject, consumption in these programmes is very much grounded in contexts of social relations and communities. In both of the television series discussed here, the individual 'stars' of the programmes quickly realize that they will be heavily reliant on the support of the local community in their quest for a more sustainable existence. Te Radar states in the final episode: 'there's no self in self-sustainability. Well, there is, but it stands for selflessness because what I've learnt is that you can't be sustainable without a community.' Neighbours and locals in both programmes provide skills, information and manual labour, they contribute plants, animals and produce, as well as conviviality and moral support. In both programmes thanks for such community support occurs in the regular representation of convivial, celebratory meals. *River Cottage Autumn* also depicts a range of 'taste communities', where practices of consumption are indissolubly linked to specific contexts and a commitment to ethical consumption and environmental sustainability. Such 'taste communities' vary widely in the profile of their participants and their modes of operating, from 'fringe' practices and lifestyles to integrated involvement in local government. Examples shown include a community working to eradicate an introduced American crayfish from the rivers in their region, an organization working with their local council to transform public green space into edible gardens freely available to the community, and a group involved in scrumping wild apple trees, with the produce used not only to make cider for the group but to supply free fruit to kindergartens.

Against the myth of the autonomous individual and the sovereign consumer, these programmes represent dependence – rather than *in*dependence – as a desirable social quality in the sense that mutual dependence within networks of social relations are shown both to enhance productivity and knowledge and to provide a source of emotional sustenance in trying conditions. Whereas Gill provocatively contends that 'Self-sufficiency is not an admirable goal, it's small-minded, selfish, mean, mistrustful and ultimately fascist. It ends up with people waving shotguns at strangers over their garden gates', it is often the permeability of fences that is apparent in these programmes. More soberingly, the programmes assert that sustainability is not achievable as an individualistic enterprise but requires a collective engagement to be viable as a mode of consumption.

As we have discussed previously (Parkins and Craig 2006: 82), the idea of 'community' sits oddly in contemporary urban and global contexts and the reactionary ideal of community that denies difference between subjects has rightly been critiqued (for example, Young 1990; Massey 2004; DuPuis and Goodman 2005). In media representations, the pleasures associated with representations of 'community life' are clearly enhanced by their placement in rural settings and the countryside often figures as the privileged site where the practices of sustainable consumption, and the temporalities they require, are picturesquely represented. The slowness associated with sustainable consumption may be more easily attained in rural contexts where an awareness of the specificity of place and a material relationship to an environment and a community may be more obvious, and is certainly more appealingly visualized in such locations. While the portrayals of community in both programmes are uniformly positive, however, there is also sometimes a 'self-reflexivity' to such representations, particularly in *Off the Radar*, that undercuts any sense of a mythical ideal of community. In *Off the Radar* talk about the importance of contemporary community is ironically set against black-and-white documentary footage of a small town dance which deliberately presents the provincialism of such a community as a source of amusement to viewers and in the final episode members of the rural community near Te Radar's farm are shown watching footage of themselves in earlier episodes, to their great amusement.

The knowingness with which *Off the Radar* presents 'community' as always a representation or a construction co-exists with its explicit valuing of social connectedness as an ethical value in a way that undercuts the potential simplification to which such programmes could easily succumb. The Bristol neighbourhood in *River Cottage Autumn* is similarly not represented as a homogeneous, idealized collective but comprises members who bring widely divergent levels of emotional investment, expenditure of labour, and levels of expertise to the allotment project. Even within families, the levels of response and engagement fluctuate between members of a couple, and between parents and their children, demonstrating the complexities of achieving an alternative approach to growing and eating food when even those who have assented to such a project differ so markedly in the degree and duration of their commitment. Regardless of how one might evaluate the representations of community in these programmes, they nonetheless demonstrate that in forms of slow living consumption is not 'extracted' or divorced from processes of production and the social contexts in which such consumption occurs.

Conclusion

Programmes that feature and advocate forms of sustainable consumption – which include, for example, *Jamie Oliver's Ministry of Food* and *Jamie Oliver at Home* in addition to the programmes discussed here – have provoked much public debate over and above Gill's diatribe and are open to a range of possible evaluations. Such programmes can be critiqued as examples of the neoliberal shift of responsibility for environmental and social problems away from governments and on to individuals, although the recent trend in Oliver and Fearnley-Whittingstall's series to engage communities, corporations and governments at every level in issues of food ethics does begin to challenge such assertions. Equally, the political and cultural effects of such programmes are often premised upon a subject who has the financial means and the time to engage in forms of sustainable consumption, despite both Fearnley-Whittingstall and Oliver explicitly acknowledging issues of class and wealth in their representations of producers and consumers. The affordability of sustainability remains a significant issue, however, even as Fearnley-Whittingstall has sought to counter these kinds of charges by stating 'you can't budget your way out of the ethics' and declaring that the contexts of such debates need to shift focus to fair compensation for farmers (Richards 2008).

We have sought here to investigate the representations of time – its different manifestations as well as the pleasures and activities associated with different uses of time – and the intrinsic significance of temporality to forms of sustainable consumption in the popular television programmes *River Cottage Autumn* and *Off the Radar*. From a cultural studies perspective, we believe that the popularity of such programmes warrants attention for the way they present *experiments* in slow living as bound up with questions of how we use and value time in everyday life. Te Radar leaves his paddocks at the end of the series to return to the city but the ethical impetus of his project is not left behind. Instead, the knowledge he has gained about sustainability in a rural setting is posed as the necessary foundation for a continuing interrogation of his urban everyday life. In this way, *Off the Radar* explicitly connects the host's experience with that of his implied audience and suggests a mutual and ongoing investment in sustainable consumption. The provisional nature of this engagement with sustainable consumption is less pronounced than with Fearnley-Whittingstall's substantial farm and commercial infrastructure although this is balanced by the presentation of the Bristol smallholding and the challenges the local residents encounter in its establishment and maintenance.

There is a pedagogy to such programmes but they do not impose upon viewers a choice of *either* modern consumer subjectivity *or* an alternative form of sustainable living (the kind of binary that is always invoked in rhetoric – such as Gill's – that seeks to dismiss the progressive potential of forms of sustainable consumption as 'greener-than-thou' sanctimony). Rather, the programmes provide representations of the kinds of negotiations involved in the temporal exigencies of modern living for subjects who would attempt to put into practice a form of 'ethical glocalism' (Tomlinson 1999) in their consumption practices. In this sense, what some have seen as the apparently oxymoronic status of 'ethical consumerism' (Paterson 2006: 225) should be understood less in terms of competing ideological standpoints – that yield either celebratory, utopian visions or world-weary and cynical dismissals – and more as a particular distillation of the dilemmatic status of contemporary living. The experiments in sustainable living that are offered in the programmes discussed here are examples of a 'search for a new vocabulary of virtue' (Rutherford 2000: 66) that cannot be dismissed as a mere lifestyle aesthetic. Instead, such experiments represent the performance and playing out of the kinds of ethical dilemmas that inevitably shape the work, leisure and relationships of everyday life in late-modern consumer culture.

Bibliography

Cross, G. (1993) *Time and Money: The Making of Consumer Culture*, London: Routledge.

DuPuis, E.M. and Goodman, D. (2005) 'Should we go "home" to eat?: toward a reflexive politics of localism', *Journal of Rural Studies*, 21: 359–71.

Ehrenfeld, J.R. (2008) *Sustainability by Design*, New Haven, CT: Yale University Press.

Gill, A.A. (2008) 'The guilt-inducing *River Cottage Autumn*', *Times Online*. Online. Available HTTP: http://entertainment.timesonline.co.uk/tol/arts_and_entertainment/tv_and_radio/article5002168.ece (accessed 13 May 2009).

Gleick, J. (1999), *Faster: The Acceleration of Just About Everything*, New York: Pantheon Books.

Halberstam, J. (2005) *In a Queer Time and Place: Transgender Bodies, Subcultural Lives*, New York: New York University Press.

Massey, D. (2004) 'Geographies of responsibility', *Geografiska Annaler*, 86B(1): 5–18.

May, J. and Thrift, N. (2001) *Timespace: Geographies of Temporality*, New York: Routledge.

Parkins, W. and Craig, G. (2006) *Slow Living*, Oxford: Berg.

—— (2009) 'Culture and the politics of alternative food networks', *Food, Culture & Society*, 12(1): 77–103.

Paterson, M. (2006) *Consumption and Everyday Life*, London: Routledge.

Richards, S. (2008) 'River Cottage Spring', *Telegraph.co.uk*. Online. Available HTTP: www.telegraph.co.uk/culture/tvandradio/3673645/River-Cottage-Spring.html (accessed 28 May 2009).

Rutherford, J. (ed.) (2000) *The Art of Life: On Living, Loving and Dying*, London: Lawrence and Wishart.

Tomlinson, J. (1999) *Globalization and Culture*, Cambridge: Polity.

Young, I.M. (1990), 'The ideal of community and the politics of difference', in L. J. Nicholson (ed.) *Feminism/Postmodernism*, New York: Routledge.

14 Ethical consumption begins at home

Green renovations, eco-homes and sustainable home improvement

Fiona Allon

Introduction: climate change is coming home

In *Climate Change Begins at Home: Life on the Two-way Street of Global Warming*, climate change scientist and popular science author, Dave Reay, presents a series of guidelines for helping average, developed-world families reduce their greenhouse gas emissions. Calling on ordinary, middle class consumers to 'do their bit', the book aims to help households reflect upon their levels of energy consumption and lower contributions to climate change. Consistent with the book's focus on individual initiative, Reay describes his own journey of cutting global greenhouse emissions:

> The politicians may have been dithering, but I was going to cut my own emissions – to do my bit . . . Along the way our big car was swapped for a Smart car, low-energy bulbs spread through the house, and the mail-order composting worms arrived (a fun evening in, I can tell you).
>
> (Reay 2006: xvi)

With chapters ranging from 'The Power of One' to 'Home Start', it is clear that Reay's agenda is firmly centred on ideas of *self-help*, *individual responsibility* and *empowerment* as the best strategy for tackling environmental problems. Understandably, given this emphasis on personal autonomy and self-reliance, the book also suggests that the privatized sphere of the home is the most appropriate arena for action: 'The challenge that we now face is that, like it or not, climate change is coming home – and we have to act before the house gets washed away by the oncoming tsunami' (Reay 2006: xiv).

Many of Reay's interventions concern the environmental consequences of everyday practices such as overfilling kettles, leaving taps running, and not turning off appliances and lights. However, he also advocates changes to the very shape, form and design of the house itself, focusing in particular on the kinds of renovations and improvements that can be adopted 'to make our home life more climate-friendly'; as Reay forcefully reminds his readers, 'an extension [rather than a new house] wins hands down climate-wise' (Reay 2006: 66).

Reay's book is one of the many guides to 'greener' homes that have appeared in large numbers in recent years.[1] A thriving segment of the book publishing industry – and print media more broadly – green home renovations is now a market of considerable size and sales volumes. The 'green revolution', however, has been *mediatized* across an exceptionally wide range of information media, materializing and taking shape within the modes of address and dissemination formats currently in favour: info-tainment, expert advice and instruction, self-help and DIY. Unsurprisingly, then, green home renovation is also a prominent topic on lifestyle television. Recently incorporating a varied range of (eclectically defined) 'green' issues, lifestyle television has begun covering the *greening* of everything from cars and houses to celebrities and reality TV shows (see Lewis 2008). However, a specific focus on green consumption within the home in particular has also developed, with programmes providing educational advice on how to achieve more environmentally sensitive lifestyle habits and consumption patterns, especially through energy-efficient home improvements. The *eco-makeover*, for example, has become one of the most popular formats of lifestyle television programming.

Building upon the success of the makeover television show format during the 'makeover takeover' (Moseley 2000) of the late 1990s and early 2000s, the eco-makeover has again proved to be enormously popular worldwide. The *EcoZone Project*, a television series featuring the green makeover of the homes of a number of high-profile celebrities, screened in the US in 2007. *Code Green Canada*, a six-part television series that offered 'homeowners across Canada invaluable information on how to reduce energy consumption in their own homes' (www.cbc.ca/codegreen/), proved such a hit it aired over two seasons. Called a 'Home Renovation Challenge', the series showed contestants competing to reduce their greenhouse emissions by making their homes more energy efficient. In Australia, there has been a flurry of environment-focused lifestyle shows aimed at educating homeowners on how to reduce energy consumption, including *Carbon Cops* and *Eco House Challenge*. Meanwhile, themes of sustainable housing have also appeared in more mainstream 'property television' such as in *Grand Designs*, the highly successful British TV series that is also broadcast in Australia, New Zealand, the Netherlands and Germany. There are countless websites devoted to sustainable homes, eco homes, zero-carbon houses and zero-energy building, as well as online DIY clubs and forums discussing the array of green home improvement and retrofitting techniques.[2]

The rise of 'lifestyle cultures' such as DIY home renovation has undoubtedly contributed to the increasing significance of the home – culturally, symbolically, financially, and now, environmentally. The aspirational culture of home ownership has also become a salient site for new formations of identity and belonging linked to consumption and economic enterprise (Allon 2008; McElroy 2008; Smith 2008). This spotlight on the home is also part of much wider shifts in discourses on the environment, society and government. Worldwide, the growing recognition of the scale of the environmental crisis and global climate change has seen a shift of focus of public discourses from 'big' questions of production and supply to finding ways of reducing energy consumption through strategies of domestic *demand management*. The reinvention of government and the emergence of new strategies of 'governing at a distance' have also intersected with the privatization of services and energy utilities, and ongoing critiques of the supposed inefficiency of the public sector and cumbersome state bureaucracies. This has led to a reconfiguration of the relationships between domestic 'end-user' households and large, bureaucratic and centralized authorities – once considered the most rational entity for managing essential resources and services like electricity and water – and a greater reliance on neoliberal market principles and pricing mechanisms.

Alongside these shifts has been the emergence of a political climate placing greater emphasis on personal responsibility and consumer choice, a political rationality that values, and even demands, self-enterprise and individual initiative. Nikolas Rose, for example, suggests that contemporary liberal regimes of rule promote individual and national well-being 'through the entrepreneurship of autonomous actors – individuals and families, firms and corporations' (1999: 139). These broader shifts in discourses of governance find a common point of intersection in the private space of the home: the home, after all, is precisely where practices of self-reliance and self-sufficiency (socially, economically and environmentally) can be most effectively developed, demonstrated, and actively encouraged.

This intensified focus on the home and domestic-based consumption has been interpreted as the consolidation of a privatized politics that sees a disturbing withdrawal into private life and a retreat and disengagement from public and civic responsibility. The hegemony of home life in recent decades has therefore come to represent the very negation of ethical commitment, political activity and progressive citizenship (see Connolly and Prothero 2008). However, what I'd like to suggest here is that many contemporary practices of consumption concerned with the environmental sustainability of the home unsettle many of the assumptions underpinning these popular theories of privatization and individualization (Giddens 1991; Putnam 2000). I'd also like to question the separations between home and citizenship, and between consumption and public-minded or civic responsibility, that such theories assume, providing evidence for some of the new links between home, self and ethical living that are unfolding in the present and that will need to be addressed in greater detail in the future. In essence, I'd like to suggest that practices of consumption concerned explicitly with reconfiguring everyday life and the home to make it less environmentally damaging, such as green home renovations, have become one of the primary arenas in which questions of ethical conduct and *responsibilized* citizenship are being worked out today. In this sense, both the home and the citizen become co-actors in an ethical project of home/self improvement designed to create new modes of private autonomy *and* public connection.

Branding sustainability

The household today is very much a meeting place for a range of new expectations about individual and collective behaviour across a number of scales, from the private-domestic to the environmental-global. These include the micropolitics of the household and the minutiae of everyday behaviours and practices (the moral imperative to recycle), government programmes to encourage green living (rebates for Energy Efficient Homes and Green Renovation Packs, for example), and injunctions to value and protect 'the environment' more generally (Macnaghten 2003). This reinforces the importance of addressing the 'little tactics of habitat' as much as the 'grand strategies of geopolitics' (Foucault 1980: 149) when it comes to attempting to understand the position of the home in the contemporary world. As a point of intersection for the complex negotiation of personal interactions and institutional demands, the home becomes a hybrid of materials, markets, moralities and meanings. The most interesting question therefore is 'what makes this hybrid "work" – financially, politically, socially, and domestically' (Smith 2008: 2).

'Sustainability', 'passive design', 'carbon neutral', 'embodied energy', 'photo-voltaics', 'smart meters', 'renewables' – this battery of technical terms is rapidly becoming part of ordinary language with the concerted push to put environmental issues on everyday social and political agendas. For the homeowner embarking on a green renovation they are merely one small part of the arsenal of knowledges, technologies, technical systems and know-how to be encountered in the process of making a house more environmentally friendly. Governmental initiatives to improve the environmental performance of residential housing have undoubtedly contributed to the increased public interest in issues of green living. 'Green loans' and other subsidies for home improvements designed to improve the energy and water efficiency of housing have also put ideas of sustainability on the domestic radars of households, if not to an uptake of actual green products and services.[3]

One of the biggest influences on the current trend for all things green, from fashion (green is the new black) to socially and environmentally responsible investment, is the idea that 'sustainability' has gone mainstream and has 'rapidly become the buzzword on everyone's lips' (Parr 2009: 15). A brief perusal of consumer culture confirms the pervasive commercial interests at stake. One newspaper article, 'Home, sweet (green) home', describes it this way: 'Clever design means we don't have to give up creature comforts to live more sustainably, and developers are getting in on the act' (Elliott 2007: 12). A recent update on home interior design trends confirms the financial force behind the fashion for eco living: 'along with the environmental awareness comes a new eco-consciousness. When design king Ralph Lauren announces he is going green, even Mother Earth takes notice' (Groer 2007: 22). The business incentives behind the demand for environmentally friendly housing are especially significant, as one property developer clearly states: 'It is fair to say that the market is far more savvy than ever before. Everyone is looking to reduce their footprint' (cited in Elliott 2007: 12).

For cultural theorist Adrian Parr, this new strain of eco-branding is simply part of the 'hijacking' of sustainability culture by the logic of late capitalism. The marriage of commercial convenience between environmentalism and consumerism has provided the corporate world with a bounty of new opportunities and images to position an expanded range of goods and services within a competitive global market. In these terms sustainability culture's call to 'make a difference' becomes the valued difference upon which the niche marketing of a profit-maximizing corporate capitalism both depends and thrives. Sustainability's commodification produces a mass market of vacuous eco-chic consumers making superficial gestures towards environmentalism but more seriously concerned with branding themselves with a badge of green distinction.

Parr is certainly not alone in pointing out the seemingly endless strategies of cooption involved in 'greenwashing'; similar arguments are to be found in an extensive body of critical work questioning whether the prism of 'consumer choice' is the best way of responding to globally interconnected, widespread, and collectively shared environmental crises (Slater 1997). Sustained critiques have likewise been made of the figure of the individual consumer that tends to dominate much environmental and social policy. 'Green' ways of life, for example, succeed in encouraging consumers to be mindful of environmental concerns and, in a sense, to make 'the environment' their preferred brand when choosing products and consuming resources. However, as Elizabeth Shove argues, this approach also 'reinforces a model of isolated individuals whose variously green identities are expressed through a precisely calibrated and increasingly extensive palate of green consumer choice' (Shove 2003: 7). It does very little to challenge the assumptions about standards of living that govern practices of consumption in the first instance. By leaving aside the question of how needs and wants come to be socially and culturally constructed at any given time, and how they then go on to shape demand and drive expectations and conventions of use, collective norms and current practices are left pretty much in place and unchecked. Fitting out an eco-designed house with a battery of solar panels and state-of-the-art '5-Star Standard' energy efficiency rated domestic appliances, for example, may make a considerable lifestyle statement, but it will have relatively little environmental consequence if standardized and ingrained practices of use do not also change accordingly.

This seems to suggest that much green consumer culture just succeeds in producing 'passive landscapes of consumption' rather than 'active and affective landscapes conducive to sustainable ways of life' (Parr 2009: 15). Yet posing the terms of the debate as a simplistic choice between 'passive landscapes of consumption' or 'active and sustainable ways of life' somewhat misses the point. The recent appearance of the figure of the 'consumer-citizen', for example, challenges the assumptions attached to this kind of dialectic: the consumer as necessarily self-interested and privately egoistic, in contrast to the active, civic-minded, reflexive citizen (Bennett 1998; Micheletti 2003; Clarke 2007; Soper 2007).

Despite these shifts, home life still generally continues to be seen as a space dominated by a logic of privatized consumption. Iris Marion Young, for instance, views the home as by and large shaped by a 'consumer-driven desire of civic privatism' that inevitably leads to a litany of consumer sins, but most worrisome of all – the paralysing pall of political quietism:

> House and home occupy central places in this consumer consciousness as
> the core of personal property and a specific commodity-based identity
> . . . The commodified concept of home ties identity to a withdrawal from
> the public world . . . Freedom consists in release from work and public
> responsibility in activities of leisure, pleasure, and consumption.
>
> (Young 1997: 142)

Young correctly identifies that in this age of consumer capitalism the resources
that can be devoted to the home have never been greater. Over recent decades the
house has certainly become the place of an intensified kind of aspirationalism,
labour and investment: from the 'sweat equity' involved in home renovations
to the house itself as a sign of status and prosperity in which everything – life
savings, identity, sense of self – is invested (Allon 2008).

In modern Western societies it seems that the house owes its continuing
cultural and emotional power precisely to this 'capacity to separate itself
ideologically from the public spaces of everyday life' (Moran 2004: 608). In this
sense, home and citizenship appear as oppositional domains of activity and action,
understood through a much wider field of oppositional relationships between
public and private, universal and particular, republican and domestic, production
and consumption, and ultimately, between male and female. This is clearly
revealed in the origins and etymology of the term 'citizenship': as Toby Miller
points out, *Citadin*, *citoyen*, civic, civil, citizen – all were related to notions of
a refined public civilization intimately connected to the public spaces of the city
(Miller 1983: 19).

Yet home and home ownership in particular have long existed as powerful
forces for individual and collective identity formation and self-definition, playing
a crucial role in constructions of citizenship and national identity in particular.
Owning a home is an experience strongly linked to morality, character and
identity, and is widely regarded as a concrete illustration of an individual's
commitment to citizenship, the community, and to the nation. Green home
renovations (an activity usually undertaken only by owner-occupiers) continue
this tradition of home and home-making as ethical, democratic, political
engagement – albeit under very different modes of governance and governmentality. The home after all is not only the primary place of consumption; it is
also the space where most of us live and negotiate belonging and citizenship. The
techniques of enterprising, ethical and responsible consumption that ecological
and sustainable home improvements represent today suggest a *reinvention* of
citizenship and patriotic duty more than its retreat and withdrawal.

Eco-homes and ethical selves

If eco-homes and sustainable houses continue the tradition of responsible
homeowning citizenship championed most strongly by liberal government in the
twentieth century, they do so within the very different political conditions and
circumstances of the twenty-first century. Since the 1980s most Anglo-American

countries have undergone comprehensive processes of socio-economic restructuring. One of the results has been a widespread transformation of the relationships between the state, the economy and the individual, characterized by a marked transition towards principles of economic privatization and individual self-governance. Along the way, the meanings of home and home ownership have subtly changed, and the relationships between autonomy, freedom and security have been redrawn and reconfigured.

In addition to previous imaginings of home that drew a direct line of connection between owner-occupation and citizenship, foregrounding it as both a cultural norm that led to national integration and community cohesion, newer meanings of the home hinge on the calculative performances of the enterprising and responsible individual. Inspired by Michel Foucault's work of governmentality and the 'care of the self', a number of studies have outlined how the 'ethicalization of existence' (Rose 1989: 263–64) is especially central to contemporary forms of self-governance, positioning the individual as active in making choices to attain self-realization and a self-directed ethical life, and as personally responsible for managing and asserting control over any risks that may be encountered (Barry *et al.* 1996; Dean 1999; Ouellette and Hay 2008). This is an ethics understood not so much as obedience to a morality and 'the inculcation of externally validated morals and obligations' but rather as 'the practices, techniques and styles of self-reflection and self-management necessary for the active construction of an ethical life' (Rose 1999: 191).

The green home, in this sense, functions as one among many personal projects of self-actualization which the individual uses to fashion ethical existence and identity. From this perspective, 'green consumption' becomes the matrix as it were of a large number of social relations and forms of activity in which ethical conduct can be practised. Similarly, eco-homes can be seen as a cultural technology of self that integrates ethics (conduct and behaviour) with self-government in order to develop a capacity for autonomy and independence. A notion of self-reliance has become pivotal to the political rationalities of liberal government, summed up as both a code for responsible living and the means by which to achieve an autonomous, self-sufficient and secure life. In interviews I conducted with homeowners undertaking green renovations or sustainable building practices, ideas of self-reliance and self-sufficiency appeared again and again. As one homeowner states:

> Well, we were interested in sustainable home design . . . [but] my particular motivation was that I wanted to get away out of the city somewhere we could be a bit more self-reliant and ultimately learn to grow some of our own food and look after ourselves a bit instead of having to depend on specialists for everything . . . [And] personally one of the strongest motivations was the feeling that our lives are going to change whether we want it or not and it is far better to take control and make them change in a good way than to slide into chaos . . . I am the one in our immediate family that has got the power to do anything about this. If we've got a few acres, we've got a sustainable

house that doesn't cost too much to run, keeps us warm and comfortable and healthy, if times did ever get tough we should be able to look after ourselves much better than in a city house. That was a big part of my motivation, to be able to look after ourselves if times do become tough. The other side of it is the feeling that for ethical reasons we've got to live better and stop taking more than our fair share . . . Also we are all in this together, the world is a closed system, if we don't do something about it we are going to trash the world.

The ethics of taking care of oneself that underpins the government of the self by the self stresses the importance of 'managing one's own existence' and 'preparing oneself for events that are going to occur' (Foucault 1990: 28). For this interviewee, the prospect of 'peak oil', as well as perhaps the imminent onset of environmental catastrophe, required above all a greater level of independence and autonomy. As a consequence, she had begun a perma-culture course and joined the Transition Movement:

basically it is a plan for changing lifestyle so that you are less dependent on energy from oil. It is more localisation, more local production of food, more re-skilling of people so that they know how to do things to look after themselves instead of having to get a tradie or some kind of specialist in for every little thing. A lot of it is to do with local food supplies but also being able to supply housing, suitable transport, all the things you need to live.

As this statement shows, there is a strong sense that the individual must be equipped to be able to respond to future environmental catastrophes, and that security, autonomy, and at least some degree of self-sufficiency is a way of both preparing for but also hopefully avoiding the prospect of a grim Hobbesian state of nature where all are against all:

The idea is the oil is going to run out, we don't know how fast but it is going to run out and maybe faster than we think, but the idea is not to sort of hunker down and just tough it out as best you can but to prepare for it ahead of time and to create a good lifestyle so that you are not going from this wonderful high life that you'll regret for the rest of your life to something very basic, more that you are creating a different kind of lifestyle where things are really good for you. You are well fed, you've got interesting things to eat, you've got plenty to eat, a comfortable home, you've got a good sense of community, you are able to take care of all your basic needs and enjoy life . . . [We need to build] a bridge to a future that is going to be pretty different from the way we live today. We don't want to move into a state of chaos or a state of deprived living, it is much more creative I think to make a really good lifestyle out of living with less and doing really good things with it.

While this may seem like an extreme point of view, other homeowners also invoked dystopian Hobbesian images:

> It's going to be a nasty future. We still are a little bit hopeful of possible change but really we agree, it is not going to be a nice future. We don't want to look back, in twenty years time when the future is not as nice as it is now, we don't want to look back and say, 'We should have done this and should have done that,' we want to feel proud that we did what we could and lived the best way we could and weren't contributing to environmental issues and doing our very best.

This interviewee described the sense of impending environmental catastrophe as one of the biggest motivations for people's interest in green home improvements and sustainable living more generally:

> They can see the world falling apart around them, global warming and natural systems failing, excessive consumption leading to rises in petrol and whatever else is happening in our society. It is all kind of coming all at once now and people can see it, they don't particularly want to pay to fix it but they'd like to be able to do something . . . Green living is now more accept-able because people can see how bad things are getting even though there are sceptics out there. Basically people think there is something wrong and they want to be able to do something about it . . . I think this has sunk in too for a lot of people, that we are living off the fat of the earth and it can't be sustained.

For these interviewees, the desire to live sustainably was inseparable in fact from the desire to live ethically:

> [In our eco-home] we're not self-sufficient, we'll never be self-sufficient, but we're more sustainable, making a lighter footprint overall . . . I suppose it is basically keeping our footprint as low as possible. The world is over-populated and we want to consume as little as possible to walk as lightly as we can . . . Not that we live uncomfortably though, we are still very comfortable. People live even more comfortably than we do on less than we have. You don't need huge houses and lots of possessions to be happy.

When viewed through the lens of self-governance, it is clear the way in which these homeowners are positioning themselves within an ethical discourse of self-realization. Importantly, however, both home-life and ethical conduct are conceived here *relationally* as connections between humans, material objects, technical systems, the environment, and the dwelling in which they all come together. The remodelling of the home and the incorporation of energy-saving devices such as solar panels, dual-flush toilets, reduced flow showerheads, and grey-water systems is part of a concerted effort to make explicit an ethical engagement with environmental sustainability and a commitment to changing ordinary habits, routines and ways of living. The intimate entanglements between technologies, energy resources and everyday relations, that govern the use of a whole range of banal material things and objects, from showerheads and light bulbs to water meters and electricity bills, are at the same time brought to the surface, demystified and de-routinized (see Marres 2009):

> It is obvious to us if we've got solar panels on the roof [and] the monitor there is telling us we are generating power and our bill is actually less, you don't actually need to know how much less every day. [But] the electricity bill came yesterday and we had quite a good pore over it, what did this mean, what did we get for that, was it less than last time, that sort of thing . . . Whatever we produce now, in the day, if we boil a jug the panel goes into boiling the jug, if the fridge comes on when you are doing a load of washing, it powers that first. Then it goes out to the grid and we get paid for that and we just have a bit of a laugh but at least we've sold something.

Green homes and responsible citizens

The figure of the self-empowered citizen, taking on responsibility where government is either floundering or failing, appears prominently in much of the popular literature on green home improvements and retrofitting. In Michael Mobbs' *Sustainable House: Living for Our Future*, green home improvements are pitched to the citizen in precisely these terms:

> Perhaps the big improvements to our environment will happen when existing houses are rebuilt to use energy, water and waste water in self-sustaining ways, but it is possible when adding or altering an existing house for homeowners and builders to achieve sustainable housing by themselves independently of governments. Our Sustainable House illustrates this and we hope that this project can help empower homeowners to take control of their own pollution and consumption of water and energy.
>
> (Mobbs 1998: 15)

The message here is that the individual must develop both an ethics of existence and a style of citizenship that is *independent of government* and appropriate for a post-welfare state world where the individual is now required to look after his or her own well-being and advancement. In this new regime of the actively responsible self, the individual takes on the responsibilities, and also the risks, previously managed by the state. Reinforcing this idea of personal responsibility, the implementation of sustainability policies in urban areas relies heavily on the practices of individuals and households in the contexts of decentralization and privatization, community learning and neighbourhood action (Nelson 2008). These transitions also dovetail neatly with increasing household interest in more diverse mixes of supply and demand side technologies for essential resources such as energy and water. Decentralized 'co-generation' systems, for example,

are increasingly feasible substitutes for traditional centralized electricity generation enabling households to sell power back to the national grid. Renewable
energy sources also tend to be dispersed, variable and diffuse in their market
frameworks, facilitating further socio-technical shifts in the balance of responsibilities between domestic users and supply systems. Nearly all of the green
homeowner-renovators who were interviewed for this research had installed water
harvesting and recycling systems and grid-interactive photovoltaic panels in an
effort to become more actively self-reliant in their energy consumption.

At a time when privatization, personal responsibility, and consumer choice are
promoted as the best ways to govern in liberal capitalist democracies, it is not
surprising that an ethics of enterprise and autonomy underpins the numerous
intersecting forces encouraging us to conduct and empower ourselves as self-
directed citizens within the home. This is clearly registered in the simultaneously
ethical and entrepreneurial motivations for green home renovations. Alongside
an ethic of self-sufficiency what is also striking about *Sustainable House* is the
explicitly entrepreneurial rationality that runs throughout the book, linking
the improvements of the house to its resale value and the expectations of potential
buyers:

> We made it clear that while we wanted better environmental results . . . we
> also wanted a house that looked the same as any other in the street and had
> the highest possible resale value . . . we had to make the house appealing to
> potential purchasers for its location, design and attractiveness.
>
> (Mobbs 1998: 19)

The financial consequences of the renovations were highly significant for Mobbs
– 'Yes, but can we sell the house if we do that?' – as were the future economic
rewards: 'we will no longer pay any electricity bills' (Mobbs 1998: 93). This
kind of entrepreneurial 'enterprise rationality' has often been closely associated
with the conceptions of self and citizenship invoked in neoliberal modes of
government. Green renovators also position their home improvements in these
terms, viewing them as an entrepreneurial exercise in investment that will yield
returns in a number of ways, from the financial benefits of self-sufficiency ('I can
sell electricity to the grid') to the steadily increasing home equity in their valuable
eco-house. This style of *eco-preneurialism* is now integrated within many
environmental issues, where it is used to demonstrate how enterprise and good
economic judgement can be linked to an ethical commitment to sustainability in
order to form a model of contemporary civic-minded conduct and behaviour on
business principles.[4]

While this may appear as yet another technical exercise in commodified
privatization, it must be remembered that all of the green homeowner-renovators
quoted in this chapter, including Mobbs, open their houses to the public in various
kinds of eco-homes tours. So alongside the rationality of private enterprise and
individual autonomy motivating sustainable home improvements, there is also
frequently an accompanying experience of 'living our private lives in public'

(Mobbs 1998: 19) that arises from the display of green homes, which itself stems from a deep-seated sense of public responsibility and the desire 'to give a good example'. The *responsibilization* of the self that green renovations represent gives rise to ethically complex, politically charged, and often very contradictory entanglements between the materiality of housing and the meanings of home. However, this should by no means be interpreted simply as a retreat from civic activity and political responsibilities – an ethics of withdrawal. The care of the self that Foucault examined did not necessarily represent a waning of political activity; rather, it was a matter of 'elaborating an ethics that enabled one to constitute oneself as an ethical subject with respect to these social, civic, and political activities, in the different forms they might take and at whatever distance one remained from them' (Foucault 1990: 94).

Conclusion: bringing it all back home

Increasingly, moral and political discourses summon up the simultaneously ethical *and* financial subjectivities of the green citizen-consumer, linking the initiative and enterprise that is now expected of a 'good' civic-minded and responsible individual with an ethics of self-improvement and care of the self. In this sense, green home improvements enable the environmentally concerned homeowner to respond to increasing governmental demands for environmentally sustainable practices of self-reliance and self-sufficiency while at the same time developing a style of living that achieves self-actualization and realization – a better self *and* a better house. As a project of combined home/self improvement, green renovations materialize, quite literally, a set of techniques and technologies that enable the homeowner to construct an ethical subjectivity and ecologically sensitive form of *dwelling*. The renovated house along the way becomes an interface between individual identity and global environmental considerations, part of a practice of ethical engagement that is personal and social, individual in focus but collective in orientation.

Notes

1 See, for example, Wilson, A. (2006) *Your Green Home: A Guide to Planning a Healthy, Environmentally Friendly New Home*, Mother Earth News Wiser Living Series; Wigley, D. (2005) *Making Your Home Sustainable: A Guide to Retrofitting*, Melbourne: Scribe.
2 See www.ecozone.tv/ and www.cbc.ca/codegreen/.
3 In 2008 the Australian government announced its 'Green Loans for Aussie Homes' scheme – low interest loans for green home improvements. Designed to 'set Australian households on a long term path to sustainability', the loans are specifically intended for the installation of solar, water and energy efficient products in owner-occupied homes. Participating homes receive a Green Renovation Pack and household sustainability assessment report that contains 'information on green home improvements, estimates of how much money could be saved by households implementing the ideas in the report and details of the benefits these changes will have for our environment'. Australian Labor Party (2008), 'Green loans for Aussie homes – media statement', 14 May. www.alp.org.au/media/0508/msenh140.php.

4   See, for example, Ivanko, J. and Kirivist, L. (2008) *ECOpreneuring*, British Columbia: New Society Publishers.

Bibliography

Allon, F. (2008) *Renovation Nation: Our Obsession with Home*, Sydney: New South.

Barry, A., Osborne, T. and Rose, N. (eds) (1996) *Foucault and Political Reason: Liberalism, Neoliberalism and Rationalities of Government*, Chicago, IL: University of Chicago Press.

Bennett, L. (1998) 'The uncivic culture: communication, identity, and the rise of lifestyle politics', *PS: Political Science and Politics*, 31: 740–61.

Clarke, J. (2007) 'Unsettled connections: citizens, consumers and the reform of public services', *Journal of Consumer Culture*, 7(2): 159–78.

Connolly, J. and Prothero, A. (2008) 'Green consumption', *Journal of Consumer Culture*, 8(1): 117–45.

Dean, M. (1999) *Governmentality: Power and Rule in Modern Society*, Thousand Oaks: Sage.

Elliott, S. (2007) 'Home, sweet (green) home', *Australian Financial Review*, Lifestyle Section: 12–13.

Foucault, M. (1980) 'The eye of power', in C. Gordon (ed.) *Power/Knowledge*, New York: Pantheon.

—— (1990) *The Care of the Self*, London: Penguin.

Giddens, A. (1991) *Modernity and Self Identity*, Cambridge: Polity Press.

Groer A. (2007) 'Eco living', *Sydney Morning Herald*, (Essential Home): 22–24.

McElroy, R. (2008) 'Property TV: the (re)making of home on national screens', *European Journal of Cultural Studies*, 11(1): 43–61.

Macnaghten, P. (2003) 'Embodying the environment in everyday life practices', *The Sociological Review*, 51(1): 63–84.

Marres, N. (2009) 'Testing powers of engagement: green living experiments, the ontological turn and the undoability of involvement', *European Journal of Social Theory*, 12(1): 117–33.

Micheletti, M. (2003) *Political Virtue and Shopping: Individuals, Consumerism, and Collective Action*, New York: Palgrave Macmillan.

Miller, T. (1983) *The Well-Tempered Self*, Baltimore, MD: The Johns Hopkins University Press.

Mobbs, M. (1998) *Sustainable House: Living for Our Future*, Marrickville, NSW: Choice.

Moran, J. (2004) 'Housing, memory and everyday life in contemporary Britain', *Cultural Studies*, 18(4): 607–27.

Moseley, R. (2000) 'Makeover takeover on British television', *Screen*, 41(3): 299–314.

Nelson, A. (ed.) (2008) *Steering Sustainability in an Urbanising World*, Abingdon, UK: Ashgate.

Ouellette, L. and Hay, J. (2008) *Better Living through Reality TV*, Malden, MA: Blackwell.

Parr, A. (2009) *Hijacking Sustainability*, Cambridge, MA and London: MIT Press.

Putnam, R. (2000) *Bowling Alone*, New York: Touchstone.

Reay, D. (2006) *Climate Change Begins at Home: Life on the Two-way Street of Global Warming*, New York: Macmillan.

Rose, N. (1989) *Governing the Soul: The Shaping of the Private Self*, London and New York: Routledge.

—— (1999) *Powers of Freedom: Reframing Political Thought*, Cambridge: Cambridge University Press.

Shove, E. (2003) *Comfort, Cleanliness and Convenience*, Oxford and New York: Berg.

Slater, D. (1997) *Consumer Culture and Modernity*, Cambridge: Polity Press.

Smith, S.J. (2008) 'Owner-occupation: at home with a hybrid of money and materials', *Environment and Planning A*, 40: 520–35.

Soper, K. (2007) 'Rethinking the "good life": The citizenship dimension of consumer disaffection with consumerism', *Journal of Consumer Culture*, 7(2): 205–29.

Wigley, D. (2005) *Making Your Home Sustainable: A Guide to Retrofitting*, Melbourne: Scribe.

Wilson, A. (2006) *Your Green Home: A Guide to Planning a Healthy, Environmentally Friendly New Home*, Gabriola Island, BC, Canada, Mother Earth News Wiser Living Series.

Young, I.M. (1997) *Intersecting Voices: Dilemmas of Gender, Political Philosophy, and Policy*, Princeton, NJ: Princeton University Press.

15 Cultivating citizen-subjects through collective praxis

Organized gardening projects in Australia and the Philippines

Kersty Hobson and Ann Hill

Introduction

> One cannot live on cookies alone . . . me now know that cookies is 'sometimes' food . . . me had crazy times in the '70s and '80s . . . me like the Robert Downey Junior of cookies.

This self-admonishing confession of the lovably infamous Cookie Monster aired in 2008 on the US-based Comedy Central's *Colbert Report*.[1] Cookie Monster – a key character on the American children's programme *Sesame Street* that in 2009 celebrated forty years of continuous programming – was being interviewed by Colbert about forsaking his eponymous gorging and wasting of high-fat and high-sugar biscuits in front of millions of children and their parents/guardian/ carers around the world. With a cheeky comparison to the actor Robert Downey Junior's well-documented drink and drugs addictions of the 1990s, Cookie Monster launched his own rehabilitation and reintegration into public life by advocating a more measured consumption of fruit and the designation of cookies as a 'sometimes food'.

While a seemingly popularist and trivial move, such shifts in discourse and practice by well-known entities can arguably be seen as part of a panoply of recent interventions, which aim to confront public and policy anxieties about rising obesity levels and junk food consumption among both adults and children. These concerns in turn intersect directly with worries over food security, as well as the loss of knowledge, skills and spaces of self and collective provisioning. Indeed, in the US, while Cookie Monster was transforming his *raison d'être*, the recently installed First Lady, Michelle Obama, was marking out her own public persona, which included an appearance on *Sesame Street* on the subject of healthy eating and transforming the White House lawns into a vegetable garden. This latter project took place with the assistance of one local school and the hope that, as the First Lady is reported to have commented, 'through children, they will begin to educate their families and that will, in turn, begin to educate our communities'.[2]

How then is one to read such moves by well-known individuals, both human and puppet? On the one hand, it could be argued that they symbolize gradually shifting norms around health, community and food. Or they could arguably be read as a form of cultural tokenism with little ability to make inroads into the complex causes of unhealthy eating, which include 'food deserts', fluctuating global markets and insecure land tenure. Scholarly analysis however requires that neither default extreme is automatically rehearsed. Hence, the recent academic upsurge in explorations of community gardening projects wherein multiple methods, conceptual interpretations and case studies provide a by-now rich field of writing and debate.

In this chapter, through case studies of 'organized garden projects' (Pudup 2008) in urban Australia and peri-urban Philippines, we engage with recent work that analyses such projects through a governmentality approach. Here, the Cookie Monster's confessions of his heady past can be positioned as just one of many diverse interventions that aim to foster and normalize the figure of the disciplined, educated and responsible citizen-subject around the issues of food, community and gardening. Adopting a 'realist governmentality' (McKee 2008) approach that questions the actual outcomes of such interventions 'on the ground', we argue that – although these projects do indeed display the intention of constituting a very specific and circumscribed 'field of action' (Howard 2007) – participants' reactions and on-going collective praxis far exceed such intentions, thus expanding their political, geographical and ethical ambit. In short, this chapter aims to show that a Foucauldian governmentality approach *can* illuminate key aspects of organized gardening interventions. However, to provide insight into its impacts on intended subjects and practices, it requires expansion and both conceptual and empirical supplementation by attention to the embodied and collective 'care of self' practices that subjects undertake as part of their ongoing participation in these projects (see Cupples and Ridley 2008; Rutland and Aylett 2008, for further comment on the conceptual expansion of governmentality).

Interpreting organized gardening projects: surveying recent interventions by social researchers

Organized gardening projects such as Michelle Obama's transformation of White House lawns are without doubt nothing new. Interventions that aim to increase the involvement of citizens in the growing of food for either individual or collective consumption have varied historically and geographically, including attempts to circumvent the ugliness of urban spaces in the early 1900s and 'digging for victory' during WWII (see Armstrong 2000; Pudup 2008). Recently, there has been a renewed proliferation of such projects in both the post-industrial North *and* the Global South, which aim to address and intervene in a number of problematic arenas, touching on issues of community, labour, nutrition and food security, to name but a few.

Given the diversity of the aims and modes of enactments of these organized garden projects, the analytical approaches adopted by scholars researching them have likewise been diverse, with the strongest empirical focus to date being on the US and the UK. There have been evaluations of the impacts of community gardens through the lens of ecological restoration (e.g. Irvine *et al.* 1999). Attention has also been given to health outcomes, both in terms of individuals' activity and nutrition levels, and gardens as triggers for further positive community development (see Armstrong 2000; Wakefield *et al.* 2007). Taking up more prosaic debates among social researchers, Schmelzkopf (2002: 337) utilizes Lefebvre's work on 'trial by space' to argue that public contestations over land use in New York – in particular the demolishing of gardens to allow the sale of land to developers – are not merely tussles over housing availability and exchange value. They fundamentally concern 'control over public space, about who has (or does not have) the right to space, and about the right to be a part of the public'. In addition Guthman's (for example, 2008: 433) work on why community food projects 'appear to lack resonance in the communities in which they are located' suggests that questions of economic and social privilege, in particular the racialized histories of these interventions, are often omitted from studies of 'alternative food practices'.

Many more examples of empirical and conceptual engagements with organized gardening projects exist; rather than rehearse them all here however, in this chapter we take up one recent engagement with such projects through a governmentality analytics. In particular Pudup (2008), writing in a US context, makes the argument that there was a subtle but noted shift in the 1990s from organized garden projects as a form of resistance to a form of governmental intervention. That is:

> The agents of neoliberal roll-out gardening technologies . . . are less neighbourhoods rising up to reclaim their communities and resist their marginalization and rather more a variety of non-state and quasi-state actors who deliberately organize gardens to achieve a desired transformation of individuals in place of collective resistance and/or mobilization.
>
> (2008: 1230)

Indeed, one does not have to look too far to find evidence of Pudup's claims in particular around the panoply of actors involved today in organized garden projects. For example, Not for Profit organizations like the Australian Stephanie Alexander Kitchen Garden Foundation (School Kitchen Gardens) – which will be discussed more below – aim to 'see the Kitchen Garden model and approach to pleasurable food education integrated into the primary school curriculum across Australia'.[3] Along similar lines is the work of the Chez Panisse Foundation (The Edible School Yard) in the US that aims to foster a 'new generation' through the principle that 'good food should be a right and not a privilege', and that 'growing, cooking, and sharing food at the table gives students the knowledge and values to build a humane and sustainable [food] future'.[4]

Such interventions are of course not the sole purview of countries like Australia and the US. Indeed, in the Global South organized gardening interventions are gaining momentum, but often with agendas that focus more on meeting basic needs, such as giving marginalized families opportunities for income generation and livelihood improvement alongside benefits to health and wellness. For example, the Philippines-based Peri-Urban Vegetable Project (PUVeP: which will also be discussed in greater detail below) is 'empowering urban poor communities through integrated vegetable production in allotment gardens', while the Not-for-Profit 'Garden Africa' aims to encourage and support people to cultivate their own food rather than rely on food aid.[5]

What then is one to make of this diverse array of interventions? From a pragmatic perspective, it can easily be argued that together they respond to pressing needs for further food security and improved nutrition around the world: which indeed, they do. But such assertions tell us little about *how* these projects function. That is, what exactly their aims and intentions are; how they aim to achieve these; through what means; and to what effect (see Legg 2006). Indeed, what are some of the possible 'desired transformations' at work that Pudup speaks about? Adopting a governmentality approach to such questions has the potential to provide a form of analytics that we now discuss, highlighting both its usefulness and its limitations in examining specific organized garden projects in Australia and the Philippines.

What we wish to emphasize here are the ways in which governmentality writings detail the changing functions of the state. That is, they claim that both traditional governing functions and governance actors have been supplemented by a plethora of indirect governance techniques and new actors, which together 'seek to promote active agency, responsible self-governance and the state as an enabler as opposed to provider of services' (McKee 2008: 184). The empirical question thus suggested by this thesis concerns how particular governmental rationalities or programmes are 'translated, practiced, performed, and produce particular effects' (Merriman 2005: 237). But rather than suppose one can automatically 'read-off' outcomes from the intentions of interventions (Rutherford 2007), scholars have of late drawn attention to the 'potential disjuncture between top-down, universalistic plans and empirical reality at the micro level' (McKee 2008: 186). Hence, a recent 'realist governmentality' turn is now gaining momentum, which looks to combine the 'concern of governmentality theory with how the "subject" is discursively constituted, and more ethnographic methods' (McKee 2008: 186).

What then can a realist governmentality approach illuminate about particular organized garden projects? In the following section, we introduce two examples of such projects in Australia and the Philippines, and tell the stories of four key actors in these projects: a fitting level of analysis given realist governmentalists' emphasis on ethnographic and 'micro' explorations, which aim to temper and critique the distanced and often-sweeping claims made by some previous utilizations of a governmentality approach (see Hobson 2009; Rutherford 2007). We examine the ways in which these interventions do indeed work to constitute a particular field of 'appropriate' discourse, subjectivities and practice, aiming to foster active, responsible and disciplined individuals around the pressing issues of food, nutrition and being a 'productive' citizen in the neoliberal world. However – as is often the case – there are more to these projects and individuals' stories that any 'just so' governmentality story suggests, particularly when we explore how, and to what ends, subjects are affected by their enrolment in organized gardening interventions. Thus, we argue below that as key actors become involved in the ongoing processes of articulating the shape and form of 'their' communal gardening intervention – although they do not necessarily re-shape the basic aims of the interventions – they enact praxis and create further potential that exceeds the spaces, peoples, and the political and social ambit of the original aims of these organized garden projects.

The Stephanie Alexander Kitchen Garden Foundation (Australia) and the Peri-Urban Vegetable Project (the Philippines)

We begin the empirics of the chapter by introducing the two case study projects, along with some individuals who became involved with them.[6] To begin in Australia, in 2009 Majura Primary School in the inner suburbs of the nation's capital, Canberra, received a A$100,000 Federal Government grant to become the Australian Capital Territory (ACT) Demonstration School for the Stephanie Alexander Kitchen Garden foundation (SAKGF): a foundation that now works Australia-wide, operating in almost one hundred schools. As mentioned above, SAKGF aims to significantly alter the food-related behaviours of children and their families through active engagement in the processes of growing, harvesting, preparing and eating school-grown food, and below we meet George and Chris, who were both coordinators in the project.

> George Main is a Canberra-based environmental historian and museum curator. He played an integral role in establishing the Majura Kitchen Garden in 2009. George assumed the volunteer role of 'garden coordinator' in the project's infancy with a view to stepping back once the project's garden specialist came on board. George remains an active participant in this garden project is a regular attendee of working bees and meetings.

> Chris Stanilewicz is a Canberra-based policy officer in local government, with a background in community development and experience in early childhood policy development, and being an ex-chef, she brings many skills and experiences to her role in the Majura Kitchen Garden project. She began as the sponsorship and fundraising coordinator, then stepped down from this role mid 2009. However, she is still very much an active supporter and was instrumental (along with George) in shaping this project.

In terms of outcomes of this project to date, for Majura Primary it is still early days. As we write, the kitchen – which is an integral part of the SAKGF project – is being built, and the garden is in the process of becoming a productive foodscape. Plus, the project has recently employed a garden 'specialist' who – along with 'a kitchen specialist who will help the children prepare the recipes and cook food' – 'comes with the Stephanie Alexander programme' (School Principal: Majura Video Story[7]).

And then there are Luminoso and Jimboy, allotment gardener representatives of the one hundred families who have received income and health benefits through the Peri-Urban Vegetable Project (PUVeP) of Xavier University, which is located in Cagayan de Oro, in the north of the island of Mindanao, the Philippines. To explain, the PUVeP intervention supported the development of nine allotment gardens in Cagayan de Oro City and has been many years in the making, now being well beyond its initial funding cycle (Holmer *et al.* 2008). Of these nine gardens, the Saint Niño Allotment Garden in the barangay (ward) of Lapasan was launched on 11 December 2003. It was co-funded by the Asia Urbs Project of EuropeAid (2002–04) and the Peri-Urban Vegetable Project of Xavier University. This funding was provided for the establishment of the garden and for the first two croppings only: a period of about six months. Since then – other than occasional donations – gardeners have had to self-fund their allotment production. The Saint Niño allotment that Luminoso and Jimboy work is presently managed by ten families. Sometimes they work together in the form of collective voluntary labour or 'pahina' but mostly they work their own plots.

Luminoso Rosal is an allotment gardener who has worked his allotment in the Saint Niño Allotment Garden since 2003. He began with no prior knowledge or experience in vegetable crop production or gardening, and has subsequently become one of the most successful allotment gardeners in Cagayan de Oro City, winning 'The Best Allotment Gardener of Cagayan de Oro City Award' in 2007. He is the president of the Saint Niño allotment gardeners' association and is actively engaged in addressing issues related to the future of the communal garden such as ensuring continued access to land.

Jimboy Eugenio is a teacher at the Lapasan National High School in Cagayan de Oro. He is also an allotment gardener who like Luminoso has worked his allotment in Saint Niño since 2003. He is a highly enthusiastic and energetic member of the association and an advocate for urban agriculture across the city.

Although both case studies are organized gardening projects that aim to increase self-provisioning – through facilitating knowledge and skills of how to garden, as well as marking out spaces for these activities – Saint Niño Allotment Garden differs from the Majura Kitchen Garden in many respects. Poor and marginalized communities were targeted for the PUVeP programme, households within those communities such as Lapasan, where Saint Niño is located, then applying to become allotment gardeners. By contrast the suburbs surrounding the Majura School are relatively (although not uniformly) affluent and membership of the SAKGF project mostly (but not solely) comes through children's enrolments in the Majura School. In addition, the PUVeP is an intervention to improve health *and* sanitation. This was achieved through the installation of composting toilets and household waste composting facilities in the gardens, as well as increasing the amount of fresh produce in the diet of participants and local communities. In addition, PUVeP aims to provide income generation opportunities for participants, with seventy per cent of the produce grown being sold and the remaining thirty per cent being used for self-provisioning and gifting within the community.

However, the aim of this chapter is not to compare the two case studies, directly evaluating them against one another. Rather, they are outlined briefly so we can ask what then are we to make of both of these organized garden projects, in terms of their governmental aims, mechanisms and outcomes? To return to Pudup's claim – that gardening projects are no longer about collective resistance per se but aim to 'achieve a desired transformation of individuals' – it can be argued that the SAKGF project for one aligns with other forms of socializing and disciplining interventions, in the Foucauldian sense.

For example, there were concerns expressed by participants of the Majura project that the garden and kitchen had to be sympathetic to the ethos of the school; to meet the curriculum requirements of the ACT Department of Education and Training; and to find amicable existence amidst many other programmes and activities already operating at Majura Primary. Early in 2009 participants expressed anxieties that the garden project could detract from children's learning. In response, the Head of the school was clear this was not the case, stating that:

> One of the things Majura does very well is it has a very strong sense of what its core business is. Our core business is literacy and numeracy. The Stephanie Alexander programme enhances that core business rather than competes with it.
>
> (Majura video diary)

Therefore this suggests that the SAKGF project works alongside other forms of interventions such as formalized education, which aims to foster particular types of young citizens, who are responsible, productive and active citizens-in-the-making (Ferreira 2000). Indeed, the Majura project – again, in line with Pudup's claims – could not be framed as a form of collective mobilization in the 'bottom-up' sense, as organized resistance through gardening projects may once have been. Instead, participants were happy, and indeed grateful, to be part of an established philosophy, label and methodology. For example, George and Chris recognized that the SAKGF hands a particular structure to the Majura School, one designed to instil confidence in taking the venture on. They state it is like 'a pillar or a lifeline' and George says that it is:

> based on almost ten years' experience in almost fifty schools down in Victoria. And there's so much that's of value there. And I'm grateful to the foundation for what they're offering. I think it's extraordinary, it's generous.
> (Majura video diary)

However, that the SAKGF seemingly aligns with Pudup's claims does not mean that we can conclude such projects are yet another governmental mechanism that seeks – and indeed succeeds in this – to forge subjectivities and practices within particularly prescribed confines (Rutherford 2007; see Bang and Esmark 2009). As Raco (2003) for one has argued, there is a tendency in governmentality-based studies to make interventions, such as the Majura project, appear logical, coherent and able to achieve desired outcomes with little deviation. But in reality governmental agendas are far from totalizing: indeed, they are contested by the actions of subjects who respond to governing intentions in a variety of ways, including failure, resistance, and the realignment of governmental aims to suit other agendas.

In terms of the case studies in this chapter, there was certainly evidence of some (mild) resistance by participants to the rigours of the project. For example, Chris took on a role of sponsorship coordinator: a role that she was not wholly comfortable with. Or as she said: 'As soon as I was in the role I knew I didn't want to be in it but I knew someone had to be so I just plodded.' She indeed tried to get 'regular monthly meetings of all the coordinators so we could keep issues on the agenda' but 'there was quite a lot of resistance to that more structured stuff . . . comments about [it being too] bureaucratic'.

Beyond that, is there then evidence from these case studies for some 'potential disjuncture between top-down, universalistic plans and empirical reality at the micro level' (McKee 2008: 186)? We argue here that the idea of 'disjuncture', while a useful starting point, misdirects in terms of what is taking place in both the case studies presented. 'Disjuncture' is a noun that suggests separation, disconnection or disjoining. However, as we will argue in the final section of this paper, the praxis developed by participants is partially in line with the governmental aims and therefore does not represent a disconnection or overt separation per se. Instead, they exceed the aims of the interventions in ways that are unpredictable, overflowing the 'field of action' (Howard 2007) they aim to establish and thus present actual and potential ground for the development of further ethical praxis around gardening, food and collective provisioning.

Exceeding the 'field of action' through ethical communal praxis

Before proceeding to detail the empirical evidence for the above claims, it is first necessary to pause briefly to reflect upon how ideas of ethical praxis relate conceptually to the tenets of governmentality. For one, claims could be made that the participants of both the SAKGF project and the PUVeP are already 'ethical' people. That is, they are the 'usual suspects' or minority of people who are already active around and committed to environmental and/or community issues. However, social researchers have argued that such claims – although there is often an element of veracity in some cases – miss the point that ethics are not a separate/innate/pre-cognitized sphere of practice that belongs to a few and thus stands outside of governmentalizing impulses. Rather, ethical practices are both articulated and 'worked-up' through diverse forms of governmental inter-vention. Or as Dean (1994) outlines, governmentality bridges the political and ethical dimensions of subject creation, as there are 'governmental' and 'ethical' self-formation processes working in conjunction. Here the former are means by which conduct, aspirations, etc. are shaped and individuals enlisted in particular strategies and goals, and the latter, the means by which individuals seek to know, decipher and act on themselves, draws on discourses and practices from governmental self-formation interventions in the process.

And yet, in later work on the 'care of the self', Foucault made the case that the development of one's own ethics may be one way to resist such governmental imperatives: that is, to somehow step outside of governmental self-formation imperatives. Fundamentally, he argued that particular practices could enable individuals to form ways of being or 'practices of freedom', which could contend with contemporary techniques of power that aim to discipline and suppress (Myers 2008). The aim here was the development of individuals' capacities to conduct themselves 'properly' in relation to others. How this might be done, according to Foucault, involves various forms of self-reflection and the uptake of self-directed practices that aim to constantly ask 'what do I aspire to be?' (see Cordner 2008).

However, as a strategy for political action, Foucault's 'care of the self' theory is not without problems. Myers (2008) for one has pointed out a distinct dis-connect between Foucault's thesis and collective political strategies for more equitable, open and responsive power relations. Or as Cordner (2008: 593) posits:

> The ethical subject described in Foucault's later writings is too self-concerned: Foucault's ethics does not sufficiently acknowledge the authority of 'the other' in our ethical interaction.

In short, Foucault presents us with a picture of individuals, standing in isolation from others and thus unable to ultimately alter the forms of power they are working to reconstitute themselves against. However, these comments have been made by political theorists whose text-based exegesis of Foucault's work has done little to test such claims empirically (Hobson 2009). As we explore below, the ways in which individuals 'work up' their own ethical practices *can* allow them to connect with others. For example, having to work with and consider actors as diverse as parents, children, the plants, the Stephanie Alexander Foundation and the Majura curriculum, as well as consumers, other gardeners, landowners and their crops in the PUVeP case, means 'the other' that Myers claims is missing in Foucault's work is already present through the embodied practices of these projects. Thus, while 'the other' may be conceptually absent in writings on the 'care of self' – making it thus appear as a dead-end in terms of forging collective ethical praxis – in practice they are uncompromisingly present due to the fundamental requirements of the governmental interventions of organized garden projects.

So what evidence is there that for participants of the PUVeP and the SAKGF project the links between these two modes of forging 'political subjectivities' (Dean 1994) are discernible, wherein ethical self-formation works to exceed, but is not disjointed from or wholly resistant to, governmental aims? As already suggested, evidence of the governmental aims of producing particular types of subjects through organized garden projects are present in these case studies. For the PUVeP, the aim of this intervention is arguably to create self-reliant and productive subjects, who create surplus and generate income by gaining access to local markets in the face of unstable global food markets and sparse state welfare support. The two participants featured here had indeed managed to attain these goals, becoming in part the profitable and entrepreneurial citizens that many argue neoliberal interventions seek to create. At the same time, Luminoso and Jimboy discuss how they have both developed new ways of viewing themselves and acting, wherein the goals of the intervention have been internalized, re-evaluated and in many ways surpassed, in terms of their own sense of self-worth and praxis. Indeed, both Luminoso and Jimboy constantly indicate that they have developed a new sense of pride in themselves – a consciousness of their dignity that exceeds purely economic calculations. Luminoso states that he is now considering extending his new practices into other spaces. This is in part because he does not own the land he currently works, and the landowner may take the land back. Thus, Luminoso is hoping to become a communal farmer working with others to further his own goals and skills *and* improve collective well-being, if suitable farmland is found in Bukidnon, Mindanao; or else he will continue to garden and look for another area to have an allotment. Thus, despite the tribulations and vulnerabilities of access to land and insecure tenure, it does appear that the communal gardener subject position is now firmly part of Luminoso's understanding of himself. Even though he is still at the whims of markets and landowners, he appears to feel some ownership now for the process of gardening and selling, claiming his ethical self-formation as one of choice, as – given the expiry of project funding – it is now wholly Luminoso's decision to be and to keep becoming a communal gardener.

Rather than inhabiting a lone position or venture however – an individualized and isolated 'care of self' tactic – he has worked in conjunction with others, and now invites them to join him on his journey. In a similar vein, Jimboy is now going door-to-door around his local area, to encourage people to begin gardening and to think about the importance of urban food production: taking on the role not only of self-provisioner but of community educator. As he states:

> Selling the fresh vegetables from house to house, it's a very good option for us to spread [information] all about the project. That is one of my techniques in having this allotment garden, to be known as an allotment gardener as part of the project here . . . [and to] inculcate in their minds about urban agriculture.

In the Majura project – while not working to subvert or disconnect from the intentions of intervention – there has been the generation of additional outcomes wherein participants have collectively worked up the political and ethical ambit of the project in ways that exceed and expand upon its original aims. For one, as George explains 'there is space for a lot more to hook in and energize' the kitchen garden project. Participants are 'flavouring' the project with what they want to get out of it as well, as Chris puts it. Indeed, for Chris the kitchen garden is, among other things, an opportunity to build and strengthen the community, to build resilience through local food production and develop skills that will help us live 'post-peak-oil' and climate change. She explains:

> we've got some pretty significant emerging environmental and global crises in terms of peak oil and climate change. We really need to be working collectively to build resilience so that when they emerge we're prepared.

And for George there are other considerations, as he states:

> One direction I am trying to explore and see whether we can build on, that I think is a bit different to the Stephanie Alexander vision, is to see whether we can build on the heritage that exists within the school, the social justice angle and in particular the Aboriginal reconciliation activity . . . I wonder whether we can really respond to that heritage in a creative way and bring something . . . that is different to the foundation. This is something that has come up independently though the Indigenous families. One Aboriginal woman who's a parent in particular . . . She's hoping that we can bring into the programme awareness that there are different ways you can engage with land. But how you engage land and grow food is determined by or shaped by culture and history and stories.

In this quote, we can therefore see how the Majura project and its clearly defined aims and mechanisms are being exceeded by participants to include the contentious and pressing issues of social justice and Aboriginal reconciliation. How this is happening is obviously an outcome of dialogue, negotiation and debate among participants, as well as other modes of engagement. For example, the above comment on 'engaging' the land speaks to the affect of embodied, hands-on experiences as key to altering praxis (for example, see Hitchins and Jones 2004). Indeed, the SAKGF website states that it favours a 'hands on' approach to behaviour change as:

> We believe that no-one embraces change in their behavior if they think it will be unpleasant, uncomfortable or too difficult. Cautionary messages that food is 'good-for-you' or 'bad-for-you' do not resonate with young people.

As researchers have recently argued, the somewhat disembodied and text-based focus of many governmentality studies have missed the ways in which the 'doing' of new practices are key to changes in individual and collective praxis (Cupples and Ridley 2008). Along similar lines, the practice of participants putting themselves 'at risk' appeared in the fieldwork data as a visceral and also productive experience. That is, whereas the political strategy ascribed to Foucault around the 'care of the self' is arguably about creating a circumscribed and highly personal and safe space as a form of political action, in taking on projects like the SAKGF, participants have no alternative but to enter into 'unsafe' and risky territory, in terms of being able to discern and foresee outcomes. As Chris explains:

> to get anything to move I think you need people who are willing to follow a process even though you don't know where it is going to head, but to have faith that people can come together and create change.

And George also states:

> I think faith is a really key word because I mean we don't know if this is going to work. We hope it is, and are imagining it will, but we don't know. People may not become volunteers next year . . . we are taking risks.

Thus for participants of organized garden projects like the SAKGF intervention, there is a desire and willingness to (for the most part) comply with the structure of the project, for example hiring specialists, constructing a kitchen, etc. At the same time, participants are – and indeed feel like they have little choice, in terms of taking the project forward – opening up spaces for thinking and acting outside the desired outcomes, allowing for uncertainty and possibility to enter in. Many dynamics inevitably surfaced in moving a group of people towards 'the thing' as Chris refers to it, particularly once the initial project enthusiasm wears off. There are expectations from the school and the foundation, and there are personality differences and different agendas among project participants: 'What's kept us going is the vision, dream and all our individual passions, plus our individual skills sets to move us all towards the thing,' says Chris. So while the SAKGF is a 'pillar and lifeline', both the Majura project and PUVeP participants are more than the sum of the intervention and their individual passions and 'skills sets', which exist outside of and prior to the intervention. Rather, these form the basis to initiate and move the project forward, and in turn are furthered, extended *and* exceeded by their involvement in the project.

Conclusion: the on-going work of organized garden project interventions

Both organized garden projects discussed in this chapter are undoubtedly works in progress. At the time of writing, the Majura project continues to grow, and the participants of the PUVeP are moving their livelihoods in diverse and unpredictable directions, made less certain by their reliance on access to markets and insecure land tenure. From an intervention perspective, both projects to date can be considered successful, in terms of enrolling the targeted individuals to meet many of their goals. However, there are concerns about the sustainability of the interventions: for example, with regards to keeping the 'community energy' that the project relies upon going beyond initial 'passion' and interest, as well as the PUVeP participants' search for new land.

However, even if these projects ultimately do not become sustained interventions, they have affected participants in ways that may not be immediately obvious if one undertakes a governmentality analysis 'from afar'. That is, if one adopts an analytical methodology that focuses on the intentions of interventions via texts and policies, rather than following the impacts of these interventions through to empirical outcomes. Thus, this chapter has examined two organized garden projects through a 'realist' governmentality approach, which aims to explore how, why and in what ways particular interventions create effect 'on the ground'. As previous analyses adopting a similar perspective have shown, no intervention that aims to foster particular forms of citizen-subjects ever fully attains its goals. There are resistance, failure and divergent enactments of goals, as the complexities of individual psychology, collective negotiation and contemporary polities intervene. But as this chapter has argued, this does not mean that the rationalities and aims of interventions like organized garden projects are negated or become totally disconnected and disjointed. Rather, through embodied acts of working up ethical subjectivities in common with others, and taking 'risks' along the way, the projects detailed herein come to exceed their original governmental ambit. Subjects *do* become enrolled in the enactment of specific political subjectivities, for example productive and responsible citizens. But this works in conjunction with, not against, the cultivating of collective ethical praxis that suggest other sites and modes of engagement that expand the governmental aims into new, and potentially fertile (politically, ethically and agriculturally speaking) areas.

Notes

1 See www.colbertnation.com/the-colbert-report-videos/174545/june-19-2008/cookie-monster.
2 See www.nytimes.com/2009/03/20/dining/20garden.html.
3 For further information see www.kitchengardenfoundation.org.au.
4 See www.chezpanissefoundation.org/home.
5 See http://puvep.xu.edu.ph/index.php and www.gardenafrica.org.uk/why_africa_charity.htm, respectively.
6 The chapter draws on qualitative interview and participant observation data collected by Ann Hill in April 2009 in Mindanao. It also draws on a video story produced in February to May 2009 and interviews conducted in November 2009 in Majura, Canberra, as part of Ann's doctoral research project 'Growing community food economies for a twenty-first century world'.
7 This information was obtained as part of Ann Hill's PhD data collection, in the form of a video diary with members of the Majura School Kitchen Garden project.

Bibliography

Armstrong, D. (2000) 'A survey of community gardens in upstate New York: implications for health promotion and community development', *Health and Place*, 6(4): 319–27.
Bang, H. and Esmark, A. (2009) 'Good governance in network society: reconfiguring the political from politics to policy', *Administrative Theory and Praxis*, 31(1): 7–37.
Cordner, C. (2008) 'Foucault, ethical self-concern and the other', *Philosophia*, 36(4): 593–609.
Cupples, J. and Ridley, E. (2008) 'Towards a heterogeneous environmental responsibility: sustainability and cycling fundamentalism', *Area*, 40(2): 254–64.
Dean, M. (1994) '"A social structure of many souls": moral regulation, government, and self-formation', *Canadian Journal of Sociology*, 19(2): 145–68.
Ferreira, J. (2000) 'Learning to govern oneself: environmental education pedagogy and the formation of the environmental subject', *Australian Journal of Environmental Education*, 16: 31–35.
Guthman, J. (2008) 'Bringing good food to others: investigating the subjects of alternative food practice', *Cultural Geographies*, 15(4): 431–47.
Hitchings, R. and Jones, V. (2004) 'Living with plants and the exploration of botanical encounter within human geographic research practice', *Ethics, Place and Environment*, 7(1–2): 3–18.
Hobson, K. (2009) 'On a governmentality analytics of the "deliberative turn": material conditions, rationalities and the deliberating subject', *Space and Polity*, 13(3): 175–91.
Holmer, R.J., Santos Jr., C.A., Sol, G.Y., Lee, S.O., Elorde Jr., E.G., Aquino, A.A., Guanzon, Y.B., Achas, D.M.D., Caseria, J.A., Factura III, H.S., Miso, A.U., Oclarit, R.A. and Montes, A.A. (2008) 'Philippine allotment garden manual with an introduction to ecological sanitation', Periurban Vegetable Project, Xavier University College of Agriculture, Cagayan de Oro City.
Howard, C. (ed.) (2007) *Contested Individualization: Debates about Contemporary Personhood*, New York: Palgrave Macmillan.
Irvine, S., Johnson, L. and Peters, K. (1999) 'Community gardens and sustainable land use planning: a case-study of the Alex Wilson community garden', *Local Environment*, 4(1): 33–36.

Legg, S. (2006) 'Governmentality, congestion and calculation in colonial Delhi', *Social and Cultural Geography*, 7(5): 709–29.

McKee, K. (2008) 'Transforming Scotland's public sector housing through community ownership: the reterritorialisation of housing governance', *Space and Polity*, 12(2): 183–96.

Merriman, P. (2005) 'Materiality, subjectification, and government: the geographies of Britain's Motorway Code', *Environment and Planning D*, 23(2): 235–50.

Myers, E. (2008) 'Resisting Foucauldian ethics: associative politics and the limits of the care of the self', *Contemporary Political Theory*, 7(2): 125–46.

Pudup, M.B. (2008) 'It takes a garden: cultivating citizen-subjects in organized garden projects', *Geoforum*, 39(3): 1228–40.

Raco, M. (2003) 'Governmentality, subject-building, and the discourses and practices of devolution in the UK', *Transactions of the Institute of British Geographers*, 28: 75–95.

Rutherford, S. (2007) 'Green governmentality: insights and opportunities in the study of nature's rule', *Progress in Human Geography*, 31(3): 291–307.

Rutland, T. and Aylett, A. (2008) 'The work of policy: actor networks, governmentality, and local action on climate change in Portland, Oregon', *Environment and Planning D*, 26: 627–46.

Schmelzkopf, K. (2002) 'Incommensurability, land use and the right to space: community gardens in New York City', *Urban Geography*, 23(4): 323–43.

Wakefield, S., Yeudall, S., Taron, C., Reynolds, J. and Skinner, A. (2007) 'Growing urban health: community gardening in South-East Toronto', *Health Promotion International*, 22(2): 92–101.

16 Lifestyle television

Gardening and the good life

Frances Bonner

A fundamental characteristic of lifestyle television is that it operates to promote consumption as the vehicle to a fully realized identity. The ethical position for most shows of this type relates to the individual's duty as an entrepreneur of the self, to reveal the 'true self' and to make sure the self is kept in tune with lifestyle indicators. Personal makeover shows repeatedly demonstrate how new clothes and hairstyles bring out a person who previous only existed *in potentia*, needing the expertise provided by the programme to be realized. Both the products displayed and the services of the experts or similar others are promoted in such shows.

This chapter will consider how a different ethical stance, one involving a 'green' consciousness, has found a space within lifestyle television. For the most part it is to be found in food and gardening programmes with the former stronger in the UK and the latter in Australia. The term 'green' is being used here to talk of environmentally conscious ethical practices including reducing energy use, recycling, following organic and sustainable practices, localism, Fair Trade and water wisdom. It can also name a concern for the welfare of the animals that people regard as food.

My focus is specifically on the advice given to viewers by television presenters, seeing them as cultural intermediaries in Pierre Bourdieu's sense, acting to pass on information and advice to a wider population. In his introduction of the term, Bourdieu explicitly lists television presenters as examples, although most subsequent work has ignored them. He was uncompromising in his distaste for the new petite bourgeoisie, his alternative term for cultural intermediaries, and was opposed to and alarmed by the practices and the dispositions of this then emergent group.

One of the prime characteristics of the new petite bourgeoisie, and one that feeds into Bourdieu's disdain, is its place in consumption. He concludes his central discussion of this grouping by suggesting that they may be 'in the process of supplying the economy with the perfect consumer whom economic theory has always dreamed of . . . by inducing him to consume and to consume the latest thing' (1984: 371). He had previously described them as '"need merchants", sellers of symbolic goods and services who always sell themselves as models and as guarantors of the value of their products, and who sell so well because they believe in what they sell' (1984: 365). Nor was this simply a matter of Bourdieu's opinion of the 1970s or of the 1960s when the surveys of cultural tastes that ground his empirical work were conducted. In a lecture delivered in 1996 on the role of intellectuals, he still spoke of cultural intermediaries as the enemy, with their work in the media causing intellectuals to retreat from public debate, thus 'depriv[ing] ordinary mortals of their knowledge, their competence and their values' (2002: 4). While this lecture blames the press, other 1996 lectures on the topic were published as *On Television*.

I do not subscribe uncritically to Bourdieu's evaluation, believing, like Sean Nixon and Paul du Gay, that cultural intermediaries have the capacity 'to condense and focus broader questions about social and cultural change' (2002: 499). This may or may not involve increased consumption. It is possible to see a clear Bourdieuian example of a pro-consumption position in television presenters who host personal makeovers involving cosmetic surgery. These programmes showcase the terminological shift from 'plastic' to 'cosmetic'; the diminution of shame in admitting to using it; the shift in take-up from celebrities and the wealthy, to lower middle and even working class individuals; the imbrication of changes in access to easy credit; and the centrality of a mutable appearance to identity and self-worth. Much social and cultural change is encapsulated here, though presenters are clearly not responsible for all of it.

Certainly cultural intermediaries are complicit in encouraging consumption of new products and services. High-profile presenters know that if they recommend a new product and it is not commercially available in sufficient quantities, complaints will be made to the programme, so they act in concert with suppliers, alerting them sufficiently far in advance. A notorious instance of inadequate alerting occurred in 1990 when British food presenter Delia Smith, giving a recipe for truffle torte, caused a run on liquid glucose that led to a nationwide shortage.

The inevitability with which Bourdieu sees cultural intermediaries promoting greater and greater consumption and the conception of this as a prime source of pleasure and identity raises difficulties where continual consumption itself is being questioned, at least among the middle class of developing countries. In what follows I want to try to consider a degree of disarticulation of continually escalating consumption from the activities of the new petite bourgeoisie by looking at presenters who explicitly advocate ethical consumption.

Bourdieu's work provides little explanation of why viewers would pay attention to the words of cultural intermediaries, nor does it distinguish between different examples – television presenters say, rather than advertising executives. Work synthesized by Shaun Moores on social para-interaction explains the way in which viewers develop relationships with regularly appearing presenters that, despite the absence of possibilities for easy reciprocity, exhibit similarities to conventional friendships (2005: 74–90). Advice is subsequently domestically received in familiar contexts marked by sociability and pleasure.

Kate Soper has developed the idea of 'alternative hedonism' to describe a shift in anti-consumerism where people both avoid contributing to the destructive aspects of affluent consumption and seek to gain sensual pleasure by consuming differently (2008: 571–72). The presenters considered here are consistent in emphasizing the fun they are having and the pleasures of the practices they promote. It is unsurprising: the broad term for their programmes is infotainment, a coinage which acknowledges the contemporary requirement for information provided through television to be also entertaining.

'Life experiment' and food programmes

My principal focus will be on gardening programmes, but I also want to consider food shows and some that appear to combine both concerns. Few of them make explicit their focus on green issues. Those few explicitly green shows have been produced operating according to two broad formulas. In one, a series of household groups, usually families, are challenged to improve their practices by one or more experts who monitor their behaviour for a limited period of time across a range of areas – utility use, waste production and disposal, and transport use being the most common. Examples include the Australian programmes *Carbon Cops* and *Eco House Challenge* and the British *No Waste Like Home*. The other type of programme increases the personalization by following an individual or a family as they embark on a long-running programme of reducing their carbon footprint and increasing their environmentally sensitive behaviour. An example of this is the UK's *It's not Easy being Green*. Both types are members of the larger category Annette Hill calls 'life experiment programmes' where ordinary people try out changes to their normal ways of life, sometimes welcoming the new, more often being critical of it (2005: 36–37). The green experimenters tend (eventually) to welcome the suggested changes, but appear mainly in short-lived series, occasionally being recommissioned for a second series or allowed revisits, but not carving out a continuing niche in the schedule.

The American situation is somewhat different, thanks to the pay channel Planet Green (a Discovery subsidiary) which, as its name indicates, specializes in the area, combining lifestyle programmes with nature documentaries. One of its lead shows is *Living with Ed* in which environmentally responsible behaviour is modelled through the conflicts between a Hollywood couple – Ed Begley Jnr and his wife, the less green Rachelle Carson. There are also food shows like *Emeril Green* hosted by celebrity chef Emeril Lagasse, and makeover programmes such as *Renovation Nation*, the aim of which is to make existing buildings more environmentally responsible. The concentration here, however, will be primarily on British and Australian mainstream primetime programmes screened on free-to-air TV and thus available to the majority of a nation's population and watched by a significant section of it.

Food presenters offer advice in far more areas than just advocating the purchase of a greater range of food items. Their comments about knives and chopping boards encourage kitchen safety and food hygiene. There may be advice on thrift, though less since the departure of Delia Smith from the screen, and on maintaining a work/life balance, largely in terms of recipes that can be made quickly on return home from paid work and on the role of food in the care for others. These last are part of an emphasis on healthy nutrition that is a constant refrain.

All of these have ethical bases, but none requires an explicit green foundation. More relevantly, running through most of the primetime shows is an assumption that organic food is better and that it is preferable in health terms to consume it whenever possible. It is not often brought to the fore, except in programmes more centrally focused on health like Gillian Keith's *You are What You Eat*. Localism is a different matter. It is central to programmes like Rick Stein's *Local Heroes* and others celebrating British food producers from presenters like Nick Nairn or Clarissa Dickson Wright. While these could be seen to advance a green stance where food travels only short distances and is quite often organic, these positions are subsumed in discourses of quality and distinction. Jamie Oliver's *Jamie at Home* series, in which he cooks food he has grown in his own garden, is similar. The foods are presented as preferable mainly because they taste better. The group of programmes is also compromised by omnipresent class restraints. The rare breed meats, heritage vegetables and free range organic produce are generally produced by the middle class for middle class consumption, because of both cost and limited availability. Jamie's own home grown fruit and vegetables, furthermore, are tended by his gardener.

Australian shows operate similarly to an extent, although the much greater land mass means that localism is rarely advanced as an ethical touchstone. 'Australian-grown' becomes rather a nationalist characteristic, which to be fair is a subtext in the British programmes as well. The Australian *The Cook and the Chef*, presented by Maggie Beer and Simon Bryant is consistent in referring to the desirability of organic produce from the Barossa Valley where Beer lives, but also ranges over the whole continent for non-local foodstuffs. The key ethical distinction for both countries' programmes is encapsulated in the word 'fresh'. Good food is fresh, but while this may be seen to involve green elements, it is truly in opposition only to readymade, pre-prepared, fast food.

The discussions which try to negotiate the comparative worth of organic or sustainable practices, explore how localism causes problems for Fair Trade, or question GM foods seem more to be found in newspapers or on-line than on television, and across all media are stronger in the UK than in Australia. Most food programmes are designed to show the preparation of several individual dishes across an episode, rarely presenting food preparation as an ongoing practice of ethical decision-making and often relegating the relevant, more considered reflections to the accompanying books.

A very particular case of green lifestyle programming is represented by the long-running sequence of British programmes presented by and featuring Hugh Fearnley-Whittingstall, starting in 1999 with *Escape to River Cottage* and continuing through *Return to River Cottage*, *Beyond River Cottage* and many more, up to the most recent seasonally named River Cottage series which Craig and Parkin discuss in this volume as contributing to a dissemination of ideas about slow living. Fearnley-Whittingstall had started as a television presenter with adventurous tastes in 1995 on the Channel 4 programme *A Cook on the*

Wildside, which involved him foraging for wild foods across the UK, but with the appearance of what was to become the River Cottage brand, he consolidated this into a focus on his own lifestyle as he established a smallholding with the aim of being as self-sufficient as possible. Lyn Thomas discusses the first series as an example of a downsizing narrative replete with 'nostalgic images of rurality' (2008b: 690–91). She used it, together with the green life experiment shows, to identify a new genre: 'eco-reality' (2008a).

Over the years Fearnley-Whittingstall's programmes have moved from an initial, rather idiosyncratic, emphasis on improving his self-sufficiency in food (while he continued to work in London), to being able to be seen within a broader environmental frame. This has been a change not so much in his ambitions, as in the prevalence of green television programmes, which enabled his to be seen in a more suitable context. The shift from growing enough for his own needs and a small amount of barter, to running a farm shop and taking in food tourists was a shift from hobbyist to local employer. In part because he runs his own production company, the many series have been able to follow the slow development of establishing a greener lifestyle and trace his cultivation of friendships and other connections in the community into which he had moved. Shorter investigations tend to show only the inevitable difficulties in getting set up. Most usefully for the current paper, however, has been his move from an inward-looking tending of his own garden according to ethical premises (while demonstrating the desirability of his practices to large numbers of distant others through his programmes) to highly explicit campaigning work.

In this he has been aided by his programme's location on Channel 4, which has become a prime site for food campaigning, broadcasting not just Fearnley-Whittingstall, but also Jamie Oliver. Both high-profile presenters came together over their respective campaigns against factory farming of chickens, each appearing at some stage on the other's programmes: *Jamie's Fowl Dinners* and *Hugh's Chicken Run* (both 2008), followed by *Chickens, Hugh and Tesco Too* (2009). The strap line for the part of the Channel 4 website which contains information on these shows is 'How to eat well, and ethically'. This encompasses Jamie's programme paralleling the chicken shows but looking at pig farming, his work aimed to improve children's eating practices in *Jamie's School Dinners* and his attempt to extend the percentage of the British population cooking fresh food through his *Ministry of Food*. It also includes several programmes presented by less well known presenters trying to change people's fondness for junk food.

While the BBC does screen many food programmes, it is less concerned with ethical inflections in the programmes, though its website, like Channel 4's, provides significant quantities of information on the area. The significance of associated websites in providing hard data about green issues to people attracted in the first instance by television programmes would be well worth separate investigation.

Neither Hugh nor Jamie really suggests consuming less; rather it is consuming well instead of badly that is their interest. Taking part in the outreach part of the *Ministry of Food* campaign requires buying the book as a first step.

Fearnley-Whittingstall however is concerned with a more thorough-going practice which requires continuous application and is able to cover a broader range of ethical concerns, though he acknowledges that he is still seen as a posh bloke telling people what to do. How successful his practice would be without the underpinning of the television programmes in which he stars, which are made by his production company and sold not just within the UK but internationally, not to mention the associated books and DVDs, is impossible to assess.

The advice of the principal presenter of Australian SBS programme *Eco House Challenge* (2008, 2009) Tanya Ha, a green journalist and author, is typical of green life experiment programmes in its suggestion of consuming fewer carbon-emitting, water-requiring commodities through consuming differently. Without dismissing the considerable value of her advice, it is certainly possible to see it as arguing that we can continue to enjoy our current lifestyles by being more thoughtful about what we consume. While I have problems with Bourdieu's moralism, aspects of his argument can be used to explain what is happening with Ha and the British presenters. Consider his core statement about the operation of the new petite bourgeoisie: '[s]eeking its occupational and personal salvation in the imposition of new doctrines of ethical salvation, the new petite bourgeoisie is predisposed to play a vanguard role in the struggles over everything concerned with the art of living' (1984: 366). Bourdieu then discusses child-rearing, but it now seems particularly apt to talk of the intermingling of advice about practical measures to prepare for and combat climate change with the ethical frame about our duty to change current practices. Most life experiment shows depict 'bad' individuals (for example, those remiss in their parenting practices) needing to be brought into sociocentrality by the presenter's advice. In contrast, Thomas admires the green life experiment programmes for their collective basis, since the solution to the issue being addressed – heedless use of utilities – can only be effective if collectively adopted (2008a: 695). The problem with approaching this through a life experiment show, though, is that the structure and the narrative are individually driven, by, for example, the incentive of being given money saved by the adopted green efficiencies.

The distinction between consuming differently and consuming less is worth making, though both can be ethically based in green principles. Jo Littler warns against overly simplistic valuations of reduced consumption that is more easily engaged in by middle class home owners who can operate an 'enclave politics'. Nonetheless she notes the value of (some, British) newspaper columnists disseminating news about this more widely throughout a population (2009: 108–09). Given how very many more television viewers than newspaper readers there are, and their greater social diversity, the importance of television presenters' advice and examples deserves consideration. Television is very useful for disseminating ideas that are in the process of becoming commonsense, which is why presenters are so clearly cultural intermediaries. Usually these ideas are well advanced, but with some of the green concerns television can intervene a little earlier.

Garden makeovers and gardening programmes

Garden programmes and their presenters have strong potential to advocate green-centred ethical consumption. The concern with organic practices is a major overlap with food programmes, but there are also significant differences. (Fewer of the presenters become celebrities and there are also simply fewer shows. American pay channel Planet Green screens no garden programmes.) The major differentiation between garden programmes rests on the matter of time: there are the fast and finite garden makeovers, and those concerned with the ongoing practice of gardening. A British variant of the latter is the garden documentary visiting existing, sometimes public, gardens, such as *Around the World in 80 Gardens* (BBC 2008). In their discussions with the gardeners responsible for producing the plantings, presenters repeatedly draw out the continuous labour required. They are thus, despite the apparent centrality of a finished product, focused on garden*ing*. It is this focus on the continuing practices of preparing the soil, planting, cultivating and repeating all the attendant processes that is at the heart of the way these programmes are able to best represent ethical consumption on lifestyle television.

Since about 2006, garden makeover programmes, especially standalone ones, have become rare, although there have been some Australian examples, such as *Domestic Blitz* (Channel 9, 2009). In keeping with the earlier, more popular examples, these continue to stress design aspects, low maintenance gardens, and gardens as entertainment spaces, while minimizing the labour involved. Australian commercial programme *Guerilla Gardeners* (2008) presented an allegedly public spirited series where dull areas of various cities were enlivened by unlicensed plantings and ornamental features. The ethical issues involved in this, however, went no further than aesthetic ones and joy in the illegality of the activity.

British gardening has become a concern solely for the BBC; Channel 4 screened both gardening and makeover programmes at the turn of the century, but has stopped doing so. Even dedicated lifestyle channels on digital free-to-air and pay TV ignore gardens, getting no closer than repeats of the River Cottage series. The Australian situation is more diverse. *Better Homes and Gardens* (Channel 7, 1995–) is a commercial Australian magazine programme with garden segments, often involving small makeovers, while the Lifestyle pay channel screens repeats of shows first broadcast on free-to-air and commissions its own. This last example includes the major green exception to the commercial picture so far. The Lifestyle channel has retained landscape architect Brendan Moar for over ten years across a number of programmes, currently *Moar Gardens* and *Dry Spell Gardening*. The latter constructs new gardens along green guidelines and talks about elements gaining or losing 'eco-points'. While technically a makeover, the presenter works for the clients, who remain on-site, his fee is discussed, and there is no reveal (the conventional concluding surprise revelation of the new look).

Ethical consumption is far more evident on the Australian public broadcasters, the ABC and the multicultural broadcaster SBS, both through the espousing of organic practices and the avoiding of fast, cosmetic makeovers. If either of the long running flagship gardening shows, the BBC's *Gardeners' World* and the ABC's *Gardening Australia*, transform a garden, it is a long process followed over several seasons or even years. On all the public broadcasters' shows, organic practices represent the default mode of good gardening. The espousing of organic practices has had a longer run in British culture, with Geoff Hamilton, chief presenter of *Gardeners' World* from 1979 to 1995, being credited with 'almost single-handedly taking organic gardening out of the realm of the cranky and into the mainstream' (Search 2003: 71). Nor was it just BBC at that time; Bob Flowerdew presented the *All Muck and Magic* sequence of organic gardening shows on Channel 4 from 1987 until 1990. Nowadays it is seen as so much commonsense that the word is rarely uttered on *Gardeners' World* although it is still the omnipresent mode. Carol Klein, normally a *Gardeners' World* presenter, explicitly introduced organic practices in her short series *Grow Your Own Veg!* because it was designed to teach people to garden productively from scratch.

Australia has a somewhat less established organic culture, so *Gardening Australia* is characterized by heavy reiteration of the virtues of being organic and all that that entails. Until his retirement at the beginning of 2009, this was centred on the lead presenter Peter Cundall's vegetable plot in the Hobart Botanical Gardens, but accompanied by a sustainable garden in Brisbane tended by associate presenter Jerry Coleby-Williams and a permaculture one in Perth belonging to another presenter, Josh Byrne. Both these gardens continue to be featured on the show. The programme has followed the establishment of both, giving different refinements on contemporary organic practices and providing a narrative framework that allows advice to be repeated within a new framework.

Both sustainable gardening and its more hard-core fellow, permaculture, operate from a position antithetical to lifestyle culture. The degree of incompatibility may not be immediately apparent, because green approaches are being presented as fashionable elsewhere, in magazines and newspapers for instance. Yet the continuing televisual presence of the once counter-cultural activities should not be seen as just part of this. The key words 'sustainable' and 'permanent' mark a refusal to adopt the ideology of fashionability and the rapid turnover of identity indicators that underpin lifestyle. In contrast *Dry Spell Gardening* may discuss the environmentally positive and negative qualities of all the components used, but Moar is usually called in to update the appearance of a garden to match a renovated house.

Gardeners' World and *Gardening Australia* locate gardening at the centre of a life well lived, with television gardeners able to demonstrate not just persistent green behaviours including thrift and resourcefulness, but also clear instances of care for both the family and the community. This is even more the case with the two SBS gardening programmes: *Vasili's Garden* in 2008 and *Costa's Backyard Odyssey* in 2009. The presenters' Greek names are the first indication that these programmes are fulfilling the channel's multicultural brief, though in different ways. Vasili Kanidiadis, who had previously presented the show on a Melbourne community channel, visited mainly Greek and Italian immigrant gardeners and talked about their fruit and vegetable gardens, naming their practices organic but not explaining what this involved. He was more intent on persuading his viewers of the importance of growing as much of their own food as they could. Costa Georgiadis examines gardening practices across a wider range of backgrounds (immigrant, indigenous and refugee) and includes regular visits to community gardens. He is quite emphatic in promoting organic practices, but his interest in community gardening is the locus for the most distinctive ethical component. Green concerns are not framed by fashionability or individualized consumption, but are shown as continuing communal responsibilities. The joy that all these presenters have in engaging with and promoting sustainable modes of gardening places them firmly as advocates of an alternative hedonism.

Waterwise gardening

As cultural intermediaries, garden show presenters disseminate contemporary 'wisdom' from various sources – including trendsetters, big corporations, public health officials or their own professional training – to those sections of the wider society that watch their shows or talk about them. Because of the mainstream status of their primary medium, they are unlikely to mediate cutting edge advice, but they do have the potential to reach large numbers of ordinary people. Much more substantially than their concern with organic gardening, all the Australian programmes have promoted waterwise gardening as a specific separate topic.

In essence waterwise gardening has now become an inescapable part of Australian television advice. Whether programmes are screened on commercial or public broadcasting, they have to take account of the too long disregarded situation that Australia is a drought-prone country. This status has been brought home by the consequences of the extensive drought that has been evident across Australia for at least seven years and, with the uncertainties about precisely how climate change will alter rainfall, may well become intensified.

Perhaps the fondness of standalone garden makeover programmes for water features and instant lawn to produce the required visual transformation contributed to their disappearance in Australia. Yet despite their fondness for water thirsty elements, even the older Australian shows occasionally had waterwise moments, particularly centring on plant selection, especially of striking dry climate examples. Makeover shows – and shorter makeover segments – are primarily concerned with fast garden design rather than with the practice of gardening, so selection is the key activity. A 2008 segment in *Better Homes and Gardens* that was promoted as instructing viewers on making a waterwise garden, involved making an (expensive) chequerboard of paving and succulents. The frequency with which commercial TV garden presenters advocate hard surfaces is in line with the unsurprising tendency of commercial television programmes to suggest consuming new products to solve existing problems.

By contrast when *Gardening Australia* talks of waterwise gardens, it tends to follow one of two patterns; the first involves garden visits, to large and often public gardens to recommend plants and practices for home use. The other pattern involves items shot in the homes of the two presenters who have been demonstrating sustainable and permaculture gardens and both of whom are concerned with waterwise practices, especially careful recycling of grey water. Because viewers have been shown the development and installation of these gardens, they are aware that starting off these garden styles is not a cheap option, however much their costs are amortized in the long run. Both commercial and ABC programmes then have tendencies to promote water wisdom through consuming differently, with the ABC suggesting environmentally responsible products.

The real alternative comes with SBS shows, where water use is central. *Vasili's Garden* was shot in Melbourne and the intractable materiality of the drought and water restrictions there meant that gardeners needed to have developed ways of coping if they were to grow the desired fruit and vegetables. Vasili repeatedly asked the usually working class gardeners visited how they maintained their gardens despite the restrictions. Even though the same response came week after week, each gardener was asked and consistently answered: storing rainwater. The containers shown were crude and improvised; there were no designer tanks (butts), drip irrigation or recycling systems. People made do with what they had.

Costa addressed drainage problems as well as responsible use of water resources. The regular pattern was for him to provide solutions to poor drainage, but to be instructed in water wisdom by the community gardeners. The result was that drainage was placed in the hands of professionals, but ethically desirable ways of watering gardens became a matter of sharing knowledge from a range of ordinary people all of whom valued frugality. While many water tanks were shown, they were obviously valued for their utility rather than aesthetic contributions to garden design.

The pattern then is established. Commercial shows unsurprisingly promote consumption. Water wisdom involves buying new tanks, more pavers or other hard surfaces and new plants. The ABC is less concerned with consumption, though its persistent display of the installation of systems to reuse grey water endorses the lifestyle of the green consumer. SBS, probably because it bought the community television ethos along with its first programme, is close to anti-consumption; people recycle in ways reminiscent of the 1950s or they operate communally. What is most distinctive about waterwise gardening though is the level of unanimity underlying the differences I've noted. The inescapable combination of drought and water restrictions has meant that advice must address ways to garden differently. Furthermore, because watering is a continuing requirement for any garden, this involves ongoing ethical investment.

In addition to water wisdom being a component of existing garden shows, the past two years have seen the growth of green programmes dealing specifically with water. There have been one-off commercial programmes such as *Great Water Challenge* and *Water Forever*, while existing programmes like the ABC's *The New Inventors* and the commercial *Garden Gurus*, usually a garden tips show close to advertorial in style, have aired water specials. Drought has required television to 'work through' changes to water use, to use John Ellis' term (2000:

74–86). The inclusion of water wisdom within the green life experiment shows already mentioned is another place where these issues are worked through.

Waterwise gardening had little presence on British television before 2006 and the term is still little known. However, in that year, sections of the UK were experiencing a drought and living under water restrictions involving hose bans and in consequence waterwise gardening featured occasionally on *Gardeners' World*. One episode talked about the use of grey water; another announced the team's commitment to using only grey water and rain water on the long borders at their main site; but it was a minor concern and one of the clearest differences between the two countries' approaches.[1]

Social action

In an article on the growth of the ecologically aware consumer, Michael Maniates wrote, not happily, of the 'growing allure of consumption-as-social-action' (2001: 38). The green reality challenge shows might be implicated here even though they are explicitly constructed to encourage emulation. Maniates was concerned that consumption of green products would be regarded as sufficient, replacing involvement in activities producing substantial social change. Those programmes following the installation of expensive reticulation systems to reuse water or wholesale conversion to permaculture are not presented as if more is required than adopting them. *Costa's Garden Odyssey* is probably the only garden show to be comparatively uninterested in consumption and consistent in suggesting social action.

The campaigning work on food issues I noted being conducted through television by Fearnley-Whittingstall and Jamie Oliver among others would seem to provide instances where both consumption and social action were evident. There are no Australian equivalents of these explicit campaigning vehicles and given the paucity of British gardening programmes and presenters with sufficiently high profiles for one or two to engage this way, campaigning on garden-related matters might be considered unlikely. There are, however, two areas where it can be seen. The first cannot be regarded as advocating consumption as it is being discussed here, though it was undoubtedly green. It was a programme by the then lead presenter of *Gardeners' World*, Monty Don, entitled *Growing out of Trouble*, in which working on a smallholding was trailed as therapy for a group of young people who were 'prolific offenders', mainly drug addicts. The activities were closer to Fearnley-Whittingstall's farming than actual gardening, but the practices followed were organic, indeed at one stage also biodynamic.[2]

The second acknowledges a campaign to increase the production of home-grown food, most evident through Carol Klein's *Grow Your Own Veg!* and her continuation of this advocacy on *Gardeners' World*. While there are no stand-alone Australian programmes, promotion of home garden food production for healthy nutrition, and sometimes for thrift, can be found in most shows other than garden makeovers. The rhetoric that accompanies all of this stresses the desirability of knowing what goes into the food, in other words it is underpinned by a suspicion of agribusiness. The recently retired chief presenter of *Gardening Australia*, Peter Cundall, was an active campaigner on environmental and human rights issues, but the only trace to be found in his television work was his advocacy of organic practices and school gardens. There are differences between advocates for the green lifestyle demonstrating by example and instruction, campaigners targeting a particular practice trying to change industrial and personal practices, and the regular presentation of ethically informed practice as common sense, but all could be regarded as promoting social action to some extent.

Conclusion

This examination of British and Australian lifestyle programmes has demonstrated that while television presenters certainly do act as cultural intermediaries introducing viewers to 'new doctrines of ethical salvation' as Bourdieu says, these are not necessarily only in the service of increased and heedless consumption. Both food and gardening presenters, not to mention those more explicitly naming themselves green, act to disseminate information and by example encourage both consuming differently and consuming less. I have suggested that those presenters who talk about and demonstrate gardening as an organic and (in Australia) waterwise and communal practice are likely to be advancing the greatest ethical change in consumption because of the continuing rather than one-off character of the activity. It might seem that the same should be able to be said of cooking, but these programmes are rather about food and the production of individual dishes. Gardening is represented as a continuous engagement with the earth, the seasons and the botanical world. The key activities of propagation and composting, repeatedly discussed in the shows, recycle existing materials in the greenest of ways. And, whether or not every gardener in the real world is having fun doing it, on television, they certainly are.

Notes

1 I compare the two countries' gardening programmes at greater length in Bonner (2008).
2 An associated charity was established to further this work. Since having to leave his presenting role due to ill-health, Don has accepted the Chair of the Soil Association, returning him to a campaigning role.

Bibliography

Bonner, F. (2008) 'Digging for difference: British and Australian gardening programmes', in G. Palmer (ed.) *Exposing Lifestyle Television: The Big Reveal*, Aldershot, UK: Aldgate.
Bourdieu, P. (1984) *Distinction*, trans. R. Nice, London: Routledge.
—— (2002) 'The role of intellectuals today', *Theoria*, June: 1–6.
Ellis, J. (2000) *Seeing Things: Television in the Age of Uncertainty*, London: I.B.Tauris.

Hill, A. (2005) *Reality TV: Audiences and Popular Factual Television*, London: Routledge.

Littler, J. (2009) *Radical Consumption: Shopping for Change in Contemporary Culture*, Maidenhead, UK: McGraw Hill/Open University Press.

Maniates, M.F. (2001) 'Individualization: plant a tree, buy a bike, save the world?', *Global Environmental Politics*, 1(3): 31–52.

Moores, S. (2005) *Media/Theory: Thinking about Media & Communication*, London: Routledge.

Nixon, S. and du Gay, P. (2002) 'Who needs cultural intermediaries?', *Cultural Studies*, 16(4): 495–500.

Search, G. (2003) *Gardeners' World: Through the Years*, London: Carlton Books.

Soper, K. (2008) 'Alternative hedonism, cultural theory and the role of aesthetic revisioning', *Cultural Studies*, 22(5): 567–87.

Thomas, L. (2008a) 'Alternative realities', *Cultural Studies*, 22(5): 680–99.

—— (2008b) '"Ecoreality": the politics and aesthetics of "green" television', in G. Palmer (ed.) *Exposing Lifestyle Television: The Big Reveal*, Aldershot, UK: Aldgate.

17 'Caring at a distance'

The ambiguity and negotiations of ethical investment

Cathy Greenfield and Peter Williams

Introduction

Ethical investment sits alongside a concern with ethical consumption through its common implication in the ethical agency available to people in the twenty-first century. It entails specific forms of consumption of finance industry services and products. In addition, ethical investment indicates alternatives to dominant arrangements in which narrowly figured economic rationalities insulate the daily work of consumption and production from political and ethical considerations. Thus at a time when the dispositions and practices that characterize financialized economies have become seemingly entrenched, ethical investment presents a particular negotiation, if not contestation, of these practices, based around an exhortation to individuals to ethical agency. It is on these grounds, rather than simply its proclaimed increasing size as a proportion of all financial investment, that ethical investment deserves attention. Consideration of what it consists of, its historical formation and current practices, actors and relations, of debates and controversies concerning it, and of its possible achievements, can tell us something about the ways in which people's agency has been assembled in recent decades. Our argument – that the apparently 'free' choice to invest ethically is heavily pressured and underpinned by a dominant finance culture as well as longer-running connections between credit and conscience – begins by noting a particular tradition of connections between ethics, financial activity and formations of personhood, then discusses some recent examples of exhortations to ethically invest, considering as it does so the complexities of what the term 'ethical investment' entails.

History lessons

Ethical investment presumes that investment is a practice which needs to be shaped in a *certain* way in order to be ethical, but also that this *can* be done. The notion that investment can be an ethical pursuit is one that depends historically on establishing finance as a legitimate professional domain, that is, distinguishing it from gambling. As De Goede's (2005) genealogy of finance chronicles, this shift entailed numerous and lengthy struggles, such as those over the US bucketshops, or small betting shops, of the late nineteenth century, where it was possible to bet on the movements of stock prices without actually purchasing stocks. Along with futures trading, bucketshops were the focus of ongoing legislative and wider debates which attempted to resolve the ambiguity between gambling and speculation, the latter defended by its supporters as involving intellectual effort not found in gambling's faith in fortune.

De Goede traces these debates as 'the slow articulation of money making as a calm virtuous pursuit' (2005: 34) and focuses on the 'paper wars' exchanges (1698–1734) between Defoe, Swift and Pope with their characteristic 'sexualized public discourse on credit' (De Goede 2005: 27). Especially in Defoe's writing about 'Lady Credit', new knowledges emerged about finance as something that may be engaged in while keeping one's virtue. The means to this active mastery and control of credit were the techniques of double-entry book-keeping – a way of producing knowledge of one's overall financial position by creating visibility for those actions performed in the most distant areas of one's household (Quattrone 2009: 99). At the same time, the book-keeper conducts ethical work on himself:

> to Defoe accounting and the 'casting up of books' are moral technologies that will not only reveal the truth of the tradesman's circumstance, but that will also guarantee the cleanliness of the tradesman's conscience.
>
> (De Goede 2005: 36)

The practices of self-monitoring and self-control associated with book-keeping, as 'books to be practiced' (Quattrone 2009), were part of wider, initially Protestant, 'practices of self' or ethical techniques, involving other forms of reading and writing such as diary keeping and providence literature, which shaped the conscience of the practitioner (Hunter 1989: 220–21). This consciencization, linked to the financial accounting of book-keeping, suggests the basis for an ethico-financial practice or literacy which is reprised and intensified in the contemporary proliferation of ethical investment. Thus the conduct of the individual ethical investor is systematized through a conscious and thoughtful management of their relation to the current imperative in financialized economies to be financially responsible and to invest.

Shifting circumstances and responses

It is within such financialized economies – that is, economies in which the finance sector has been made dominant – that ethical investment has grown rapidly, according to its various reporters and promoters.[1] The current capitalist crisis of circulation, commonly known as the Global Financial Crisis, offers an exemplary moment for critical consideration of ethical investment and of the broader ethics–investment nexus within which it is located. The crisis has thrown up a range of perspectives and responses, as the following quotations indicate:

The biggest challenge in the present crisis is whether we can recover some sense of the connection between money and material reality – the production of specific things, the achievement of recognizably human goals that have something to do with a shared sense of what is good for the human community in the widest sense.

(Archbishop of Canterbury cited in BBC 2008)

'Great fortunes will be made in this market' Peter Hall – Sydney, March 2009. A savage bear market offers wonderful opportunities – and we are hunting for bargains. Through 15 years of market ups and downs the Hunter Hall Value Growth Trust has achieved a compound annual return of 13.9%.

(Hunter Hall advertisement 2009a)

The first quotation is from a widely reported story in which the Archbishop of Canterbury condemned a financial system that produced 'no concrete outcome beyond profit for traders' and issued a call to rejoin financial outcomes with 'just outcomes' (BBC 2008). The second is from a series of newspaper advertisements run by Australia's 'largest dedicated ethical investment manager' (Hunter Hall 2009b), alerting potential clients to both the opportunities afforded by the Crisis and to high rates of return for their services – highlighting that ethical investment is, after all, investment. The 2008–09 global economic downturn has prompted reconsideration of investment strategies (by those in the financial sector), calls for more responsible investment (by politicians, regulators and some journalists), and calls to re-balance financial outcomes with ethico-social outcomes (by church and community leaders). Nevertheless, what is more important – as well as more certain – than what the Global Financial Crisis means for ethical investment and for the ethics–investment nexus, is the location of ethical investment as a possible, persuasive form of agency within the wider and established phenomenon of financialized economies, of which the current crisis is a particularly dramatic aspect.

Financialization and ethical investment

The financialization of economies has entailed a growth regime organized around equity or 'shareholder value' rather than production (as in the earlier Fordist growth regime) (Aglietta 2000), a complex financial technology characterized by the innovations of securitization (the conversion of risk into contractual packages) and new forms of derivatives enabled by computerization and ICTs, as well as a substantially altered finance culture. This culture (Greenfield and Williams 2001; 2003; 2007; Martin 2002; Langley 2008) has involved promotion of the importance, accessibility and benefits of the world of finance to the general populations of especially Anglo-American countries and produced, over the past two or more decades, a saturated media environment accustoming those populations to the requisite dispositions, norms and practices for their willing or mandated participation in investment opportunities; individuals called on to take responsibility for their own finances; and the widespread aspiration to 'secure' one's own financial futures and freedom. Thus, investment advice, superannuation, insurance, home mortgages, consumer credit, specialized retirement advice, financial counselling, internet banking and stock-market trading are products and services that through the 1990s and the first decade of the 2000s became routinized topics of consumer conversation and knowledge. The growing emphasis on the need for everyone to possess financial literacy occurred at the same time as savings were increasingly channelled into the capital market through the expansion of defined contribution pension plans in the US in the early 1980s, the equivalent growth in British pension funds (Minns 2001), and in Australia with the introduction of compulsory occupational superannuation in 1992.

There are by now numerous questions concerning the outcomes of this concerted promotion of finance and responsibilization of populations for their financial well-being, a claimed 'democratization of finance'. Over a decade ago, Leyshon *et al.* (1998) questioned the adequacy of provisions for financial literacy given the financial risks these developments had transferred to individuals. Further, Aldridge (1998: 9–15) describes the 'passive individualist' participation in investment that neoliberal finance regimes have actually achieved, as opposed to their rhetoric. He sees this passive individualist participation as the alternative habitus to that of the 'active consumers' demanded by the rhetoric of neoliberal finance regimes, and the result of their failure to provide, and thus for broad populations to acquire, the 'cultural capital' or expertise needed for 'active consumption'. Such participation is based in branded, commodified, mass-based, costly, and opaque provision of finance products, products which, notably, exclude the possibility of ethical investment as anything other than a market brand (Aldridge 1998: 12–15). Langley has extended this description of the ways in which 'everyday' savers and borrowers feel 'at home' in financialized economies, identifying the conditions and realities that lead to their existence as 'uncertain subjects' (2008: 88–112), unable to attain the reduction in uncertainty about their financial futures which the new finance culture promises. In many cases individuals are struggling to participate in investment because of stop-start contractual work conditions, and are forced to negotiate contradictory exhortations to participate in heavily promoted consumer credit.

The point of establishing these elements of financial literacy, finance culture, and the broader financialization of which they are a part is that it helps us understand some key conditions within which people are assembled as 'ethical investors'. First, if the role of 'ethical investor' is now on the horizon for more people (more, that is, than just those wealthy individuals who have historically had the capital as well as the know-how to be both investors and philanthropists),[2] it is a specific inflection of their formation *as investors*, equipped with both the disposition to accept the risks attendant to investment, rather than the risk avoidance attached to earlier practices of saving, and with the disposition of 'waiting' for future returns.[3]

A second condition for ethical investment which derives from financialization is that the complex financial technology and innovations that it involves, such as finance-based derivatives,[4] provide the potential for new, monetized forms of 'caring at a distance' (Silk 2000: 303). The financial innovations of the late twentieth century have produced new and monetized time-space relations connecting social groups in different ways. For example, forward-based derivatives, particularly futures and swaps, link the present and the future of different places, 'by interest rates and the expectations held by traders about the future' (Pryke and Allen 2000: 272). If these new social relations are more often in the news for the problems they cause (for example, pensioners' savings in one country jeopardized by financial collapse of funds in another), they also provide the connections for new forms of 'caring' for others, where 'we take the crucial step actively to do good' (Silk 2000: 304), others with whom the one caring does not have face-to-face contact or share a locale or community. Like the forms of ethical consumption enabled by Fairtrade, social finance organizations such as Triodos and Charity Bank 'emphasise connectivity over localism' and 'the cultivation of forms of "caring at a distance"' (Buttle 2007: 1078).[5] But what precisely is meant by 'caring' in twenty-first-century investment?

This question hinges on a third condition deriving from the financialization of economies within which people are assembled as ethical investors: the normalized practices of calculation of return on what is owned. These practices build, extend on and intensify agency organized around equity or ownership, informed by the possessive individualism that has characterized liberal regimes of government. In this doctrine, the individual is 'essentially the proprietor of his own person and capacities, for which he owes nothing to society' (Macpherson 1962: 263). In the later neoliberal regimes of government which underpin financialization, this ethic of autonomy is enabled and buttressed by further ownership of careers, of lifestyles, of relationships as social capital, and of equity in homes, retirement funds, and diverse enterprises. The resulting form of agency is one which, when moved to do good, involves caring in ways which are conditional on returns, not just for the recipients but also for the carer's bank balance as well as psychological state. For this is one of the key issues in ongoing debates about and scrutiny of ethical investment, that whatever else this form of activity is, it *is* 'investment'. It must be calculated to return a profit. This normative limit to what ethical investment entails is apparent in debates over the legal implications for trustees assisting clients with ethical investment. While working with ethical or social criteria such as avoidance of the armaments or tobacco industry or support of recycling or affirmative action employment policies, a major legal argument is that their primary agenda must be financial performance, distinguishing them, for example, from the trustees of charities (Ali and Gold 2002: 7), and the calculations involved in another adjacent activity, corporate activism. The primacy of the calculation of profit is also evident in the ongoing scrutiny of the rate of return enjoyed by ethical investment, relative to market benchmarks (for example, Keefe 2008: 5–7; Kurtz 1997).

While in some ways this seems to be the statement of a truism (ethical investment must be investment), it is important to make visible the normalized imperative of getting a return from ownership. This places a particular conditionality on the ethics involved. When this conditionality is considered, the form of caring at a distance enabled by ethical investment seems less like the state of affairs promised by win-win rhetoric, with its egalitarian and socially cohesive connotations, and instead becomes recognizable as a definite power relation between owners and 'others'. This observation does not rule out or contest any beneficial outcome that might be achieved by ethical investment for those 'others', but it does notice that ethical investment's caring at a distance entails both the distance *inserted* between carer and recipient by the mediation of their relation through the instruments and practices of a financial technology, as well as the geographical distance between investors/carers and those invested in, which this technology routinely involves.

Noting the consequences of this particular kind of caring at a distance is not to demand a personalist, face-to-face localism in caring for people, but to indicate that it does little to contest the privatization which has eroded other arrangements of social cohesion and well-being. We are thinking, for instance, of those organized through practices of social security funded by taxation, in which 'a relation of obligation between citizen and society [is] enacted and regulated through the mediating party of the State' (Miller and Rose 2008: 87). Having noted these parameters and limits, let us turn to closer consideration of how ethical investment is understood by its promoters and participants.

Definitions

We have already indicated that ethical investment is not charity, philanthropy or corporate activism, despite adjacencies with and intersections between these kinds of financial activity given their shared social or ethical concerns, and despite a regular rhetorical blurring of them. How is ethical investment positively distinguished and defined? For Spagnolo, author of *The Ethical Investor: Make Money and Feel Good about it* (2007) – only the latest in a long line of such practical guides – ethical investment is a 'kind of umbrella description of an approach to investing where investments are screened or filtered according to your personal values and beliefs' (2007: 5–6). The 'umbrella' here indicates that ethical investment may mean any or all of the following: 'socially responsible investment', 'social investment', 'screened investments', 'mission-based investment', 'values-based investment', 'sustainable investment' or 'green investing'. The area, as well as the terminology, has a considerable history and continues to develop.[6] From the seventeenth-century Quaker refusal to profit from war and slavery (Weigand *et al.* 1996: 36) to Anglican and Methodist Churches' adoption of ethical prohibitions on particular types of investment in the early twentieth century, ethical investment gathered momentum in the 1960s with churches and social movements investigating ways to restrict investment in companies involved in apartheid South Africa or complicit in the Vietnam War (Mackenzie 1997: 59).

Sparkes considers the changing usage of 'ethical investment' across this history. While at first it referred to the ethical considerations taken by some churches in making investments, ethical investment later denoted the growing range of commercial investment products utilizing screening processes, while by the late 1990s the term 'ethical investment' was increasingly joined by that of 'socially responsible investment', which foregrounded the evaluation of companies 'not just by their financial performance, but . . . [by] also assessing how they achieve such profitability' (1998: 5). More recently, 'sustainable investing' has been promoted as an 'emergent financial discipline' with a distinguishing focus on the 'materiality' and 'outcomes' of environmental, social and governance factors rather than previous emphases on 'values' (Keefe 2008: 8; see also Kessel 2009).

Given these shifts in terminology, we advance a working definition of ethical investment that entails how investment is made in a company with reference to its involvement in, and its record of relating to, a diverse list of activities, products and concerns.[7] Combinations of research and 'screening' are used to discriminate between those companies to be avoided and those to invest in; for example, 'negative screens' are used to exclude particular companies from the 'entire universe of investable securities' in which an investor can participate (Ali and Gold 2002: 9), while positive or inclusionary screens 'identify and encourage the progressive policies and practices of corporations' to the same end (Weigand *et al.* 1996: 39).

If ethical investment can thus be defined *without* prioritizing values in the way exemplified by Spagnolo's popular definition, a framework of 'personal values' nevertheless does underpin one major form of address found in the promotional culture of the ethical investment sector.[8] Here is just one example of this from a finance expert speaking about ethical investing:

> Recent studies suggest that there's very little difference [in yields] between investing to make money and investing to make money and express your values. The hard part may be finding *which* values you want to express, and then matching those values to a particular fund.
>
> (American Public Media 2007)

In line with this values-oriented concept of ethical investment, techniques of personal testimony and personalization are common at both the leading and more modest end of the sector. The pioneering mutual fund manager Domini, for instance, presents its origin through the story of Amy Domini, a stockbroker:

> One of Amy's clients, an avid birdwatcher, sought Amy's advice on what to do with [her stock in] a large paper company she held that endangered the birds she loved . . . Amy began to realize that a new way of looking at investments was emerging, and she realized how much sense it made.
>
> (Domini 2009)

Another example of personal testimony comes from Steven Whipp, of Berkshire Securities, speaking to camera of his own experience as an ethical investor as well as his fiduciary role as an ethical investment advisor. He concludes: 'what better way to build a relationship with a client than to define what their values are, what really makes them tick' (Heartmindmoney 2007). This values discourse routinely sits alongside the theme of 'making a difference', in which the stories of impacts and outcomes in local or distant communities or in the global environment are presented as the realization of personal values through the mechanism of selective investment.

A more analytical definition of ethical investment than Spagnolo's is provided by Mackenzie, as 'the practice of investing funds on the basis of a set of ethical criteria' (1997: 59). This has the virtue both of being inclusive of a range of investment practices and of not reducing these necessarily to 'personal values and beliefs'. For Mackenzie, this allows the distinction between, on the one hand, 'investor-led' funds, that choose which companies to avoid or to invest in on the basis of market research into general ethical concerns as well as clients' ethical profiles, and, on the other, 'deliberative funds', where typically a committee structure carefully researches and deliberates about the positive and negative aspects of each company and constructs a definite ethical argument concerning reasons for avoidance or selection.[9]

Arguments and ambiguity

Mackenzie's distinction attempts to answer some of the criticisms that right-wing commentators and think-tanks in the UK, the US and Australia have directed at ethical investing: that it routinely and simplistically embraces 'fashionable causes' and 'pre-empt[s] complex moral arguments in favour of a particular foregone conclusion' (Anderson 1996). It is through the 'definitional ambiguity' and subjective nature of its ethical criteria, these critics contend, that ethical investment has 'devolved into an exercise in tactics and liberal sentimentality' (Entine 2003: 358; see also Hoggett and Nahan 2002). Such attacks take aim at the 'aggressive simplicity' (Anderson 1996) of the more populist end of ethical investment rhetoric, that is, the presentation of ethics as intrinsic personal values to which individuals simply align their investment activity.

We shall return to the problems with this populism below, but it is important to note that ethical investment's right-wing critics are also keen to debunk the 'calculation and politics' that they argue characterizes ethical investors and advocates: 'not . . . ethics at all' (Anderson 1996). This concerted attack on ethical investment for its liberal politics identifies the area as a touchstone of concern for neoliberal think-tanks, keen to expose what, in their view, is a connection between ethical investment and social engineering (Hoggett and Nahan 2002: 3). The diagnosis of ethical investment's appeal and of its threat to free markets is that, while profit 'may have undergone a partial rehabilitation . . . residual hostility is still capable of inflaming the puritan conscience' when it comes to some *kinds of* profit (Anderson 1996). Ethical investment is thus taken as a doctrinal threat to the asserted rhetorical autonomy of the economic, contradicting as it does Milton Friedman's dictum that 'there is one and only one social responsibility of business

– to use its resources and engage in activities designed to increase its profits so long as it . . . engages in open and free competition, without deception and fraud' (Friedman cited in Mackenzie 1997: 12).

Yet the think-tanks' detection of residual hostility to profit runs counter to the dual aspects, or paired but distinct imperatives, of ethical investment. The second form of address commonly used to hail audiences as potential ethical investors is the emphasis on the ethical investment sector's ability to match or outperform traditional portfolios. For example, a case study in Spagnolo's *The Ethical Investor* recounts the story of Malcolm, who

> didn't have particularly strong ethical leanings, but had heard that ethical investments perform well. He also accepted that incorporating 'triple bottom line accounting procedures' . . . could contribute to the financial success of a company. This became the basis of the ethical screens in Malcolm's portfolio.
>
> (Spagnolo 2007: 15)

In a different register, Pax World Investments greets readers with the promise of outperformance:

> In our view, Sustainable Investing has the potential to deliver higher returns with lower risk over the long term. We believe it is a superior and potentially transformative investment approach that better serves investors, markets and society.
>
> (Pax World 2009)

Meanwhile, ethical investment fund manager Australian Ethical shouts its performance, exploiting ethical investment's duality of address as a double entendre, in its newspaper advertisement headline 'Did Good? Did *Really* Good!', announcing 'Almost 15 years of outperformance from investment in sustainable companies' – '*pure*investment*performance*' (Australian Ethical 2009).

Thus, the two paired forms of address, one to people's conscience, the other to their prudence or financial self-interest, attempt to persuade interested audiences to contemplate and pursue ethical investment. While ethical investment's slogans, for example, 'doing well while doing good' (Social Funds 2009a), seemingly unite conscience and prudent accumulation, an ethical investor may not, in fact, be moved by both interpellations. The investor who is seeking financially beneficial diversification in their portfolio by selecting ethical investment products may have no ethical involvement – in the sense of a personal intention to do good or to avoid doing harm – except for consumption of the services and products of the ethical investment sector.

The duality of these paired forms of address ('doing well while doing good'), we are suggesting, is something of a marker of ethical investment more generally. The different ways this duality is negotiated means the domain of ethical investment is complex, diverse, at times ambiguous, and sometimes unstable. The negotiation of ethical and financial investment may be accomplished by leading with personal values, or prioritizing the outperformance promised by the environmental, social and governance factors in 'best of class' screening, or balancing the two. Ethical investment is complex because of its different rationalities and associated devices, such as screens and investor profiles, as well as because of the different communication strategies used to promote ethical investment.[10] It is diverse, in terms of the purposes and kind of investors involved. It is at times ambiguous because of the variety of possible motivations driving the ethical investor. Ethical investment is also sometimes unstable in terms of being able to keep the promise to perform ethically. For example, Pax World incurred a US$500,000 penalty for 'taking stakes in companies involved with alcohol, gambling and military contracting' (Lieber 2008). For critics, this instability is more usually taken as hypocrisy or as proof of the inevitability of the investment world's requirement of ethical compromise. At the same time, this tendency towards compromise can ironically serve to broaden the appeal of ethical investment through highlighting its alignment with general finance sector practice more broadly. Another way of thinking about the ambiguities, complexities, instabilities and diversity of ethical investment is to understand it as a financial technology.

A financial technology of ethical investment

The definitions, underlying knowledges, lists of ethical issues, promotional artefacts, forms of address and other communicative techniques discussed above are parts of a recognizable financial technology of ethical investment. This is in the sense Raymond Williams seminally defined 'technology', as a set of techniques (or particular skills and applications of such skills), the technical inventions or devices developed from these techniques, the knowledges associated with both the development and application of these techniques and devices, and the knowledges and conditions for their practical use (1981: 226–27). What this view of ethical investment adds to our understanding is that individuals are formed as ethical investors *within* this technology, contrary to the populist presentations of ethical investment as a more or less straightforward and intuitive expression of personal values, from which people then proceed to organize their financial activity. The difference between these views is shown by the examples above of a values discourse, where we emphasized that values are something that require considerable work to *identify* (in American Public Media 2009) or to *discover* within the investor–advisor relation (Heartmindmoney 2007). Similarly, in Spagnolo's *The Ethical Investor*, a good proportion of the book is spent *exploring* personal values (2007: 29–58).

The technology of ethical investment comprises a heterogeneous set of elements. Setting these out in list form, they range from: specific knowledges such as religious doctrines, financial knowledges (for example, modern portfolio theory) and research into corporate social, environmental and ethical performance; legislation requiring disclosure of the use of social, environmental or ethical considerations in making investments; devices such as screens, questionnaires administered to companies, ethical investor profiles, and software such as Calvert Investments' 'Know What You Own Service' (Calvert Group 2009); purpose built indices such as the FTSE4Good; SRI products, ethical trusts, community development financial institutions, green funds, and so on; actors such as fund managers, socially responsible investment researchers, ethical/socially responsible investors, both individual and organizational; and the various media forms, strategies and techniques comprising the information and promotional culture of ethical investment.

One important part of the technology of ethical investment's promotional culture is the concept and presentation of the 'ethics investment problem'. That is, the 'problem' that motivates or 'requires' ethical investment for its solution can be seen as a constituent part of the technology of ethical investment, rather than outside and authoring it. This 'problem' is commonly formulated as the possibility or presumed likelihood that, without careful scrutiny and accounting of where one's money is going, support may be being unwittingly given to companies, products and practices that harm others (Mackenzie 1997: 116–33). Ethical investment is given its rationale largely as a response to the problem of 'support'.[11] A striking rendition of the 'problem of support' can be seen on YouTube in Futerra Sustainability Communications' video, 'One Minute' (FSC 2006). The premise of the video is that power is possessed by the individual, who is presented as able to 'make a difference'. A brief but intensely atmospheric narrative takes the viewer into a young British woman, Katy's, kitchen where, surrounded by a succession of interlocutors whom the viewer sees and hears though she doesn't, Katy boils the kettle (while a power worker tells her of the green energy they've developed), makes a mug of coffee (while an African woman describes what Katy's purchasing of a Fair Trade product means to her distant community), and then opens and reads her bank statement (while a menacingly confiding executive, machine gun in hand, details how armaments profits have been good this year, keeping her interest rate high). The concluding narration, 'What will happen in the next minute? You don't know your own strength' dramatizes a scenario of personal integrity undermined by 'the problem of support' – the harm being done to others through the support we give by investing in companies involved in unethical or injurious practices – which can be solved by Katy paying the same ethical attention to where she invests her money as to where she buys her coffee and her electricity.

The problem of support emphasizes that the ways in which the personal values that are brought into connection with the knowledges, practices, relations, devices and organizations of ethical investing do not begin with the fully formed ethical individual simply choosing this kind of action. The kind of agency produced here is assembled within a specific financial technology of ethical investment. It is an agency that entails a particular, watchful negotiation of the duality of or distance between ethics (rhetorically constituted as values) and practices of financial investment. For example, the webpage of First Affirmative Financial Network introduces readers to Sustainable Investing by emphasizing the practice as a careful, thoughtful application of the investor's values and choices. In sections such as 'Profiting from a Conscious Choice' and 'Transformative Investing' readers learn that 'You can make a positive difference by consciously directing your investments'. They are addressed as potentially one of the 'many thoughtful people choos[ing] not to profit from behaviour in others that they find objectionable in themselves' (FAFN 2009). As we began this chapter by outlining, this care and scrutiny, a marker of distinction for its practitioners, is connected to a longer history of consciencization.

Conclusion

We have sought to establish how the agency of the always organizationally embedded individual ethical investor is assembled, in order to emphasize that, while 'choosing' ethical investment may be presented in voluntarist terms by the populist end of the ethical investment culture, this 'free choice' is heavily pressured by current cultural persuasions to invest, as well as underpinned by long-established connections between the management of credit and the management of individual conscience. To notice the limits of the individualized and privileged character of much ethical investment rhetoric and practice is neither to dismiss it nor condemn it necessarily to the 'defensive realm of static sanctimoniousness' (Littler 2009: 15). It may be the case that ethical investment has some agency in a more '"affirmative" and "open" moral struggle as part of a collective project' (Littler 2009: 15). Here Mackenzie's point comes to mind: that 'the mere existence of a substantial ethical fund industry shows the financial community that there is reasonably substantial interest in ethical issues' (1997: 146).

That said, the prospects of ethical investment as a form of collective action for rearranging the power relations of current credit practices and of caring for others are constrained by three factors which have been succinctly described by Langley (2002; 2008: 127–35). Ethical investment is a 'choice' only for those with sufficient capital; ethical investment is increasingly dominated by 'major market institutional networks'; and those networks effectively decide what is counted as ethical (Langley 2002: 159–60). This last constraint suffuses contemporary discussion of what is possible in the area of progressive social change, casting social relations, friendship, knowledges and skills as so many forms of privatized 'capital' to be accumulated. Departing from this, what more broadly and fully democratic practices and relations of caring at varying distances, of social security and of *socio*-economic equity (as distinct from narrowly measured economic equity) might be calculable, policy programmable and possible? These are matters for democratic and political decision-making, not market contingencies.

Notes

1 The scale and importance of ethical investment is routinely in dispute. Eurosif (2008) estimated the Global Social Responsibility Investment market at approximately €5

trillion, with the US making up thirty-nine per cent, Europe fifty-three per cent and the rest of the world eight per cent.

2   Ali and Gold (2002: 3) point out that the availability of such investment strategies to the 'general community of investors . . . [rather than] wealthy individuals and charitable foundations' dates in the UK from 1984, in Australia from 1986 and earlier in the US.

3   'Waiting' is a trope in the rhetoric of neo-classical economics to the effect that value is derived not only from labour but also from 'waiting'. Waiting 'means owning wealth and the "sacrifice" is not consuming it' but lending it at interest (Robinson and Eatwell 1973: 39). 'Waiting' is tantamount to capital and the capitalist disposition that ensures its further accumulation.

4   Derivatives are the means by which companies lay off risk to those who want to acquire it. Finance-based derivatives (e.g. Collateral Debt Obligations) emerged in the 1980s.

5   Social finance organizations balance their consideration of their clients' financial risks with specific social objectives (Buttle 2007: 1078), such as providing finance to a local microfinance bank in, say, Tanzania.

6   Social Funds (2009a), '[t]he largest personal finance site devoted to socially responsible investing', provides users with a Social Investment Timeline of key developments. Targeted at personal finance writers, it exemplifies the sector's assiduous promotional work and the importance of giving investors a sense of belonging to a tradition (Social Funds 2009b).

7   These include alcohol, tobacco, gambling, pornography, armaments, employment policies, corporate relations with the community, diversity, pollution, uranium mining/nuclear power, recycling, energy use, genetic modification, product quality, human rights, animal rights, abortion/birth control, involvement in Sudan (a current issue) and so on.

8   A promotional culture that includes websites, magazines, newsletters, online videos, practical guides, news articles and public relations material.

9   The research needed for such deliberation can be complex. For example, ethical investors wishing to make a positive difference to food crises in poor countries would need to know how their investments affect 'commodity prices, indigenous farming, biofuel development, and funding and logistical assistance for feeding programs' (MacDonald 2008).

10 These range from the more professional or 'polished', for example Pax World, with its connotation of a close relation to the 'traditional' or 'neutral' investment sector, to the more personalized, and trending to folksy and populist style of *Greenmoney journal*.

11 Though increasingly, this problem is being joined by that of 'how to positively support ESG initiatives', for example, Keefe (2008). Both problems are, of course, paired with the EI problem of how to make a prudent investment, that is, a return on capital.

Bibliography

Aglietta, M. (2000) 'Shareholder value and corporate governance: some tricky questions', *Economy and Society*, 29 (1): 146–59.

Aldridge, A. (1998) '*Habitus* and cultural capital in the field of personal finance', *The Sociological Review*, 46 (1): 1–23.

Ali, P.U. and Gold, M. (2002) 'An appraisal of socially responsible investments and implications for trustees and other investment fiduciaries', Centre for Corporate Law and Securities Regulation, University of Melbourne. Online. Available HTTP:

http://cclsr.law.unimelb.edu.au/go/centre-activities/research/research-reports-and-research-papers/index.cfm (accessed 22 October 2008).

American Public Media (2007) 'Ethical investing', YouTube. Online. Available HTTP: http://au.youtube.com/watch?v=eZHNaN52_Ic&feature=related (accessed 4 December 2008).

Anderson D. (ed.) (1996) 'What has "ethical investment" to do with ethics?', Social Affairs Unit. Online. Available HTTP: www.bwz.com/BWZ/9604/learn.htm (accessed 22 June 2009).

Australian Ethical (2009) Advertisement, *Australian Financial Review*, 27–28 June: 37.

BBC (2008) 'Archbishops attack City practices', *BBC News*, 25 September. Online. Available HTTP: http://news.bbc.co.uk/2/hi/uk_news/7634641.stm (accessed 29 May 2009).

Buttle, M. (2007) '"I'm not in it for the money": constructing and mediating ethical reconnections in UK social banking', *Geoforum*, 38: 1076–88.

Calvert Group (2009) 'Know What You Own Service'. Online. Available HTTP: www.calvertgroup.com/kwyo.html (accessed 29 June 2009).

De Goede, M. (2005) *Virtue, Fortune, and Faith: A Genealogy of Finance*, Minneapolis, MN: University of Minnesota Press.

Domini (2009) 'The Domini story'. Online. Available HTTP: www.domini.com/about-domini/The-Domini-Story/index.htm (accessed 29 June 2009).

Entine, J. (2003) 'The myth of social investing: a critique of its practice and consequences for corporate social performance research', *Organization and Environment*, 16: 352–68.

Eurosif (2008) 'SRI study: 2008 global SRI data'. Online. Available HTTP: www.eurosif.org/publications/sri_studies (accessed 23 June 2009).

First Affirmative Financial Network (FAFN) (2009) 'More about us'. Online. Available HTTP: www.firstaffirmative.com/consumer.jsp (accessed 28 June 2009).

Futerra Sustainability Communications (FSC) (2006) 'One Minute', YouTube. Online. Available HTTP: http://au.youtube.com/watch?v=LG9nj5OGIJQ&feature=related (accessed 4 December 2008).

Greenfield, C. and Williams, P. (2001) 'Finance advertising and media rhetoric', *Southern Review: Communication, Politics & Culture*, 34(2): 44–66.

—— (2003) 'Globalization and the neo-liberal culture of finance capitalism', in L. Kerr (ed.) *Cultural Citizenship: Challenges of Globalization*, proceedings of the International Conference on Cultural Citizenship: Challenges of Globalisation, 5–8 December 2002, Geelong, Vic.: Deakin University.

—— (2007) 'Financialization, finance rationality and the role of media in Australia', *Media, Culture & Society*, 29 (3): 415–30.

Heartmindmoney. (2007) 'Socially reponsible investing – Steven Whipp', YouTube. Online. Available HTTP: www.youtube.com/watch?v=lZs81gQQgUM&NR=1 (accessed 29 June 2009).

Hoggett, J. and Nahan, M. (2002) 'Ethical investment – deconstructing the myth', *IPA Review*, September: 3–6.

Hunter, I. (1989) 'Providence and profit: speculations in the genre market', *Southern Review: Literary and Interdisciplinary Essays*, 22 (3): 211–23.

Hunter Hall. (2009a) Advertisement, *Australian Financial Review*, 2 June: 2.

—— (2009b) 'About us'. Online. Available HTTP: www.hunterhall.com.au/group-profile/about-us (accessed 3 July 2009).

Keefe, J. (2008) *Sustainable Investing as an Emergent Financial Discipline*, Keynote speech, Sustainable Investing 2008 Conference, NYC. Online. Available HTTP: http://paxworld.com/about/presidents-corner/ (accessed 27 June 2009).

Kessel, B. (2009) 'Sustainable Investing 2.0', *Greenmoneyjournal*. Online. Available HTTP: www.greenmoneyjournal.com/article.mpl?newsletterid=45&articleid=621 (accessed 27 June 2009).

Kurtz, L. (1997) 'No effect, or no *net* effect? Studies on socially responsible investing', *Journal of Investing*, 6 (4): 37–49.

Langley, P. (2002) *World Financial Orders: An Historical International Political Economy*, London: Routledge.

—— (2008) *The Everyday Life of Global Finance: Saving and Borrowing in Anglo-America*, Oxford: Oxford University Press.

Leyshon, A., Thrift, N. and Pratt, J. (1998) 'Reading financial services: texts, consumers, and financial literacy', *Environment and Planning D: Society and Space*, 16: 29–55.

Lieber, R. (2008) 'Socially responsible, with egg on its face', *New York Times*, August 22. Online. Available HTTP: www.nytimes.com (accessed 22 June 2009).

Littler, J. (2009) *Radical Consumption: Shopping for Change in Contemporary Culture*, Maidenhead, UK: Open University Press.

MacDonald, G.J. (2008) 'How can investors help the hungry?', *The Christian Science Monitor*, August 25. Online. Available HTTP: www.csmonitor.com/2008/0825/p13s01-wmgn.html (accessed 22 June 2009).

Mackenzie, C. (1997) 'Ethical investment and the challenge of corporate reform', unpublished thesis, University of Bath. Online. Available HTTP: http://staff.bath.ac.uk/hssal/crm/phd/crm-phd.pdf (accessed 2 June 2009).

Macpherson, C.B. (1962) *The Political Theory of Possessive Individualism: Hobbes to Locke*, London: Oxford University Press.

Martin, R. (2002) *The Financialization of Daily Life*, Philadelphia, PA: Temple University Press.

Miller, P. and Rose, N. (2008) *Governing the Present*, Cambridge: Polity.

Minns, R. (2001) *The Cold War in Welfare: Stock Markets versus Pensions*. London: Verso.

Pax World (2009) 'About Pax World'. Online. Available HTTP: http://paxworld.com/about/about-pax-world/ (accessed 29 June 2009).

Pryke, M. and Allen, J. (2000) 'Monetized time-space: derivatives – money's "new imaginary"?', *Economy & Society*, 29 (2): 264–84.

Quattrone, P. (2009) 'Books to be practiced: memory, the power of the visual, and the success of accounting', *Accounting, Organizations and Society*, 34: 85–118.

Robinson, J. and Eatwell, J. (1973) *An Introduction to Modern Economics*, London: McGraw-Hill.

Silk, J. (2000) 'Caring at a distance: (im)partiality, moral motivation and the ethics of representation', *Ethics, Place and Environment*, 3 (3): 303–22.

Social Funds. (2009a) 'Introduction to socially responsible investing'. Online. Available HTTP: www.socialfunds.com/page.cgi/article1.html (accessed 29 June 2009).

—— (2009b) 'Social investment timeline'. Online. Available HTTP: www.socialfunds.com/media/timeline.cgi (accessed 29 June 2009).

Social Investment Forum. (2003) *2003 Report on Socially Responsible Investing Trends in the United States*, Washington, DC: Social Investment Forum. Online. Available HTTP: www.socialinvest.org/resources/research/ (accessed 22 June 2009).

Spagnolo, A.-M. (2007) *The Ethical Investor: Make Money and Feel Good about it*, Camberwell, Vic.: Penguin.

Sparkes, R. (1995) *The Ethical Investor*, London: HarperCollins.

—— (1998) 'Through a glass darkly: some thoughts on the ethics of investment', The Beckley Lecture, GK Chesterton Centre for Faith and Culture, Oxford, *Epworth Review*, 25(3): 1–9.

—— (2001) 'Ethical investment: whose ethics, which investment?', *Business Ethics: A European Review*, 10(3): 194–205.

Weigand, E.M., Brown, K.R. and Wilhem, E.M. (1996) 'Socially principled investing: caring about ethics and profitability', *Trusts & Estates*, 135, 9 August: 36–41.

Williams, R. (1981) 'Communications technologies and social institutions', in R. and E. Williams (eds.) *Contact: human communication and its history*, London: Thames & Hudson.

18 The moral terrains of ecotourism and the ethics of consumption

Robert Melchior Figueroa and Gordon Waitt

Introduction

In this chapter, we provide a brief overview of Western philosophical ethics as they may pertain to tourism. Our discussion then turns to one of the most popular attempts to address sustainability across the globe: ecotourism. Ecotourism as distinct from tourism writ large is earmarked by appeals to concepts and ethical practices pertaining to sustainability (in all its varied meanings), consumption, preservation, and the politics of colonialism and the dynamics of global development strategies. In order to bring the ethics of consumption into the context of ecotourism, we provide a case account of ecotourism that represents one of the more popular versions, national park tourism, and the exchanges that occur over what we call the 'moral terrains' of ecotourism. At Uluṟu-Kata Tjuṯa National Park ecotourism pertains to market dynamics, colonialism, adjacent and conflicting heritage, challenges to environmental identity, micro-management strategies aimed at cultural reconciliation and political agency, as well as the ethics of entertainment that plagues tourism as a human form of consumption. We conclude with sections addressing the elevation of the ethics of ecotourism to a quandary of global environmental justice and utilize the controversy of the Uluṟu-climb to exemplify normative demands on today's quest for sustainable tourism.

Tourism, ethics, and consumption

'When in Rome', the saying goes, 'behave as the Romans do.' It is perhaps one of the most common Western expressions that conveys one of the oldest philosophical ethics of the civilization, hearkening back to Aristotle's guidance in achieving the 'good (virtuous) life'; his bottom line: to be virtuous, behave like the virtuous person. As the classic motto indicates, adventuring to learn different customs reflects an educated-informed and ethically sensitive traveller – an ethical tourist. Thus, conceived of in terms of tourism, Aristotle's prescription for the 'good life' translates easily to this human practice of cultural exchange as a form of entertainment, and hence, a form of consumption. Changing our behaviour to the virtue of the 'Romans in Rome' – as it were – is part of the enjoyment of being there; we are permitted to change our 'homeland ethics' in all sorts of ways, and this in itself becomes a form of cultural entertainment, and hence, a form of cultural consumption. Moreover, just as theatre, film, and place-based literature stretch the moral imagination, travel, and especially tourism, allows us to consider alternative ways of achieving the 'good life' while permitting for moral transgressions from 'homeland ethics'. By converting space, place, and human interactions into a form of entertainment, tourism informed by the code 'When in Rome' sets off a guide to alternatives in virtuous living across different cultural traditions, norms, mores, and political behaviour. However, if bracketing homeland ethics and our stretching moral imagination is part of the tourist experience this raises deeper questions about what constitutes good tourist practice.

Certainly behaving in *every way* like the Romans do will not produce ethical tourism, even if such mimetic behaviour is intended as a display of cultural respect. Cultural respect is indeed ethical behaviour, but contextually, acting exactly like people of different cultures does not yield ethical behaviour in itself. Likewise, not all behaviours that tourists encounter are necessarily good simply because it is done in that culture; thus, 'When in Rome' is not a virtue intended to slide into ethical relativism. There are limits to this virtue, or any virtue, as Aristotle warns us, because uncritical and unreflective attempts to achieve any virtue can easily turn into a vice. Far from the proper ethics of virtues, respect, conduct, and fairness, 'tourism' is often susceptible to the universalizing tendencies that follow most forms of industrial consumerism. Many a place transformed into a tourism destination relies heavily upon the reproduction and verification of Western and non-Western perceptions of racial, gender, and sexual stereotypes. For example, politicians in Egypt who are anti-gay tourists like to emphasize homosexuality as a Western form of corruption to the Islamic state. To discipline the collective will of the nation these politicians imagine a past and future without the subject of the homosexual. Hence, gay tourists are represented by the Egyptian media in the all too familiar tropes of 'alien', 'degenerate' and 'threatening'. In 2001, fifty-two Egyptian men were arrested during the raid of a well-known discothèque housed in a boat on the Nile for allegedly meeting with Western 'gay tourists'. Subsequently, the International Gay and Lesbian Rights Commission mobilized on the streets of Barcelona, Geneva, London, Manila, New York, Oslo, Toronto and Washington, DC to resist state sanctioned homophobia while the *Lonely Planet Egypt* (2002) guide asked all tourists to boycott travel to Egypt in protest against the heightened police persecution.

Since the interplay of ethics and politics is itself one of the entertaining aspects of tourism, the contemporary tourist is confronted with numerous unique ethical problems, because tourism is now global in so many respects and thus abides by patterns of consumption and resource allocation to a magnitude beyond what was historically possible. Many forms of contemporary tourism confront global social and environmental injustices by invoking a spatial-irony: the irony that much tourism is sold as a 'problem free' environment. Tourists certainly do not consume a 'problem free' environment, regardless of the tourist industry's wish to extinguish daily ethical and political problems from the tourist experience; instead, tourism itself is an ethical and political problem that we willingly (though perhaps unreflectively) take on as part of the challenge and excitement.

The spatial-irony of tourism produces contradictions for most attempts at ethical tourism. Walking into certain international hotel chains there is an effort to achieve consumer familiarity regardless of where you happen to be: Rome, Sydney, Mumbai or Dubai. Spatially extensive tourism chains are carefully managed and planned to certain Northern base-line standards of comfort, cleanliness, service, décor and ambience. As Edensor (1998) has ably argued these are enclavic tourist spaces. Indeed, the spatial boundary of such resort spaces may often be regulated by guards, guides and surveillance cameras. These techniques reconfigure the boundaries of the touristic bubble by banishing potentially offensive sights, smells, and sounds, or encounters with the poverty lurking just outside. Order is maintained down to the manicured lawns. When stepping across the threshold to be surrounded by the familiar consumptive comforts provided in-house there is no necessity to conscientiously reflect on the world beyond the threshold of the resort.

Cocooned within familiar enclavic spaces there is no necessity to question the unethical presumptions of colonialism that are often deployed to market destinations in the global Southern world. Rather than dismantling gender, racial, sexual, cultural, or religious stereotyping, the staged in-house shows that feature at such resorts often appropriate and circulate this knowledge through performances of the familiar tropes of the non-Western world as a timeless, wild place inhabited by noble savages. Similarly disillusioning are habitual Northern consumptive-style practices that get transposed to areas throughout the global South that could never sustain such living conditions and comforts for its own citizens. Like the palatial grounds/buildings of former Haitian leaders (of the pre-2010 earthquake era), or the mansions and limousines of the political and economic elite of the poorest nations in the world, the transnational corporate tourist industry has generated countless highly monitored pockets of Northern consumption. Habitual practices of everyday life re-consume the tourist by displacing the locally lived experience with that of the experience of the global consumer.

Given these environmental and socio-economic façades and contradictions, how are we to determine which modes of tourist existence, values, behaviours, and encounters are 'good' or 'bad'? Of course, this is exponentially more difficult to assess than the question tends to imply, in part, because one common meaning of the 'tourist' already presupposes a person who is fundamentally disrespectful to the 'local' people, place, decorum, or the environment as a whole socio-ecological nexus. This meaning of the 'tourist' conjures up a visitor who is morally degenerate. As an act of socio-ecological consumption – that is, consuming both culture in its many expressions and resources in its many environmental and ecological expressions – the tourist of today is a living ethical dilemma, steering between ethically good and bad features of cultural exchange and contemporary tourist industry practices, encounters and ideas that constitute simultaneously local and global scales.

One of the most obvious scalar ethical contradictions for the contemporary conscientious traveller is the global environmental impact of modes of transportation made 'affordable' by transnational corporations; that is, airlines. How do we go about ethical tourism when the first leg of the holiday requires some rationalization of the carbon dioxide emissions of air travel itself? An intriguing and complex utilitarian calculus determining the greatest happiness (preference satisfaction) for the greatest number of moral subjects besets the conscientious tourist in the first moments of holiday excursion. The moral dilemma increases exponentially by the mile travelled, in large part because there is a fundamental connection between big business tourism and the consumptive behaviours of contemporary tourists that serve to aggravate the connotation of the tourist as morally insensitive. In particular, rather than simply being perceived as naïve or crass travellers, the social and environmental injustices related to global market forces produce much greater moral obstacles for the contemporary tourist to navigate than the virtues of 'When in Rome'. Big business and global forms of tourism impact ecologies and economies across geographical scales, and threaten cultures in ways that render social and environmental injustices inseparable. As a global industry that criss-crosses scalar obligations to human societies and non-human species and ecosystems, the ethical responsibility for the conscientious traveller can be daunting. It involves voyeurism and commercialization, consuming traditional environmental knowledge of others while also invading the spaces and situated experiences of others. Resolving the conundrum of economic development, environmental sustainability, and cultural sustainability in an industry that relies on inputs and outputs along a supply chain that stretches across international borders is a constant challenge to even the most conscientious traveller.

Sustainability, ecotourism, and moral terrains

Fortunately, the individual tourist is not merely left to her own devices to initiate conscientious travel. Indeed, scores of documents, inter-agency initiatives in the United Nations, and collaborative efforts in the tourist industry have brought the inspiration of sustainable development from the likes of Agenda 21, the model policy established in the UN Rio 'Earth Summit' 1992, to the tourism table. While much criticism can be made against the development strategies from Agenda 21, importantly it led to the UN charging the World Tourism Organization (WTO) with a mandate to foster sustainable tourism. A complex web of committees, offices, background papers, and corporate partnerships emerged from this mandate including the establishment by the UN's Economic and Social Council of 2002 as the International Year of Ecotourism. One agency response to this declaration of the 'year of ecotourism' was the WTO-sponsored World Ecotourism Summit, Quebec, in 2002. Another output from corporate partnerships around the world is the *Global Sustainable Tourism Criteria*, which stipulate a list of objectives under the influence of the UN Millennium Development Goals: 'Poverty alleviation and environmental sustainability – including climate change'. Offering a code of best practices in the global tourism industry, the criteria include demonstrating effective sustainable management, maximizing social and economic benefits to local communities and minimizing negative impacts, maximizing benefits to cultural heritage and minimizing negative impacts, and maximizing benefits to the environment and minimizing negative impacts. Another major effort for branding and certification of sustainable tourism is captured in the world's largest cooperative, Green Globe International, Inc., which offers a symbol and criteria of its own for tourist activities that promote environmental protection and responses to climate change.[1]

As a result of this extensive international attention, sustainable tourism – or more specifically ecotourism – may actually be one of the more popular forms of conscientious global citizenship. While it can be defined in a number of ways, at heart 'ecotourism' tends to concentrate on principles of environmental sustainability, empowering tourism service providers, and educating the traveller to become culturally sensitive and environmentally aware. In education terms, the conscientious ecotourist is a critical thinker who is open to challenging his/her own perceptions about the people and places he/she encounters. In consumptive terms, the conscientious ecotourist makes a definitive choice to economically, socially, and environmentally value the people and places visited, as well as to behave beneficently towards human and non-human others. These virtues and normative goals are well beyond the mere platitude of developing the local economy. Instead, principles of sustainability, locally empowered development (both in terms of recuperating goods for infrastructure and decision-making), consideration for ecosystems, and a desire to encounter difference – cultural, religious, ethical, etc. – are the focus of touristic experiences. In political and economic terms, ecotourism includes a transformative ethic intended to provide competition around 'good practice' through consumer choices, which grow individually and collectively to a form of boycotting industry players engaging in 'bad practice'.

However, since ecotourism has been broadened and/or normalized from its origins as part of a sustainable tourism development platform in the wake of the 1992 Rio Earth Summit (Weaver 2004), it has also inherited the subsequent ways in which 'green marketing' – aimed at capitalizing on green consumer sentiment – functions as a strategic force in tourist consumption; ecotourism has thus become quite problematic despite its efforts towards a transformative ethics. The corporate tourism industry has deployed its own interpretations of ecotourism marketing to reproduce, rather than challenge, mainstream tourism industry practices, strategically targeting the self-proclaimed environmentalist, ethical, conscientious, individual consumer (McMinn 1997; McNamara and Gibson 2008). By targeting the tourist who self-identifies with an ethical intent, ethical labels like 'ecotourism' and 'sustainable tourism' can be appropriated by corporations while generating moral blindness to the underlying controversies of consumption practices. McMinn (1997: 135) argues the term 'sustainable tourism' has provided 'a philosophical base and a positive public image upon which to promote development, in particular newly discovered tracts of the world, where "regular" tourism might otherwise be seen as having negative impacts'. Purchasing holidays marketed as 'ecotourism' by mainstream companies in 'remote' places in the global South often enables affluent, well-educated, and conscientious consumers to continue with their affluent lifestyle and differentiate themselves from mass tourists, while feeling good that their holiday supposedly utilizes environmentally sensitive products and practices (Khan 2003).

Other authors offer similar warnings that 'eco' consumer preferences are insufficiently focused to create fundamental restructuring of social and environmental performances (Johnson 1998; Ross and Wall 1999). Honey (2008: 46) adds that 'the conscientious traveller can have a difficult time sifting tourism's wheat from the chaff to find a genuine ecotourism product'. For Honey, corporate 'green-washing' strategies allow tourism business practices to continue 'as usual' with only lip-service paid to the short- and long-term implications of increased visitor numbers to a particular destination (Williams and Ponsford 2009). The work of Font (2003), Font and Harris (2004) and Goodwin and Francis (2003) illustrates how green-washing practices are often exemplified by sustainable tourism branding polices and certification schemes. McNamara and Gibson (2008) argue these regulatory techniques offer directions to businesses, but have no legislative authority over practices. Indeed, Wheeler (1995) observes that regardless of contemporary labels, tourist industry marketing is often fitted to various forms of ethical abuse associated with discrimination and environmental abuse. As this growing scholarship in tourism testifies, tourists focusing on conscientious travelling remain situated in their own global context, forcing the questionable ethics and politics of neoliberal perspectives on development to fold back on to even the most conscientious, feel-good tourist.

In contrast, one example of a UK-based international organization that has made extensive efforts to work on many of the UN principles of sustainable tourism is Pro-Poor Tourism. Pro-Poor Tourism pursues its activities behind one of the latest inroads in sustainable tourism – the Pro-Poor Tourism movement. These charities have established community-based tourism initiatives in different parts of the global South to specifically address the environmental and social disrespect associated with the transnational corporate tourist industry. But even the latest efforts in conscientious, sustainable tourism can be conflicted by the perils of post-colonial ethical conundrums. As Fennell (2006: 103–4) observes, 'although the basic tenets of the Pro-Poor tourism platform are sound in principle, knowing what is good or right for tourism in the lesser developed countries, and instituting measures from the most developed countries, may seem to some to be patronizing'. The Pro-Poor Tourism movement may serve as an instance of the privileged position assumed by the global North. Admittedly, Pro-Poor Tourism is only one instance of international organizations putting forth moral standards for global tourism and tourists. But they serve to show that despite international principles, corporate cooperatives and initiatives for sustainable tourism, and new conscientious tourism movements, tourism itself is riddled with ethical politics in ways that are simply 'built into' the nature of travel and tourism.

However, one cannot be an absolute moral sceptic about the various movements towards sustainable and ecological tourism. Certainly, there are other numerous instances of conscientious tourism that diametrically oppose the moral and political flaws of neoliberal global tourism, and these instances do reflect numerous positive ethical advances in this arena of human interaction. To add to the positive advances in tourist ethics made by the efforts and labour of many across the globe, we offer yet another, perhaps alternative, way of assessing this conundrum of touristic ethics and consumption in a post-colonial world where sustainability in all its meanings involves new global obligations to the traveller – the metaphorical configuration of *moral terrains*. We have introduced the concept of moral terrains in the broadest sense of ecotourism in several writings (Waitt *et al.* 2007; Figueroa and Waitt 2008; Waitt and Figueroa 2008), as a 'strategy to break from theoretical boundaries that have kept tourism geographies from embodied knowledge and broader notions of place ethics'. Such a reading of the ethics of tourism, especially ecotourism, through the lens of shifting moral terrains has several implications, specifically in terms of embodied-situated ethics, the critical place of emotions and affective experiences for ethics, the ethical reconciliation of difference, and the capacity for orienting to a relational environmental ethics.

Many Western ethical philosophies have been unable to appreciate the variability of bodily responses to tourism places. Every place-based interaction between peoples indicates different situated experiences, different dimensions of related power, and different ways of perceiving values and conducting oneself. It is through situated encounters with other bodies (human and non-human) that individuals make sense of both themselves and their worlds. Some encounters will evoke emotions that will strengthen a sense of self in the world, while others will evoke bodily responses that will become a source of reflection and offer potential for an alternative future. By considering the capacity of bodies to be affected where moral terrains intersect, we can better engage in the nuances and situated experiences of place-based ethics. Such thinking alerts us to the importance of bodies as more than containers of ideas; this has drawn our attention in our research to the importance of the affective capacity of emotions such as sadness, joy, disgust, embarrassment, guilt, fear, shame and pride (Probyn 2005). Like ideas, embodied experiences of shame and joy can help disrupt the existing power structures between those individuals constituted as host and visitor.

Admittedly, the global economic nature of most ecotourist endeavours is rife with contradictions and navigating the ethical pathways across differences (economic, political, cultural, religious, and environmental) is never easy or without fundamental messiness. However, adding the obligations of conscientious tourism opens gateways to alternative experiences of excitement that forge new alliances, thus increasing visitors' capacity to change their behaviour. The virtues of 'world-travelling' in the sense that Lugones uses the term then are not cut and dried but require constant ethical tuning:

I am a plurality of selves. This is to understand my confusion because *it is to come to see it as a piece* with much of the rest of my experience as an outsider in some of the 'worlds' that I inhabit and of a piece with significant aspects of the experience of non-dominant people in the 'worlds' of their dominators.

(Lugones 1987: 14)

This plurality is part of the shared experience that generates a new moral terrain between resident and visitor reflective of the general benefits of human interaction with other humans, their places, and ways.

Another facet of the moral gateways opened up by the moral terrains framework is the foregrounding of new ethical relationships between humans and non-humans, tourists and their ecological values, human-to-human interactions, and the intrinsic value of place. The crux of these moral gateways rests on realizing the intrinsic value of place, as opposed to the instrumental value of place. Both tourist and resident relate to the moral status of place intrinsically in the sense that it acts uniquely on differently situated agents, and in many respects may actually present a version of its own 'agency'. Whether it be the deepest rainforest or the National Park experience – in terms of a method of sustainability, a cultural-ecological context, and a choice through which the tourist can operationalize the impacts of her consumerism – the place, sometimes the very rocks and setting, has an agency of acting upon and moulding the affective and ethical experiences of the human agent.

The concept of moral terrains as an inherently relational ethic thus reconceives moral agency: it is no longer reduced to a conscious subject acting upon the object. From this moral and ontological stance, the relational ethic of moral terrains is anti-dualistic, where dualism imposes an oppressive structure socially forged on to the place and spaces of moral agents and subjects. In the context of place or rocks or mountains or ecosystems, the relational ethic does not assume that consciousness is required, in order to act in a moral exchange. Thus, the tourist, the resident, the place, and non-human entities are seen as possessing their own capacities for agency. This relational ethic is one of the variants of the ecotourism vision, that place is worthy of sustainability in its socio-ecological heritage, and that supporting local political and economy agency are intrinsically important to sustaining relationships to place.

Scaling ecotourism to global environmental justice

Given what we have said of tourism and global consumption thus far, the ethical frame that best fits this arena of human activity lies beyond a strictly individualistic notion of the moral agent. Instead, justice, as a form of collective ethics, collective responsibility, and impacts that are collectively borne, is the proper moral scale. More precisely, environmental justice, and even more specifically global environmental justice, is the appropriate framework for understanding the collective moral terrains of tourism – a global consumption of place ethics.

A general concept of environmental justice has been alluded to earlier in this chapter in relation to the 'conceptual connections and causal relationships between environmental issues and social justice' (Figueroa and Mills 2001). Global environmental justice extends to the context of global market dynamics, development paradigms, scales of global, national, and local levels, and equity in the transnational benefits and burdens of the issues at hand. The local/regional or domestic scale of environmental justice is related to the global scale in a variety of ways. For instance:

> Domestic and global environmental justice come together in the environmental justice struggles of indigenous peoples. For centuries indigenous groups who have maintained traditional, non-industrialized, self-subsisting, environmentally friendly, and spiritual lifestyles with their natural environments have experienced waves of colonial and industrial conquest, carried out for the explicit purpose of wresting away control over their natural resources.
>
> (Figueroa and Mills 2001: 436)

In terms of the many concepts that form under the rubric of justice, both the scales of domestic and global environmental justice are bound by two interpenetrating, broad dimensions of justice – the distributive dimension and the recognition dimension (Figueroa 2001; 2003; 2007; 2009). Distributive justice, broadly construed, concerns fairness in the distribution of environmental benefits and burdens, as well as the proper compensation and redistribution of resources in order to repair inequities or ultimately to ameliorate an unfair arrangement. Recognition justice, broadly construed, concerns identities, heritage configurations, and a proactive participatory parity of direct involvement in the (environmental) decisions that impact everyday activities. Recognition justice encompasses restorative versions of justice that allow differently situated agents to reconcile and restore respect for the varying ways that identities are associated with place. Thus, on the axis of scalar environmental justice – domestic and global – and the axis of dimensions of justice – distributive and recognition – the environmental justice frame best represents the feature of collective action and responsibility that encompass any case of ecotourism. In turn, what counts as ecotourism and ethical tourist consumption shifts into a dramatic complexity that defies many of the standard dualisms of environmental ethics.

In the US, for example, the national park most favoured by avid rock climbers is 'Devil's Tower', referred to by indigenous tribes of the Kiowa and Crow, among others, as 'Bear's Lodge' and a vital part of their creation story and environmental heritage. In an effort of reconciliation, the US government proposed compromise by maintaining the park and abiding by indigenous religious tradition. That is, until the law of the land (the *US Constitution*) was applied to the dispute and the courts ruled in favour of an interpretation of separation between church and state, and lifted the prior claim of the American Indian tribes to the normative and ethical authority over the practices of tourists (in this case the climbers). Despite the efforts of many conscientious climbers to respect the Bear's Lodge tradition of honouring the sacred ground during solstice, which required avoiding physical contact in the manner of climbing, a number of the avid climber tourist population believed it to be their right of constitutional heritage to climb the public space. Burton (2002) provides a detailed account of this case in his book *Worship and Wilderness: Culture, Religion, and Law in Public Lands Management*, and, among other similar cases throughout the US, he recognizes the issue is in large part the co-evolution of cultures and different environmental heritage. These clashes are indicative of different moral terrains occupying the same space in different place-related identities.

In effect, if environmental problems are seen co-existing and co-originating in social problems, the scope of global environmental justice broadens to ethical questions surrounding the emergence, conscience, and aspirations of ecotourism. The virtues of ecotourism are bound by the relational ethics between humans, non-humans, and place. If the argument that the global trend towards ecotourism is best understood at the level of global environmental justice, then one benefit for our understanding of global environmental justice is that justice can be seen to pertain to the non-human others and ecosystems that house, sustain, and allow them to flourish. Global environmental justice also helps us to better understand the scope of ecotourism to include postmodern touristic activities, such as visiting the neighbourhoods of extreme poverty in developing nations (also referred to as 'poverty tourism' or 'poorism') (Selinger 2008). The practice of 'toxic tours', a vital experience in the grassroots strategy for environmental justice, and even the more notorious practice of 'disaster tours', fits the range of ecotourism if we recognize that 'eco' has many meanings, despite the popularization of it referring to post-Enlightenment equivalences of nature, wilderness, remote, and preserved biosystems. Poverty tourism, for instance, considers the environmental sacrifice zones of colonization, global consumption and resource distribution, failed sustainable development rhetoric, and moral blindspots in mainstream environmental values, especially those myopically focused on non-anthropocentric frameworks. Toxic tours educate visitors on the environmental impacts of modern industrial society, typically the sites of transnational corporate manufacturing and waste, and on the most disenfranchised citizens, typically from historically marginalized races, ethnicities, and the poor. In the wake of Hurricane Katrina in 2005, 'voluntourism' became an alternative for conscientious ecotourism, organizing many citizens to take their vacation time in New Orleans and the surrounding region of evacuation and disaster, in order to assist in the clean-up (mostly toxic) of the homes and properties of the victims of the hurricane. Meanwhile, bus companies and entrepreneurs generated an industry of disaster touring, where visitors paid upwards of US$60 per person to board a bus and tour the neighbourhoods ravaged by the storm. This too is an ecotourism that illuminates everything from the impacts of climate change, to a heritage of environmental racism in the worse-impacted district of New Orleans, to the legacy of failed federal response, and the emergent identity of environmental refugees.

Joint management at Uluṟu-Kata Tjuṯa National Park and the ethics of environmental heritage

The above discussion illustrates that global environmental justice need not be limited to some elite concept of the 'global', but should also extend the relational ethics between humans and non-humans in place. To exemplify this scale of relational ethics under global environmental justice and conclude the chapter we focus on the ongoing and recent controversies in the joint-management structure of Uluṟu-Kata Tjuṯa National Park in the Northern Territory of Australia, commonly known as 'Ayers Rock'. Our exploration of this case here stands as an example of issues confronting ecotourism more generally. Even though this is not one of the typical 'rainforest' cases, it highlights indigenous struggles, state-sponsored agency interaction, and the ways in which colonial tourism obfuscates conscientious tourism in the global marketplace. Our specific focus is on the ways in which the moral terrains of the Park are played out through the ongoing debate over climbing 'the Rock' – Uluṟu, itself.

Indigenous nations, tribes, and communities are confronted with the political recognition of sovereigns within a sovereign nation, and that makes them particularly vulnerable to domestic colonial values and behaviours, as well as international colonial practices represented by global touristic perspectives. In the case of Uluṟu, this is reflected in the clash between the national heritage of settler Australian identity and the socio-religious-environmental law that constitutes the *body ethos* (as opposed to the body politic) of the recognized traditional owners of Uluṟu: the Aṉangu community. As we discuss below, moral concerns around climbing Uluṟu stretch back as far as tens of thousands of years in the Aṉangu environmental heritage, but the collision of moral terrains between the indigenous peoples and the tourist climber have existed only since the nineteenth-century settler colonization of the Australian continent. On the moral terrain of Aṉangu tradition, or *Tjurkurpa*, Uluṟu presents a cultural mapping of norms, law, heritage, ritual, and identity that grounds vital portions of the Aṉangu ethic. This ethic is inseparable from any account of environmental ethic as the Aṉangu *Tjurkurpa* is a relational ethic, that does recognize an anthropocentric/non-anthropocentric distinction. Given the rock itself carries agency in the collective moral activity of the community, the Aṉangu ethic exemplifies the deepest form of environmental justice. In this tradition exists multiple moral terrains for the Aṉangu: the rock can only be climbed by particular family groupings, specific licence is given only to males who have passed through particular rites of passage available only to specific elders, and the rock can only be climbed in particular windows of time. Surrounding the rock are a number of sacred sites that cordon off approach from different gender groups – men must respect the sites of women's rituals (business) by staying at a distance and turning their gaze away, and vice versa for appropriate behaviour of Aṉangu women with respect to the sites of men's rituals. A complex cultural map exists in this moral terrain, but this code is vastly different from dominant touristic activity that has been normatively guided by the tourist industry and Western colonial environmental heritage – the legacy of owning and disassociating from the land in order to control and conquer nature.

Elsewhere we have detailed the history of Uluṟu-Kata Tjuṯa National Park; the crucial summary is that since the Park was opened in the 1950s, a climb to the top of Uluṟu has been established and become a national heritage for settler Australians (see Figueroa and Waitt 2008). The Park and the tourist industry around Uluṟu has always been centred around the attraction of the climb, which, unlike the Bear's Lodge/Devil's Tower case, can be ascended with the assistance of a chain link by most able-bodied tourists. In recent history, the Anangu were returned the area that designates the Park under the provisions of the *Aboriginal Land Rights (Northern Territory) Amendment Act 1985*, which led to a 'handing back' of Uluṟu in 1986 (*National Parks and Wildlife Conservation Amendment Act 1985*). The climb debate, if there ever was a public debate, was buried with the colonial ruin that the Anangu suffered, until the 'handing back' publicly revived the debate, as the Park now came into a joint-management structure between the Commonwealth and Aboriginal governance; ultimately, the site appropriately became a mixed designation (cultural/natural) World Heritage Site.

Today, a cultural centre exists for better understanding the environmental heritage and moral terrain of the Anangu, since all visitors considerate of Anangu law receive a *Pukulpa Pitjama Ananguku Ngurakutu* (Welcome to Anangu Land) in the form of a visitor pass that is written in both the Anangu language and English. The sign at the base of the climb requests in many languages that visitors avoid the climb, and provides numerous reasons for this, mostly out of cultural and environmental respect, directing tourists to alternative activities with the rock and its environs. The sign boldly states, 'We Don't Climb', which gives rise to a fundamental problem in environmental justice, identity, heritage, and the dynamics of moral terrains – who is included in this 'We'? The global tourist, the settler Australian, the Anangu, or some appeal to a universal 'we'? The insight that Burton gives of the Bear's Lodge/Devil's Tower debate is that the 'we' is a co-evolving subject; and in the case of Uluṟu the dilemmas of consumption ethics in the contemporary ecotourist are further complicated by the ethical task of reconciliation. Indeed, the Park, and Uluṟu perhaps as its central symbol, has become a site of reconciliation and 'sorry saying' or restorative justice, between the settler citizenry and the Aboriginal community.

As we write this chapter, Australians of all moral terrains have re-engaged the debate over permanently closing the climb to tourists, although the Environment Minister Peter Garrett estimates it will be some years before the Australian Federal Government succeeds in closing it. The reasons added to the signage at the base of Uluṟu identify dangers to climbers (including the annual number of fatalities), environmental erosion, degradation by litter and vandalism, and the cultural requests by the traditional owners. Despite the Anangu ownership of the Park, the joint-management scheme places the Environment Minister at the helm for setting criteria to determine the climb's closure. Criteria depend on significant drop-off in climbers, alternatives to dominance of the climb for international tourists, and options available for the tourism industry. However rational these criteria sound, especially on behalf of the international tourism industry, the climb closure rhetoric outside the circle of federal politicians is often far more diverse and inflammatory due to the different moral terrains and concepts of justice as they apply to the different heritage constructions. Elsewhere we have indicated the moral terrains of colonialism, overt racism, generalized disrespect, and apathy, if not disdain, for the norms of the reconciliation process (see Waitt *et al.* 2007; Waitt and Figueroa 2008). Likewise, we have documented the moral terrains of co-evolution towards a place of reconciliation from the individual tourist to the collective behaviour of tourist resistance in defence of cultural and ecological respect (see Figueroa and Waitt 2008). According to some reports, the Park is witnessing a drop-off of tourist climbers already, as visitors are conscientiously taking up the alternatives, most of them culturally informed of the moral terrain of the Anangu, while the traditional owners are remaining resolute for environmental justice to take place.

Far to the north, in Arnhem Land, a vast territory that is predominantly Aboriginal Land, an elder reveals to a group of international tourists the magnificent ancient rock drawings of his ancestors: 'We share so you can understand; you cannot understand if we don't share.' What are we to understand from this sharing? That is partly up to the tourist, but it requires an ethical stance that recognizes the global implications and historical struggles of the place and its people. Back at Uluru-Kata Tjuta National Park the conscientious tourist is confronted with more than the biodiversity and sustainability argument, but also with questions about whose moral terrain to embrace, the settler heartland and colonial interpretations of nature, the traditional land and law of indigenous people, or the entertainment factor and tourism industry that the climb offers the consumer? Are we obligated to equally reconcile all perspectives on the climb? Certainly, the moral activity here cannot simply succumb to ethical relativism, because some moral terrains are the path of oppression and environmental injustice. For the tourist then, consuming ethics depends on consciously relating to the moral terrains of place, in order to determine the appropriate course of action.

Note

1   For further information on these initiatives see the following URL sites: www.un.org/ esa/dsd/susdevtopics/sdt_susttour.shtml; www.un.org/documents/ecosoc/res/1998/ eres1998-40.htm; www.sustainabletourismcriteria.org/index.php?option=com_content &task= view&id=58&Itemid=188; www.world-tourism.org/sustainable/IYE-Main-Menu.htm; and www.greenglobeint.com/.

Bibliography

Burton, L. (2002) *Worship and Wilderness: Culture, Religion, and Law in Public Lands Management*, Madison, WI: University of Wisconsin Press.
Edensor, T. (1998) *Tourists at the Taj*, London: Routledge.

Fennell, D. (2006) *Tourism Ethics*, Clevedon, Buffalo, Toronto: Channel View Publications.

Figueroa, R. and Mills, C. (2001) 'Environmental justice', in D. Jamieson (ed.) *A Companion to Environmental Philosophy*, New York: Basil Blackwell Publishing.

Figueroa, R.M. (2001) 'Other faces: Latinos/as and environmental justice', in L. Westra and B.E. Lawson (eds) *Faces of Environmental Racism: Confronting Issues of Global Justice*, Lantham: Rowman and Littlefield.

—— (2003) 'Bivalent environmental justice and the culture of poverty', *Rutgers Journal of Law and Public Policy*, 1(1) Summer: 27–42.

—— (2006) 'Evaluating environmental justice claims', in J. Bauer (ed.) *Forging Environmentalism: Justice, Livelihood, and Contested Environments*, New York: M.E. Sharpe.

—— (2009) 'Environmental justice', in J.B. Callicott and R. Frodeman (eds) *The Encyclopedia of Environmental Ethics and Philosophy*, New York: Thompson Gale.

Figueroa, R.M. and Waitt, G. (2008) 'Cracks in the mirror: (un)covering the moral terrains of environmental justice at Uluru-Kata Tjuta National Park', *Ethics, Place, and Environment: A Journal of Philosophy and Geography*, 11(3): 327–49.

Font, X. (2003) 'Labelling and certification: benefits and challenges for sustainable tourism management and marketing', *International Ecotourism Monthly*, Year 5, 50, July, *Ecoclub*. Online. Available HTTP: http://ecoclub.com/news/050/expert.html#1 (accessed 5 December 2003).

Font, X. and Harris, C. (2004) 'Rethinking standards from green to sustainable', *Annals of Tourism Research*, 31(4): 986–1007.

Goodwin, H. and Francis, J. (2003) 'Ethical and responsible tourism: consumer trends in the UK', *Journal of Vacation Marketing*, 9(3): 271–82.

Honey, M. (2008) *Ecotourism and Sustainable Development: Who Owns Paradise?*, 2nd edition, Washington, DC: Island Press.

Jamieson, D. (1994) 'Global environmental justice', in R. Atfield and H. Belsey (eds) *Philosophy and the Natural Environment*, Cambridge: Cambridge University Press.

Johnson, D.B. (1998) 'Green businesses: perspectives from management and business ethics', *Society & Natural Resources*, 11(3): 259–66.

Khan, M. (2003) 'Ecotourists' quality expectations', *Annals of Tourism Research*, 309(1): 109–24.

Lugones, M. (1987) 'Playfulness, "world"-travelling, and loving perception', *Hypatia*, 2(2): 3–18.

McMinn, S. (1997) 'The challenge of sustainable tourism', *The Environmentalist*, 17: 135–41.

McNamara, K.E. and Gibson, C. (2008) 'Environmental sustainability in practice? A macro-scale profile of tourist accommodation facilities in Australia's coastal zone', *Journal of Sustainable Tourism*, 16(1): 85–100.

Plumwood, V. (2002) *Environmental Culture: The Ecological Crisis of Reason*, London: Routledge.

Probyn, E. (2005) *Blush: Faces of Shame*, Minneapolis, MN: University of Minnesota Press.

Ross, S. and Wall, G. (1999) 'Evaluating ecotourism: the case of North Sulawesi, Indonesia', *Tourism Management*, 20(6): 673–82.

Selinger, E. (2008) 'Ethics and poverty tours', *Philosophy and Public Policy Quarterly*, 29(1/2): 2–7.

Waitt, G. and Figueroa, R.M. (2008) 'Touring the moral terrain of Uluru: pathways of shame and pride', in V. Frank, J. Malpas, M. Higgins and A. Blackshaw (eds) *Making Sense of Place: Exploring Concepts and Expressions of Place through Different Senses and Lenses*, Canberra: The National Museum of Australia.

Waitt, G., Figueroa, R.M. and McGee, L. (2007) 'Fissures in the rock: rethinking pride and shame in the moral terrains of Uluru', *Transactions of the Institute of British Geographers*, 32(2): 248–61.

Weaver, D. (2004) 'Tourism and the elusive paradigm of sustainable development', in A. Lew, C.M. Hall, and A. Williams (eds) *A Companion to Tourism*, Oxford: Blackwell.

Wheeler, M. (1995) 'Tourism marketing ethics: an introduction', *International Marketing Review*, 12(4): 38–49.

Williams, P.W. and Ponsford, I.F. (2009) 'Confronting tourism's environmental paradox: transitioning for sustainable tourism', *Futures of Tourism*, 41(6): 396–404.

Index

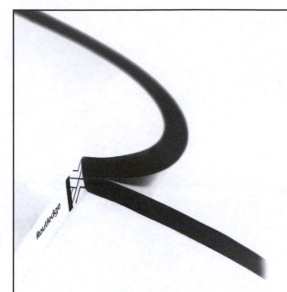

Routledge
Paperbacks Direct

Bringing you the cream of our hardback publishing at paperback prices

This exciting new initiative makes the best of our hardback publishing available in paperback format for authors and individual customers.

Routledge Paperbacks Direct is an ever-evolving programme with new titles being added regularly.

To take a look at the titles available, visit our website.

www.routledgepaperbacksdirect.com